Sleep Difficulties *and* Autism Spectrum Disorders

D0023876

by the same author

An A–Z of Genetic Factors in Autism
A Handbook for Professionals
ISBN 978 1 84310 976 1

An A–Z of Genetic Factors in Autism
A Handbook for Parents and Carers
ISBN 978 1 84310 679 1

Dietary Interventions in Autism Spectrum Disorders
Why They Work When They Do, Why
They Don't When They Don't
ISBN 978 1 84310 939 6

of related interest

Children with Autism
Diagnosis and Intervention to Meet Their Needs
2nd edition
Colwyn Trevarthen, Jacqueline Robarts, Despina
Papoudi and Kenneth J. Aitken
ISBN 978 1 85302 555 6

Sleep Difficulties *and* Autism Spectrum Disorders

A Guide for Parents and Professionals

Kenneth J. Aitken

Jessica Kingsley *Publishers*
London and Philadelphia

Front cover image supplied by istockphoto.com

First published in 2012
by Jessica Kingsley Publishers
116 Pentonville Road
London N1 9JB, UK
and
400 Market Street, Suite 400
Philadelphia, PA 19106, USA

www.jkp.com

Copyright © Kenneth J. Aitken 2012

All rights reserved. No part of this publication may be reproduced in any material form (including photocopying or storing it in any medium by electronic means and whether or not transiently or incidentally to some other use of this publication) without the written permission of the copyright owner except in accordance with the provisions of the Copyright, Designs and Patents Act 1988 or under the terms of a licence issued by the Copyright Licensing Agency Ltd, Saffron House, 6–10 Kirby Street, London EC1N 8TS. Applications for the copyright owner's written permission to reproduce any part of this publication should be addressed to the publisher.

Warning: The doing of an unauthorised act in relation to a copyright work may result in both a civil claim for damages and criminal prosecution.

Library of Congress Cataloging in Publication Data
Aitken, Kenneth J.
  Sleep difficulties and autism spectrum disorders : a guide for parents and professionals / Kenneth J. Aitken.
       p. ; cm.
  Includes bibliographical references and index.
  ISBN 978-1-84905-259-7 (alk. paper)
  I. Title.
  [DNLM: 1. Sleep Disorders--therapy. 2. Child Development Disorders, Pervasive--complications. WM 188]
  LCclassification not assigned
  616.85'882--dc23

                                        2011030451

British Library Cataloguing in Publication Data
A CIP catalogue record for this book is available from the British Library

ISBN 978 1 84905 259 7
eISBN 978 0 85700 550 2

Printed and bound in Great Britain

I dedicate this book to Cucina and Cuba, the sister Goddesses who were thought by the Romans to watch over children in their cradles and beds as they slept.

This volume has been carefully produced and edited. Nevertheless, the author, editors and publishers do not warrant that the information is entirely free from errors. The reader is advised to bear in mind that all statements, data, illustrations and details may contain inadvertent inaccuracies.

The term 'ASD' is used widely throughout. ASD is an acronym that stands for Autistic Spectrum Disorder. The term ASD, which is being introduced in the DSM 5 system, replaces previous diagnoses for all people who would have been given diagnoses such as autistic disorder (autism), Asperger's disorder, childhood disintegrative disorder or pervasive developmental disorder not otherwise specified.

CONTENTS

List of Tables

List of Figures

ACKNOWLEDGEMENTS

I have studied and worked in child and adolescent mental health for over 30 years, with a specialist interest in neurodevelopmental disorders. In this time I have had the good fortune and opportunity to work with and help a large number of families with sleep-disordered children and adolescents. I have also been fortunate to be able to discuss clinical cases and issues with a wide range of other clinicians and researchers.

As with many things, my interest in sleep disorders developed initially through chance meetings and discussions.

I remember in the early 1990s attending a meeting of the Society for the Study of Behavioural Phenotypes in Wales and getting talking with Roger Freeman, a Consultant Child and Adolescent Psychiatrist from Vancouver. He had a particular interest in sleep problems. His group had been getting highly promising results by using melatonin supplements in the treatment of sleep disorders in children with various neuro-developmental issues, including ASD, visual impairments and global learning difficulties. I discussed the role of melatonin with my neurology colleagues in Edinburgh and we gradually started using it with children who had sleep difficulties, often in association with seizures, ASD and ADHD. At that time it had been used as a supplement for getting over jet lag and by shift-workers, while adjusting to night shifts or time off, but was relatively unknown as a treatment for clinical conditions. Melatonin has gone on to become a mainstay in the treatment of several of the sleep difficulties we will discuss in this book. At that time melatonin was available in the UK as an unregulated over-the-counter food supplement. It has since been reclassified as 'medicinal by use' and is now only available in the UK on prescription, and is not commonly available in Canada. In the US melatonin always has been and continues to be available as an over-the-counter supplement.

I can also remember meeting with Tom Anders, a Child Psychiatrist working in Denver and discussing his longstanding interests in sleep problems. At the time he was a Consultant and was working on the development of the International Classification of Sleep Disorders. The following year I found myself working with him at the Institute of Psychiatry in London when he did a sabbatical swap with Michael Rutter. He went on for a time to head up the MIND Institute in Sacramento, one of the world's leading clinical and research centres on ASD.

As with any book of this type, I am grateful to the many clinicians and families from whom I have learnt and to those colleagues who have taken the time and interest to comment on drafts of the manuscript. I accept full responsibility for all errors and inaccuracies found herein.

I would like to take the opportunity to thank Jessica Kingsley and Karen Ings for early discussions and encouragement over this project, Claire Cooper who guided and smoothed the production process from Jessica Kingsley Publishers, and my longstanding friend and colleague Bill Taylor who acted as a sounding board for many of my ideas on the text and gave valuable feedback at various stages of the development of the manuscript.

Dr Ken Aitken
Edinburgh
July 2011

INTRODUCTION

This is a short(ish) and I hope a fairly practical introduction to the sleep issues often seen in people with ASDs (Autism Spectrum Disorders), and to what can be done about them when they cause problems. Sleep difficulties are a common and often distressing aspect of life for many people with ASDs.

Most people pick up a book on sleep difficulties either because they have a sleep problem themselves or because they are trying to help someone else who has one. This book discusses the more 'usual' sleep problems that are likely to be a cause for concern for people with an ASD.

There is no shortage of general books on sleep problems, some of which I have listed in a short appendix at the back of the book. The large number of volumes that have been produced is more a reflection of how commonly people are affected by sleep problems than because any given book on the subject has been found to be especially helpful.

Surprisingly, there is only one book that I have been able to find that focuses on sleep problems in people with special needs (Durand 1997). This is a good introduction, but pre-dates many of the important developments in our understanding of sleep problems and of how best to manage them. A therapist manual and an accompanying parent workbook on sleep were written more recently by the same author (Durand 2008a, 2008b). Both of these later works are more general in their aims and coverage and focus primarily on behavioural interventions.

Sleep problems should not be dismissed or trivialized. They are neither benign nor an issue only for the poor sleeper themselves.

Sleep difficulties are related to phenomena as diverse as increasing the risk of breast cancer (Batt 2000; Verkasalo *et al.* 2005), the likelihood of being involved in industrial accidents (Dorrian, Baulk and Dawson 2011) and the risk of impulsive aggression (Lindberg *et al.* 2009). Both jet lag and shift work have been found to increase the risk of breast cancer, cardiovascular problems and stroke (Harrington 2010). Those with poor sleep have poorer academic performance (Willis 2009), tend to develop poorer executive functions (Friedman *et al.* 2009) and are also more likely to engage in adolescent risk-taking behaviours (Catrett and Gaultney 2009) than their peers.

There are significant negative effects of children's sleep problems on a wide range of family processes (Polimeni, Richdale and Francis 2005). In boys, early sleep problems can be a significant predictor of early onset substance-abuse problems (Wong, Brower and Zucker 2009). Sleep problems are often associated with challenging behaviours in the developmentally disabled (Lenjavi *et al.* 2010), including those with ASD (Goldman *et al.* 2011; Henderson *et al.* 2001), and are common in children with psychiatric disorders (Alfano and Gamble 2009; Alfano *et al.* 2010).

In one study of women with sleep-disordered breathing, their sleep problem was cited as a cause of divorce or social isolation in around 40 per cent (Guilleminault *et al.* 1995).

The societal cost of unrecognized and untreated sleep problems is only beginning to be recognized and assessed. One recent Canadian study estimated that, in addition to the hefty direct health costs, the losses in productivity alone in Quebec resulting from insomnia amounts to £3.2 billion per annum (Daley *et al.* 2009).

The most difficult and distressing problems to deal with are those that are difficult to understand or predict. Having to care for someone with a severe sleep problem when you can't fathom what is causing it can be much more physically exhausting and demoralizing than dealing with something you understand. A good starting point in trying to sort things out is trying to understand why they might be happening.

Trying to identify why a problem first arose is often the focus of detailed history taking. Sadly, however, finding out what started a problem is not usually enough in itself to produce any kind of solution. When trying to get to the root of a sleep problem, it is more important to focus initially on current sleep issues, rather than on what may have led up to them – getting a clearer understanding of what is happening now is the most important thing in developing a successful management plan. This often seems a little strange but it is important to identify what is keeping a problem going when we are attempting to change it, not why it might have started off. The genesis of the problem may be fascinating but our conclusions will always be speculative and, even if correct, will ultimately be unchangeable. Things that are in the past have an annoying habit of staying the same, although our understanding of such events may change and this can alter how we deal with current and future situations. Understanding why something continues to be a problem is often the first step to fixing it.

With nightmares, the content (where a dream seems to recall specific distressing events, for example) may overlap with actual traumatic events, and investigating the genesis of the problem often has high 'face validity' (it seems to make sense) to the person affected and to their family. By focusing on the onset and history of the problem, however, we can give too much emphasis to unchangeable events, and seem to justify why the problem keeps going.

> Jim who is 15 has recurring nightmares about being attacked by a group of boys in a back alley and being badly kicked and bruised. Jim had been the victim of an attack similar to the one in his nightmares, which occurred shortly before the nightmares started. Jim has been seeing a therapist who has reassured him that the nightmares are a normal consequence of the trauma: 'Obviously you will have unresolved issues around the assault and that is why in your nightmares you seem to replay the attack again and again'.

The explanatory approach above seems to make some sense, but I would imagine that what Jim really wants is a solution that reduces or stops his nightmares. He wakes screaming at 2.00 every morning and can give a vivid account of being set upon and doesn't want to be doing it. At one level he wants to know why they occur, but ideally he would prefer the nightmares to stop. We will return to a discussion of nightmares later in the book.

This is a book that discusses sleep problems in ASD across the age range. Most discussion is around sleep problems in infants, children and adolescents, and many of the approaches are applicable with adults. There is far less published work on and experience in the treatment of adult sleep problems in ASD.

The book is in five sections:

> Section A deals briefly with some general questions about sleep: what it is, how we currently understand it and how too much or too little sleep can affect our minds and bodies.

> Section B covers sleep disorders in general – the types of problems there can be and how commonly they present.

> Section C deals more specifically with sleep problems in ASD, why some are more common than they are in others and how they evolve over time.

> Section D deals with a range of issues that can affect sleep and may cause sleep problems to occur or get worse.

> Section E, the longest section deals with the specific sleep problems seen in ASD, what can be done to treat them and the various approaches that are currently advocated. It describes the most common sleep issues in ASD, what they are, how common each seems to be, how likely they are to respond to treatment and their outcomes.

I have tried as far as possible to explain complex, technical or unusual words in the glossary.

It is how common sleep problems are overall that singles out those with ASD as a particularly troubled group rather than any marked difference in the nature of the sleep difficulties themselves. There are specific biological differences reported in ASD and we will come on to discuss these; problems when they occur also tend if left untreated to last longer and to be more difficult than the same problems in others. Many of the approaches that have proven effective for others can, however, work equally well for those with an ASD.

As far as possible I have tried to discuss approaches where there is published literature demonstrating their effectiveness in ASD. For some of the approaches where there isn't a strong evidence base I have drawn on my clinical experience of methods that I have found to work, often when more conventional approaches have not.

Tried and tested published methods can help in many cases, but children with ASD have not always read the books and don't always respond as expected. For some problems there are as yet no effective methods.

If a problem is stressful and there are no well-recognized effective treatments this does not mean that nothing is going to help. It is important to realize that 'absence of evidence' (the fact that nobody has published on something and there are no treatment trials showing what might work) is not the same as 'evidence of absence' (that there is published evidence showing that things don't work). In the present climate of 'evidence-based practice' there is a tendency to do nothing where there is insufficient evidence to make a strong recommendation based on published evidence. There should be greater emphasis in clinical practice on how to help in situations where there is an absence of evidence, particularly when different approaches may have 'biological plausibility' and a problem is causing distress. There may be limited evidence of effectiveness, but it is often as important to know whether there is any evidence that an approach does not work, any evidence of possible side-effects and any evidence of possible harmful effects.

I have tried to produce brief overviews to help the reader focus on key information. Specimen recording sheets are included in Appendix 4 to show how to record a sleep diary, and details of and sources for a number of the main rating-scales that can be useful in discussing difficulties with clinicians. These can be helpful in clarifying the problem and monitoring responses to intervention.

Finally, there is a Resources section including support organizations with their websites and contact details and suppliers for some of the materials mentioned in the main part of the book.

SLEEP AND WHAT WE KNOW ABOUT IT

CHRONOBIOLOGY

This book deals with something that is often called chronobiology. 'Chronos' is the ancient Greek word for time and 'biology' is the study of life. Chronobiology is sometimes also referred to as 'chronoastrobiology' (Halberg *et al.* 2009) because it is the study of biological rhythms and typically of those rhythms that correspond to the solar and lunar cycles.

We live on the earth, the third closest of the eight planets to the sun. Earth rotates in an elliptical orbit around the sun. In addition, the sun and the earth rotate on their own axes, and our moon rotates around the earth. All of these processes happen in a precise pattern that has changed only minimally over the time that life on earth has taken to evolve. Our species and our own human bodies have evolved to expect the changes in light, heat and humidity brought about by the pattern of day and night, the solar cycle, and the resulting changing but predictable pattern to the seasons.

As the earth rotates on its axis, at any time half the world is bathed in sunlight (cloud-cover permitting) while the other half is in darkness. Our day–night cycle is due to the rotation of the earth relative to the sun. Life on most of the earth has had to evolve to cope with the diurnal cycle of night and day and the seasonal variations in day length and temperature. A year is the period of time it takes the earth to return to the same position from which it started relative to the sun and the stars (there are slight differences in how this is calculated giving the tropical/solar year (365.242 days) and the sidereal year (365.256 days)). The differences through this cycle and in the orientation of the earth relative to the sun result in the seasonal variations in the earth's climate. In the Arctic and Antarctic regions, where predictable lengthy periods of seasonal darkness are experienced, seasonal variations in light and temperature are more important than daily ones and many animals have evolved patterns of hibernation to reduce energy expenditure during darker periods of the year. In the extreme circumpolar regions where even daily fluctuations cease to apply, life forms, as we commonly think of them at least, have failed to take hold.

Before the reader starts to think that this is going to be a book on astrology or on how horoscopes might help with sleep problems, pause to consider a couple of examples of chronobiological processes. One such biological pattern entrained to the solar cycle is menstruation (the period of differential rotation of the sun on its axis is approximately 25.6 days); another process typically entrained with the rotation of the earth is the daily cycle of melatonin levels that is driven by changes in ambient light (a lunar day is approximately 24 hours 50 minutes 28 seconds). The consequent pattern of melatonin release is an important factor in promoting drowsiness and in alerting us that it is time to sleep.

Whether we like it or not, our bodies follow patterns governed by the motion of the earth, its moon and its sun. These temporal patterns in our physical states are functions of how and where we have evolved in the universe. If our species had evolved on Saturn, a planet with a solar year of about 29.5 years longer than that of earth that is thought to rotate on its own axis every 10.5 hours, our chronobiology would inevitably have been very different.

As life has evolved on earth it has achieved a balance in coping with the predictable cycles imposed by our habitat. Our adaptation to the effects of these external cycles depends on a number of processes.

To date, two types of internal mechanism have been identified that regulate sleep – the circadian system, which is governed by genetic mechanisms known as biological clocks (for helpful discussions see Foster and Kreitzman 2005; Gillette and Abbott 2009; Jolma *et al.* 2010), and a homeostatic process that is affected by the length of time we spend awake – the more 'sleep-deprived' we are, the more tired we get (for a more detailed discussion of how these mechanisms interact see Wulff *et al.* 2009). There are other chronobiological systems yet to be identified that help us to sleep, some of which do not rely on translation–transcription feedback loops and are not yet fully understood (see, e.g. O'Neill and Reddy 2011).

WHAT ARE BIOLOGICAL CLOCKS?
Biological clocks are the genetically controlled cellular mechanisms that allow our bodies to keep track of time and adapt our behaviour and metabolism to environmental changes.

The first recognition that genetic mechanisms were involved in sleep–wake cycles came in 1971 when Konopka and Benzer identified three clock gene mutants that drastically affected the 24-hour rhythm of fruit flies (Konopka and Benzer 1971). The same genes were found to be involved in controlling sleep–wake cycles in a wide range of other species and seemed to be highly conserved from flies to mammals. The first evidence for similar genetic mechanisms in mammals came in 1988 with the identification of a genetic mutant of the *tau* gene in the golden hamster. This gene mutation reduced its free-running day–night period from 24 to 20 hours. When external circadian cues were removed, and there was constant light, it developed a shortened sleep pattern compared to others (Ralph and Menaker 1988).

Clock genes can play a critical role in controlling energy balance. This has been shown in recent research with mice where disruption to the mPer2 clock gene has been shown to interfere with appetite control and to increase their risk of obesity (see Yang *et al.* 2009). Related issues is how active genes are at different times (Porkka-Heiskanen 2003) or in response to factors such as sleep deprivation. Clock genes control much of the daily fluctuation in our body chemistry (Holzberg and Albrecht 2003). There is mounting evidence for reciprocal effects of clock genes on neuroimmunology (Coogan and Wyse 2008).

A reciprocal process is that the activity of some genes seems to be affected by sleep pattern. One study in mice found that 2090 cortical and 409 hypothalamic genes that were involved in a range of molecular functions were specifically up or down regulated by sleep or sleep deprivation (Mackiewicz *et al.* 2007).

The similarities in the genetic mechanisms involved across species suggests both that sleep is a necessary or important process across the animal kingdom and that sleep abnormalities found in animal research will often have implications for human sleep disorders (Cermakian and Boivin 2003). The similarities in the underpinning biological processes, across the animal kingdom, are allowing significant developments in our understanding of human sleep to be made through the study of its development in other 'model organisms' such as *Drosophila melanogaster* (the fruit fly) and *Danio rerio* (the zebrafish) (Hendricks, Sehgal and Pack 2000).

In addition to sleep–wake cycle issues, mood disorders including unipolar depression and seasonal affective disorder are typically due to abnormalities of the circadian system (McClung 2007; Monteleone and Maj 2008).

There is a growing body of evidence that circadian abnormalities are seen in a large proportion of individuals with ASDs (Glickman 2010). Methods for the reliable assessment of human circadian rhythms are now available and in use (see Hofstra and de Weerd 2008).

Variations in cognitive ability follow a circadian pattern and are affected both by endogenous circadian clocks and external factors that vary the amount and timing of actual sleep (Kyriacou and Hastings 2010).

WHAT IS SLEEP?

A useful starting point in understanding and unravelling sleep problems is trying to get a basic idea of what sleep is, why we might do it and what it might be for.

We should start by defining what we mean by sleep. There are many definitions to choose from. Here is a selection:

> Sleep is a reversible condition of reduced responsiveness usually associated with immobility. (Cirelli and Tononi 2008, p.1605)

> ...sleep is that golden chain that ties health and our bodies together. (Thomas Dekker, *The Gull's Hornbook* 1609)

> Sleep is the interest we have to pay on the capital which is called in at death; and the higher the rate of interest and the more regularly it is paid, the further the date of redemption is postponed. (Arthur Schopenhauer)

> Sleep that knits up the ravelled sleave of care,
> the death of each day's life,
> sore labour's bath,
> balm of hurt minds,
> great nature's second course,
> chief nourisher in life's feast. (William Shakespeare, *Macbeth,* Act II, scene ii)

Most of us will spend roughly a third of our time alive on earth in sleep. Few, if any, of us really understand why. At first glance it seems dangerous – closing down our sensory awareness and making us sitting (or lying) targets and physically unproductive for a large period of our lives. Why would such a process have evolved at all? Sleep is a state in which any animal is highly vulnerable to predation, attack or accident and is one that involves a range of changes to level of arousal and metabolism. Despite its obvious drawbacks, sleep is virtually ubiquitous across the animal kingdom. It is seen in all creatures studied to date but can vary in form and extent (see Siegel 2005a, 2008; Staunton 2005).

During REM (rapid eye movement) sleep, when we are at our most vulnerable, most higher animals have evolved a mechanism that disconnects cortical activity from motor control. This method of limiting movement during REM sleep should make sleeping safer (see Lima and Rattenborg 2007) – an animal in REM sleep is less likely to be spotted by a predator and is less likely to move and put itself into danger by falling from a safe position or making a noise to alert others.

Sleep is something we all do, that every one of us has personal experience of and that we all have our own thoughts and beliefs about. It is surprising for such a pervasive aspect of human life, one that is found across all human cultures and which figures heavily in our art and literature, that we know so little about it.

Sleep is a social phenomenon; our sleep patterns are entrained with those of our mothers well before we are born. As we grow in the womb we are acutely aware of changes in our own and our mother's heart and respiratory rate, her fluctuating levels of hormones and peptides, and of changes in the light levels and sounds that surround us. For most humans, from birth on, we rarely sleep alone. When people sleep together their sleep patterns tend to synchronize, as do other cyclical aspects of our biologies. Most research, however, has treated sleep as if it were exclusively a solitary activity, and tends to focus on sleep in the individual.

Babies will often sleep best when able to hear the heartbeat of an adult, and in most societies infants co-sleep with their mothers in the early years of life (see discussion in Morelli *et al.* 1992).

A range of factors has been identified that affect the development of sleep. Some of these are essentially fixed – genetic factors such as clock genes, and environmental factors such as the orbits of celestial bodies; others have altered over the generations. In this latter category are factors such as cultural change (things such as group recreational activities happening after dark; the trend for discouraging mother–infant co-sleeping; changes to diet) and scientific innovation (things such as the discovery of fire, the wearing of clothes, the light bulb, central heating and the television) (see Jenni and O'Connor 2005; Wrangham 2009).

In most land mammals, sleep appears to have evolved along similar lines. The length of time regularly spent asleep is correlated with physical morphology (Siegel 2005a), physiology (Elgar, Pagel and Harvey 1988), and life history (Lesku *et al.* 2006). The biological processes involved appear to be highly conserved–that is, they have a similar basis across a broad range of species (Allada and Siegel 2008). The genetic basis to this process is gradually yielding its secrets to systematic research (see Winrow *et al.* 2009).

Animals that have shorter sleep patterns are also those that have a higher risk of being eaten while asleep. This fact could merely be because smaller mammals have higher metabolic rates, need to spend more time searching for food and are also more typically found at the bottom of the animal food chain. If sleep duration is under genetic control, it may also be an effect of evolutionary selection – at any level in this hierarchy those who sleep less are more likely to survive to the next day to pass on their genes so should outbreed their sleepier competitors, all other things being equal.

It is important to learn early in life from your parents, siblings or peers to sleep when and where it is safe. Babies today are born by and large into safe environments. In evolutionary terms this security is a recent improvement that came about with the shift from hunter-gatherer to agrarian living around 10,000 years ago.

It seems probable that our present-day sleeping patterns evolved largely before our discovery of reliable sources of night-time light and energy that artificially alter our day–night cycles. Our sleep patterns definitely developed prior to the advent of many of our other recently self-imposed sleep issues such as jet lag and night-time shift work.

In birds, however, most of the correlations we can see across other land and aquatic species do not appear to hold true (Roth II *et al.* 2006), with the exception of the negative association with predation.

Why do we sleep?

However we do it, there seems to be a strong biological need for all animals to repeatedly enter a sleep state, gearing their bodily patterns to the patterns of the planet.

The 'best guess view' on why we all sleep is not very enlightening. It is essentially that sleep must be very important because otherwise we wouldn't do something quite so risky. So far, however, no one is quite certain what it is that sleep is very important for.

> If sleep does not serve an absolutely vital function, then it is the biggest mistake the evolutionary process has ever made… (I. Allan Rechtschaffen, University of Chicago Sleep Laboratory, Smithsonian Institute, November 1978)

> Sleep remains one of the great mysteries of biomedical science. Few physiologic processes are as fundamental to health and function, so universal in daily experience, and so poorly understood… (Tractenberg and Singer 2007, p.1171)

Sleep patterns are not due simply to the motions of the planets. From fruit flies (Ganguly-Fitzgerald, Donlea and Shaw 2006) to humans (Ueno *et al.* 2009), sleep patterns are affected by a range of factors that include stress, exercise and diet.

Some have argued that sleep is trivial and is just something to do when we are resting and there is no better alternative on offer (see, e.g. Rial *et al.* 2007). Others have argued that sleep has to be an essential process as otherwise it would have been selected out by evolution (Rattenborg *et al.* 2007). Arguments can be advanced for a balance between benefits in terms of selective memory enhancement and energy conservation and the reduced ability to engage in other activities at these times (see Roth II, Rattenborg and Pravosudov 2010).

I have an intuitive difficulty in accepting the 'sleep is a trivial and non-functional way of filling in time' view. It is similar to saying that we only have a brain to stop our ears from banging together. Even if sleep were an epiphenomenon, it is such a widely embracing one that the physiological processes it parallels must be highly important.

Environmental factors are important influences on sleep, but our sleep patterns also seem to be genetically determined to a significant degree (see, e.g. Heath *et al.* 1990). Accepting that sleep is under a degree of genetic control, it carries such significant risks that it would be selected against unless its benefits outweighed them, or was inextricably linked to other processes that conveyed a selective advantage. By this I mean that if the time we spent asleep increased our risk of being killed before we manage to pass on our genes, this would lower our chances of reproducing. People who slept less or did not sleep would have a competitive edge, and be more likely to parent and successfully rear children with further copies of their more successful shorter-sleep genes. The consequence would have been a selection pressure to evolve shorter and shorter sleep patterns, or even for sleep to disappear altogether. This is of course unless we sleep for a reason.

The argument would be different if there were no such obvious disadvantages to being asleep. Once we lived in secure houses with less chance of being killed while we slept, the selection pressure against sleeping would have reduced. There is no historical or fossil record of how much sleep people had at different times in our past – behaviour leaves no such traces.

Various theories that claim to account for why we have evolved a behaviour pattern that includes sleep have been proposed:

1. *Sleep is a time that our brains can consolidate learning experiences gained when we are awake* (Hill, Hogan and Karmiloff-Smith 2007; Sejnowski and Destexhe 2000). Sejnowski and Destexhe suggest that the alternation between fast and slow wave electrical activity seen in sleep helps us to store new memories – they suggest that slow-wave activity opens molecular pathways that enhance plasticity. A small structure in the limbic system called the hippocampus could be a key physical component in this process. Some supporting evidence comes from the cyclical changes in hippocampal electroencephalogram (EEG) that were observed during sleep in five patients undergoing evaluation for epilepsy surgery. They all demonstrated a pattern of cycling between fast hippocampal activity during REM and flattened slow-wave activity during NREM (non-REM) sleep (Moroni *et al.* 2007). There is further support from animal research on maze learning in rats. Rats brain activity while trained on a novel maze and during subsequent sleep, showed that the same assemblies of hippocampal neurons were activated in both states (Wilson and McNaughton 1994).

2. *Sleep may be an unnecessary endpoint to a physiological cascade of events.* Sleep may result from altered input–output relationships between small groups of highly interconnected nerve cells induced by chemical growth factors that are themselves the result of other patterns of neural activity (Krueger, Obal and Fang 1999). On this view, we don't need to sleep but we need to alter our metabolism in the period leading up to it that makes sleep an inevitable by-product (this could be called the 'you can't make an omelette without breaking eggs' model).

3. *The role of sleep is to restore brain energy that has been depleted during wakefulness,* a theory advanced by Benington and Heller (1995). The original model focused largely on two neurochemicals – adenosine and glycogen – both of which show clear circadian patterns. This 'energy hypothesis of sleep' has been revised and extended to include discussion of a range of other metabolic processes that also show circadian patterns (Scharf *et al.* 2008).

    There is considerable evidence from animal research that the parts of the brain that metabolize more while awake are subsequently recorded as having a greater intensity of slow-wave activity during sleep. This suggests that there is some role for sleep in replenishing the energy that has been expended during the more active waking use of the specific brain regions involved (see Rector *et al.* 2009).

    There is ongoing debate about the function of sleep and also about the effects of variation in sleep pattern. In our increasingly obese and weight-obsessed population, one aspect that is of interest is that sleep variations seem to predict likelihood of future weight gain (Laffan and Punjabi 2008). Sleep restriction increases both appetite and ghrelin levels and decreases leptin levels (ghrelin is a recently discovered hormone that affects appetite, while leptin is involved regulating energy metabolism through the metabolism of certain types of body fat) (Spiegel *et al.* 2004).

4. *Sleep may be something that fulfilled an important function at an earlier stage in our evolution but is no longer required.* This view would see sleep as the behavioural equivalent of the appendix – a vestigial remnant of a once important system we no longer require. We can speculate, however, as with any other behaviour, even if this were correct it is impossible to test – there would be nothing left to see.

DREAMING

> ...we must also enquire what the dream is, and from what
> cause sleepers sometimes dream, and sometimes do not; or
> whether the truth is that sleepers always dream but do not
> always remember (their dream); and if this occurs, what its
> explanation is.
>
> Aristotle, 'On Sleep and Sleeplessness' (c. 350 BC)

Dreams have fascinated people for as long as we have articulated our thoughts. Most of our attempts to understand them have focused on trying to understand the psychological significance of their content rather than their biological function/s.

The philosopher Alfred J. Ayer didn't believe in dreams at all because, on his own account, he was not aware of ever having had one. For others, their dream experiences seem complex and immersive and enable the complex stories of childhood that require suspense of belief in reality to come to life in a rich internal contemplative world. Many childhood stories such as *Alice in Wonderland*, *The Lord of the Rings*, the *Narnia Chronicles*, the tales of Dr Seuss and the many stories of Roald Dahl and Philip Pullman rely for their impact on the audience being able to contemplate such rich fantasy worlds.

In the famous early twentieth-century novel *At Swim-Two-Birds* by Flann O'Brien (1937), the story takes place on several levels bridged by sleep. Layers of the story are played out by characters who live in the dreams of others. Similar devices have been used in a number of films such as *The Matrix* (Wachowski and Wachowski 1999) and *Inception* (Nolan 2010).

In *The Interpretation of Dreams* (Freud 1913) there is a graphic representation of a dream recounted by a wet-nurse. In her dream, as told to Freud, her young charge needed to urinate while they were out walking. As the boy relieved himself, his urine gradually formed into a stream then a river and finally all manner of vessels from gondolas to sailboats and liners went floating past them. She woke to hear the boy crying out to her having wet himself in his sleep. For Freud, the importance of dreams like this lay in their content, symbolism and metaphorical significance.

A large part of psychoanalytic theory developed around Freud's view of the roles played by dreams and the unconscious. There has been periodic resurgence of interest in such views on the psychic significance of dreams (e.g. Reiser 2001; Solms 2000). For Freud, sleep was 'the royal road to understanding the unconscious'. It appears that in some respects he may have been correct – the study of sleep and the metabolic activity that occurs, particularly during REM sleep, may be starting to provide us with a better understanding of the means by which the electrochemical processes occurring in the brain correspond to the processes of thought.

What do we understand today about dreams – what do we think they are, what physical processes happen when they occur, and what might they be for?

People who have been woken during REM sleep are the most likely to report their dreams. Nathaniel Kleitman and his student, Eugene Aserinsky, were the first to report an association between dreams and the REM stage of sleep (Aserinsky and Kleitman 1953, 1955). One early study established that when woken from REM sleep some children as young as two could recount dreams (Kohler, Coddington and Agnew 1968).

Although most dreams are reported by people who have been woken from REM sleep, similar dream reports are also given by around 5–10 per cent of people woken from non-REM sleep (e.g. Cicogna *et al.* 2000). There does not appear to be a direct correspondence between REM sleep and dreams (Foulkes 1962) or the ability to recall them.

Do we know why we dream?

> To sleep, perchance to dream – ay, there's the rub.
>
> William Shakespeare, (*Hamlet*, Act III, scene i)

Clinical interest in sleep and dreaming came when we had developed the means to record and interpret electrical activity from electrodes placed on the scalp.

There had been brief interest in brain electrical activity in mid-nineteenth-century Britain with the work of Richard Caton. Caton discovered that electrical impulses could be recorded from the brains of dogs, monkeys and humans that were different when they were in different states of arousal. Caton presented his work to the British Medical Association (Caton 1875, 1877, 1887).

It was 78 years later, with the opening of the first sleep laboratory in 1953 by William C. Dement, that many would argue the field of sleep research became an area of true clinical interest. Dement built on the work of Caton and of Hans Berger who had subsequently developed the EEG. Dement established the first laboratory to conduct overnight recordings of EEG and eye movements during sleep (Dement 1958; Dement and Kleitman 1957a, 1957b). A good historical account of much of this early work, covering the period up to 1964, can be found in Gottesmann (2001).

One stage in sleep that appears to be markedly different from other human sleep states occurs when the sleeper lies still but the eyes move around rapidly under closed eyelids. This stage is called 'rapid eye movement' or REM sleep.

Some have argued that in mammals such as humans, the role of REM sleep is the reorganization and adjustment of emotional behaviour (see, e.g. Cai 1991) or, more generally, in the 'modulation, regulation, and even preparation of cognitive and emotional brain processes' (Walker 2009, p.168).

From functional brain imaging, the various areas involved in REM sleep have been identified (Maquet *et al.* 1996). During REM a system that involves the pontine tegmentum, the amygdala and anterior cingulate is bilaterally activated, together with the right parietal cortex.

Occasionally individuals present clinically in whom the atonia or 'sleep paralysis' normally seen in REM sleep persists, sometimes causing the person to be aware but unable to move on waking. This temporary paralysis can be extremely distressing and may last for several minutes. The opposite dissociation can also occur – a REM sleep state without atonia – this is known as REM sleep behaviour disorder. As we will go on to discuss, in this condition, the person acts out their dreams.

There is a two-way interaction between waking mood and sleep pattern. The content of dream sleep can be affected by daytime experiences and experiences during sleep can affect our daytime affect and perception of events (Vandekerckhove and Cluydts 2010; Walker and Harvey 2010).

At the opposite end of the spectrum, there are conditions in which REM sleep does not occur. This problem is typically a consequence of changes to the function of the pontine tegmentum. Absence of REM sleep has been reported in spinocerebellar degeneration (see Osorio and Daroff 1980); with mass lesions (Valldeoriola *et al.* 1993); and by haematoma (Gironell *et al.* 1995). REM-deprivation does not appear to cause any problems with daytime wakefulness. On polysomnography, those with spinocerebellar lesions have been shown to enter a unique sleep stage called 'sleep stage X'.

Sleep seems to play an important role in the consolidation (strengthening) of memory (Drummond *et al.* 1999; Maquet 2001; Stickgold 2005; Walker, Brakefield, Hobson and Stickgold 2003; Walker, Brakefield, Seidman *et al.* 2003). It seems that even brief periods of sleep can result in significant benefits for learning and retaining information (Mednick, Nakayama and Stickgold 2003), while lack of sleep can significantly impair retention (Ellenbogen 2005).

The processes by which sleep affects learning and retention appear complex (Dahl 1996) and we are only beginning to tease out how the different phases of sleep are involved (Hobson and Pace-Schott 2002), and how these change through the course of individual development (Siegel 2005a, 2005b, 2009a, 2009b).

The proportion and amount of REM sleep alter gradually as we age (Garcia-Rill *et al.* 2008). The typical newborn spends two thirds of the time asleep and roughly half of this time is spent in REM. By 15 years of age a typical teenager spends one third of their time asleep but only 1 hour is spent in REM sleep. The major changes in sleep pattern parallel the processes of brain maturation (Marks *et al.* 1995).

For the interested reader wanting to explore this area in more depth, I would suggest beginning with some of the reviews of the nature of dream sleep and the biological mechanisms hypothesised to underpin it. There are many that go into greater detail than is possible here (see Eiser 2005; Hobson 1990, 2005, 2009; Pace-Schott *et al.* 2003; Tractenberg and Singer 2007).

REM sleep is seen in other species. In 1958 Dement reported periods of cortical arousal associated with rapid eye movements during sleep in the cat (Dement 1958). In most other mammals, the occurrence of REM sleep is preceded by a pattern of electrical activity called ponto-geniculo-occipital (PGO) spikes. This pattern can be detected on an EEG (see Kavanau 1997 for discussion). When we are awake PGO spikes appear in response to sudden external stimuli that startle us. These spikes originate from cells in the pedunculopontine nuclei of the ascending reticular activating system (ARAS). The ARAS is a brainstem structure that is critical to maintaining our state of arousal.

There are various accounts of dreaming as a psychological phenomenon that do not attempt to address the issue of dream function (see, e.g. Seligman and Yellen 1987), and there is a long history of attempts to understand dreams and how they are linked to emotional and physical health (Palagini and Rosenlicht 2010).

We will not enter the philosophical debates on whether dreams happen. We will assume agreement that there are real phenomena that most people can accept as dreams, and that for the purposes of a book like this one at least it would not be helpful to contest this proposition.

Assuming that dreams are real phenomena, there are a number of different theories about why they happen.

DREAMING AS 'THREAT REHEARSAL'

Antti Revonsuo (Revonsuo 2000; Revonsuo and Valli 2008), a Finnish research psychologist, has proposed that one role of dreaming may be to simulate and rehearse the avoidance of threatening experiences that we anticipate we may be subjected to while awake. Noting that the form and content of remembered dream experiences is not random but selective, complex and seemingly related to events in our everyday waking lives, he developed his theory to try to account for the apparent salience of our recalled dream experiences.

His view would help to account for many of the seemingly premonitionary aspects of remembered dreams that then appear to come to pass as real life events – on this view dreams are a way of mentally rehearsing different 'what if?' scenarios. This theory has some empirical support from work analysing the dream content of severely and mildly traumatized Kurdish children and comparing these to the dreams of non-traumatized Finnish children – the more traumatized the child, the more traumatic the dream content reported (Valli *et al.* 2005) – although this could be argued to be simply replaying experiences that have been undergone rather than mental preparation.

This theory has some empirical support; however, it cannot be the whole story. Many dreams have no such content link to potential or to past threatening experiences and are not easily reconciled with this being the only reason that dreaming takes place.

A further source of information that bears on the issue comes from the condition known as 'REM sleep behaviour disorder'. In this condition, affected people act out their dreams (see Budhiraja 2007). This suggests that during dreaming people really do imagine being involved in actions. They are normally prevented from physically acting these out by a process in which cortical activity is disengaged from motor control during REM sleep.

DREAMING AS RANDOM ACTIVATION

Another view of the function of dreams is the Random Activation or 'Activation-Synthesis' Theory (Hobson and McCarley 1977). On this view, dreaming is a spin-off from a physiological process during which the brain compares an internally generated pattern from the midbrain to information stored in the forebrain. During this process external information input and output resulting in physical movements other than eye movements are blocked. This is similar to the epiphenomenal view below, but here dreaming is seen as a consequence of a brain process that occurs during sleep, rather than as a consequence for the brain of other things happening in the body.

DREAMING AS 'MENTAL DECLUTTERING'

A number of clinicians have taken the view that dreaming is a form of mental feng shui, allowing the brain to weed out unwanted associations and memories. The credit for proposing this view is typically given to the German physician W. Robert (1886) whose conception was stated by Freud as being that dreams were 'excretions of thought that had been stifled at birth' (Freud 1900, p.79). A similar view was proposed by the English neurologist John Hughlings Jackson who stated that the role of sleep was to 'sweep the higher layers of the highest centres clean' of unnecessary neuronal connections, leaving or consolidating the remainder (Taylor, Holmes and Walshe 1958, p.98).

Many years ago, Francis Crick (who later received the Nobel prize for his work on the structure of DNA with John Watson) together with Graeme Mitchison suggested that dream sleep was a specific state during which undesirable neural associations were weakened (Crick and Mitchison 1983). The general idea was that dreaming was a process by which neural associations could be weakened in a form of 'reverse–learning'.

It has been suggested that the Crick–Mitchison Theory could provide a way of accounting for some of the behavioural and cognitive features of ASD and Asperger syndrome (Brown 1996).

DREAMING AS MEMORY CONSOLIDATION

In contrast to the view of dreaming as a means of selective forgetting, another prominent and almost mirror opposite view has been that dreaming is a process that aids memory consolidation.

There is a considerable body of research that shows REM sleep to be important for learning and memory. This work is not typically to do with the content of dreams but with showing that changes in the amount of REM sleep have a direct effect on the quality of learning and recall.

There is some anecdotal evidence linking dream content to the need to consolidate new information. In a task requiring subjects to play the video game 'Tetris' several hours each day for three days the likelihood of recalling dream imagery related to playing the game was inversely related to previous familiarity with the game (Stickgold *et al.* 2000). The likelihood of Tetris appearing in dreams was associated with how novel the task was.

Research on sleep and memory consolidation may lend support to several of the above views on the role of dreaming. A study on the effects of REM on memory consolidation found that increased REM sleep appeared to aid the consolidation of emotional but not of neutral memories (Nishida *et al.* 2009). This suggests a mechanism that may selectively enhance consolidation of memories linked to particular states of arousal. If correct, this could provide a simple neurochemical mechanism that results in selective enhancement of memory consolidation.

DREAMS AS 'EPIPHENOMENA'

A last view that we need to discuss briefly is that dreams are merely epiphenomena (by-products of some non-mental physiological process needed by the body) – production of growth hormone for physical repair; cortisol for stress reduction or some other such process and that dreams occur as a chance consequence and by-product of this process. This amounts to saying that there is no reason for or mystery behind the purpose or origin of dreams. We just dream because we do.

Although it is easy to speculate, and we could probably come up with a number of other possible theories for why dreaming might happen, the nature of sleep and dreaming is inherently subjective and is not open to direct scientific scrutiny. It isn't possible to get definitive answers to why sleep or dreaming occur.

What we do have access to is evidence from measurable physical processes that happen during sleep – changes in our brain activity, metabolism and body biochemistry.

WHAT CHANGES OCCUR DURING SLEEP THAT DON'T OCCUR AT OTHER TIMES?

Understanding the workings of the brain has taken many paths: in recent years these have been dictated more by the tools available, while in the past the restrictions have been more to do with religious prescription. The two major developments in our understanding to date have come from studying the electrical patterns of activity in the brain and from the growing understanding of its chemistry. An excellent overview of these apparently competing models and how they developed can be found in Elliot Valenstein's book *The War of the Soup and the Sparks – the Discovery of Neurotransmitters and the Dispute over How Nerves Communicate* (2005).

The stages of sleep

When we sleep, we are said to go through four 'sleep stages' (stages 1 through stage 3 sleep, and REM sleep). These stages typically occur in a specific sequence. The idea of distinct sleep stages was first proposed in 1937, based on observed EEG differences (Loomis, Harvey and Hobart 1937). The first agreed classification was formalized in 1968 (Rechtschaffen and Kales 1968). The classification was revised most recently in 2007 (Iber *et al.* 2007) when a distinction between what had previously been called stage 3 and stage 4 sleep was dropped.

Each sleep stage has characteristic neurophysiological features with associated behaviours. Interpretation of the EEG profile is a highly skilled procedure, because sleep and arousal change with the age of the person (see Grigg-Damberger *et al.* 2007). Changes in non-REM slow-wave electrical activity are associated with the stage of structural maturation and synaptic development the brain has reached (Tononi and Cirelli 2006). These developmental differences are being used in studying the pattern of cortical development through childhood and adolescence (Kurth *et al.* 2010).

Other techniques such as functional magnetic resonance imaging (fMRI) allow changes in cerebral oxygenation to be correlated with changes in brain electrical activity (Czisch *et al.* 2002, 2004). This research is enabling accurate differentiation of phases within sleep stages which so far have been based largely on movements observed during sleep. Ever more sophisticated methods such as 'optogenetic deconstruction' are being developed to tease apart the basis to sleep biology (see Adamantidis, Carter and de Lecea 2010).

Studies of brain metabolism during sleep report reduction in both blood flow and metabolic rate (Braun *et al.* 1997; Maquet 2000; Maquet *et al.* 2005). Although there is reduced metabolism, the higher order networks in the brain continue to function and to show functional connectivity (Larson-Prior *et al.* 2009).

An early study (Tanguay *et al.* 1976) reported on 16 autistic children (aged 3 years–5 years 2 months) and 30 controls (3 months–5 years 8 months). They collected EEGs from the first three periods of REM sleep on each subject. The control group showed a clear developmental effect, with the amount of REM sleep reducing with age. The autistic group failed to demonstrate this effect with immature REM patterns that were more like those seen in pre-18-month controls.

It has been suggested that the differences in EEG spectra between awake and REM sleep seen in autism indicate difference in thalamocortical connectivity when compared to normal controls (Daoust *et al.* 2004).

So, what are these different sleep stages? In awake and sleeping states, there are several clear stages of sleep and arousal that can be identified from EEG.

When you are awake, an EEG recording would typically show variable electrical activity that is low voltage and high frequency. When you start to sleep, this pattern changes, going through a number of characteristic and well defined stages.

STAGE 1 SLEEP

In the first stage of sleep there is increased lower frequency activity on the EEG. This ranges from alpha waves (8–13 Hertz) to theta waves (4–7 Hertz). This is a 'light' stage of sleep from which someone can easily be aroused. There is some decrease in muscle tone compared to the awake state, but physical twitches and jerks are commonly seen.

REM SLEEP

Through sleep, there are periods of what is usually called REM (rapid eye movement, 'paradoxical' or 'dream') sleep that occur interspersed with stage 1. The first period of REM sleep is unlikely to occur in an adult until they have been asleep for 90 minutes or more except when they are overtired (this is typically referred to as being 'sleep-deprived'). In infants and neonates the period of sleep preceding REM can be fleeting. This compressed sleep cycle is why babies can often seem to cope with sleep patterns that exhaust their parents.

In infancy we sleep for longer overall and REM sleep accounts for a far higher proportion of our time spent asleep than when we are older. A neonate will spend roughly 50 per cent of its time asleep in REM sleep while adults will spend less time asleep of which less than 20 per cent will be in REM (Roffwarg, Muzio and Dement 1966).

A key part of the nervous system involved in REM sleep is a midbrain nucleus called the 'locus coeruleus'. This was one of the first structures reported to mediate sleep pattern (Jouvet and Delorme 1965). Abnormalities in the formation of the locus coeruleus have been shown in mouse models of Rett syndrome (Taneja *et al.* 2009).

REM sleep can be detected in the developing foetus before birth from around the 30th week post conception, and until birth is largely entrained with maternal sleep cycles (see Mirmiran, Maas and Ariagno 2003).

The existence of REM sleep was first noted in infants in 1953 (Aserinsky and Kleitman 1953; for discussion, see Aserinsky 1996). It is typically when roused from this type of sleep state that people appear able to describe dreams. Dreams are reported by around 70 per cent of people awakened from REM sleep who are able to give a verbal report. During REM sleep, a complex pattern of brain metabolic activity involving neocortical and basal-forebrain hypothalamic structures is seen (Nofzinger *et al.* 1997).

There are two distinct phases to REM sleep. These are known as tonic REM and phasic REM. In the tonic REM phase there is some degree of cortical response to external stimuli, while in phasic REM there is no reaction to environmental stimuli. During phasic REM there is clear evidence from fMRI of a functionally isolated thalamocortical loop with significantly increased thalamic and temporal lobe metabolism (Wehrle *et al.* 2007) – this would seem to be a clear physical basis to dreaming – a complex pattern of brain activities that would otherwise happen during interactions with the world that are effectively occurring in isolation.

Autistic children take longer to enter REM sleep and show both a relative and an absolute deficiency in REM (both the amount and proportion of sleep spent in REM is lower) in children with autism when compared to both developmentally delayed non-autistic and normally developing controls (Buckley *et al.* 2010).

STAGE 2 SLEEP

In stage 2 sleep a number of different types of electrical activity occur – sleep spindles (typically 12–14 Hertz, also known as the sensori-motor rhythm or SMR) and 'K complexes'. The presence of these two types of electrical activity is used to define stage 2 as a non-REM stage of sleep. In stage 2 sleep muscle activity decreases and the person shows no awareness of what is going on around them. During non-REM sleep there are alternating phases known as the cyclic alternating pattern (CAP) (see Bruni, Novelli *et al.* 2010).

Sleep spindles seem to be important in screening out external noise – the more sleep spindles, the better able someone is to sleep through external noises (Dang Vu *et al.* 2010). This is something which will have had evolutionary pressures – where awareness of predators/attackers is important, rapid arousal from sleep would be selected for, while in safer or noisier environments being able 'to sleep through anything' might be more advantageous.

STAGE 3 SLEEP

Stage 3 sleep consists principally of low frequency (0.5–2 Hertz) slow or delta waves. This is when many sleep problems such as night terrors, rhythmic movement disorder, bruxism, nocturnal enuresis (bedwetting), sleepwalking and somniloquy (sleeptalking) are all most likely to occur.

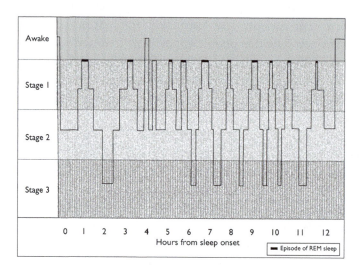

Figure A.1 Sleep stages

The stages of sleep are usually described in terms of their changes in electrical activity. As we will see, there are also corresponding changes in brain chemistry.

An additional sleep stage is occasionally seen that has been called sleep stage X. This has been reported in individuals who lack REM sleep as a result of defects in the pontine tegmentum (see Osorio and Daroff 1980).

There is clear evidence that the circadian cycles that can be seen in the electrical activity of the brains of primates are entrained by ambient light levels and that this process is initiated in mid-pregnancy (Rivkees 2003).

In a study of 27 able ASD adults without sleep complaints and 78 healthy comparison controls group-matched on age and sex, in the autistic group subjective ratings of their own sleep demonstrated insomnia or a phase-advanced sleep cycle – sleeping later than the controls (Limoges *et al.* 2005). In a case-matched subset of 16 ASD and 16 controls, a range of differences were reported as significantly different in the ASD group – they took longer to get to sleep, woke more often, had lower sleep efficiency (the amount of time asleep compared to the amount of time spent in bed), an increased duration of stage 1 sleep, decreased non-REM and slow-wave sleep, fewer stage 2 EEG sleep spindles, and fewer rapid eye movements during REM sleep.

EEG fluctuation typically referred to as the CAP (a pattern seen in non-REM sleep) is often slower in conditions such as autism (Miano *et al.* 2007) and Asperger syndrome (Bruni *et al.* 2007), in disorders of arousal, in learning difficulties and in ADHD (attention-deficit hyperactivity disorder) (Miano *et al.* 2006). Differences in CAP are reported in a range of clinical disorders and conditions (see Bruni, Novelli *et al.* 2010).

In addition to changes in brain electrical activity there are also systematic changes in levels of a number of endocrine compounds. These are chemicals that are detectable in body fluids, the best-studied of these being growth hormone, thyroid stimulating hormone, cortisol and melatonin (for review, see Haus 2007). Excellent general overviews of the relationship between endocrine factors and sleep can be found in McCarley 2007; Rutter, Reick and McKnight 2002 and Vorona 2008). There is good evidence that these vary in systematic ways and that these processes interact. Further biological factors that show a circadian pattern and may be implicated in control of sleep are adenosine and glycogen.

The circadian patterns in electrical and chemical activity develop at an early stage. Differences between REM and non-REM sleep in the foetus can be detected during the last 10 weeks of pregnancy (see Mirmiran *et al.* 2003).

In addition to these chemical and electrical changes in activity within the brain, they are also paralleled by changes in other factors such as respiration and body temperature (see Mazzoccoli *et al.* 2004).

Biochemical changes associated with sleep

GROWTH HORMONE (SEE FIGURE A.2)

This is a peptide hormone involved in stimulating both cell growth and regeneration. It is important throughout the lifespan. The largest pulses of growth hormone secretion occur during stage 3 sleep (Takahashi, Kipnis and Daughaday 1968), with over half of our growth hormone being secreted at these times (Mehta and Hindmarsh 2002), in tandem with the production of melatonin. One study has shown that there is a strong association between the proportion of slow wave sleep and the level of growth hormone in men (Van Cauter, Leproult and Plat 2000).

Excessive levels are associated with sleep-disordered breathing and are implicated in obstructive sleep apnoea. Elevated growth hormone may also play a role in narcolepsy (see Vorona 2008).

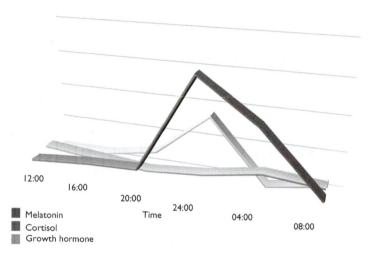

Figure A.2 Circadian hormonal fluctuations

CORTISOL (SEE FIGURE A.2)

Cortisol is a steroid derived from cholesterol and produced through mitochondrial enzyme activity in the adrenal glands. Cortisol levels appear to have a fairly fixed circadian rhythm that is affected by sleep pattern and by daytime levels of arousal (Balbo, Leproult and Van Cauter 2010). It shows a circadian pattern of release in both boys and girls with the highest levels being found in serum around waking and the lowest levels in the early stages of sleep (Knutsson *et al.* 1997).

A study of urinary cortisol levels in 18 high-functioning autistic boys aged 4–14 reported that they all showed a normal circadian pattern, with slightly elevated daytime cortisol levels in a small number (Richdale and Prior 1992).

THYROID STIMULATING HORMONE (TSH)

TSH, also known as thyrotropin, is a peptide hormone synthesized in the anterior lobe of the pituitary gland. It is involved in the control of thyroid function.

An early study (Rose and Nisula 1989) examined variation in TSH in 96 children aged 5–18 and established that there was a clear circadian pattern with the highest levels being recorded between 21:00 and 06:00. TSH is produced in distinct pulses with an average of 9 pulses in a 24-hour period in the adult, which cluster with the greatest TSH levels being found between 2 and 4 am (Brabant *et al.* 1990; Nicolau and Haus 1994). The pattern is paralleled by other biochemical factors such as free levels of the thyroid hormone triiodothyronine (Russell *et al.* 2008).

Abnormal TSH levels have been linked to a number of sleep problems. These include obstructive sleep apnoea, restless legs syndrome, sleepwalking and insomnia (for review see Vorona 2008).

MELATONIN (SEE FIGURE A.2)

Melatonin is a biologically active compound derived from the dietary amino acid tryptophan. Tryptophan is first converted to serotonin and then from serotonin to melatonin.

In adults, melatonin levels in body fluids such as blood and saliva show a clear circadian pattern with high circulating levels in the period before sleep. Levels gradually reduce through the night and waking occurs typically when it has returned to daytime levels. The critical role of melatonin in human circadian rhythms has been used to argue for the use of melatonin supplements and the development of melatonin agonists in the treatment of sleep disorders (Turek and Gillette 2004).

ADENOSINE

Adenosine is one of the four nucleosides in ribonucleic acid (RNA); in addition in its free state it has a number of metabolic functions.

There is good animal evidence for circadian fluctuation of adenosine concentrations in a range of body tissues and is important in maintaining energy homeostasis (Chagoya de Sanchez 1995). Adenosine is thought to play a key role in the regulation of sleep (Basheer *et al.* 2004), a view supported by research showing that adenosine agonists induce sleep while adenosine antagonists decrease sleep (see Bjorness and Greene 2009).

Free adenosine levels are affected by both caffeine and chocolate intake which suppress REM sleep. Cases have been reported where REM sleep behaviour disorder has been linked to ingestion of caffeine (Stolz and Aldrich 1991) and chocolate (Vorona and Ware 2002).

PROLACTIN

A hormone produced by the pituitary gland, prolactin is involved in a variety of functions including the stimulation of lactation after birth. Prolactin shows a circadian rhythm with elevated levels during sleep and lower levels on waking (Spiegel *et al.* 1994).

A number of animal studies suggest that prolactin levels are directly correlated with REM sleep (e.g. Obál *et al.* 2005; Roky *et al.* 1995).

TESTOSTERONE

Testosterone shows a characteristic circadian rhythm in men, with a peak level at around 08:00 and a trough at around 20:00 (Plymate, Tenover and Bremner 1989). Diurnal rhythms are clearly established well before puberty and have been reported in samples as early as 4–5 years of age (Mitamura *et al.* 1999).

The pattern of testosterone secretion is disrupted when sleep becomes fragmented (Luboshitsky *et al.* 2001) and levels of testosterone are reduced in conditions such as obstructive sleep apnoea (Luboshitsky *et al.* 2002).

There is a close correlation between fluctuations in the level of circulating testosterone and in the level of luteinizing hormone (Rowe *et al.* 1975). In women a rapid rise in luteinizing hormone, an anterior pituitary hormone, triggers ovulation.

LEPTIN

Leptin is a hormone that is involved in fat metabolism. It shows a clear chronobiotic pattern in the general population. The highest levels are found at night and the lowest levels around midday. Levels are twice as high in women as they are in men, but with similar periodicity (Licinio *et al.* 1998). Levels are also higher in obese than in lean individuals (Sinha *et al.* 1996).

There is evidence for a direct association between leptin levels and seizure control in epilepsy (for discussion, see Diano and Horvath 2008).

Leptin levels correlate inversely with markers of pituitary-adrenal function such as adrenocorticotropic hormone (ACTH) (Licinio *et al.* 1997).

GHRELIN

Ghrelin is found in the hypothalamus and also in the stomach. It is a peptide involved in appetite control. It shows a circadian pattern with increased night-time and lower morning levels (Dzaja *et al.* 2004; Schuessler *et al.* 2005).

In animals plasma ghrelin levels have been found to correlate with the central nervous system (CNS) levels of serotonin (Nonogaki, Ohashi-Nozue and Oka 2006), affecting synapse formation in the midbrain (Abizaid *et al.* 2006). Abnormalities have been reported in association with inflammatory bowel disease (Peracchi *et al.* 2006), seizures (Berilgen *et al.* 2006) and immune dysfunction (Dixit and Taub 2005), all of which have been linked to ASD.

Ghrelin is a sleep-promoting factor. Higher levels correlate with increases in slow-wave sleep (Weikel *et al.* 2003).

INSULIN

Insulin is a pancreatic hormone that controls blood glucose levels. Abnormalities in this process can result in diabetes. It is involved in the regulation of the body's metabolism of carbohydrates and fats.

Fluctuations in insulin levels appear to vary with sleep stage (see, for review, Simon and Brandenberger 2002). Lower levels have been reported during REM and higher levels during non-REM sleep (Kern *et al.* 1996).

GLYCOGEN

Glycogen is used in the body to store carbohydrates for its future energy requirements. Genes involved in glycogen metabolism play an important role in mammalian circadian rhythm (Itaka *et al.* 2005).

Prolonged periods of wakefulness deplete brain glycogen (in the rat, 12 hours without sleep will deplete brain glycogen by about 40 per cent. This is reversed with around 15 hours of sleep. See Kong *et al.* 2002). Sleeping leads to the accumulation of glycogen in CNS tissue. Most glycogen is found in astrocytes, not neurons. It is mobilized and used as an energy source on waking. Glucose provides the major source of nervous system energy and glycogen plays a relatively minor role; however, its circadian fluctuation suggests that it is likely to be more reflective of the energy demands of the brain in different states of wakefulness (see Brown 2004).

Do circadian patterns emerge as we develop?

From well before birth the human foetus has steadily developing sensory functions. A number of studies show the development of foetal abilities and the increasing ability to recognize and learn from sensory input (Lecanuet and Schaal 2002/1).

A variety of maternal factors such as nutrition, psychological stress and the use of drugs affect foetal growth and development. Low bodyweight and ponderal index at birth predict lower melatonin production in adulthood and increase the risk of obesity (Kennaway *et al.* 2001).

These external biological factors, and exposure to the range of neurochemical and sensory, circadian and ultradian patterns 'fine tune' the inherent rhythmicity in the developing foetus. In particular, they impose temporal patterning on brain systems such as the suprachiasmatic nucleus (see Kennaway 2002).

There is evidence for the development of circadian rhythms in the human infant from as early as 30 weeks post conception (Mirmiran and Kok 1991; Mirmiran *et al.* 1992; Mirmiran *et al.* 2003). Patterns in both body temperature and heart rate are apparent at least from this stage.

The first study to clearly document foetal behaviour tracked a group of 14 healthy pregnancies from 32 to 40 weeks at fortnightly intervals. It recorded body and eye movements using ultrasound, and foetal heart rate using cardiotocography. Until 36 weeks these varied independently but by the 38- and 40-week sessions they changed in concert and four clear behavioural states could be identified equivalent to the states that can be differentiated in the newborn. There is progressive elaboration of behavioural states postnatally (Pillai and James 1990), and it is clear that the basis to the sleep–wake pattern and circadian patterning of active behaviour emerges before birth.

A fifth behavioural state, equivalent to crying in the neonate, has not been observed in free records of the foetus. It has been described in response to vibroacoustic stimulation in a study where this was being used to examine the effects on foetal responsiveness with recent maternal exposure to tobacco and cocaine (Gingras, Mitchell and Grattan 2005).

From as early as the 32nd week of pregnancy, circadian patterns are detectable in the electrical activity of the foetal brain, with REM and non-REM sleep patterns being clearly discernible (Visser *et al.* 1987).

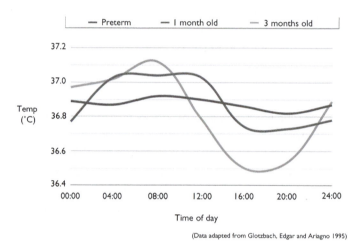

Figure A.3 Infant circadian temperature variations

The infant's progression from an unstable to a circadian pattern

Towards the end of pregnancy, the foetus shows a well-developed ability to learn and remember sounds. As the sounds that they will hear most will be their mother's voice, but distorted through the amniotic fluid, this is most likely to be achieved by using prosodic features rather than things such as pitch and tone. The newborn infant already has a learned preference for the speech and movement patterns of its own mother (DeCasper and Fifer 1980; DeCasper and Spence 1986).

While still in the womb, experience of other sounds can also lead to recognition and preference. For example, babies exposed through abdominal headphones to particular music during the last 3 days of the pregnancy showed greater alerting, more heart rate variation and spent more time awake when exposed to this music after birth compared with matched babies with no prior exposure *in utero* (James, Spencer and Stepsis 2002).

The above studies have direct implications for enhancing the social responsiveness of infants with less *in utero* exposure to cues such as mother's voice. This would be seen in infants born prematurely, with congenital deafness, or with other sensory issues.

After birth, circadian variations in light levels, tryptophan, melatonin and SCFAs (Short-Chain Fatty Acids) in breastmilk, and ambient sound and temperature (Figure A.3) all help to establish the infant's endogenous circadian patterns. This is consistent with the fact that breast-fed babies generally develop better sleep patterns than those who are bottle-fed (Lucas and St James-Roberts 1998).

There are increased risks of ASD associated with the use of formula feeds (Schultz *et al.* 2006), and with prematurity or low birthweight (Limperopoulos *et al.* 2008). These suggest that the importance of these sorts of factors has been given insufficient emphasis to date.

Chronotypes are particular patterns of body function, normally simplified to morning types and evening types. There is some biological validity to this differentiation. For example, performance is associated with biological rhythms in factors such as melatonin (Gibertini, Graham and Cook 1999). Chronotype can be assessed on children and there is a validated assessment tool for 4–11-year-olds – the Children's ChronoType Questionnaire (CCTQ) (Werner *et al.* 2009).

Developmental changes in chronotype seem to occur at two distinct times: first at around 12 years (Díaz-Morales and Sorroche 2008) when there is a transition corresponding to the final major increase in brain growth at adolescence; and second at around 20 years when a second abrupt change in sleep pattern occurs, from progressively later to earlier chronotypes. This second change can be used to mark the transition from adolescence to adulthood (see Roenneberg *et al.* 2004).

Chronotype patterns show large individual differences and are affected by age and sex. Within the individual they tend to be stable over time other than the changes at the beginning and end of adolescence.

THE BRAIN AT REST

Our brains are very difficult to investigate, particularly when we are alive. We believe them to be the very essence of our lives – we can exist without, or with replacements for, most other parts of our bodies but, unlike our other organs, our own brains seem to be essential to who we are. As the most critical and delicate part of our anatomy, it is little wonder that they are the best protected from injury, the least accessible and the hardest to study.

After we die, our brains rapidly lose electrophysiological activity and our neurochemical systems start to break down. These make postmortem assessment of functional aspects of the brain all but impossible. This is largely due to the dependence of the CNS on external sources of energy. Neurons lack the subcellular organelles known as mitochondria that are present in most other cells in the body. Mitochondria provide chemical energy sources such as adenosine triphosphate (ATP) inside most other living cells. The other exceptions to this cellular energy rule are mature erythrocytes (red blood cells). Lacking such internal sources of energy, the nerve cells of the brain are dependent on receiving their energy through the bloodstream and their supporting cells, such as glia and astrocytes, hence their rapid loss of function when the heart stops beating and circulation of the blood stops.

In studying the living person a wide range of problems beset the brain researcher. Not the least of the difficulties is that the organ of interest is entirely encased in bone. This makes it difficult to access or to study the brain using techniques such as X-rays (it was only with the development of CAT (computerized axial tomography) scanning that computer analysis of multiple X-rays enabled us to start imaging the living brain inside the skull with any degree of detail, while MRI (magnetic resonance imaging) by providing a system that images water content rather than more dense structures has taken this type of structural imaging to new levels of definition). Systems such as the EEG which measures electrical activity, MRI which allowed clearer structural definition, and the recent revolution in techniques such as fMRI, PET (Positron Emission Tomography) and SPECT (Single-Photon Emission Computerized Tomography) which look at metabolism, and techniques such as DTI (diffusion tensor imaging) (a method that can identify fibre tracts within the brain by fractional anisotropy, a way of mapping non-random water movement within the brain) have begun to allow us to access this complex system.

There have been huge strides in our ability to image brain structure, metabolism and electrical activity in recent years. There is an emerging consensus on how human brain functions can best be studied (Biswal *et al.* 2010). The various approaches that can be used to study brain structure and function in the living brain have, as we will see, begun to help us to understand the issues involved in understanding sleep. One model that amalgamates much of the research on neurophysiological analysis of sleep with cellular and molecular findings is the Cellular-Molecular-Network model (Datta and MacLean 2007).

There is still very limited information on brain function during sleep in ASD. This is a fast developing area and promises to yield helpful information on brain development in ASD and how it links to clinical presentation (see Pierce 2011).

IS OUR SLEEP AFFECTED BY WHAT WE EAT?

Let me have men about me that are fat;
Sleek-headed men and such as sleep o' nights:
Yond Cassius has a lean and hungry look;
He thinks too much: such men are dangerous.

William Shakespeare, *Julius Caesar*, (Act I, scene ii)

Shakespeare seems to have been aware that there was a link between sleep, the shapes of our bodies and our behaviour. Like many others since, however, he got the link the wrong way round. He assumed that people who were overweight would sleep more soundly, and slim people would sleep less. In fact obesity is usually associated with sleeping less not sleeping more, probably as a consequence of things such as the higher intake of food through snacking which can go along with spending less time asleep (Nedeltcheva *et al.* 2009). A large part of why exercise helps in weight loss is to do with occupying yourself in something other than consuming food at times when you would otherwise be more likely to eat rather than simply burning off calories.

The Greek philosopher Aristotle is the person usually credited with recognizing a link between sleep and nutrition (Aristotle c. 350 BC). Most of us know from experience that eating a large meal can induce drowsiness. This is something that may be familiar from overindulgence at times of celebrations such as Christmas, Thanksgiving or the end of Ramadan. For many the effect can be compounded by alcohol. So much for anecdote, is there any evidence that our diets affect our sleep?

As infants we all began by drinking milk for nutrition, either from our mothers or as a prepared infant formula. There is good evidence that normally there are marked circadian rhythms in both the melatonin (Illnerova, Buresova and Presl 1993) and tryptophan levels (Cubero *et al.* 2005) in human breastmilk. The circadian rhythm of breast-fed infants' endogenous melatonin pattern gradually becomes entrained with those of their mothers. There are also circadian changes in the levels of antioxidants in breastmilk as was shown in a study of expressed milk provided on day 1–5 (colostrum) (Cubero *et al.* 2009).

Breast-fed babies typically develop better sleep patterns than those who are formula-fed (Lucas and St James-Roberts 1998), and it is known that the child's own circadian rhythm of melatonin production is not established until around 3 months after birth (Ardura *et al.* 2003).

The likelihood both of breastfeeding and of persistence with it are associated with the likelihood of the mother and infant co-sleeping (Ball 2003). As breastfeeding encourages establishing a sleep pattern in the infant, and also improves immune function, this is a pattern that may have evolved through its beneficial effects on offspring survival.

Early circadian changes in the dietary intake of melatonin and tryptophan for the young breast-fed baby are dependent on the fluctuations in levels in the mother's breastmilk. There are no such variations in the levels of intake for a baby receiving formula feeds.

Tryptophan from breastmilk affects sleep in infancy and, as the child gets older, levels of tryptophan from diet still seem to be important for sleep. A recent Japanese study on over 2000 infants and school children showed a strong association between the amount of tryptophan that is ingested at breakfast, diurnal rhythm and subsequent sleep quality (Harada *et al.* 2007).

Tryptophan is an amino acid that is found in many foods. Bananas, chocolate, oats, dates, milk, yogurt, cottage cheese, red meats, eggs, fish, poultry, various seeds and nuts are particularly high dietary sources. Tryphophan is the dietary factor used by the body to produce melatonin.

Dietary factors affect behaviour and sleep in many individuals with ASD (see Aitken 2008). ASD and abnormal brain electrical activity have been reported together in a number of studies, and both are associated with an increased risk of epilepsy (see Canitano 2007). Sleep problems are also overrepresented in those with epilepsy. The role of lipid metabolism in seizure activity has been shown to be significant and can respond to dietary changes.

One small study of 18 therapy-resistant epileptic children looked at the effects of a ketogenic diet (this is a specialized diet low in carbohydrate that causes ketones to be excreted in urine). It was found to reduce daytime sleepiness, improve sleep quality and increase REM sleep while decreasing seizure frequency and severity at 1-year follow-up in all 11 children who were able to continue with it (see Hallböök, Lundgren and Rosén 2007).

A small sub-group of those with ASD have comorbid coeliac disease and are completely unable to tolerate dietary gluten (a molecule found in wheat and some other grains). It has been shown that those with coeliac disease have poorer sleep but that their sleep problems do not improve with a gluten-free diet alone (Zingone *et al.* 2010).

Perhaps the most surprising link between ASD and diet, if it is replicated, is between the use of formula feeds and risk of subsequent autism (Schultz *et al.* 2006). In an Internet survey study carried out by a San Diego-based research group, 861 families of children with ASD and 123 families of controls provided information. The study found that formula feeds supplemented with omega-3 fatty acids (to mimic the essential fatty acid profile of human breastmilk) were associated with a significantly increased risk of ASD (OR 2.48) when compared to breastfeeding for at least 6 months. The use of unsupplemented formula feeding was associated with an even larger increase in regressive autism (OR 12.96). (OR stands for 'Odds Ratio' – in the first study example here, this indicates that if you were not breast-fed, you were 2.48 times as likely to be autistic compared to an infant who was breastfed.)

In subsequent discussion and analysis of these results, most emphasis has been placed on the resultant differences in essential fatty acids when comparing breast to formula feeding and the possible link to ASD (see, e.g. Brown and Austin 2009). As we have seen, this is only one difference between the supplemented and unsupplemented formula-fed groups. No direct study of the effects of circadian differences in melatonin, tryptophan or of differences in other essential nutrient levels in ASD have so far been published.

A wide range of other factors is known to have nutritional effects on circadian rhythms in animals and man including the function of genes important for the metabolism of cholesterol, amino acids, lipids, glycogen and glucose (Froy 2007).

Several studies have implicated a role for B vitamins in the modulation of sleep. It has to be acknowledged, however, that this has to date been surprisingly poorly researched (Lichstein *et al.* 2008). Most B vitamins are initially provided in infant milk and in breast-fed babies levels are heavily affected by maternal diet.

In vegans, a mother's breastmilk lacks vitamin B12 as this is an essential vitamin derived entirely from animal products. Vitamin B12 cannot be made by our bodies. It has been reported that B12 deficiency can cause developmental regression (Casella *et al.* 2005). Vegan breastmilk is also deficient in taurine (Rana and Sanders 1986). Taurine is a compound derived from the conditionally essential amino acid cysteine, a sulphur-containing amino acid found at higher levels in animal proteins (Furst and Stehle 2004; Pohlandt 1974).

There is direct evidence for a role of B vitamins in sleep. Two studies (Ohta *et al.* 1991 and Okawa *et al.* 1990) have shown vitamin B12 to shorten the sleep–wake cycle, and a further study has found a vitamin B complex to be helpful in the treatment of nocturnal leg cramps (Chan *et al.* 1998).

One 3-month randomized controlled trial in a small group of autistic children (8 active vs 7 placebo) described parent-reported significant improvements in sleep and GI (gastrointestinal) issues with a multimineral/multivitamin supplement compared to placebo control. Although interesting, the study as it stands is too small to draw any useful conclusions (Adams and Holloway 2004) and should be replicated.

Iron deficiency has been linked to 'restless legs syndrome' (Earley *et al.* 2000), and more generally to sleep problems in infancy (Peirano, Algarín, Garrido, Algarín and Lozoff 2007; Peirano, Algarín, Garrido and Lozoff 2007; Peirano *et al.* 2009, 2010). Iron and zinc supplementation have both been found to lengthen infant sleep in nutritionally deprived populations (Kordas *et al.* 2009).

Orexins (also known as hypocretins) are neuropeptides that are produced in an area of the brain called the posterolateral hypothalamus (see Martynska *et al.* 2005). They are highly conserved across mammalian species and are involved in the control of food intake and energy expenditure. Recent research has shown that certain sleep disorders – particularly narcolepsy (Kok *et al.* 2002; Mignot *et al.* 2002) and obstructive sleep apnoea (Sakurai *et al.* 2004) can be associated with orexin abnormalities.

As we discussed above, REM sleep behaviour disorder has been linked in case reports to both excessive ingestion of caffeine (Stolz and Aldrich 1991) and chocolate (Vorona and Ware 2002). Caffeine will be discussed later, under herbal treatments, where its effects on sleep are discussed in terms of the role it can play in sustaining alertness and attention.

ALCOHOL CONSUMPTION

Drinking alcohol can interfere with sleep. This is not a common issue in childhood but becomes more of an issue in adolescence. Alcohol remains the most common drug used by Western adolescents (see Johnston *et al.* 2006).

The effect of alcohol on sleep in adolescence has only recently become a subject of clinical research interest (Comasco *et al.* 2010; Shibley, Malcolm and Veatch 2008). There is increasing evidence for an association between substance abuse (including alcohol and tobacco) and sleep difficulties, learning problems and executive function difficulties in adolescence (see, e.g. Fakier and Wild 2010).

Clock genes have been found to affect how our bodies deal with alcohol. PER2^{Brdm1} mutant mice have a defect in the glutamate system in their brains that is associated with increased alcohol consumption (Spanagel *et al.* 2005). Variations in the PER2 gene in humans have also been found to be associated with poorer regulation of alcohol intake (Perreau-Lenz, Zghoul and Spanagel 2007; Spanagel *et al.* 2005).

In one recently reported study, differences in the PER2 clock gene (2q37.3) were associated with both excess alcohol consumption and sleep problems in Swedish adolescent males (Comasco *et al.* 2010).

DIET, GENETICS AND BRAIN DEVELOPMENT

Many people may be surprised to learn that in addition to the effect that genetics has on our appetites and metabolism, our diet has a reciprocal and direct effect on how our genes express themselves (for discussion of how diets, nutrient differences and medication can affect epigenetic processes, see Junien 2006; McGowan, Meaney and Szyf 2008). The fact that changes in environmental factors such as diet can alter gene expression has caused a major change in our understanding of genetics.

Changes to diet can alter the phenotype over a number of generations and affect how genetic mechanisms can result in a particular phenotype or in a disorder such as a cancer (see Skinner and Guerrero-Bosagna 2009).

Research in rats has shown that circadian variation of the nutrients in formula feeds can affect the pattern of expression of certain genes important for brain development (Puigjaner *et al.* 2007).

Increasing our understanding of the mechanisms that operate in these overlapping areas – genetics, neurochemistry, diet and their interactions – is helping with the development of better targeted and more effective treatments for sleep disorders (Mignot, Taheri and Nishino 2002).

SOCIAL INTERACTION AND SLEEP

A further area that is important in the development and regulation of sleep is the role of social interaction and, particularly in the early stages of development, of the mother–infant relationship (Donlea and Shaw 2009).

We know that there is a strong association between sleep problems in individuals with ASD and parental stressors (Doo and Wing 2006), and more specifically with maternal stress (Hoffman *et al.* 2008).

Why a mother's laughter is probably one of the best medicines for the growing baby

> Laughter is the tonic, the relief, the surcease for pain.
>
> Charlie Chaplin (quoted in Strean 2009, p.965)

As everyone would probably assume, laughter is good for you. We may not know why – it doesn't seem to achieve anything or produce anything but it feels good to laugh. What is laughter for? Presumably we laugh, chortle, guffaw and giggle for a biological reason.

One possible explanation is that we find it is difficult to be aggressive when we laugh so maybe it is a signal that tells others that we are relaxed, that we feel safe and are less likely to be agressive.

In the Moriguchi-Keijinkai Hospital in Osaka, Japan, a researcher from the Allergy Department, Hajime Kimata, showed a roomful of mothers an 87-minute DVD of Charlie Chaplin's film *Hard Times*. After watching the film the mothers all fed their babies. They went on to provide milk samples over the next 12 hours that were analysed for their levels of melatonin.

A second group of mothers also had the pleasure of watching an 87-minute DVD. To most people, their film would be less entertaining; it was a compilation of unremarkable weather forecasts. As with the first group of mothers, after viewing the film, they all fed their babies and provided milk samples over the next 12 hours.

What was this supposed to achieve? All of the babies whose mothers were taking part in the study had allergic dermatitis. The study was looking at the levels of melatonin in the mothers' milk, how these varied, whether this was affected by watching either of the DVDs, and whether any observed differences had any effects on their babies or their babies' skin problems.

The mothers had a clear preference for viewing *Hard Times* and found the film funny. Dr Kimata's analyses found that the mother's laughter at the film and the levels of melatonin in her breastmilk were strongly associated – having a fit of the giggles increases the melatonin levels in her breastmilk (Kimata 2007). The extent of allergic responses to both latex and house dust mite in the infants whose mothers had watched the Chaplin film significantly reduced, so one result of maternal amusement was an improved immune response in her infant.

Laughter enhances the functioning of our immune systems (Atsumi *et al.* 2004; Berk *et al.* 2001), and reduces allergic skin reactions (Kimata 2001, 2004). This suggests that being happier is likely to reduce infection risk so may be a factor in controlling the spread of disease within groups.

While laughter and feeling happy seems to have positive effects, the corollary would seem also to be true – prenatal maternal depression and anxiety (O'Connor *et al.* 2007) and postnatal depression or low mood state (Armitage *et al.* 2009) are both associated with poorer infant sleep (although no one has yet looked at whether maternal depression reduces breastmilk melatonin levels or whether formula-fed babies of postnatally depressed mothers are less likely to show sleep difficulties). Postnatal depression has been linked to lowered maternal immune function (Groer and Morgan 2003) and to an increased rate of sleep problems in mothers (Dørheim *et al.* 2009).

Infants of depressed mothers are less socially responsive (Field, Diego and Hernandez-Reif 2009) and effects are more strongly related to lifetime parental depressive history than to current affect (Forbes *et al.* 2004).

Taken together these findings argue for the importance of maternal mood state in establishing and maintaining the infant sleep–wake cycle.

Mother–infant co-sleeping

Many aspects of sleep have received little study but are often described in authoritative terms in parenting books. Co-sleeping (sleeping with another person) is just such an issue, and one that has aroused considerable emotion both for and against. Most adults co-sleep (Troxel 2010) but sleep is usually studied as if it were a solitary activity.

Many children share rooms with siblings, and then go on to share their bed with a partner, often for the rest of their lives. In many respects it makes more sense to view sleep as a social activity than as a solitary one, and some form of co-sleeping is the norm rather than the exception.

The pattern of infant sleeping is different when sleeping with the mother than when sleeping alone, although the amount of sleep does not seem to differ (Mao et al. 2004). Infants who co-sleep with their mothers are found to waken more frequently through the night than infants who sleep alone, but overall they spend the same amount of time asleep. Co-sleeping leads to more frequent but shorter periods of night-time waking and to faster settling back to sleep.

Co-sleeping seems to induce synchronized levels of arousal in sleepers and may be important in both alerting mothers to infant sleep disturbance and in accelerating the maturation of infant sleep patterns by entraining them to those of their mothers (McKenna, Ball and Gettler 2007; McKenna and Mosko 1994; McKenna et al. 1990, 1993).

An early sociodemographic study in Cleveland (Lozoff, Wolf and Davis 1984) of 6-month to 4-year sleeping patterns in 150 families found that co-sleeping was routine in 34 per cent of caucasian and 70 per cent of black families. In the caucasian group only, co-sleeping increased in prevalence with the age of the child, was associated with increased stress and lower education and was more common when the child did not fall asleep in bed.

The limited amount of data on co-sleeping in children suggests that around 10 per cent of babies sleep with their mothers/parents in the first year, with a gradual rise in rates through the preschool period, peaking at around 4 years of age when around 38 per cent of children are reported as co-sleeping once or more per week (Jenni et al. 2005). This is data from a longitudinal study which followed 493 children from 1 month to 10 years of age. The study found that at around 4 years of age more than half of all children studied spent at least one night per week in their parent's bed. No link was shown between bed-sharing and sleep problems (Jenni et al. 2005), but there was a close correlation between the frequency of bed-sharing and night waking.

Not surprisingly, breastfeeding mothers get less sleep when they sleep separately from their babies than do bottlefeeding mothers (Quillin 1997). In contrast, when co-sleeping, breastfeeding mothers get better sleep than those who are bottlefeeding (Quillin and Glenn 2004).

For several decades, particularly in the US, there has been a strong lobby against co-sleeping (typically defined as mothers sleeping with their babies in the same bed). The argument for this view has been that there are increased risks to the infant of problems such as sudden infant death syndrome (SIDS) from unintentional suffocation (for discussion, see McKenna and McDade 2005). This lobby against co-sleeping runs contrary to most of the evidence about the evolutionary development of human sleeping patterns (McKenna *et al.* 1993).

If anything, the data suggest that co-sleeping in a normal bed actually reduces the risk of SIDS. Most incidents of infant fatality related to co-sleeping are in infants whose parents are drug abusers. These have typically involved sleeping prone on a couch or in a high-risk bed such as a waterbed that can more easily restrict infant breathing (McKenna and McDade 2005).

INFANT SELF-SOOTHING

A number of behaviours that children often engage in before sleep come under the category of 'self-soothing'. These are things such as thumbsucking; rolling hair between fingers; rhythmic body-rocking and the use of things such as soothers, teddy bears, dolls and blankets as 'transitional objects' when going to sleep. Favourite objects that young children hold or stroke while going to sleep are often referred to as 'transitional objects' as they appear to aid the transition from wakefulness to sleep.

A lot has been written about the role of these types of activities and objects. Benjamin Spock, the paediatrician and author of *The Commonsense Book of Baby and Child Care* (1946), wrote that activities such as thumbsucking and the use of transitional objects were related. He viewed them as substitutes used by children who had not been allowed to breastfeed enough by their mothers. This was a tremendously influential volume that first appeared in the post-Second World War baby boom and sold over 50 million copies (it was often cited as being the next most popular book after the Bible).

Spock cited work suggesting that babies who were breast-fed more regularly were less likely to suck their thumbs. Spock's work remains popular and has recently appeared in a posthumous updated eighth edition (Spock and Needleman 2004).

There is very limited evidence on the issue. Infants who seem poor at self-consoling or at using a transitional object are more likely to develop infant sleep disorders and are more likely to rely on parental consoling to get to sleep (Holliday, Sibbald and Tooley 1987). All infants would appear to use some sorts of transitional aids, whether these are external objects, self-consoling or parental contact, to help them in getting to sleep (Burnham *et al.* 2002). It is not clear how the use of such activities helps infants in getting to sleep, or whether there is anything to be gained or lost through trying to get the infant to 'break the habit'.

Mary Ainsworth, a Canadian developmental psychologist who pioneered the concept of 'Attachment Theory', suggested that children who were 'insecurely attached' to their mothers would be more likely to make use of these sorts of soothing activities to calm themselves. Subsequent research has shown, however, that there is no association between attachment and use of soothing activities such as thumbsucking or transitional objects (Van Ijzendoorn *et al.* 1983).

Some of the transitional behaviours that seem essential for some children to get to sleep run the risk of causing them physical damage (pulled out patches of hair; calloused, reddened or bleeding skin that has been sucked, chewed or bitten, and even permanent scarring or tissue damage).

One girl I worked with some years ago chewed her skin so badly at night when getting to sleep that she had exposed the tendons on the backs of her hands, and her parents dreaded the blood-stained pillows that greeted them each morning. Her problem was treated quickly and effectively using an endorphin-blocking medication coupled with a behavioural programme to redirect her into less distressing activities.

Some behaviour can also be invasive or difficult to tolerate for others. I remember one boy in particular who seemed only able to fall asleep while rubbing and pulling at his mother's ear. This pattern responded well to the introduction of an alternative calming activity and a graded approach to sleeping in his own bed.

Typically these sorts of patterns will respond to behavioural intervention – things such as substituting an alternative object and coupling the introduction of this with the use of a simple reward scheme. This is most easily worked through with support from someone knowledgeable in behavioural approaches with children, such as a child clinical psychologist or a nurse behavioural therapist.

One study (Miano *et al.* 2007) compared the use of transitional objects in getting to sleep in a small group of 31 ASD children and an age and sex matched control group of 893 normal controls (all aged 3.7–19 years). The authors reported a non-significant difference (25.81% of the autistic children and 18.2% of the controls used a transitional object when getting to sleep).

OTHER FACTORS THAT CAN AFFECT SLEEP

A variety of other factors affect infant sleep. Maternal smoking, for example, has been shown to impair infant arousal (Richardson, Walker and Horne 2009). Maternal alcohol ingestion prior to infant breastfeeding, even at low levels, markedly reduces infant activity during sleep, with compensatory increases in motor activity during subsequent sleep (Mennella and Garcia-Gomez 2001).

One study (Lopez-Wagner *et al.* 2008) looked at sleep problems in parents and their children in both normally developing and autistic children. It compared parents of 106 autistic children (aged 4–16 years) to parents of 168 typically developing children (aged 4–15 years) using the Pittsburg Sleep Quality Index (Carpenter and Andrykowski 1998) to assess parental sleep problems and the Children's Sleep Habits Questionnaire (Owens, Spirito and McGuinn 2000) to assess the children. In both groups there was an association between the two measures. As in other research we discuss, the rate of sleep problems was higher in the autism group. The rate of sleep problems in autism was higher both for the children and for their parents. In addition, in a child with autism a given level of sleep disturbance was associated with a greater degree of sleep disturbance in the parents than in the controls. This study suggests first, that there may be a genetic basis – an issue that warrants more detailed genetic study, and second, of more direct practical relevance, in this population help for the child's and parent's sleep problems is likely to be of greatest benefit when both are addressed in tandem.

HOW MUCH SLEEP IS NORMAL?

The range of what is seen as 'normal' varies in a variety of ways including by country – the average person in France sleeps, or at least reports sleeping, an hour longer than the average person in Korea and half an hour longer than the average person in the UK. There is limited information on children but there also appear to be distinct differences between the sexes with girls sleeping for longer and with less physical movement (e.g. Sadeh, Raviv and Gruber 2000).

There is evidence that our sleep patterns are affected by a range of external factors such as where we live in the world (our physical latitude and longitude) and the climatic conditions to which we are subjected. Differences are reported between populations from the same ethnic background depending on whether they are living in temperate, subtropical or tropical regions (Randler 2008) and between different ethnic groups living in the same areas (Javo, Ronning and Heyerdahl 2004).

Studies have varied wildly in their estimates of how much sleep is normal and how much is required. The range of what is reported as typical varies by several hours per night within the general population.

DO WE NEED TO SLEEP AT ALL?

Some people have deliberately kept themselves awake to try to make it into the record books. The world record for staying awake without artificial stimulants is currently held by Randy Gardner, an American who in 1964 set the record at 264 hours (11 days). This is an exceptional time without sleep, but was presumably exceptional for Randy himself as well as being unusual in general so is not the upper limit of what is 'normal' but the upper limit of what has so far been thought possible.

Some people do seem regularly to require much less or much more sleep than others. It has been recognized for many years that some individuals take very little sleep but without any of the difficulties that would normally be seen if the same sleep restriction was imposed on others. They appear to have a pattern that has been described as 'healthy insomnia' (see, e.g. Jones and Oswald 1968).

It seems clear that some sleep is an essential component of the human day, but there are wide individual variations in the amount required. In adults, prolonged sleep loss or restriction impairs the formation of new nerve cells in the hippocampus (Meerlo *et al.* 2009). This structure is crucial to the formation of new memories. Sleep loss also increases the circulating levels of C-reactive protein, which in turn increases cardiovascular risk (Meier-Ewert *et al.* 2004).

DEC2 has been identified as a transcription repressor gene that regulates the amount of mammalian sleep (He *et al.* 2009). One study has identified a DEC2 mutation (hDEC2-P385R), in two members of the same family. This difference was associated with significantly shortened sleep when compared to the sleep pattern of other members of the same family. Similarly shortened sleep patterns can be found in animal models that mimic this hDEC2-P385R gene difference (He *et al.* 2009).

WHAT DO WE KNOW ABOUT THE NORMAL RANGE OF SLEEP IN CHILDHOOD?

Our sleep patterns change as we get older. Such developmental changes in brain electrical activity need to be taken into account in any assessment (Crabtree and Williams 2009; Grigg-Damberger *et al.* 2007).

There is a wide variation in the range of what is 'normal'. You might think that a child has an unusual sleep pattern but it may still be within the normal range. In this context, knowing the range of typical sleep can be important (Figure A.4).

A number of cohort studies have reported that as children get older they sleep for shorter periods. The following diagram shows the percentages of children at 8, 10 and 12 years of age sleeping for different amounts of time each night. This is data from a cohort study on 140 Israeli children (Sadeh, Raviv and Gruber 2000). It is clear that although the graphs overlap, at 8 years the typical night's sleep is 9–9.5 hours, by 10 this has dropped to 8 to 8.5 hours, and by 12 it is 7.5 to 8 hours.

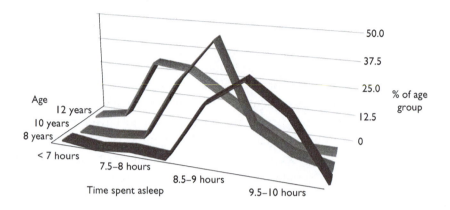

(Data adapted from Sadeh, Raviv and Gruber 2000)

Figure A.4 The normal range of sleep in childhood

Cohort studies provide cross-sectional data – they look at large numbers of children of different ages collected at the same point in time. Such studies could mask variability over time in individuals within these groups. Ideally longitudinal data would provide a better view of things such as stability over time in the sleep pattern of the individual.

There are now some longitudinal data on this issue. One particular research group based in Switzerland has systematically measured sleep patterns and physical growth in children they have followed for over two decades. The Zurich longitudinal study has collected detailed information on 493 children in the first two years and further annual data on the same group through to the age of 16 (Iglowstein *et al.* 2003).

Figure A.5 shows the percentage of children taking daytime naps from 0.5–7 years and Figure A.6 shows the range of values for night-time and daytime sleep combined at different ages between 1 year and 16 years. The typical or average length of time gradually reduces with age. At all ages, there is a wide normal range – the range of 'normal' could be anything between 6 and 12 hours of night-time sleep at 1 year, with the range dropping to between 6.75 and 8.6 hours by 16 years.

In a more recent study, a separate cohort of 305 children were followed over the period from 1 to 10 years alongside data collected on their physical growth (Jenni *et al.* 2007).

One of the most important findings to emerge from these studies has been the wide variation in the amount of sleep seen in normal infants and young children: from less than 6 to more than 14 hours in normal 1-month-olds, narrowing to between 9 and 13 hours at 1 year then gradually falling through the following decade and a half until by 16 years the typical person sleeps for somewhere between 6.75 and 8.5 hours a night.

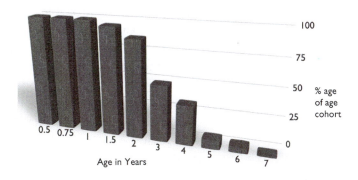

Based on data from Iglowstein *et al.* (2008)

Figure A.5 Percentage of children taking regular daytime naps by age

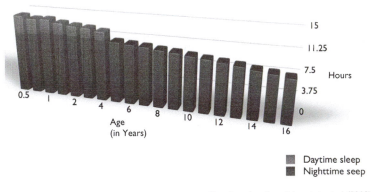

Based on data from Iglowstein *et al.* (2008)

Figure A.6 Sleep duration by age

It is easy to see that there is a wide 'normal' range. It is important not to leap to the assumption that you should be aiming to help your child to achieve some expected sleep pattern that is typical of the population, especially if this is not typical of your family. A number of sleep issues, such as insomnia and familial advanced sleep phase syndrome, seem to be genetic and heritable and to lead to patterns of sleep that are different from what would be normal for the general population.

WHAT DO WE KNOW ABOUT NORMAL PATTERNS OF SLEEP?

Through the first year of life, night waking is frequent, and more often than not, the infant requires adult attention to get back to sleep (Goodlin-Jones *et al.* 2001). Without treatment, frequent night waking is a reasonably stable problem over time (see, e.g. Bernal 1973) and creates increasing strains on the family.

The 2004 'Sleep in America Poll' (Mindell, Meltzer *et al.* 2009) surveyed a sample of 1473 parents and caregivers. Late bedtime and parental presence in the room while the child was falling asleep were strongly associated with poor sleep patterns.

It is possible that neither factor is a cause – correlation does not prove causation. Parents might stay up at the bedside because the child is having difficulty falling asleep, and parents might allow children to stay up later if they don't seem to be tired or they are unlikely to go to sleep when put to bed. It is also possible that the parents' behaviour may be contributing to or even causing the presenting problem.

In the Sleep America Poll, the later the child went to bed, the longer the time between going to bed and going to sleep, and the shorter the time spent sleeping. When parents were present in the bedroom, this was associated with more frequent night waking. In children over 3 years of age, the lack of a consistent bedtime routine was associated with shorter sleep, as was a television in the bedroom. From the age of 5, regular consumption of caffeinated soft drinks was also linked to shorter sleep.

SLEEP PROBLEMS IN GENERAL

What do we mean by 'sleep problems', how do we define them and what are the differences between them?

Before a problem can be treated it is usually helpful and often important to define what it is. This can help to identify approaches that have been useful for others with similar problems; studies where the evidence suggests that certain approaches may not be as helpful; and studies that have shown that particular approaches are difficult to implement, or even that some approaches might make things worse.

Let's begin by looking at the two main ways of classifying sleep difficulties. The one that is most widely used is the second edition of the International Classification of Sleep Disorders (ICSD-2) (American Academy of Sleep Medicine 2005). This system was last revised in 2005 and recognizes eight main types of sleeping difficulties (not including night-time enuresis and encopresis). The main psychiatric classification system is the Diagnostic and Statistical Manual of the American Psychiatric Association (DSM for short). The latest version, DSM-5, was published in its final draft form in August 2011 and should be formally adopted in May 2013.

HOW SLEEP PROBLEMS ARE CLASSIFIED

The ICSD-2 used a slightly different grouping to the earlier DSM-IV-Tr criteria that were published in 2000. The Diagnostic and Statistical Manual, 5th Revision (DSM-5) has appeared in draft form and various other classifications are used in the clinical literature.

Table B.1 compares the ICSD-2 to the proposed DSM-5 classification at the time of going to press, and to some other terms used in the current clinical literature.

The below classifications are not exhaustive. 'New' types of problems are regularly being described. For example, 'night-time eating disorders' (Howell, Schenck and Crow 2009) have recently made an appearance in the sleep literature.

TABLE B.1 SLEEP PROBLEM CLASSIFICATIONS

ICSD-2 classification American Academy of Sleep Medicine (2005)	DSM-5 proposed classification American Psychiatric Association (2013)	Reported sleep problem/disorder
Insomnia	Primary insomnia/insomnia + substance abuse/insomnia/ insomnia + sleep efficiency comorbid mental health disorder	Settling difficulties; co-sleeping issues; night waking; long sleep latency; early waking; difficult bedtime routines; daytime sleepiness
Parasomnias	Parasomnia disorders	Nightmares; awakening screaming; nocturnal enuresis
Hypersomnias of central origin	Kleine-Levin syndrome; primary hypersomnia	Kleine-Levin syndrome; hypersomnia; daytime sleepiness
Sleep-related breathing disorders	Obstructive sleep apnoea-hypopnoea syndrome; primary central sleep apnoea; primary alveolar hypoventilation	Obstructive sleep apnoea
Sleep-related movement disorders	Restless legs syndrome	Periodic limb movements in sleep (PLMS); restless sleep
Isolated symptoms, apparently normal variants, and unresolved issues		Short sleep; early waking
Other sleep disorders		Abnormal objective sleep patterns (on actigraphy)
Circadian rhythm sleep disorders	Circadian rhythm sleep disorder – delayed sleep phase type; jet lag type; shift work type; free-running type; irregular sleep–wake type (all of the above are subsumed under a new category of narcolepsy-cataplexy)	Late sleep onset; long sleep latency; early waking; irregular sleep–wake patterns; free-running sleep

HOW COMMON ARE SLEEP PROBLEMS?

Sleep problems are not uncommon in the general population, being reported in upwards of 25 per cent of all children (see, e.g. Kerr and Jowett 1994; Mindell 1993; van Litsenburg *et al.* 2010), with some studies reporting rates as high as 50 per cent (Polimeni *et al.* 2005). Specific problems can have a high prevalence. Habitual or daily snoring is seen in approximately 10 per cent of the child population (Ng *et al.* 2006). Unfortunately in many settings sleep problems in children often go ignored and undiagnosed (Blunden *et al.* 2004).

A detailed longitudinal review of sleep development over the first 4 years of life in 68 infants (Gaylor *et al.* 2005) suggests that some 19 per cent could be classified as having a sleep problem by the age of 2 years but that the rate of problems tended to reduce with age.

One survey study of the electronic records of 154,957 0–18-year-old children and adolescents in Philadelphia reported on well-child visits in 2007 (Meltzer *et al.* 2010). Sleep disorders were found in 3.7 per cent. In this survey, ASD, ADHD and physical growth problems were all associated with an increased likelihood of having sleep problems.

So sleep problems are fairly common in children and adolescents and can lead to a range of other difficulties when they are not identified and treated.

It may be helpful at this point to read a simple introduction to the recognition of sleep difficulties and their management. I would recommend Ivanenko and Patwari (2009) as a brief recent paper reviewing the recognition and management of paediatric sleep problems.

IS IT IMPORTANT THAT SLEEP PROBLEMS ARE ADDRESSED?

Sleep problems are common, with significant sleep disturbance affecting around 20–30 per cent of all children, but are they important? Would it matter if things were just left to take their natural course or is it important to address sleep problems if they are present?

We know that secondary age pupils who report getting less sleep consistently achieve poorer exam results even when they come from similar backgrounds and study for the same length of time as those who achieve better results (Wolfson and Carskadon 1998, 2003).

Significant sleep restriction can markedly affect immune function (Moldofsky *et al.* 1989). Even modest levels of sleep deprivation have effects on daytime sleepiness, cognitive performance and physiological markers such as levels of inflammatory cytokines (Vgontzas *et al.* 2004).

Sleep problems are common across a range of psychiatric disorders and it seems probable that similar approaches may produce benefits across a number of conditions (see Harvey 2009; Harvey *et al.* 2010).

In general, there is an association between daytime challenging behaviour (things such as aggression, defiance, non-compliance and self-injury) and sleep problems, with a broader range and greater severity of behavioural difficulties being shown by those with sleep problems (Wiggs and Stores 1996). This is observational data, and it is possible that cause operates in the opposite direction with challenging behaviour resulting in impaired sleep. It seems intuitively more plausible that poor sleep would result in greater tiredness and irritability leading to a higher likelihood of someone being likely to present with challenging behaviour.

We know that sleep processes are intimately involved in the development of neural wiring, and that interference with normal sleep patterns can affect synaptic plasticity (see Miyamoto and Hensch 2003; Tononi and Cirelli 2006). This implies that the amount and type of sleep someone has will have a direct effect on their brain development.

THE IMPORTANCE OF ADEQUATE SLEEP FOR BRAIN DEVELOPMENT

The importance of normal sleep for optimal brain development has been appreciated for some years (see Graven and Browne 2008 for a recent review).

Much of the early work in this area evolved through studies on the effects of disruption to early sleep organization in premature infants. A number of key factors have been identified that can help with the development of sleep–wake cycles in premature infants. These include the beneficial effects resulting from varying the lighting levels in special care baby units (Hao and Rivkees 1999; Rivkees *et al.* 2004) and the effect of increased close physical skin-to-skin contact with a caregiver (see Feldman *et al.* 2002).

A recent overview from Canada (Jan *et al.* 2010) has raised significant concerns over the likely effects of longer-term sleep problems on children's brain development and on learning.

Sleep problems are an often neglected component of behavioural assessment that can have an important bearing on other aspects of behaviour and development (see Schreck 2010).

SLEEP PROBLEMS IN ASD

HOW COMMON ARE SLEEP PROBLEMS IN ASD?

Sleep problems appear to be more common in those with ASDs than in the rest of the population, with over 70 per cent of those with ASD experiencing difficulties compared with around 50 per cent of age and sex-matched controls (Allik, Larsson and Smedje 2006a; Clements, Wing and Dunn 1986; Johnson, Giannotti and Cortesi 2009; Patzold, Richdale and Tonge 1998; Polimeni *et al.* 2005; Richdale 1999; Richdale and Schreck 2009; Souders *et al.* 2009).

A number of literature reviews, overviews of this area and cohort studies have appeared (Allik, Larsson and Smedje 2006a, 2008; Cortesi *et al.* 2010; Harrell, Schreck and Richdale 2008; Honomichl *et al.* 2002a; Johnson and Malow 2008a, 2008b, 2008c; Johnson *et al.* 2009; McGraw *et al.* 2007; Malow and McGrew 2008; Ming and Walters 2009; Reynolds and Malow 2011; Stores and Wiggs 1998; Williams, Sears and Allard 2004).

In 1984 a Japanese questionnaire survey of 79 parents of autistic children found that 49 (65%) reported that their children had sleep problems (Hoshino *et al.* 1984). The likelihood of reported sleep problems was associated with the severity of autism.

A 1998 questionnaire survey of 88 autistic children in Tokyo (Taira, Takase and Sasaki 1998) reported 56 (65.1%) with sleep disorders. Difficulties settling to sleep were reported in 23 (26.1%), with bedwetting in 22 (25%), night waking in 19 (21.6%), and early morning waking in 11 (12.5%). Most problems were reported to abate when the children began nursery with 10 persisting into primary school and 2 into secondary education. Unfortunately the age range of the sample is not given. A further report by the same group (Takase, Taira and Sasaki 1998) used 28-day sleep logs to describe the sleep patterns in a cohort of 89 autistic subjects aged 3 to 20 years during summer vacation. A high proportion of their subjects went to sleep later and rose earlier than normal, with one girl showing an unusual non-24-hour sleep–wake pattern.

One study found an increased prevalence of parent-reported sleep problems (in 12/22 autistic children). Typical problems were frequent night-time and early morning wakening, but parent report was poorly corroborated by actigraphy (Hering *et al.* 1999). The actigraphy measures, showed a pattern in these children that did not differ from the general population, and these authors concluded that the high rate of reported problems was due to parental oversensitivity. Actigraphy itself correlated poorly with other measures such as videosomnography (Sitnick, Goodlin-Jones and Anders 2008), so it may be that the implication of this study is that actigraphy is a less sensitive measure than parental report rather than that parents of autistic children are overly sensitive.

A separate study (Schreck and Mulick 2000) compared ratings by five groups of parents – those of children with autism (38); PDD-NOS (pervasive developmental disorder not otherwise specified) (17); learning difficulties (22); undiagnosed but attending special education (49); and age matched normal controls (43). In this study all groups rated their children on an unpublished 107 item questionnaire, the Behavior Evaluation of Disorders of Sleep (BEDS) (Schreck 1997/1998). All groups were reported to sleep for comparable amounts of time, but parents of those with ASD indicated a greater prevalence of dyssomnias and parasomnias and of specific problems such as screaming and disoriented wakening.

A polysomnography study carried out on 17 children and adolescents with autism (Elia *et al.* 2000) found that social relating and daytime activity level were correlated with amount of REM sleep, while visual response and non-verbal communication correlated with sleep fragmentation and total time spent asleep. This is interesting in view of the correlations between ADHD and polysomnography that also shows a correlation between reduced levels of REM sleep and daytime activity level (Gruber *et al.* 2009).

The Children's Sleep Habits Questionnaire (CSHQ) (Owens, Spirito and McGuinn 2000), and the Parenting Events Questionnaire (see Crnic and Greenberg 1990) and sleep diaries were used in a 2002 study (Honomichl *et al.* 2002a) that evaluated sleep and sleep problems in 100 2–11-year-old children with clinical diagnoses of Pervasive Developmental Disorder (PDD) (these children would currently be diagnosed with ASD). The PDD children took longer to get to sleep and once asleep they had more fragmented sleep than age-matched controls.

A Canadian survey from Southwest Ontario (Couturier *et al.* 2005) also used the CSHQ. They reported that 78 per cent (18/23) of the PDD children were reported to have sleep problems by their parents, compared to 26 per cent (6/23) of a matched comparison group and the problems reported were more severe.

An Oxford study (Wiggs and Stores 2004) used the Simonds and Parraga Sleep Questionnaire (Simonds and Parraga 1982) and actigraphy to assess sleep in a group of 69 5–16-year-old autistic children. On parental report, 46 had sleep problems, 22 of whom had complex sleep problems. At the time the questionnaire was completed the most prevalent reported issue was fear of the dark. Sleeplessness was reported by a high proportion of families; however, the pattern was unusual, as 'the sleeplessness patterns of a large minority of children could not be classified by conventional diagnostic criteria' (p.372).

The measures used can be important in whether problems are recognized. A Norwegian study in 15 adolescent and young adult autistic and Asperger individuals (Øyane and Bjorvatn 2005) used a combination of sleep questionnaires, sleep diaries, actigraphy and polysomnography. Fourteen young men and one young woman, aged 15–25 took part. On the actigraphy and polysomnography measures, over 80 per cent of the sample showed evidence of a diagnosable sleep disorder. This contrasted with the parental and self-report measures – five parents rated their child as having a sleep problem (1 in 3 of the sample), and sleep diary and Epworth Sleepiness Scale reports were comparable to the general population.

A survey of sleep patterns in 106 autistic and 168 community controls using the CSHQ (Owens, Spirito and McGuinn 2000) reported elevated scores in their autistic group on most CSHQ subscales (bedtime resistance; sleep onset delay; sleep duration; sleep anxiety; night wakings; parasomnias and sleep-disordered breathing). The only rating on which there were no significant differences between the two groups was the Daytime Sleepiness Scale (Hoffman *et al.* 2006).

In a survey of 187 ASD children (144 male, 43 female) aged 8.8 years (SD (standard deviation) 4.2), almost daily significant problems with sleep were reported in around 86 per cent. The problems, in order of prevalence, were insomnia (56%); bedtime resistance (54%); parasomnias (53%); problems getting up in the morning (45%); daytime sleepiness (31%) and sleep-disordered breathing (25%) (Liu *et al.* 2006). The authors suggest that sleep problems have a high prevalence in the ASD population. As there were no control prevalence rates the only valid conclusion is that sleep problems are commonly seen in association with ASD.

In a study of 17 individuals with learning disability and ASD and 14 individuals with learning disability but no ASD, aged 26–58 years, actigraphy recording was not able to show differences in sleep movements between the groups (Hare, Jones and Evershed 2006).

A Boston group (Dominick *et al.* 2007) compared 67 children with ASD to 39 with a history of language impairment (HLI), in terms of their likelihood of showing 'atypical' behaviours. All the children were aged between 4 years 2 months and 14 years 2 months and were part of a larger CPEA (Collaborative Programes of Excellence in Autism) project. In both groups sleep problems were associated with depression as diagnosed on the KSADS (Kiddie-Schedule for Affective Disorders and Schizophrenia) – 32 per cent of those with sleep problems also had depression as compared to 13 per cent of those without sleep problems. In the ASD group, 34 (63.6%) were reported to show abnormal sleep patterns as compared to 15 (41%) of the HLI group. In the ASD group the likelihood of sleep problems was greater with lower IQ, lower expressive language, more social deficits and higher levels of repetitive behaviour.

A survey of sleep problems reported on 68 autistic, 57 non-autistic children with developmental delay and 69 normal controls (Goodlin-Jones *et al.* 2008). They reported significantly poorer sleep in both of the clinical groups compared to the controls, but also found marked differences between parental reports of sleep problems (which tended to correlate with measures of parental stress) and actigraphy measures of insomnia.

A further study from the same research group (Krakowiak *et al.* 2008) reported on sleep in 303 ASD (167 male/136 female), 63 children with non-autistic developmental delay (46 male/17 female), and 163 typically developing children (134 male/29 female) at a mean age of 3.5 years. This was part of a larger epidemiological cohort study called CHARGE (Childhood Autism Risks from Genetics and Environment) (see Hertz-Picciotto *et al.* 2006). Frequent sleep problems were reported in 53 per cent of the ASD, 46 per cent of the developmentally delayed and 32 per cent of the controls. Cognitive levels as assessed on the Mullen Scales and adaptive level on the Vineland Adaptive Behavior Scales were not associated with sleep problems. Settling and night waking problems were proportionately more common in the ASD group.

One fairly recent study (Souders *et al.* 2009) compared 40 typically developing children to 59 children with ASDs. For each of the children, a Children's Sleep Habits Questionnaire (CSHQ) (Owens, Spirito and McGuinn 2000) was completed and they underwent 10 nights of sleep where actigraphy data was collected (using a device called the AMI 'MicroMini MotionLogger Actigraph' (see AMI 2009). This was used to quantify a number of features of their sleep – level of activity while sleeping; sleep latency (how long between going to bed and falling asleep); the number of night-time awakenings; sleep efficiency and total time spent asleep.

On these measures, approximately 45 per cent of the typically developing control group were rated as having mild sleep disturbance, while 66 per cent of the ASD group were rated as having moderate sleep problems, with 57.6 per cent of families expressing concerns. Both the prevalence and the severity of sleep difficulties were greater in the ASD group. The most commonly presenting sleep problems in the ASD group were 'insomnia of childhood – sleep association type' (12/59 or 20%); 'insomnia due to a mental disorder' (11/59 or 19%) and difficulties in getting to sleep ('behavioral insomnia sleep-onset/limit-setting type') (6/59 or 15%).

The breakdown of sleep problems in the ASD group is shown in Tables C.1 and C.2 (some of these categories overlap).

According to the American Academy of Sleep Medicine, there are two main types of paediatric insomnia: the first is *sleep-onset association type,* and is the most common type of sleep difficulty reported by Souders *et al.* (2009) in children with ASD (reported in 20% of their sample). This is where the child will only fall asleep when taken through a particular routine (this could involve being held or rocked), a particular object (a 'comfort object'/holding onto someone/a bottle) or in a specific setting (such as the parents' bed), and cannot fall asleep otherwise.

The other insomnia category is the *limit-setting type*, which was reported by 10 per cent of their ASD group. This is where the child will not go to bed or sleep without strict, explicit, clearly stated and reinforced bedtime rules.

TABLE C.1 ASD SLEEP PROBLEMS I

Sleep diagnosis	Number (N = 59)	Percentage of total ASD group
None	9	15
Sleep-disordered breathing	1	2
Inadequate sleep hygiene	2	4
Parasomnias (linked to night waking)	3	5
Insomnia of childhood – limit-setting type	6	10
Insomnia possibly due to medical condition (seizures (1); asthma (3); GERD (1))	6	10
Insomnia due to pervasive developmental disorder	11	19
No sleep problem – on active sleep medication *	11	19
Insomnia of childhood – sleep association type	12	20

GERD: Gastro-oesophageal reflux disease
* melatonin (4); Catapres (clonidine) (1); risperidone (4); aripiprazole (2)

Another clinical survey (Mayes *et al.* 2009; Table C.2) detailed parental reports on a large cohort of 477 children aged 1–16 of varied IQs (their IQs were reported as from 9–146). In this survey it was reported that sleep problems were common and their prevalence was largely independent of individual and sociodemographic variables such as age, IQ, gender, race, parent occupation, neuropsychological functioning and learning ability. An overall rating of sleep disturbance was computed as was prevalence of specific types of sleep problem. A significantly higher proportion of children with ASD were reported to have sleep problems; 151 children (32%) were on psychoactive medication, and those receiving stimulants or medication for sleep problems were rated as having greater sleep disturbance than those who were not. No attempt was made to assess whether the medication was thought to have resulted in any clinical benefit.

One Australian study (Polimeni *et al.* 2005) found a high prevalence of sleep problems in their controls (50%) with significantly higher rates of problems reported in both their autism and Asperger groups (73%), with parasomnias (nightmares, enuresis and waking in distress), tiredness and disorientation after waking all being more common in the Asperger group. The general conclusion reached was that both the prevalence and severity of sleep problems was greater in ASD than in the general population.

TABLE C.2 ASD SLEEP PROBLEMS II

Sleep diagnosis	Number	Percentage of total ASD group
Sleeps more than normal	67	14
Daytime sleepiness	100	21
Sleepwalking/sleeptalking	167	35
Bedwetting	172	36
Nightmares	186	39
Sleeps less than normal	205	43
Waking too early	215	45
Frequent night waking	238	50
Restless when asleep	267	56
Difficulty falling asleep	286	60

Data from Mayes *et al.* 2009.

A Swedish study (Allik *et al.* 2006a) surveyed a group (N = 32) of 8–12-year-old children with diagnoses of Asperger syndrome or high-functioning autism (AS/ HFA). Those with AS/HFA had more difficulties getting to sleep and had higher rates of daytime sleepiness compared to their controls. The authors noted a higher rate of insomnia in the adolescents with ASD than in their peers. In the ASD group the sleep problem was often comorbid with daytime behavioural difficulties. Ten of the ASD children but none of the controls fulfilled the criteria for childhood insomnia (Glaze, Rosen and Owens 2002), and this finding was associated with higher rates of teacher reported emotional and hyperactive symptoms and higher levels of parent reported emotional and autistic symptoms.

Various reviews and cohort studies of sleep difficulties in ASD have appeared (Allik *et al.* 2006a, 2008; Cortesi *et al.* 2010; Johnson *et al.* 2009; Johnson and Malow 2008a, b; Malow and McGrew 2008; Ming and Walters 2009).

In Asperger syndrome, higher rates of sleep problems are also reported. Comparing a group of 52 5–17-year-old children with Asperger syndrome to 61 group-matched controls (Paavonen *et al.* 2008), shorter sleep duration (59% vs 32%) and difficulties getting to sleep (53% vs 10%) were reported by parents in a significantly higher proportion of those with AS. On self-rating, 58 per cent of the AS children and 7 per cent of the controls rated themselves as having sleeping difficulties.

One study looked at overnight urinary melatonin levels in 23 4–10-year-old autistic children (Leu *et al.* 2010). The children also underwent two night-time EEG recordings, and their parents completed the Children's Sleep Habits Questionnaire and the Parental Concerns Questionnaire. Higher urinary levels of the melatonin metabolite 6-sulfatoxymelatonin were associated with decreased daytime sleepiness, increases in stage 3 sleep and decreases in stage 2 sleep.

There are a number of measures that can be helpful in characterizing sleep problems in ASD. Profiles on the Childhood Sleep Habits Questionnaire (Malow, Marzec *et al.* 2006) show associations with both actigraphy (measures of movement during sleep) and polysomnographic recording (sleep EEG) (see Goldman *et al.* 2009).

Although carrying out an EEG is often difficult with children who have an ASD, the results can be helpful in clarifying the nature of the problem. To help in carrying this out, structured preparation can considerably ease the process (see Slifer, Avis and Frutchey 2008; DeMore *et al.* 2009).

Sleep problems in ASD children are associated with a higher level of daytime problems with increased levels of parental concern, higher levels of stereotyped behaviours and higher scores on the Child Behavior Checklist when compared both to ASD children who are good sleepers and to normal population controls (Goldman *et al.* 2009).

There is some evidence to suggest that shorter sleep is associated with a greater severity of ASD symptomology (Schreck, Mulick and Smith 2004).

In summary, sleep disorders are significantly more common in ASD than in the general population. They are reported in approximately 2/3 of children and adolescents with ASD.

Certain problems such as nightmares and bedwetting appear to be very common when compared to the rest of the population, and are both seen in approximately 1/3 of cases. Behavioural insomnias (difficulties with settling to sleep) constitute the largest single subgroup of sleep difficulties, affecting around 60 per cent of people with an ASD.

IS IT IMPORTANT TO ADDRESS SLEEP PROBLEMS IN ASD?

Clearly problems such as nightmares and bedwetting can be distressing to the child and worrying and inconvenient for carers, and settling difficulties can be demanding on carers, but is there any indication that they are likely to present more of a problem than this?

In an early study of sleep in children with autism (Richdale and Prior 1995), sleep difficulties were found to be associated with the severity of social difficulties rather than with comorbid learning difficulties.

More recently, studies from one group suggest that there may be an association between poorer sleep and greater intensity of daytime autistic symptomology. Studies from Penn State University-Harrisburg and Columbus Children's Hospital in Ohio have found an association between length of sleep and problems such as night-time screaming on the Behavior Evaluation of Disorders of Sleep (BEDS) (Schreck, Mulick and Rojahn 2003), and the overall level of autism and severity of social skills deficits on the Gilliam Autism Rating Scale (GARS), in a group of 55 5–12-year-old autistic children. This is a cross-sectional observational study and cannot indicate the direction of causation, but it does suggest that children with more severe autistic symptomology also tend to have poorer sleep.

A further paper on the same sample (Schreck *et al.* 2004) looked in more detail at specific aspects of the presentations seen this group. A number of features seemed to interact. Shorter sleep was associated with greater autistic symptomology, poorer social skills and a higher rate of stereotypies. Increased sensitivity to stimuli in the bedroom (a seven-item factor on the BEDS scale related to worries and anxieties around getting to sleep – e.g. fear of noises; needing a night-light left on) was related to several issues such as communication and fewer developmental sequence disturbances.

As sleep issues are related to the severity of daytime behaviour problems, impede learning, are more common and more severe in ASD, and when not addressed are more persistent, it is important that they are identified and appropriately treated when present.

ARE THERE REASONS WHY SLEEP PROBLEMS SHOULD BE MORE LIKELY IN ASD?

As discussed in the last section, sleep problems seem to be more common in people with ASD than in the rest of the population. What, if any, are the possible reasons for this difference?

Some people with ASD have genetic differences that interfere with the production or metabolism of melatonin, an important component of our sleep pathways.

A further biological basis that could predispose to problems with the sleep–wake cycle in ASD is genetic disruption to the development of cells called cortical interneneurons. Gamma-aminobutyric acid (GABA)ergic inhibitory interneurons are sensitive to a range of genetic factors, and predispose, in animal models at least, to a range of issues such as behavioural disturbance, epilepsy and to sleep–wake cycle abnormalities (Levitt, Eagleson and Powell 2004; Powell *et al.* 2003). This suggests that ASDs may, in some cases at least, be 'developmental disconnection syndromes' (Geschwind and Levitt 2007) where the normal patterns of brain connections have not formed.

People with autism are in general less aware of social cues than others (see, e.g. Tager-Flusberg 1999) and would be less likely to recognize or respond to social cues concerning sleep.

There are differences in the patterns of brain activation seen in autistic toddlers during 'bedtime stories' with a reversed pattern of cortical activation compared to what is seen both in chronological and mental-age matched controls at age 3 (Redcay and Courchesne 2008). This may be part of a broader difference in selective social interest. Preferential looking towards animated geometric patterns when given the choice between this and animated children engaged in dancing or yoga could discriminate ASD toddlers from as early as 14 months (Pierce *et al.* 2010).

A recent study of brain activation during bedtime stories in a 3-year-old autistic toddler showed little change in the activity in the left of the superior temporal gyrus with some activation on the right in marked contrast to the bilateral increases with most change in the left hemisphere seen in controls (Pierce 2011).

There is clearly a need for more work on this area, but these early findings suggest that this could be an important focus for early identification and intervention that links some of the social difficulties in ASD to problems around the social cueing that is important in sleep initiation in infancy.

───── ❊ ─────

REASONS SLEEP PATTERNS MAY HAPPEN OR CAN BE MADE WORSE

MATERNAL MOOD STATE AND BIOLOGY

Depression and anxiety in parents are both common issues in ASD. These can make consistent parenting more difficult.

Parental mood is a significant predictor of subsequent infant and toddler sleep patterns (O'Connor *et al.* 2007). Developmental difficulties can be associated both with low maternal (see Murray and Cooper 1997) and low paternal mood state (Davé *et al.* 2009). Higher levels of parental anxiety and depression predict greater levels of sleep disturbance in the child.

Infant sleep disturbance can be predicted to some extent from the level of maternal distress that is in evidence even before the baby is conceived (Baird *et al.* 2009). It is possible that these findings are due to the continuing presence of the factors that led to antenatal distress. There is also mounting evidence for an association between antenatal stressors and likelihood of subsequent development of autism (Kinney, Miller *et al.* 2008; Kinney, Munir *et al.* 2008).

Another factor that has received surprisingly little attention is the association between parental sleep pattern and child sleep disorders. One study of 107 families of 2–12-year-old children who presented with sleep difficulties found an association between the complexity of the child's presenting difficulties and the probability of parental excessive daytime sleepiness, with a stronger association with maternal than paternal presentation (Boergers *et al.* 2007). At face value this could merely be that having a child who sleeps poorly stresses mothers out more, but it could also be evidence for a genetic/biological factor underpinning both presentations.

THE NEUROBIOLOGY OF SLEEP

There is a complex biological system that is the basis to all of our sleep-wake cycles. Recent research has clarified the functional neuroanatomy, neurochemistry and electrophysiology of this system (see Rosenwasser 2009). Much of this process is driven by a light-dependent process called photoentrainment. The role of ambient light as an important factor in health and disease is becoming more clearly appreciated (Schmoll *et al.* 2010). Other factors are involved which are not light dependent, but these play a relatively minor role (Klerman *et al.* 1998).

Differences in melatonin (N-acetyl-5-methoxytryptamine) metabolism

Melatonin is a chemical released by the pineal gland, a cone-shaped endocrine structure that sits deep in the midbrain. Melatonin output from the pineal alters in response to changing light levels. The biological pathway is that retinal input to the suprachiasmatic nucleus (SCN) in the visual pathway stimulates melatonin release into the bloodstream. This pathway and its output are under the control of changes in ambient light levels. This system acts as a driver or 'zeitgeber' for the biological process that typically initiates sleep. The system is sensitive to differences in nocturnal light levels (Zeitzer *et al.* 2000), accounting for why in some cases simple changes such as the use of blackout curtains or phasing out the use of a night-light can be highly effective. The action spectrum for melatonin production in response to ambient light shows that it does not match the pattern one would expect with scotopic-photopic changes and so is unlikely to result from effects generated by the rod and/or cone systems in the retina and is likely to rely on a separate light-responsive retinal system (Thapan, Arendt and Skene 2001).

There is good evidence that 'exogenous' melatonin provided as a supplement can be used to mimic the metabolic effects of natural release (e.g. Braam *et al.* 2009; Doghramji 2007). This can help in many cases where lower levels of melatonin are not sufficient to provide the normal stimulus for sleep. There is evidence for the beneficial use of melatonin supplements in circadian rhythm sleep disorders in children with multiple disabilities (Jan and Freeman 2004). In adults with developmental disabilities, a positive response to melatonin is associated with lower pre-treatment serum levels of endogenous melatonin (Laakso *et al.* 2007).

A review of melatonin in intellectual disability and sleep disorders (Sajith and Clarke 2007) identified six small randomized controlled trials. Five reported positive results, two with specific clinical groups – Rett syndrome (McArthur and Budden 1998) and tuberous sclerosis (O'Callaghan *et al.* 1999), both of which can be comorbid with ASD (see Aitken 2010a). Only one study, in moderate learning disability (Camfield *et al.* 1996), failed to report beneficial results.

Some people have significantly slower melatonin metabolism than most. People with this pattern show a good initial response to supplementation that tails off rapidly after a few weeks (Braam, van Geijlswijk *et al.* 2010). So far this difference has only been reported in people with a learning disability, but may occur in the general population. From the work of Wiebe Braam's group it seems that a positive response to melatonin supplementation can be re-established in many cases through a brief period off melatonin supplementation followed by use of a substantially decreased dose.

Melatonin is interesting for several reasons:

1. It is a 'chronobiotic'. This means that the circulating levels of melatonin in the bloodstream vary through the day (Nir 1995).

2. Melatonin results from the metabolism of tryptophan (an essential dietary amino acid), by a well-recognized genetic pathway that has been identified as mutated in a number of ASD cases.

3. Tryptophan is essential for the production of serotonin, a neurotransmitter whose aberrant functioning is implicated in some cases of ASD, and for which a number of specific genetic factors, linked to ASD, have been identified (Anderson *et al.* 2009).

4. Abnormalities of one melatonin receptor gene, MTNR1B, are overrepresented in the ASD population (Chaste *et al.* 2010; Jonsson *et al.* 2010), suggesting a link between abnormal melatonin binding, ASD and certain types of sleep disorder. MTNR1B is also involved in regulating blood glucose and mutations have been shown to increase the risk of type 2 diabetes by around 20 per cent (Prokopenko *et al.* 2008).

5. Several studies have identified abnormalities in melatonin production and metabolism in people with ASD (Kulman *et al.* 2000; Leu *et al.* 2010; Melke *et al.* 2008; Nir *et al.* 1995; Ritvo *et al.* 1993; Tordjman *et al.* 2005).

6. In some people with ASD, abnormal melatonin synthesis has been shown to be related to reduced activity of the enzyme acetylserotonin methyltransferase (ASMT) (Toma *et al.* 2007; Melke *et al.* 2008). ASMT converts N-acetylserotonin to melatonin the final stage in this biological pathway.

Several synthetic 'melatonin analogues' have been developed which have similar biological actions: ramelteon (Kato *et al.* 2005), agomelatine (LY 156735) (Millan *et al.* 2003; Nickelsen *et al.* 2002) and tasimelteon (VEC-162) (Rajaratnam *et al.* 2009) are the best known (for reviews of this field, see Doghramji 2007; Hardeland 2009).

NOTE: As previously mentioned, in the USA melatonin is available as an over-the-counter supplement. In Canada it is not commonly available. In the UK it is currently classified as a prescription-only medication, having been previously available, until 1997, as a health supplement. It was re-classified as 'medicinal by use' due to its use exclusively as a sleeping aid and became a prescription medication.

Visual impairments and a link to reduced melatonin levels

Retinal damage or dysfunction affects the ability of the brain to modulate melatonin release, as the level of ambient light falling on the retina controls pineal release.

Sleep disturbance is common in individuals who are functionally blind. In the blind population the rate of sleep problems is highest, as would be expected, in people with no light perception, or in conditions where the eyes fail to develop (this is called 'anophthalmia' (Tabandeh *et al.* 1998).

Impaired vision has often been reported in association with ASD behaviours (see, e.g. Hobson and Bishop 2003), and ASD is more common amongst the visually impaired. In one large survey, DSM-IV autistic disorder was diagnosed in 30 (approximately 11.7%) of 257 visually impaired 7- to 18-year-olds (Mukaddes *et al.* 2007).

These findings support the importance of biological mechanisms involving melatonin in the pathogenesis of some cases of ASD. They also give a better understanding of the rationale for the use of melatonin supplementation as a potential treatment and an understanding of the neurobiology. These pathways are involved in the metabolism of serotonin and are an important component of the link from diet to behaviour, ASD and sleep issues.

Oxytocin

Oxytocin is a further neurochemical that has been linked to sleep. It is a nonapeptide – a small peptide molecule that is formed from nine amino acids. Oxytocin is produced in various structures but particularly from specific magnocellular neurosecretory cells (others produce vasopressin) found in the supraoptic and paraventricular nuclei of the hypothalamus. It is then released into the bloodstream from the posterior lobe of the pituitary gland. This structure lies directly below and contiguous to the SCN of the anterior hypothalamus (see Gutkowska *et al.* 2000; Saper, Chou and Scammell 2001). The SCN is a key structure involved in sleep modulation, and has been termed the brain's 'master circadian clock' (Zee and Manthena 2007, p.59).

The circadian rhythms of the SCN respond to a wide range of inputs such as glutamate, pituitary adenylate cyclase activating peptide (PACAP), from the retinohypothalamic tract, GABA from the geniculohypothalamic tract, melatonin from the pineal gland, and neuropeptide Y from the intergeniculate leaflet (see Reghunandanan and Reghunandanan 2006).

There is much active interest in the role of oxytocin in social functioning and in sexuality (for a brief overview, see Lee, Macbeth *et al.* 2009), and in its effects on EEG mu/alpha beta rhythms and mirror neuron function (Perry *et al.* 2010). As mu rhythm appears to be implicated in the earliest stages of development of the neural systems involved in social cognition this is of potential importance in understanding the early development of ASD (see Marshall and Meltzoff 2010).

In female animals, oxytocin levels affect lactation and parenting. In early research it was shown that intraventricular injection of oxytocin into virgin female rats could induce maternal behaviour (Pedersen and Prange 1979).

In males, oxytocin has been found to play a major role in inducing erections and in yawning (Argiolas, Melis and Gessa 1986; Argiolas *et al.* 1989). Penile erection and yawning are functionally related and both are partially under dopaminergic control (Holmgren *et al.* 1985).

To date there has been relatively little investigation of the role of oxytocin in the sleep–wake cycle. There is some evidence for a role of oxytocin in sleep. In the male rat, intracerebral injection of oxytocin promotes sleep in stress-free situations while increasing wakefulness when the animal is under stress (Lancel, Kromer and Neumann 2003). This having been said, caution needs to be exercised in extrapolating about biological functions across species when there is uncertainty about their functional and structural parallels (Insel, Gingrich and Young 2001).

A synthetic analogue of oxytocin known as 'carbetocin' was originally developed for the treatment of postpartum haemorrhage. An intranasal spray, carbetocin has recently completed US phase 1 trials as a treatment for the core impairments in autism.

Do non-biological factors affect yawning?

Some sleep-related behaviours are affected by social context and appear to be different in those with ASD. Yawning, for example, is 'infectious' – when one person yawns others are more likely to do so too (e.g. Provine 1989). This social aspect of yawning is impaired in a number of neurological conditions including autism (Thompson 2010).

Infectious yawning in humans is a developmental function. It can only be reliably elicited by viewing videotapes of yawning from around the age of 5 years and by reading or listening to stories about yawning from around 6 years in normally developing children (Anderson and Meno 2003).

Many other species yawn, and yawning can be induced across species by human modelling. This has been shown, for example, in dogs (Joly-Mascheroni, Senju and Shepherd 2008), and can be seen within social groups in other species as well.

A Japanese study looked at yawning in children who had been asked to watch videotapes of other people yawning and in children who had watched control videos in which no yawning occurred (Senju *et al.* 2007) (Figure D.1). The children were all aged around 11 years. There were 24 children with ASD and 25 non-ASD controls who were slightly more cognitively able. In the normal controls, there was a significant increase in yawning when they had watched yawning, while in those with ASD there was no difference in yawning dependent on what they had observed.

In the general population contagious yawning correlates with empathy and performance on theory of mind tasks. The people who are most likely to yawn when they see someone else yawn also tend to show the strongest empathy and the best abilities to recognize the thoughts, feelings and emotions of others (Platek *et al.* 2003).

The probable biological basis to this system is a well-established one, linking the visual pathways to the limbic system. The structural and functional connectivities involved, between the retinal and hypothalamic systems, are extensive (see Byerly and Blackshaw 2009; Trachtman 2010) and include the commissural fibres of the SCN.

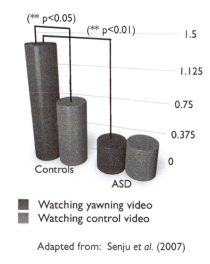

Adapted from: Senju *et al.* (2007)

Figure D.1 Yawning in autistic children

There is an extensive literature on the associations between sleep and emotion (see Baglioni *et al.* 2010). Some of this is of practical importance. For example, based on a large twin study, sleep disturbance at age 2 years is a predictor of depressive symptomology at age 10 years, and could be a useful screening measure for preventative interventions (Gregory *et al.* 2009).

A range of ASD conditions have been shown to have widespread hypothalamic involvement. The ASD conditions so far documented in which differences in these systems have been found include Biedl-Bardet syndrome; Klinefelter's syndrome;

Noonan's syndrome; Prader-Willi syndrome; Rett syndrome; Smith-Magenis syndrome and Tourette's syndrome (see Aitken 2010a,b).

DIET, SLEEP AND ASD

A more detailed review of dietary issues in ASD can be found in Aitken (2008). In addition to the general dietary factors we have discussed, a number of specific dietary differences have been reported in ASD that are potentially relevant to sleep problems.

Low levels of iron intake

Low serum ferritin levels (a measure of iron levels in the blood) have been reported in several studies in autism (Dosman *et al.* 2006; Latif, Heinz and Cook 2002). This is potentially relevant in sleep problems because one of the wide range of deleterious effects on brain development that can result from iron deficiency is disruption to the sleep–wake cycle (see Lozoff and Georgieff 2006).

There is support for a link between poor sleep and low serum ferritin in ASD (Dosman *et al.* 2007). An open-label study of 8 weeks of supplementation with 6mg/kg bodyweight of 'Supple-Forte elemental iron sprinkles' was carried out. A variety of assessments were conducted including pre- and post-ferritin corpuscular volume and haemoglobin from bloods; a measure of sleep disturbance (the Sleep Disturbance Scale for Children: Bruni *et al.* 1996); and diet diary records. A total of 33 ASD children took part in this study; 16 were preschool and 17 were of school age; 69 per cent of the preschoolers and 35 per cent of the school age childen had insufficient dietary iron intake at baseline, and 77 per cent had restless sleep. Over the group, both ferritin levels and sleep improved significantly with iron supplementation but there was no significant association within the group between changes on the two measures.

Low levels of dietary tryptophan

Tryptophan is one of the nine essential amino acids that are critical to various metabolic processes and your body must get from diet. It has an important role in sleep with a proportion of dietary tryptophan being used to produce serotonin. Serotonin is in turn converted into melatonin.

Amino acids can be divided into those which are essential to obtain from diet, those which are conditionally essential (can be produced in the body but are usually obtained from dietary sources) and those which are non-essential, being derived from diet but also produced internally in sufficient amounts to cater to metabolic need.

The essential amino acids (those which are required in the diet as they cannot be manufactured by the body) are isoleucine, leucine, lysine, methionine, phenylalanine, threonine, tryptophan, valine and histidine. The conditionally essential amino acids are arginine, asparagine, cysteine, glutamine, serine and tyrosine, and the non-essential amino acids are alanine, aspartate, glutamate, glycine and proline.

An early study on l-tryptophan supplementation in adults found an increase in the overall time spent asleep. There was also both a relative and an absolute reduction in the amount of REM sleep (Wyatt *et al.* 1970).

Tryptophan is converted into 5-hydroxytryptophan (5-HTP) by the enzyme tryptophan hydroxylase. There is some evidence that defects in the tryptophan hydroxylase gene *TPH2* can be associated with autism (Coon *et al.* 2005). One large series failed to replicate the finding, suggesting that although it may be a sufficient cause it is an uncommon one (Ramoz *et al.* 2006).

This first step in the metabolism of tryptophan to melatonin (Figure D.2) is also controlled by a co-factor called tetrahydrobiopterin (THBP4 (aka BH4)). There has been increasing interest in the role of THBP4 in ASD (Schnetz-Boutaud *et al.* 2009). Beneficial effects from treatment with THBP4 have been reported in a number of studies, beginning with early Japanese research by the pharmaceutical company Suntory dating back to the late 1980s (see, e.g. Naruse *et al.* 1989). THBP4 is an essential co-factor in the production of 5-HTP, the intermediate step in the pathway to serotonin.

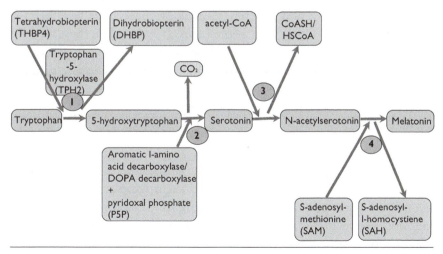

Tryptophan pathway differences in ASD linked to melatonin metabolism and sleep

Key References: 1. Coon *et al.* 2005; Schnetz-Boutaud *et al.* 2009; 2. Burlina *et al.* 2001; 3. Weiss *et al.* 2006; 4. Chaste *et al.* 2010; Jonsson *et al.* 2010.

Figure D.2 The pathway from tryptophan to melatonin

5-HTP is converted to serotonin by the action of aromatic amino acid l-carboxylase (AADC) which requires vitamin B6 as a co-factor. To date only a single case has been reported in which an aromatic amino acid l-carboxylase defect has been linked to ASD (Burlina *et al.* 2001); however, relatively few cases of AADC deficiency have been reported and the presentations have usually been complex (Brun *et al.* 2010). There is however a large literature on the role of B6 (particularly the active form P-5-P) in certain types of refractory seizure activity (see Baxter 2001) and in ASD.

Next, serotonin is converted to N-acetylserotonin. This process is controlled by the beta subunit of the platelet membrane adhesive protein receptor complex, ITGB3 (Weiss *et al.* 2006). ITGB3 has been implicated in ASD, as has an interaction between ITGB3 and SLC6A4 (Coutinho *et al.* 2007). SLC6A4 is a presynaptic serotonin transporter gene and it has been shown to be independently involved in the high levels of serotonin sometimes seen in ASD (Coutinho *et al.* 2004).

The final stage in the production of melatonin is the conversion of N-acetylserotonin into melatonin. This relies on the enzyme acetylserotonin methyltransferase (ASMT). The gene controlling the production of ASMT is abnormal in some ASD families but not in controls (Melke *et al.* 2008).

At the final step of the melatonin pathway, two studies have shown an association between ASD and melatonin receptor gene mutations (Chaste *et al.* 2010; Jonsson *et al.* 2010).

In summary then, there are a number of steps in the tryptophan metabolic pathway that result in the production of melatonin. All of the steps in this pathway are under genetic control and differences in all of these steps have been reported in association with ASD in at least some cases. It is possible, therefore, that sleep problems can arise as a result of deficient dietary intake of tryptophan while in other cases there may be problems in the metabolic pathway through which tryptophan is converted into available melatonin. Finally, there may be differences in the receptors on which melatonin operates.

Excess levels of taurine intake

Taurine is an amino acid derived from cysteine which itself is conditionally essential. Taking taurine as a supplement lowers blood sugar (Kaplan *et al.* 2004). Excessive ingestion has been suggested as a direct cause of problems in two specific cases. In one, onset of a manic episode in a 36-year-old man resulted from taking a combination of taurine, caffeine and inositol that induced a combination of manic behaviour and insomnia (Machado-Vieira, Viale and Kapczinski 2001). In the second case, toxic encephalopathy was described in the case report of a 27-year-old bodybuilder who was taking a variety of nutritional supplements including taurine, protein supplements and illegal hormones (Obermann *et al.* 2006).

Taurine is a component in many energy drinks and there is increasing concern over emerging links between energy drink consumption and the prevalence of problem behaviour in adolescents (Miller 2008).

As most of the information to date concerns excessive taurine use in combination, it is difficult to be clear about a specific effect of taurine alone; however, caution should be exercised in exceeding RDA (recommended daily amount) levels without further research.

METABOLIC AND PHYSIOLOGICAL FACTORS THAT CAN BE RELATED TO DISORDERED SLEEP

Blood pressure

A group of 238 normal adolescents, without recognized sleep apnoea or any other significant medical issues, had a variety of recordings – actigraphy, two overnight EEG records and multiple blood pressure measurements – to examine associations between demographic factors, blood pressure and sleep quality. Poor sleep quality was associated with 'pre-hypertensive' elevation of systolic and diastolic blood pressure. In this population the finding could not be accounted for on the basis of other factors such as sociodemographic variables or obesity (Javaheri *et al.* 2008).

In general with chronic insomnia there appears to be elevated night-time systolic blood pressure with smaller daytime to night-time changes in systolic pressure (Lanfranchi *et al.* 2009). This elevation in night-time systolic blood pressure is correlated with a significant increase in higher frequency EEG activity during non-REM sleep (Krystal *et al.* 2002; Merica, Blois and Gaillard 1998; Perlis *et al.* 2001).

It would appear that elevated night-time blood pressure could be associated with poor sleep independently of other possible contributory factors. As many factors related to elevated blood pressure are found more commonly in the ASD population, hypertension should be checked in all cases and treated as required when found.

Ear infections and snoring

Ear infections have been suspected as a possible cause of sleep disorders in ASD for some years (Herr 2003).

A large survey of 16,321 5- to 7-year-old Kentucky children found 1844 were reported as being habitual snorers and 827 (44.8%) of these had histories of recurrent otitis media (inner ear infection). This compared to 4247 with recurrent otitis media out of the remaining 14,447 non-snorers (29.3%) (Gozal *et al.* 2008). This gives an odds ration of 1.95 or, expressed another way, says that recurrent ear infections are almost twice as common in snorers than you would expect if there were no association between the two. The need for tympanostomy (insertion of grommets into the ear to keep the ear canal open) was also increased in the children who snored, suggesting that when snoring and a history of ear infection were both present the ear problems were likely to be more pronounced.

The metabolic syndrome

The 'metabolic syndrome' is the name given to a constellation of clinical features and lifestyle risk factors that increase the risk of diabetes and cardiovascular problems (see, e.g. Grundy *et al.* 2004). Currently a variety of overlapping diagnostic criteria are in use. These typically include dyslipidaemia, central obesity, elevated blood pressure and abnormal glucose metabolism.

Abnormal breathing during sleep and metabolic syndrome have not yet been investigated in detail in the paediatric population; however, sleep apnoea is a recognized secondary problem in cases of paediatric metabolic syndrome (see Halpern *et al.* 2010). The co-occurrence of sleep-disordered breathing in adolescents with the features of metabolic syndrome has been reported. In one screening study of 270 adolescents aged around 13.6 years (Redline *et al.* 2007), 13 of the 22 with sleep-disordered breathing also met the criteria for metabolic syndrome (59%) while this was true of only 39 of the 248 without sleep-disordered breathing (16%). This is roughly 6.5 times the number one would expect if there were no association.

A significant association has been found in adult community samples between sleep problems and presence of the metabolic syndrome (Nieto, Peppard and Young 2009). This is unsurprising as many of the factors reported as part of the metabolic syndrome have been reported in association with sleep-disordered breathing.

Hypertension (Peppard *et al.* 2000), diabetes and insulin resistance (Punjabi *et al.* 2004), abdominal obesity (Grunstein *et al.* 1993) and dyslipidaemia (Ip *et al.* 2000) have all been reported as more common in people who have sleep-disordered breathing.

Gastro-oesophageal reflux disease (GERD)

From adult research, gastrointestinal (GI) problems in general are commonly associated with sleep difficulties. In one series of chronic insomnia patients, 33.6 per cent had GI issues compared to 9.2 per cent of matched controls, while 55.4 per cent of GI patients complained of sleep problems compared to 20.2 per cent of matched controls (Taylor *et al.* 2007).

The GI tract is almost entirely alkaline with the exception of the stomach. The lining of the stomach produces hydrochloric acid and digestive enzymes that are irritating to other tissues in the GI tract.

GERD is a condition in which gastric acid from the stomach is brought up into the throat when someone is lying down or taking vigorous exercise. It results from a poorly functioning sphincter at the lower end of the oesophagus (where the upper GI tract joins the top of the stomach). This problem causes discomfort and physical irritation as the gastric acid irritates the lining of the oesophagus.

A number of studies have indicated a link between GERD and sleep problems (see Cremonini *et al.* 2009; Jung, Choung and Talley 2010). The current view is that the two conditions interact; differences in the clearance of stomach acid through saliva, swallowing and gastric motility together with adopting a prone position during sleep may aggravate GERD and worsen any problems. These are more likely in the early stages of sleep as reflux is reduced during deeper sleep stages.

A part of the US Sleep Heart Health Study (Fass *et al.* 2005) reported on a questionnaire survey of data from 6395 adults. They found that a number of factors such as sleeping poorly, having an elevated body mass index (BMI) (of 25 or over), insomnia, obstructive sleep apnoea (OSA), daytime sleepiness and higher levels of carbonated drink consumption predicted heartburn during sleep. Heartburn during sleep is in turn a feature that is strongly associated with GERD.

One study in 25 older adults with GERD (mean age 42.8) examined the effects of a specific medication, rabeprazole (a proto-pump inhibitor which reduces acid production from the lining of the stomach) (Orr *et al.* 2009). After an 8-week course of treatment, there was a significant reported improvement in upper airway function and in both objective measurement and patient ratings of sleep quality. Rabeprazole is not currently approved in the USA or the UK for use with individuals under 18 years of age.

The first paper to suggest a possible link between ASD and GERD was a clinical case series from Baltimore (Horvath *et al.* 1999). This report was on upper endoscopy (looking at the lining of the throat down as far as the entrance to the stomach with a fibre-optic device) in 36 children with autism and GI issues. The paper reported that GERD seemed to be a common finding in association with ASD, and that in these cases there was a high prevalence of sleep disorders. That a condition that causes pain and discomfort on lying down tends to co-occur with sleeping problems should not come as any surprise.

Inflammatory biomarkers and related immune issues

A number of immune factors have been implicated in sleep (see Imeri and Opp 2009; Krueger 2008). The interaction between cytokines such as interleukin (IL)-1 and neurotransmitters such as serotonin are increased at times of infection and may underlie the change in sleep patterns seen at such times.

Some immune factors are reported to be different in ASD (see, e.g. Ashwood *et al.* 2010; Croonenberghs *et al.* 2002); however, there are significant variations in some of these factors and measurement is complex as variations can be both age- (see Sack *et al.* 1998) and/or sex-dependent (Sadeghi *et al.* 2005). A recent study of daytime immune profiles of children with ASD has shown an elevation of plasma cytokine levels (Ashwood *et al.* 2010). No published study has so far attempted to correlate immune factors that are reportedly different in ASD, such as TNF-a and IL-6, with the likelihood of sleep disturbance in this group.

Experimental deprivation of sleep has a marked effect on immune markers such as tumour necrosis factor alpha (TNF-α) receptor 1 and IL-6 (Shearer *et al.* 2001); c-reactive protein (CRP) (Meier-Eweart *et al.* 2004); and IL-17 (van Leeuwen *et al.* 2009). Changes in IL-6 caused by sleep restriction are strongly associated with increased pain perception (Haack, Sanchez and Mullington 2007). The increase in CRP, which is coupled with increased heart rate and can be brought on by sleep restriction, has effects that last well after sleep has recovered and increase the risk of developing cardiopulmonary difficulties (van Leeuwen *et al.* 2009). These findings suggest that some of the immune differences reported in ASD may be reactive rather than constitutional in origin and could be secondary to persistent sleep difficulties.

The processes are complex and an increase in both pro- and anti-inflammatory markers is reported (Frey, Fleshner and Wright 2007). Increases in CRP and IL-6 are associated with increased sleep duration while increases in TNF-α are associated with reduced sleep (Patel *et al.* 2009).

Many other factors influence inflammatory markers (see O'Connor *et al.* 2009 for discussion), and it may be premature to draw any strong conclusions on the links between inflammatory factors and sleep in ASD from the literature to date. OSA, for example is associated with an increase in levels of pro-inflammatory markers, but is also strongly associated with obesity, asthma control and cardiopulmonary difficulties (Mehra and Redline 2008).

OTHER FACTORS THAT CAN INFLUENCE SLEEP
Skin disorders

As we have seen, when melatonin intake ingested by breastfeeding babies increases this can improve allergic dermatitis (Kimata 2001, 2004).

Psoriasis and other dermatological conditions that increase itchiness and scratching are associated with sleeping difficulties (see Dahl *et al.* 1995; Jafferany 2007). These problems can sometimes arise as a consequence of other medications that are taken to improve separate comorbid conditions such as ADHD, seizures and mood swings.

Relatively little research has been carried out on the possible link between skin problems and sleep (see Thorburn and Riha 2010).

Epilepsy

It is well recognized that there is a high rate of sleep problems in people who have epilepsy (see, e.g. Kotagal 2001; Manni and Terzaghi 2010; Matos *et al.* 2010) and that there is a high level of comorbidity between epilepsy and ASD (see Aitken 2010a, 2010b).

The association between epilepsy and sleep issues is thought to result from the similarity in oscillatory patterns seen in both, with epileptic discharges developing from sleep-related circuitry (Beenhakker and Huguenard 2009).

Some children who have been diagnosed with night terrors have been subsequently found to be suffering from night-time seizures that presented as night terrors (see, e.g. Lombroso 2000).

One large study (Byars *et al.* 2008) examined the interrelationships between neuropsychological functioning and sleep problems in children who had recently developed overt clinical seizures. This research reported on 331 children aged 6 to 14 who were assessed following their first reported seizures. Settling difficulties, daytime sleepiness and parasomnias were significantly more common in this group as rated on the Sleep Behaviour Questionnaire and the Child Behavior Checklist. This was in comparison both to a large sample of 225 sibling controls and to rates reported in the clinical literature. Difficulties shown on a detailed neuropsychological test battery were strongly associated with the presence of sleep problems in this population.

Fluctuations through the sleep–wake cycle are involved in a range of changes in neural functioning including synaptic plasticity. On this basis, fluctuation in seizure threshold may vary dependent on factors such as sleep state and level of sleep deprivation (Romcy-Pereira, Leite and Garcia-Cairasco 2009).

EFFECTS OF SLEEP DEPRIVATION ON BRAIN GROWTH AND STRUCTURE

Animal research on the effects of long-term sleep deprivation has demonstrated a variety of effects including damage to hippocampal neurons. The hippocampus is the brain structure most likely to sustain damage as a consequence of low oxygen levels. Hippocampal function is critical to a range of CNS processes including memory formation (Tung *et al.* 2005) and glucose homeostasis (Barf, Meerlo and Scheurink 2010).

In humans even relatively brief periods of sleep restriction can have marked effects on cognitive function. In a study comparing performance of 16 children aged 1 to 14 years who were randomly allocated to either 5 or 11 hours of time in bed in a sleep laboratory, Randazzo *et al.* (1998) reported that the children who experienced restricted sleep while not impaired on simple cognitive tasks or rote learning did show impairment on a number of tests of verbal creativity including fluency and mental flexibility and on a test of executive function (the Wisconsin Card Sorting Task).

The persistence of sleep problems at times of active brain development (i.e. when processes such as neural proliferation, dendritic arborization, dendritic pruning or apoptosis are at their most active) might be expected to have effects on brain development. These processes are most active in early childhood (Jan *et al.* 2010) and during adolescence (Casey, Duhoux and Cohen 2010).

CNS TRAUMA

Traumatic brain injuries are associated with high rates of post-injury anxiety and depression (Whelan-Goodinson *et al.* 2009). In addition, rates of sleep disorder are also higher in people who have experienced CNS trauma (Makley *et al.* 2008; Rao *et al.* 2008).

Rates of traumatic injuries, particularly to the head, are reported as being higher than expected in the ASD population (McDermott, Zhou and Mann 2008).

The literature in this area is particularly weak, however, only mentioning ASD symptomology passim (e.g. Barlow *et al.* 2004), without comment on causation or any consequent changes in presentation.

ATTENTION-DEFICIT HYPERACTIVITY DISORDER
(For reviews, see Mayes *et al.* 2009; Owens 2005, 2009.)

Certain specific sleep problems are more commonly reported in those diagnosed with ADHD: restless legs syndrome (RLS) and sleep-disordered breathing (SDB) (Cortese, Konofal and Yateman 2006; O'Brien, Holbrook *et al.* 2003; Picchietti *et al.* 1998; Picchietti, Underwood and Farris 1999) in particular. In addition, periodic limb movement syndrome and narcolepsy also seem to be overrepresented (for discussion, see Owens 2005). A subgroup of ADHD children have sleep onset insomnia that does not appear to be related to poor sleep hygiene (van der Heijden, Smits and Gunning 2006).

Overall rates of sleep disorders are high in children with ADHD (Gruber and Sadeh 2004; Gruber, Sadeh and Raviv 2000; Mayes *et al.* 2009; Walters *et al.* 2008). This may be an effect of constitutional make-up but could also be in part a direct consequence of the effects of stimulant medication (Berman *et al.* 2009; Corkum *et al.* 2008; Mick *et al.* 2000; O'Brien, Ivanenko *et al.* 2003; Sangal *et al.* 2006; Stein 1999). With few exceptions (e.g. Faraone *et al.* 2009) sleep disturbance or exacerbation of pre-existing sleep difficulties are reported in children and adolescents being treated with stimulant medication for ADHD symptomology.

Snoring, a feature of OSA, is reported to be three times as common in paediatric ADHD as in other psychiatric groups or in the general population, affecting some 33 per cent (O'Brien, Holbrook *et al.* 2003). One surprising finding is that when effectively treated, typically by removal of the tonsils and adenoids, 50 per cent of cases no longer meet criteria for ADHD at follow-up (Chervin *et al.* 2006). Unfortunately, a significant subgroup of children treated for snoring by adenotonsillectomy continues to snore (Liukkonen *et al.* 2008).

Polysomnography (sleep EEG) studies show that children with ADHD seem to sleep for less time overall and to have reduced amounts of REM sleep both proportionally and in absolute terms when compared to controls (Gruber *et al.* 2009).

There is a high degree of overlap in the symptoms of ADHD and ASD (see Ponde, Novaes and Losapio 2010). Stimulant medications are frequently used with children who show such features. The possibility of iatrogenic side effects of stimulant use in such cases should always be considered, especially if the sleep difficulties arose after the use of any such medication was begun.

CRANIOFACIAL DYSMORPHOGENESIS

Craniofacial dysmorphogenesis is a complicated-sounding term that is used to describe someone whose head and face have developed in an unusual but syndrome-typical fashion. This is perhaps best illustrated by the extreme differences in development seen with hemifacial microsomia. In this condition, one side of the face and skull develop more slowly than the other and these are significantly smaller than the features on the other side (this is seen in a number of conditions such as Goldenhaar's syndrome).

The term craniofacial dysmorphogenesis is used when describing many clinical conditions which have characteristic facial features as, for example, in Down's syndrome.

This issue is of particular relevance here when the effect is to constrict breathing and increase the risk of apnoea (Hui 2009; Lee, Chan *et al.* 2009; Lee, Petocz *et al.* 2009).

Differences in the development of the upper airway system can affect its structure and function, and, together with the lung volume and composition of the body (muscular development and level of body fat), can affect the likelihood of developing OSA.

OBESITY

It has long been suggested that diet is related to sleep. William Banting, in what is thought to be the first publication on dieting, stated that adhering to what was essentially a low carbohydrate diet 'leads to an excellent night's rest, with from six to eight hours' sound sleep' (Banting 1863, p.4).

A link between obesity and sleep pattern has been noted by many of those writing on sleep (Van Cauter and Knutson 2008). Obesity has been linked to poor sleep in a number of studies in both adults (Bjorvatn *et al.* 2007; Patel *et al.* 2006; Taheri *et al.* 2004) and children (Reilly *et al.* 2005; Seicean *et al.* 2007). Some others have disputed that there is any such link (Mehra and Redline 2008; Spruyt and Gozal 2008).

Metabolic energy control demonstrates strong circadian rhythms and is under the control of biological clocks. The genes REVERBa, RORa and PPARa/g have all been highlighted in the control of lipid metabolism (Zanquetta *et al.* 2010).

As we noted above, obesity is linked to poorer asthma control and to aspects of immune function that are involved in sleep regulation.

In older children and adults there is an association between obesity and the severity of obstructive sleep apnoea. Although the data are preliminary, this association only becomes clear from around age 7, with no strong association between the two being seen at younger ages (see Graw-Panzer *et al.* 2010).

Sleep pattern, appetite and obesity are clearly interrelated and a number of specific biological factors may account for this (Prinz 2004). These include insulin, leptin (an inflammatory marker that is involved in appetite regulation) and ghrelin. Ghrelin levels are linked to levels of serotonin. Abnormalities of ghrelin have been implicated in various conditions such as epilepsy (Berilgen *et al.* 2006), irritable bowel disease (Peracchi *et al.* 2006) and immune dysfunction (Dixit and Taub 2005) (for an overview, see Aitken 2010a, 2010b).

The issues here are to an extent circular as poor sleep interferes with normal metabolism that in turn affects the quality of sleep. Poor sleep is linked to obesity, and obesity impairs the function of insulin which in turn is associated with a greater incidence and severity of obstructive sleep apnoea and type-2 diabetes (see Trenell, Marshall and Rogers 2007).

A number of genetic conditions are associated with both ASD diagnosis and obesity. The best known of these are Biedl-Bardet syndrome, Cohen syndrome, Fragile-X syndrome, Prader-Willi syndrome and Rubenstein-Taybi syndrome (see Aitken 2010a, 2010b).

In Prader-Willi syndrome, sleep-related breathing problems improve with weight reduction; however, excessive daytime sleepiness (EDS) does not (Harris and Allen 1996). This finding suggests that some aspects of their sleep patterns are secondary to obesity, while others are not, but may benefit from adjunctive approaches (see section below on EDS).

GENETIC FACTORS

As we have discussed, some genetic factors are influenced by diet while others can influence dietary intake.

The interactions between genetic and environmental factors in neurodevelopmental disorders are complex and only beginning to be understood (Thompson and Levitt 2010). There are a number of specific genetic conditions associated with both ASD diagnosis and sleep problems, and a number of specific genes involved in sleep regulation that have been found in association with ASD.

Specific ASD-linked genetic conditions with high rates of sleep problems

A number of genetic ASD-linked syndromes present with high rates of sleep disorders compared to the rates reported in the general population (Table D.1). In particular, Prader-Willi syndrome (Miller *et al.* 2009; Williams *et al.* 2008); Angelman syndrome (Pelc *et al.* 2008); Down's syndrome (see Cotton and Richdale 2010); Rett syndrome (see McArthur and Budden 1998; Young *et al.* 2007), Smith-Magenis syndrome (Boudreau *et al.* 2009); and, much more rarely, Kleine-Levin syndrome (Arnulf *et al.* 2005; Berthier *et al.* 1992) are genetic conditions which have been reported in association with ASD. All have been shown to present frequently with sleep disorders (see, for review, Aitken 2010a, b).

TABLE D.1 GENETIC CONDITIONS IN ASD ASSOCIATED WITH SLEEP PROBLEMS

Condition	Gene locus/loci	Key references
Prader-Willi syndrome	5q11–q13; 15q12	Bruni, Verrillo *et al.* (2010); Cotton and Richdale (2010)
Kleine-Levin syndrome	6p21.3	Berthier *et al.* (1992)
Angelman syndrome	15q11–q13; Xq28	Pelc *et al.* (2008)
Smith-Magenis syndrome	17p11.2	De Leersnyder *et al.* (2006)
Down's syndrome	Trisomy 21	Cotton and Richdale (2006, 2010); Diomedi *et al.* (1999)
Rett syndrome	Xq28	Rohdin *et al.* (2007)

OTHER GENETIC FACTORS

'Clock genes'

It has been proposed that clock gene anomalies may be associated with both the timing difficulties seen in autistic social interactions and the high rate of reported sleeping problems seen in ASD (Wimpory, Nicholas and Nash 2002).

Our genetic make-up provides a number of systems that specify 'invariant features' – things that are consistent about how we are built and how we function. The best known of these are the 'homeobox'/HOX genes that specify the physical layout of our bodies (Holland, Booth and Bruford 2007). These genes have been 'conserved' across the evolutionary span, being virtually unchanged in structure and function from fruit flies to *Homo sapiens* (see Garcia-Fernàndez 2005). They are fairly general in what they specify – things such as the sequence of body parts, their midline symmetry (many structures in mammals show symmetry around a central line – our cerebral hemispheres, eyes, nostrils, arms, legs, ribs, kidneys, lungs and testes/ovaries to name a few). A few organs such as the liver, intestines and heart do not show this gross pattern of symmetry, but are the exception rather than the rule.

Many other aspects of our bodies are similarly specified by our genetic make-up. The many predictable biological rhythms of the body, from our resting heart rate and breathing pattern to circadian and ultradian rhythms, have genetic bases but these have been harder to identify. This is partly because a link between genetic structure and temporal patterning is more difficult to identify. Systems such as Laban dance notation help to specify movement in space (see Guest 2005) and musical notation to specify changes in sound. The earliest musical notation system so far identified is from Ugarit in present-day Syria and has been dated to 3400 BC. These systems, developed to specify changes in movement and sound, help us to see how a structural system such as DNA could specify an invariant pattern such as basal heart or breathing rate in a structural code.

The biology of circadian rhythms has been the subject of a large amount of research in recent decades and has begun to be much more clearly understood at the molecular and genetic level (see Foster and Kreitzman 2005). Alun Barnard and Patrick Nolan give a useful update in their 2008 paper, which looks at neurobehavioural effects of genetic disruption to circadian systems (Barnard and Nolan 2008). Some patterns may show lengthy cycles, and seasonally changing rates of sleep problems are seen in the general population (see, e.g. Pallesen *et al.* 2001), and have been reported in ASD (Hayashi 2001).

A number of genes have now been shown to orchestrate phasic temporal processes (see Bamne *et al.* 2010). These genes, which specify temporal rather than structural factors, have been termed 'clock genes'. Abnormalities in some of these genes have been identified and associated with human sleep disorders (see, e.g. Lamont *et al.* 2007; Piggins 2002; von Schantz 2008; von Schantz and Archer 2003). Clock genes have also been implicated as having possible roles in other clinical conditions such as human metabolic syndrome (Gomez-Abellan *et al.* 2008) and breast cancer (Dai *et al.* 2011). A useful general review of clock genes and sleep disorders can be found in Ebisawa (2007).

As part of a broader genetic study, 15 genes involved in the regulation of circadian rhythm have been identified that frequently show quantitative or qualitative differences in ASD, three of which are recognized clock genes (Hu *et al.* 2009).

TABLE D.2 CLOCK GENES DIFFERENCES IN ASD

Clock gene	Gene locus	Association with ASD (+/-)	Key reference
Per3	1p36.23	+	Hu *et al.* (2009)
Npas2	2q13	+	Nicholas *et al.* (2007)
BHLHb2/DEC1	3q25.1	?	Hu *et al.* (2009)
Clock	4q21	+	Hu *et al.* (2009)
RORA	15q22.2	+	Nguyen *et al.* (2010)
Per1	17p12	+	Nicholas *et al.* (2007)

The clock genes in Table D.2 have been reported in association with ASD.

Variations in some of the above are being linked to specific types of sleep problem. For example, a Per3 length polymorphism has been reported in association with delayed sleep phase syndrome (Archer *et al.* 2003).

One system known to be affected by differences in the function of clock genes is known as the hypothalamic-pituitary-adrenal (HPA) axis (Nader, Chrousos and Kino 2010), and may have an important role in the control of clinical issues such as appetite and obesity (Yang *et al.* 2009).

Differences in some clock genes, specifically the genes Per1, Per2, CLOCK, RORA and Npas2, have been reported in association with ASD (Nicholas *et al.* 2007; Hu *et al.* 2009; Nguyen *et al.* 2010).

One function of clock genes is in the modulation of CNS pathways involving synaptic cell adhesion molecules such as neuroligin 3 and neurexin 1. Another role is in controlling postsynaptic scaffolding proteins such as SHANK2, SHANK3 and DLGAP2. These provide circadian modulation of synaptic function (see, e.g. Bourgeron 2007; Toro *et al.* 2010). This process gives rise to temporal changes in the function of the nervous system that parallel diurnal changes in the environment.

A close association between clock genes and the circadian biology of adipose fats has been shown (see Gimble and Floyd 2009). This area of research is rapidly improving our understanding of cardiovascular disease. It may be an important piece in the biological jigsaw relating sleep to metabolic rate and obesity.

Improvements in genetic screening are leading to identification of novel genes involved in modifying circadian rhythm and clarifying our understanding of how these processes operate (see, for example, Hirota *et al.* 2010).

In addition to clock genes, some recent research has shown that there are clearly additional biological mechanisms involved in biological cycles. John O'Neill and Akilesh Reddy at the Metabolic Research Laboratories at Cambridge University have shown that mature human red blood cells, which have no cell nucleus and no DNA, even when kept in the absence of external cues, show circadian fluctuations in the levels of certain highly conserved antioxidant proteins called peroxiredoxins (O'Neill and Reddy 2011). The fluctuations in these protein levels are entrainable – they can be modified by changes in environmental factors such as light levels, and are temperature-compensated as are clock gene-mediated circadian patterns. Clearly some further factors that are not directly related to DNA transcription must be involved. There is still more to learn about the biological processes that underlie our biological rhythms.

—⁕—

WHAT CAN YOU DO?

A flock of sheep that leisurely pass by
One after one; the sound of rain, and bees
Murmuring; the fall of rivers, winds and seas,
Smooth fields, white sheets of water, and pure sky –
I've thought of all by turns, and still I lie
Sleepless…

William Wordsworth, 'To Sleep'

INTERVENTIONS – ASSESSING THE EVIDENCE

I hope that if you have read up to this point you now have a much clearer idea of what sleep is and what we know about it, the nature of sleep problems and the evidence that they are more common in ASD and will now have an understanding of some of the biological reasons why this might be.

When considering what might be helpful, it is useful to see what has been done before with similar problems and how well it worked. In general terms, this is what we call evidence-based medicine (EBM). This is an important and often missing stage in considering what to do.

Many treatments have been used in the past that had the desired effect but where no one considered the wider consequences (giving opium to babies to help them sleep was a common practice in Victorian England, and it worked. This would never be recommended today because of our understanding of the effects of opiates on the brain).

We will go on to consider the evidence for various treatments, but first there are a number of things that you should start to think about, particularly concerning how to evaluate evidence. So, before looking at the approaches and the evidence, I want to make a few cautionary points.

Stage hypnotists are still a very popular type of touring theatre act. When a hypnotist opens at a venue, if he has a good subject on his first night he will usually offer them free tickets to come back the following night with some friends. Often they will bring along people who also prove to be good subjects. If all goes well, by the end of the week there will be a group of susceptible people in the audience whose attendance will help the hypnotist to put on an entertaining show, and his reputation will grow. This strategy works well because we typically make friends with people who are similar to us, and this extends to often being similarly susceptible subjects for this sort of spectacle. I am pointing this out not to make a statement about stage hypnotism or to put anyone off going to see one, but to make a general point about factors that can make something appear to work.

Many medications seem effective in experimental trials with subjects who are selected on strict criteria, have nothing else wrong with them, whose compliance is closely monitored and who have been paid to take the medication. These treatments often fail to make the grade in clinical trials where the people taking them are different, often having more than one medical complaint, sometimes forgetting to take their medication and often different in a host of other ways from the subjects in the original trials.

Intensive early intervention approaches with good anecdotal or open trial results typically report on groups of families with a high level of time and financial commitment. These approaches often show poorer results in 'real-world' studies. When reports of good results are from unrepresentative families who are more affluent, more verbal and more committed to the approach, they can often prove difficult to replicate. With families who are more sceptical, less affluent and have less free time, they will often have poorer outcomes.

There is an inherent bias towards writing about things that have worked. Researchers are less prone to publish poorer outcomes and journals are also guilty of a positive publication bias. They are less likely to publish 'failed' studies (good studies that show something has not worked) than successful ones (where the treatment under study has shown good results).

Many sleep problems will spontaneously get better. If a problem is fairly common and is likely to improve whatever else happens, there will be a proportion of people who have tried an approach and where the sleep problem got better but the improvement would have happened anyway. Obviously one can never be sure if a specific individual who has become better falls into this category (these people are usually called 'false positives') but it illustrates the problem and the need for a clear understanding of how treatments are assessed and better ways of assessing what works and what doesn't.

Before embarking on any approach, it is important to be sure both that the problem is unlikely to improve quickly anyway and that there is a strong chance, based on the evidence, that what you do is likely to be of benefit.

Therapists, especially if they are commercially motivated and looking to attract business, will always try to point to cases they have seen who have improved. People whose children have attended them with sleep difficulties and have improved are also likely to believe that the improvement has resulted from the approach they have used, and satisfied client comments are often posted on websites. If someone has sought out an expensive therapist who they believe is effective there are strong incentives to believe that the results they have seen are as a direct result of what they paid for.

Sometimes this can be a 'therapist-specific effect' – a particular person seems to get good results with an approach that other people find doesn't work as well. What it is important to know is whether there is something unusual about those who improved. Maybe there is something different about the way that the therapy was implemented, or perhaps the good results were a 'cherry-picked' group, as in the hypothetical hypnotist example at the beginning of this section. If these sorts of things can be excluded, or have been controlled for, and there is good evidence that the approach works with similar people, there is a stronger chance that it might work for others.

It is important to keep abreast of the published evidence. New studies and reviews of best practice appear all the time and what should be done for a given problem changes accordingly.

Many people have an inherent tendency to prefer complementary and alternative treatments to conventional pharmacotherapy. Several reviews of complementary and alternative medicine (CAM) approaches have concluded that there are significant potential risks with many such approaches compared to conventional medicine (see Farah *et al.* 2000; Kruskal 2009; Lim, Cranswick and South 2010). Because something is natural does not necessarily mean that it is always safe or safer.

The difficulty in teasing out what works is the reason for the heavy reliance now being placed on 'evidence-based' practice. There are basic flaws, however, in always adopting a laissez-faire approach, waiting for a research group to do a proper randomized controlled trial (RCT) to show that a treatment does work.

An extreme example that illustrates why some situations do not lend themselves to an evidence-based approach and RCTs can be found in an amusing little article reviewing the evidence that parachutes are useful in preventing death or injury from 'gravitational challenge'. Having failed to find any RCTs on this important issue, the authors concluded:

As with many interventions intended to prevent ill health, the effectiveness of parachutes has not been subjected to rigorous evaluation by using randomised controlled trials. Advocates of evidence-based medicine have criticised the adoption of interventions evaluated by using only observational data. We think that everyone might benefit if the most radical protagonists of evidence based medicine organised and participated in a double blind, randomised, placebo controlled, crossover trial of the parachute. (Smith and Pell 2003, p.1459)

Just because there are no RCTs or the evidence base is weak does not automatically mean that something does not work (see discussion in Schreck 2001). I am fairly sure that breathing is important to maintaining human life and do not feel it is important to carry out a RCT to prove this hypothesis. The old adage 'absence of evidence is different from evidence of absence' often holds true. There may be reasons why an effective treatment has a weak evidence base – a patentable drug therapy usually has a wealthy backer who is anticipating lucrative rewards, often trying to be first to market a new type of medication in order to capture the lion's share of the market. In contrast, a complementary or alternative therapy usually has limited access to funding for research on its effects and limited prospects of recouping the costs of research even if it were shown to be highly effective.

There are a few caveats to be aware of and questions to ask about the evidence-based approach:

1. *Is the EBM approach appropriate to the evaluation of the particular treatment/ intervention?*

   It is important to recognize that some approaches do not easily fit with an 'evidence-based' model but may nevertheless be beneficial and can be equally well or in some respects better validated (see, for example, the discussion of Applied Behaviour Analysis (ABA) in Keenan and Dillenburger 2011).

   There is an acceptance that randomized controlled trials are useful in validating pharmacological treatments of closely matched groups of individuals with the same problem. There is also an acceptance that they are not an appropriate approach to evaluating interventions that rely on identification of individual differences rather than commonalities.

   Another thing to note is that pharmaceutical trials with clinical populations typically, though not always, assess the use of a particular dosage of medication. This 'one size fits all' approach often doesn't take into account factors such as the age, sex, bodyweight, muscle–fat ratio, diet or metabolic rate of the person, or their concurrent use of other alternative or complementary treatments. This approach oddly holds dose constant while allowing many aspects of the patients under study to vary. The aim is to assess the utility of a standard dose that can then be taken to market. With the Model-T Ford, you could have any colour you wanted as long as it was black.

   Some approaches use individual differences and single-case methods to provide more 'bespoke' interventions. This type of approach has most often been adopted for evaluation of behavioural and cognitive-behavioural methods. As these are specific to the individual they necessitate a different approach to evaluation and are not easily amenable to RCT evaluation (see, for example, Barlow, Nock and Hersen 2008).

Single-case research designs are beginning to become established not just as an alternative approach to assessment but also as an established research paradigm for biomedical research, with increasing recognition of the important role of individual differences (see Janosky *et al.* 2009). It may be that the effects of a treatment are highly specific. Rather than finding the average shoe size of a Princess, this could be similar to the quest to find Cinderella by finding which foot fits a specific glass slipper.

Reviews of ABA treatments have found that although the targets of treatment have been well specified, treatment integrity (how well specific studies have adhered to the treatment approach) have been less well specified and monitored. This problem makes generalization from the results of many studies more difficult (McIntyre *et al.* 2007). There have been significant moves towards ensuring that research designs for psychological intervention studies are improved in this respect (see Lord *et al.* 2005; Smith *et al.* 2007), by building on the use of single-case methodology in developing evidence-based practice (Horner *et al.* 2005).

A useful discussion of some of the practical issues in developing and sustaining evidence-based approaches to work with more complex populations can be found in Forness (2005).

2. *If there is RCT data supporting the use of an approach, is this information from a population that is relevant to the situation the approach is being considered for?*

Randomized controlled trials are relatively easy to conduct for therapies that can be matched (medication trials are often an ideal) with groups who all present with the same problem. Where there is good RCT evidence, however, the person who needs help is unlikely to fit the same criteria as those in the trial – RCT studies tend to take subjects from specialist clinics involved in academic research who have no comorbid problems and may be different in age, sex or sociodemographics. Any or all of these selection criteria may affect the likely success of the treatment, and it would be unsurprising if sometimes the trial design is set up to make a positive finding more likely (for example, if there was previous research suggesting that the treatment might work best with teenage boys a trial might be set up to strengthen this finding). This is partly why levels of benefit shown in RCTs often exceed those subsequently reported in clinical practice.

Most RCTs are conducted with highly selected groups. Usually they have no other problems, are not on other medication, have no other health or medical issues, and come from stable, more affluent families… This is not a good evidence base to compare against if this is not similar to the person who needs help, and it may be that there is no appropriate evidence base to indicate how likely the treatment is to work with this person here and now. Similar points can be made about the use of 'third world' populations for trials of treatments as often high rates of problems within a population (for example, rates of minor infection, diarrhoea and vomiting) can mask low but significant rates of adverse reactions to treatment.

3. *Are there explicit or implicit 'conflicts of interest' for those who conducted or funded the research?*

Almost all RCTs published to date have been carried out with pharmaceutical industry sponsorship. This may be direct and this should be declared in the article, or may be indirect through more general support to the facility or university through which the research was carried out. Many clinical journals receive substantial support in the form of advertising and some associations which publish journals have supported lectures which they then publish and which may not require to be 'peer-reviewed' but can be cited. In some circumstances the funding agency will have the right to veto publication of research thus potentially skewing the literature in favour of positive results. As this becomes more difficult in some countries, research may be sponsored more vigorously in countries where this is not the case.

Perhaps surprisingly, it remains the case that stating that a piece of research has received funding from a particular source is sufficient to allow it to be entered into meta-analyses or reviews, with equal weight being given to the conclusions as would be given to studies that were less inherently open to bias. An example of bias in research design is the use of a poorly performing medication or a placebo as a comparison against which to gauge beneficial results rather than comparing against an approach which might be a treatment of choice.

The increase in 'open access' online publication, which is not as strongly affected by the same conflict of interest issues, has led to substantial improvements in objectivity and to publication of more balanced research, which in many cases has led to more tempered claims for treatment benefits to be tempered. Much of the credit for this change has to go to Harold Varmus who pioneered much of the open access movement in biomedical research (see Varmus 2010).

Some research has been designed to highlight possible beneficial effects (Is outcome compared against placebo or against another treatment?

How long is the follow-up period? Is the study group or follow-up period unusual?...).

4. *If an approach has only been evaluated as a short-term treatment, is there a high relapse rate, or is there any evidence on this aspect of treatment?*

When a treatment has been used for short-term treatment of a condition, how often does the problem recur if the treatment is stopped? If it is seen as a maintenance treatment, are there any known or potential issues concerning longer-term use?

5. *Do RCTs tell whether a particular approach will work with a particular person?*

RCTs look to establish a probabilistic answer to the question of whether a treatment is effective. If a treatment is said to be effective at a given level of probability (say $p < .05$ on an appropriate statistical test) this means that there is a demonstrable difference in outcome between a treated and a matched untreated group that would only be predicted by chance to happen 1 time out of 20 if the study were to be repeated continually with similar groups. This type of data does not allow conclusions about whether an individual person will respond to the treatment being assessed. Individual differences may be crucial.

I hope that this section has given some pointers to be aware of when approaching the rest of the book. Evidence often sounds convincing at first hearing but, as with so much else in life, the devil is in the detail.

If I wanted to convince people that a particular drug/diet/natural light bulb/behavioural approach/whatever was likely to be helpful, and I was able to help them to implement it, I would try to present them with a convincing case. If I were convincing, this would suggest that:

1. I believed it was the best approach to take

2. I was aware of any possible problems with the approach

3. there was evidence which I could produce that it was an effective approach with similar cases

4. I was competent at using it in the same way that it was used in the published literature

5. I knew the person you wanted to use it with and I was recommending an approach that had been shown to work with similar people (at least in respect of things that might affect response like age, sex, weight and relevant medical conditions)

6. I was aware of the possible alternative approaches and the evidence for and against these

7. I was not merely doing what I felt I was competent at doing despite there being evidence that a different available approach might be better suited to the problem.

As we enter an era in which cost effectiveness is an important issue in healthcare decision-making we need to know not just that something works but that it works better than the available alternatives. If there is a marked cost difference, the greater benefit should be sufficient to justify the increased cost. This type of decision depends on a whole host of factors. To give some examples of potential costs and benefits: once the patent on a medication expires its cost typically plummets as generic products are allowed to compete for market share; psychological therapies are typically expensive as they are labour intensive, but in many areas (such as the use of cognitive-behavioural therapy (CBT) in the treatment of depression, psychosocial interventions in ADHD and behavioural interventions with infant settling and night waking) relapse rates for effective behavioural treatment are lower than with medication, thus bringing down the relative longer-term costs; little attention is given to the relative risk of side-effects or risk of secondary problems arising from treatment, and their effects on longer-term costs of treatment – these are factors which could be considered for broader aspects of care across a population of people receiving treatment but not at the individual level, except where there is a high likelihood of such collateral effects.

In what follows I have tried to be systematic in presenting what is currently being used in the treatment of sleep problems from different perspectives and orientations, what the evidence is for these approaches, where there is evidence against the use of particular treatments and where there is a lack of evidence.

There is a range of sources for systematic reviews providing evidence on treatment. I would recommend periodically checking sources such as the Cochrane Collaboration (www.thecochranelibrary.com/view/0/index.html), and BMJ Clinical Evidence (http://clinicalevidence.bmj.com/ceweb/index.jsp) for reviews on evidence-based best practice.

TREATMENT AND MANAGEMENT

We will now move on to the main focus of the book. This has three key components:

How can we assess sleep problems?

What can be done to resolve them?

How can we tell whether what we have tried has been successful?

The first deals with general aspects to assessing and managing sleep problems which are similar for all types of sleep problems – essentially working out what is going on and deciding on how to focus a management approach and tell if it is working or not.

The second summarizes the evidence for a range of approaches that are advocated for use in sleep problems, and how to access further information about them.

The third is in sections, each focused on a specific sleep problem. For each section, there is a brief problem description, followed by information on how common it is, how likely it is that someone will outgrow it, what treatments are available, and what the evidence is for their success.

I have, where this is available, provided information on the published research on any given approach and stressed the importance of looking for well-conducted research (ideally RCTs) in arriving at decisions on what is likely to be the most appropriate approach to use with any given problem.

There have been numerous general reviews of treatments for sleep problems (Kotagal and Pianosi 2006; Lozoff, Wolf and Davis 1985; Mindell 1993; Moturi and Avis 2010; Owens, France and Wiggs 1999). Typically these have emphasized the role of particular types of approach – psychological or pharmaceutical interventions in the main. Here I have tried to be broader in focus and looked for evidence on a range of approaches that people access rather than confining coverage only to those offered through standard health routes.

One important issue when considering possible strategies is the same today as it was in 1938 when the Mowrers discussed the evidence on available treatments for night-time enuresis:

> In the hands of a limited number of individuals, virtually every method that was proposed seemed to produce cures; but the inability of other persons to obtain equally good results by what appeared to be precisely the same objective procedures eventually made it clear that the effectiveness of these methods was more a function of subtle psychological influences than of the particular physical praxis involved. (Mowrer and Mowrer 1938, p.436)

It is not helpful to know that a therapy had a good result in one case that has been highly publicized or apparently gets good results when carried out by one particular therapist. What is important is to know that it has been effective when compared against others who had the same problem but didn't get the same treatment, and ideally that this result has been repeated with different therapists in different places. The level of available evidence may turn out not to be as strong as this, but I have tried to provide a review of what has been done and/or key sources from which to access further material.

Causes of sleep problems in ASD

A number of issues can be primary or contributory causes to sleeping difficulties in a child with ASD. The following are all possible factors:

- specific abnormalities of neurochemistry related to sleep such as differences in adenosine, GABA, tryptophan metabolism, melatonin receptor function and vasoactive intestinal peptide (VIP) activity

- poor sleep hygiene or more general behaviour management issues

- a neurological comorbidity such as epilepsy that in itself predisposes to sleep problems

- a sensory comorbidity, particularly affecting vision and retinal function

- GI problems such as GERD

- an unwanted side-effect of medication such as a psychostimulant, or the interaction between medications or between prescription medications and CAM treatments

- the presence of a comorbid but unrelated sleep disorder in a child with ASD (this could, for example, be secondary to an issue such as being bullied).

Before considering any of these, however, it is important to get some clear information about the nature and extent of the sleep issues. All parents worry about their children – are they worrying unnecessarily or is there a significant problem?

ASSESSING THE ISSUES AND DOING A BASIC SLEEP CLEAN-UP

Getting a baseline

The first stage in developing a management approach should be to keep a baseline record of the sleep pattern against which any changes can be compared. Without a baseline, it is often difficult to be clear whether there really is a problem and, if there is one and things are put in place to correct it, to show that any improvement has occurred.

As a first step I would recommend keeping a diary (it could be based on the one provided in Appendix 4). Ideally a record should be kept for long enough that a typical pattern becomes clear. If there are only problems on a couple of nights per week this might take 2 weeks or so; if there is a nightly pattern that is clear and consistent then keeping a diary for a week might be sufficient.

Having kept the diary, the next step is to look for any patterns that have emerged which might guide an intervention – this is known as a 'functional analysis' (see Didden *et al.* 1998).

Functional analysis

The term 'functional analysis' is a way to try to identify the likely cause or causes of the behaviour in question. This is normally seen as a behavioural formulation and the term is closely associated with behaviour therapy. It is the type of analysis of sleep difficulties that should be carried out whatever approach is to be adopted. Can a pattern be identified linked to the sleep issue we are hoping to change? Usually the main emphasis in a functional analysis involves looking at the antecedents, the behaviour itself and its consequences. This is sometimes called an ABC analysis. There are two components to carrying out a functional analysis – the first is to look at the 'setting events' (the context in which the behaviour occurs) and the second is to describe the behaviour itself (what is the nature of the sleep problem – what exactly happens?).

SETTING EVENTS

These are often talked about as the 'five Ws' – **W**ho? **W**hat? **W**here? **W**hen? and **W**hy?

Who? – Does the person share a bed or room? Do they fall asleep elsewhere and get carried to bed? Does someone stay with them until they fall asleep? Does the same person see to them if they waken and need to be settled?

What? – Is the issue always the same or does it vary? If it varies, is this consistent (e.g. do they cause more of an issue if settled by Mum/Dad)?

Where? – Do they always sleep in the same bed/place? What happens on holidays/when in hospital/at relatives' or friends'?

When? – This is where the sleep diary helps a lot – is the pattern consistent or is there a particular pattern to the variability (more broken nights after a good unbroken night/bedwetting/a nocturnal seizure)? If the problem is longstanding does it show seasonality?

Is there any link to menstrual periods – remember that this could be in the person with the sleep issue, but could also be a problem in a carer or sibling?

Why? – Does anything in the pattern of behaviour that emerges from the above suggest why the problem is being maintained?

BEHAVIOUR DESCRIPTION

People often use the acronym 'FINDS' to remember what to look at here. This stands for **F**requency, **I**ntensity, **N**umber, **D**uration and **S**ense.

Frequency – How often do they do 'it' (waking; screaming; wetting…) – every night/week/month…?

Intensity – How extreme is it when it occurs (e.g. become roused but fall back to sleep quietly/awake and sit up/fully awake and out of bed…)?

Number – How often does the problem occur in a typical night (wakes up with a nightmare several times per night; once; usually once; once every few nights; weekly…)?

Duration – How long does each episode last (hours/minutes/fleetingly)?

Sense – Does there seem to be any obvious situational factor that might be maintaining the problem (gets to go into bed with parents/their own room is cold…)?

Having collected this information, a clear pattern may now be emerging, or it may seem that there is some key issue that has not been recorded that seems to relate to the problem (let's say that night terrors have happened on nights when there has been stress during the evening due to another child arguing with you over their homework), and it may be useful to record for a bit longer to see if this is important, adding this information to the diary.

So now we have discussed how to assess the presenting problem and collect a baseline, the next stage is to ensure that there is a good bedtime routine.

Basic 'sleep hygiene' – establishing a night-time routine

> A ruffled mind makes a restless pillow.
>
> Charlotte Brontë

In some cases all that is needed is to improve sleep hygiene. In these cases a specific 'problem-focused' approach is not needed.

After collecting a baseline, a first stage should be to look at 'sleep hygiene' – this is basically looking at all of the factors (behavioural, sleep-related, dietary and other potentially contributory factors) that could form either a stand-alone treatment approach or a component of a multimodal package. In behavioural interventions these factors are often referred to as the 'setting events' (see above). Typically these factors operate in the period leading up to trying to get to sleep, and may be having an effect on sleep pattern – is there a regular routine or does anything stand out as being linked to good or poor sleep?

There is increasing evidence for associations between good sleep hygiene and better sleep patterns across the age range (see Mindell, Meltzer *et al.* 2009). Excessive use of things such as electronic media – Internet, texting, mobile phones and MP3 players – correlates with poorer sleep patterns (see Cain and Gradisar 2010).

A number of scales have been developed to assess sleep hygiene. These help to identify any simple changes to routine that might be a first stage in addressing the problem. The Children's Sleep Hygiene Scale (CSHS) (Harsh, Easley and LeBourgeois 2002) and the Adolescent Sleep Hygiene Scale (ASHS) (LeBourgeois *et al.* 2004, 2005) are scales designed to assess nine areas related to sleep hygiene:

Area	*Issues such as:*
Physiological	drinking and eating routine
Cognitive	activities that affect level of mental activity and arousal before bed
Emotional	activities that affect level of anger/distress around bedtime
Sleep environment	lights, music, TV, room temperature
Daytime sleep	naps
Substance use	ingestion of alcohol, caffeine
Bedtime routine	preparation for bed
Sleep stability	variation in pattern
Bed or bedroom sharing	sharing with parent/s, sibling/s, other/s.

Information on both the CSHS and the ASHS can be found in Appendix 4.

For some children with ASD, social stories can be used to explain the sequence of activities involved in bedtime routines (Gray and Garand 1993). These are essentially simple sequential stories taking the person through the steps involved in everyday activities. It is well established that children with ASDs are less attuned to social cues, and that materials such as 'social stories' can be useful in helping them to structure everyday activities (e.g. Lorimer *et al.* 2002). In the time leading up to bed it may be helpful to emphasize sleep routine, using a social story.

Social stories were shown to be useful in the treatment of disruptive bedtime behaviour in a small series of four developmentally normal 2–7-year-old children (two boys and two girls) (Burke, Kuhn and Peterson 2004). This was achieved using a social story called 'The Sleep Fairy' (Peterson and Peterson 2003).

In 2004 a single case study (Moore 2004) described how an 11-step social story was constructed and used nightly with a 4-year-old boy, 'Peter'. Peter had an ASD diagnosis, severe learning disabilities, expressive and receptive language delay and behavioural problems including issues around bedtime and sleep. At the start of the programme Peter would only sleep in his parents' room with his mother in close proximity, taking 1–2 hours to get to sleep, waking several times through the night and rising early every morning. He also presented with significant daytime challenging behaviours. The goal was to get him to sleep in the lower bunk bed in the same room with his brother occupying the top bunk.

Peter's social story outline

Sentence content	Pictures shown on social story page
Peter's 'night, night' story	Thomas the tank engine Peter (close up)
My name is Peter... I cuddle down at night with Mum to read my 'night, night' story	Peter (close up) Mum with Peter on lap reading story
This is me...this is my brother...this is our bedroom	Peter Brother Bedroom (all pictures cut out with velcro fixture so that child can correctly arrange the pictures each time the book is read through)
This is me in my Bart pyjamas... I put my pyjamas on before 'night, night'	Peter in his pyjamas
This is my Thomas duvet; it's soft and cosy	Thomas the tank engine duvet
Tiger is my favourite toy; I bring him to bed with me	Tiger toy in Peter's bed
I bring my bottle to bed with me... When I have finished I put it down on the table	Peter with bottle in bed Bottle on table
Mum sits next to my bed to read me the 'night, night' story one last time	Mum sitting with a book next to Peter's bed
Here I am going to sleep on my own!	Peter in bed asleep
Good morning Peter... Mum wakes me with a hug and kiss for sleeping on my own	Mum opening curtains Mum (close up)
When I sleep on my own through the night, I get a Thomas sticker like this one to stick on my Thomas chart	Thomas sticker (with velcro attachment)

(adapted from Moore 2004, Table 3, p.136)

'Peter' showed a rapid improvement in his night-time behaviour and this was maintained over a 2-week period except during a brief bout of illness. As this was used as part of a broader behavioural intervention, Moore was uncertain how much of the improvement could be attributed to use of the social story.

Sleep hygiene factors to aim for

FOR CHILDREN WITH SLEEP PROBLEMS

If possible, try to discourage playing on/in bed – try to encourage the child to associate being in bed with being calm and sleeping.

Have a clear and pre-set bedtime that is signalled by parents.

Adopt a bedtime routine – washing, brushing teeth; getting into nightclothes.

Wind down in the 40 minutes before going to bed – no laptops, computer games, texting, radio, TV or music.

Have a calm bedtime story/reading time/story tape that the child enjoys and selects.

Keep lighting low or off in bedroom.

Darken the room at bedtime.

FOR ADOLESCENTS WITH SLEEP PROBLEMS

Avoid using bed/bedroom for activities other than sleeping.

Prepare for bed when the person is starting to feel tired.

Avoid nicotine in the hours leading up to bedtime.

Avoid coffee, tea and stimulant drinks in the 2 hours before bed.

Avoid heavy exercise before bed.

Wind down in the 40 minutes before going to bed – no use of laptops, computer games, texting, radio, TV or music.

Keep lighting low or off in bedroom.

Darken the room at bedtime.

Better sleep hygiene does not necessarily help with some problems. In a study of 74 medication-naive (i.e. had not been previously treated with medicaiton) ADHD children with chronic sleep-onset insomnia and 23 ADHD controls, for example, no differences in sleep hygiene between the groups was observed on the Children's Sleep Hygiene Scale (van der Heijden *et al.* 2006).

Mindell, Telofski *et al.* (2009) looked at the effect of instituting a clear bedtime routine on sleep pattern when compared to a control group: 405 infants or toddlers were randomly assigned to routine or control groups. There was a significant positive effect of having a clear bedtime routine on the likelihood of problematic sleep, and improved sleep was associated with more positive maternal mood.

For a brief introduction to the role of improving sleep hygiene in the management of insomnia, see Stepanski and Wyatt (2003).

Drawing up a management plan

Having kept a baseline diary, clarified the problem by doing a functional analysis and made changes to basic sleep hygiene, the next stage is to decide, ideally in conjunction with the relevant health professional/s, on a treatment or management strategy. This should address as many components as have been identified as relevant and could include aspects of sleep hygiene; sleep-related behaviour management; daytime behaviour; night-time routine; diet and, possibly, medication.

Assuming that we have good sleep hygiene but still have a sleep problem, what approaches to treatment and management are available?

The following sections provide a brief discussion of different general approaches that are available, the evidence for them and further contact information where this is available.

GENERAL APPROACHES TO SORTING OUT SLEEP PROBLEMS

It is a bad plan that admits of no modification

Pubilius Syrus, First Century BC saying 469
(Lyman 1856, p.45)

Before moving on to review the various approaches that have been advocated for helping with sleep problems, we will briefly discuss a framework which may be helpful in making sense of the issues.

A framework for understanding sleep problems – finding the patterns that connect

The brilliant polymath Gregory Bateson, whose works made contributions to multiple disciplines from social anthropology to biology, psychiatry and cybernetics, stressed the importance of looking for patterns in both structure and behaviour. His famous ploy in lecturing to students was to produce two objects, an orchid and a crab, and to use these as a basis for discussing pattern in living things. When discussing behaviour, identification of patterns allows us to generalize from one situation or instance to the next, and the accuracy or otherwise of our predictions allows us to strengthen our hypotheses and hopefully become more accurate. I would recommend everyone to read his work *Mind and Nature: A Necessary Unity* (Bateson 1979), a key book that highlights many of his most important ideas.

Looking through the literature in the area of sleep problems it is easy to assume that people are talking about completely different things. Those working on behavioural interventions seem to be discussing an entirely different subject from those working on the neurophysiology of sleep, who differ again from those dealing with genetics, from CAM approaches, or from those working on psychotherapeutic understanding of dream content. As few individuals with any of these interests are familiar with the others – neurophysiologists tend not to be well-versed in dream theory and most psychiatrists are not experts on genetics – it is easy to get confused about the salient issues and it is difficult to see the wood for the trees. It is easy to become familiar with certain specific aspects of sleep problems but to fail to see the patterns that connect.

A simple approach that may help to set some of these things in an overall context is the general model developed by John Morton's group at the Cognitive Development Unit (CDU) in London (Morton 2004). I am not advocating this specific approach but present it as a way of trying to make out an overall pattern in the individual case.

This group developed a simple flowchart approach in which factors at different levels of analysis could be related to others. Most of their work dealt with issues in the areas of reading difficulties, conduct problems and autism but the general principles can be applied to almost any issue.

I have tried to illustrate the approach using a hypothetical case. Here I have differentiated between biological factors, cognition, behaviour and consequences, but different divisions could be used to highlight other things – interpersonal relationships (issues such as separation anxiety may be relevant here); emotional content/reactions (such as imagery in nightmares or dreams); family reaction (to behaviours such as sleepwalking or eneuresis) and external events (such as bullying affecting anxiety). The layout of the diagram looks as if there is a clear flow from biological factors to others; however, the aim is to highlight areas for intervention, not to imply that biological factors are necessarily involved or need to be addressed before other approaches would be effective.

In the example below I have laid out a possible analysis of sleep difficulties and then gone on to show how this might help to pinpoint specific issues that could be the focus for intervention.

'Paul' is a 9-year-old high-functioning autistic boy, who has been referred by his general practitioner with a history of insomnia. He has a self-restricted diet, a high level of performance anxiety and a significant degree of academic underachievement. His family has had some initial advice from a support group and have a regular night-time routine in place.

He has had a battery of physical tests and been found to have reduced acetylserotonin methyltransferase activity on metabolic testing and to have a gene deletion at Yp11.32. The other ASMT locus at Xp22.33 is intact. As there is some enzyme activity, his conversion of N-acetylserotonin to melatonin is reduced but not absent. Salivary melatonin has been assessed and been found to be roughly half the age-expected level but he has a normal circadian pattern. An assessment by the dietician has shown his restricted diet to provide a low intake of tryptophan (Figure E.1).

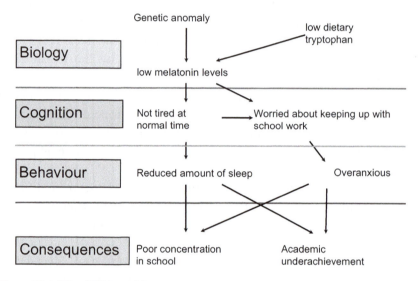

Figure E.1 The CDU model

This type of approach to analysing the issues helps to identify the most appropriate levels of assessment and intervention that may be helpful and to look at the likely chain of effects that changes to these might set in motion.

It may also help to identify issues at several levels that may need to be addressed in tandem as part of an effective treatment package.

Taking the above example, there may be relevant issues that can be identified and worked on (see Figure E.2).

Addressing all of the above issues may be relevant to the case as formulated and described. It may be the case that several or all of these issues would need to be worked on before sustained clinical improvements would be seen. It could be that none of these are necessary or sufficient, or that there are further key issues that have yet to be identified.

From this analysis, the following seem the most likely to be relevant:

- Paul's abnormal melatonin levels could indicate that supplementation may be helpful in increasing sleep, reducing anxiety and improving performance.

- Genetic counselling may be useful in explaining the presentation, in helping to make sense of the problem for Paul and his family, and may be helpful for other affected family members.

- Increasing his intake of higher tryptophan foods, particularly at breakfast, may improve sleep, reduce anxiety and improve performance. The defect in ASMT makes it less likely that this will be beneficial however as the Xp22.33 ASMT locus is intact and there is a circadian pattern of melatonin release, the earlier steps in this pathway would appear to be functioning and increasing the intake may be less helpful.

- CBT may help to address some of the issues around anxiety and performance, assuming both that Paul would be able to comply with this and his family could be engaged in the process (see Wood *et al.* 2006).

- Relaxation training could also provide Paul with a useful method for controlling his anxiety. This is a practical strategy he might use while preparing to go to bed.

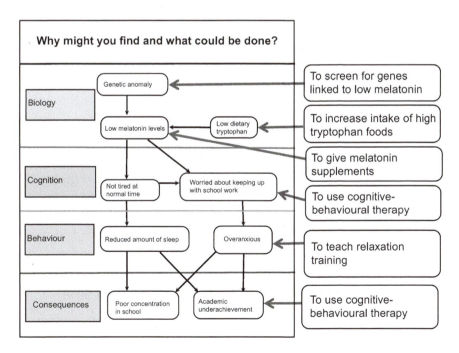

Figure E.2 A worked example of the CDU model

Sometimes a sleep issue is part of a more general pattern of difficulties in the family that is difficult to see. Often when we are in the middle of a situation it is difficult to get enough of a perspective to see what is happening – we just react to things.

COERCIVE FAMILY PROCESSES

One aspect to a situation that is often difficult to recognize is what has been called a 'coercive family process'. This is a situation where the individuals involved do not enjoy what is happening but are rewarded for their behaviour and feel that they are dealing with it as best they can. Recognizing the pattern is often a major step in sorting things.

Let's use a slightly different example to illustrate what is meant:

Susan is 3 and has a very close relationship with her mother Ellie. Every time Ellie is on the phone at home for more than a few minutes, Susan gets annoyed and starts shouting, keeping out of Ellie's reach but making enough noise that she has to finish her call and quieten her down. Usually Ellie is annoyed, Susan gets upset and neither of them enjoys what is happening (Figure E.3).

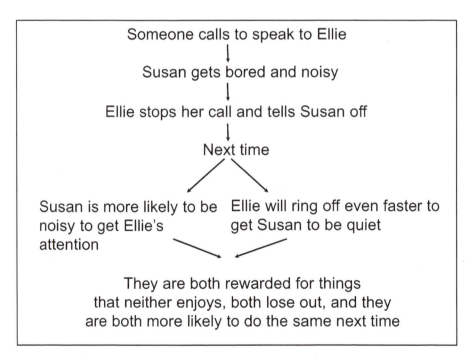

Figure E.3 Coercive family process analysis

Susan has worked out a way of getting Ellie's attention when she is on the phone, and Ellie has worked out how to get Susan to be quiet – they both get a payoff from their behaviour, but neither is really achieving what they want and neither enjoys what is happening.

Once you step back and see the pattern it is easier to find ways to change it. In this example, Ellie could pretend to call someone or prepare a friend beforehand and ignore Susan's disruptive behaviour until she was quiet. This would make it easier to ignore Susan being noisy and allow Ellie to reward Susan for being quiet, which is what she wants Susan to learn to do when she is on the phone (Figure E.4).

Once she had clarified the problem Ellie could see why she was finding it so difficult to deal with – her short-term strategy of dealing with Susan being noisy was rewarding Susan with her attention. It also helped her to see what she could to do to change it.

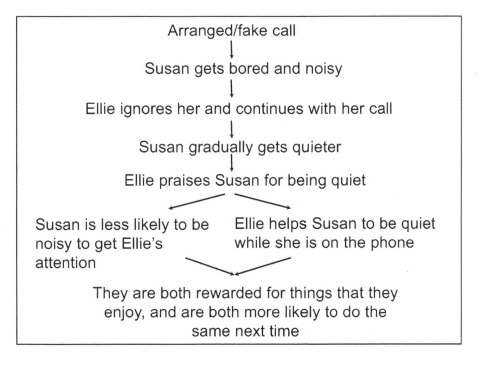

Figure E.4 Coercive family process intervention

This general model has been widely applied to behavioural problems. It was first developed for the analysis of antisocial behaviour in adolescent boys by a group in Oregon headed by Gerry Patterson (Patterson 1982).

It should be fairly easy to see how this type of pattern can be a part of a sleep issue and provides a way of understanding it and working out how to change it.

How to decide that a treatment intervention has been successful

It is important to find a way of working on the problem that has a good chance of helping. It is just as important to be able to tell if it has worked (Is the problem better? Has it improved? Has there been an acceptance that the behaviour is within normal limits?), and also when it has worked what has made the difference (for example, a complex intervention might have been anticipated but in fact improving sleep hygiene was sufficient). Sometimes people feel better about a problem because they have a consistent way of dealing with it (this can lead to fewer disagreements and people getting on better and may not be down to an improvement in sleeping). Monitoring reasons for success can be a useful discipline – it should help to remember what to do if there is a recurrence of the problem; when other issues should be addressed; or, in the worst scenario, if additional help is needed, it should help to exclude some possibilities and streamline the process.

Once a clear baseline profile of the frequency and severity of the sleep problem has been established and a functional analysis carried out as described above, this provides a good position to gauge whether or not the intervention has improved things.

There are essentially five possible outcomes from keeping such a record:

1. There is a complete improvement – the problem has resolved with no ongoing issues.

2. There is an improvement that has changed matters sufficiently that nothing further needs to be done.

3. There has been some improvement with a need for further change.

4. There is no appreciable difference between the problem now and during the baseline recording.

5. Things have got worse.

These outcomes are displayed (Figure E.5) as profiles from a hypothetical run of 8 weeks of sleep recording data (from the beginning of January to the end of February) with a hypothetical sleep problem rated as 20 at the beginning of the intervention period.

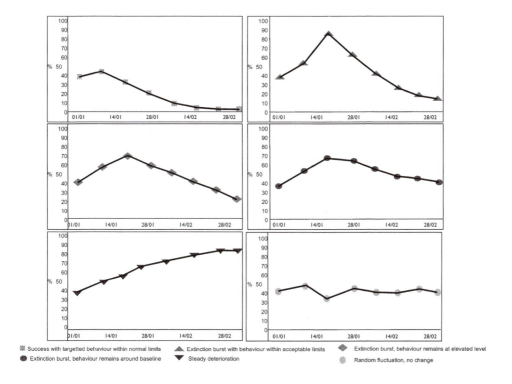

Figure E.5 Outcome data: possible patterns in sleep records

These graphs show the sorts of result you might find in your recording:

1. A slight initial deterioration was followed by steady improvement and by 8 weeks the problem has completely resolved.
2. The problems worsened over the first month, but then began to improve and have almost completely resolved.
3. The problems worsened over the first month, but then began to improve and are now better than at the start.
4. The problems worsened over the first month, but then improved, but are now much the same as they were to begin with.
5. The problems have continued to get steadily worse.

In the ideal world outcome 1 or 2 will have been achieved. The problem is better and there is a clear idea of how to tackle things should any problems recur. If outcome 3 has been achieved, the strategy is working but needs to be continued for longer, or it may need to be modified from the initial intervention to achieve the desired result. With outcome 4 an alternative approach is needed, as the formulation seems to have been incorrect – whatever was changed did not affect the problem. In outcome 5, if nothing else has changed, and sufficient time has been given for things to improve, relevant factors have been identified that influence the behaviour but not how they are operating – the changes seem to be making the problem worse for longer than would be seen with an 'extinction burst' and it is vital to see how these influences could be reversed.

The reason for emphasizing the need to leave sufficient time is that in some cases we do see what I referred to above as an 'extinction burst' – a period when there is an exacerbation of the problem before it improves. If, for example, a child wakes, cries out, and finds being consoled when wakening is rewarding, an approach could be adopted that involves ignoring this behaviour and giving more attention when they are settling to bed and in the morning on waking. It is likely that in the initial stages the problem will increase in frequency and/or severity as the child is unaware that the response has changed.

A related issue is that it is quite common clinically to see families who when various strategies are suggested respond: 'We tried that; it didn't work.' Assuming this to be true, the child will have had a lot of experience of things being tried briefly, not working and discontinued. When these are retried, the child has an expectation they will be ineffective. In this situation, effective and appropriate interventions typically take longer to produce improvements.

Maintaining improvements

Having identified the key factors that resulted in the development and maintenance of a sleep problem, changed these, and brought about an improvement, it is equally important to maintain the gains that have been made.

If this has primarily been a behavioural issue, letting the programme slip and allowing the problem to build up again will make it more difficult to succeed as quickly if it has to be worked through a second time – the child has learned that they are able to get around the programme and get what they are looking for and is less likely to respond.

It is important to maintain a watching brief, for the early weeks at least, to ensure that the problem has been successfully dealt with.

The next part of the book takes the main specific sleep issues and for each adopts a common format:

1. Defining the problem – what is it?

2. Giving a best estimate of prevalence where this is possible from the literature – how common is it?

3. Giving an idea, where this is known, of what typically happens when nothing is done to address the problem – will it get better if we just live with it?

4. What treatments are typically used; what is involved; are there any negative effects?

5. How successful is treatment?

SPECIFIC TYPES OF SLEEP PROBLEM: WHAT THEY ARE AND WHAT CAN WORK TO SORT THEM OUT

> ...diversity of sleep disorders is often not acknowledged in medical and other textbooks. Such inadequate coverage is part of the general neglect of the topic in professional training which persists despite the personal, social and economic importance of these disorders.
>
> Gregory Stores (2001)

Samuel Johnson, the eighteenth-century English polymath, held firm but misguided views on where swallows go in winter, claiming that they conglobulate and rest together on the bottoms of riverbeds (Hill and Powell 1934). There are many equally firmly held beliefs about approaches that may be beneficial for sleep problems; some of these are equally irrational.

It has been interesting to see the change in attitude of many 'mainstream' UK clinicians who previously dismissed melatonin as a 'fad' supplement used by eccentric families, but who, now that it is a prescription medication, have suddenly started talking about it as an important 'medical' treatment. Approaches fall in and out of favour and have more or less support, depending in part on whether there is a vested interest in carrying out research on them. It is unlikely that bodies other than cheese manufacturers would have funded research on the effects of cheese on dreaming. It is equally unlikely that large RCTs of medication would be conducted with funding from sources other than the pharmaceutical industry. Where there is limited evidence it is important to ask why there is so little evidence rather than to dismiss out of hand something that has apparent merit. It can be useful to consider why there may be little incentive to fund research to find out whether an approach with anecdotal support works as well as is claimed.

Looking on the Internet for information, many approaches are proposed simply as treatments for 'sleep problems'. This is like getting a garage to put petrol in a car because it has stopped working – if it is out of fuel it is an excellent approach with a high probability of getting it working again. If it has stopped for a different reason – let's say the engine has seized – it doesn't matter how much fuel you put in or how often you repeat the process, it will not work. Trying to use an approach that works for a different type of sleep problem may be a complete waste of time.

We will now look at specific types of sleep difficulties and examine the evidence for beneficial effects of different therapies, where this is available.

I have tried to be as systematic as I can in describing the various types of sleep problems as they are currently classified. This does not mean that all sleep difficulties will be neatly classified or described here – unfortunately the people with the problems don't tend to read the books first, and novel problems often present themselves. There is also a degree of overlap across the sections as a number of studies address more than one type of difficulty.

Sleep problems are often classified into two major groupings known as the dyssomnias and the parasomnias.

Dyssomnias are problems with initiating and maintaining sleep and with daytime sleepiness:

- delayed settling

- frequent night waking

- early morning waking

- excessive daytime sleepiness.

The second group, the parasomnias, are problems that interrupt the normal course of sleep:

- tooth grinding

- enuresis

- nightmares

- night terrors

- sleepwalking and sleeptalking

- headbanging.

For recent reviews of parasomnias, see Attarian (2010) and Kotagal (2009).

From keeping a baseline record a specific type of sleep pattern may have emerged. The most common sleep patterns are illustrated in Figure E.6.

This type of analysis allows circadian rhythm sleep disorders to be more easily identified such as delayed sleep phase disorder; advanced sleep phase disorder; non 24-hour sleep–wake syndrome; and irregular sleep–wake rhythm (see Barion and Zee 2007).

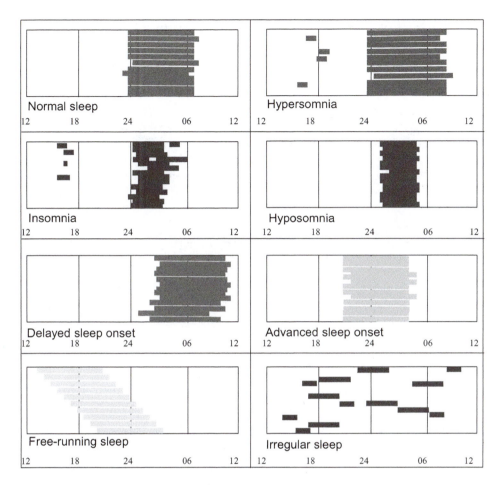

Figure E.6 Typical patterns on baseline recording
Based on Wulff *et al.* 2009

Difficulty settling to sleep and frequent night waking

'He never goes down to bed and he's up and down like a yo-yo all night long.'

'Jason' is a 5-year-old boy who has a diagnosis of ASD. His family are concerned about his sleep pattern. Every evening they give him a shower and get him ready for bed at the same time as his younger sister Diana. When bedtime arrives, he always protests that he isn't tired and gets very upset when his parents try to take him to his room.

Most nights they relent and keep him up until he falls asleep on one of them and then they can carry him through to bed – often he wakes during this process and the settling period starts all over again.

During the night Jason will typically waken his parents four or five times and unless one of them goes in to his bed to settle him he typically ends up sleeping with them from the early hours.

His parents argue a lot about how to deal with him. Often one of them (usually his dad) ends up sleeping on the couch.

WHAT IS 'DIFFICULTY SETTLING TO SLEEP'?

In infancy this is a problem where without good prospective research data identification relies on concerns being reported by parents. As many parents have little to compare against, and individual variation across babies is high, few will report difficulties, and of those who do, many will be easily reassured – there is a high perceived need to feel that one's baby is 'normal'. This could lead to a high 'false negative' rate in prevalence data from clinical samples.

Taking longer than they intend to fall asleep after going to bed is a common problem in children. It is reported as an issue by almost 60 per cent of children at least sometimes between the ages of 10 and 13 (Laberge *et al.* 2001).

WHAT IS 'FREQUENT NIGHT WAKING'?

There are differences in the extent and severity of night waking depending on methods used for assessment. In a sample of 50 9–24-month-old infants referred for frequent night waking, it was shown that parental reports and actigraphy (using a wristband that monitors infant movements) provide different but complementary pictures of sleep pattern when both are used in the assessment of interventions (Sadeh 1994).

Night waking is an issue during the phase of sleep consolidation and is the most common sleep disorder of early childhood. As children get older, night waking persists at the same frequency (there is wide variation, but the typical child will wake on average just under twice per night) at least into early adolescence. As children get older they tend to self-console and return to sleep without alerting their parents (Sadeh *et al*. 2000), again leading to a higher 'false negative' rate if one were to rely on parental report to establish prevalence.

DO THESE TWO PROBLEMS TEND TO CO-OCCUR?

In younger children it is common to see settling difficulties and night waking problems co-occur. In the Camden study both problems were seen in the same child in roughly half of their sample (see Richman 1981a, 1981b; Richman, Stevenson and Graham 1975).

The prevalence and persistence of these problems and their potential to affect development make them a key target for early intervention (Sadeh and Sivan 2009).

HOW COMMON ARE THEY?

By around 3 months of age 70 per cent of infants are reported by their parents as sleeping through the night (Moore and Ucko 1957).

Problems with getting to sleep are perhaps the most commonly reported sleeping problem at all ages. Persistent night waking is also common in small children and is thought to affect some 20 per cent of 1–2-year-olds (Richman 1981a, 1981b), and 25 per cent of all 1–5-year-olds (Armstrong, Quinn and Dadds 1994).

Persistent night waking is reported as a problem by around 20 per cent of parents of 1–2-year-olds (Richman 1981a) and 14 per cent of parents of 3-year-olds (Richman *et al*. 1975).

As we have seen, from the epidemiological data on sleep problems in ASD they are also the most prevalent issues reported by parents of those with ASD, being seen in 50–60 per cent of cases (Mayes *et al*. 2009).

In one recent study by the Children's Hospital of Philadelphia of randomly selected ASD and control children aged 4–10 (Souders *et al*. 2009), on parental report using the CSHQ, 15/59 (25%+) of the ASD children and 2/40 (5%) of their typically developing controls were assessed as having frequent night waking. Sleep onset was also delayed in the ASD group as a whole, with 'behavioral insomnia sleep-onset type' being the most prevalent diagnosis, being found in 12/59 (20.3%) with 3/59 (5%) presenting with frequent night waking as their primary diagnosis.

DO THEY TEND TO GET BETTER IN ANY EVENT?

There is a surprising lack of longer-term prospective epidemiological data on this issue.

In one prospective study of 308 mother–infant pairs followed from 8 months to 3 years (Zuckerman, Stevenson and Bailey 1987), 18 per cent of mothers reported difficulties at 8 months of whom 41 per cent still reported difficulties at 3 years of age; 26 per cent of those who did not report difficulties at 8 months did so at 3 years. The only sociodemographic factor that was associated with persistence of infant sleeping difficulties was maternal report of depressed feelings.

Another 1987 study (Kataria, Swanson and Trevathan 1987) studied 60 children aged 15–48 months and then followed up the same cohort after a three-year period. In the initial cohort, 25 of the families (42%) reported significant sleep problems (22% with night waking, 13% with difficulty settling, 13% 'bedtime struggle' and 7% with both night waking and 'bedtime struggle'). On 3-year follow-up, 21 of the original 25 continued to have significant sleep issues and the strongest association was with the presence of other significant parental stressors.

WHAT CAN BE DONE TO TREAT THEM?

There is good evidence for the effectiveness of preventive behavioural programmes for parents. Adair et al. (1992) compared 164 infants and their families enrolled in such a programme against 128 historical controls. With an intervention that consisted of two antenatal and two postnatal sessions discussing behavioural strategies, at 9-month postpartum follow-up, the intervention group were reporting half the likelihood of night waking compared to their controls. In a randomized prospective trial of 60 intervention and 60 control families, the intervention infants were reported as sleeping significantly better than the controls by 6–9 weeks of age (Wolfson, Futterman and Lacks 1992).

In an early study of 19 children aged under 5 who presented with settling difficulties, frequent night waking or both (Jones and Verduyn 1983), outcome as rated by the therapists was good. They reported 10 cases as resolved and 7 as partially resolved by the end of treatment with maintained improvement at 6-month follow-up in 16/17. Treatment was behavioural and involved gradual reduction of reinforcement.

A Swiss study (Largo and Hunziker 1984) presented results on a consecutive series of 52 children, aged 2 months to 3 years, all of whom had night wakening, 13 with associated settling difficulties, 4 with nightmares and 1 with night terrors. A 2-week sleep chart was kept and parents were then given basic sleep information about the normal course of sleep development. The approach was successful in ameliorating the problems in 44 cases (85%) with no further intervention being required based on parental report.

A study of positive bedtime routines or graduated extinction compared against non-intervention controls measured frequency and duration of night-time tantrums as outcome measures. Subjects were 36 families recruited by newspaper advert with children aged 18–48 months. Both interventions were significantly better (with an average of one tantrum per week) than non-intervention controls (with an average of three episodes per week) (Adams and Rickert 1989).

One small study looked at using a 'bedtime pass' that the child could exchange for an 'excused departure' from the bedroom after bedtime (Friman *et al.* 1999). It was initially trialled with two children aged 3 and 10 years, and acceptability with 20 parents and 23 paediatricians was evaluated. Both children responded well to the intervention with night-time crying and coming out of the bedroom reducing to zero. The approach was rated as highly acceptable by both parents and paediatricians.

An RCT examined the effectiveness of trimeprazine (alimemazine) (Simonoff and Stores 1987). A group of 18 children were selected for inclusion in the study from 59 eligible 1–3-year-old children who had been referred with night waking problems. Compared to placebo controls, those on trimeprazine were reported as having significantly fewer wakings, less time spent awake at night, and longer periods of night-time sleep.

One other behavioural approach that has been reported is the use of a 'faded bedtime with response cost protocol'. The first paper on this approach detailed treatment of four children with learning disability, self-injury and ASD; all had night-time sleeping problems and two had excessive daytime sleepiness (Piazza and Fisher 1991). All showed clinical improvement that was maintained over a variable period of follow-up. A further paper reported on the same approach in a 2-year-old developmentally normal toddler. There was clinical improvement that was maintained over a brief period of follow-up (Ashbaugh and Peck 1998).

Blampied and France (1993) reviewed the evidence on infant sleep problems, noted the high prevalence of such problems in the general population and proposed a behavioural model built around establishing appropriate stimulus control (a clear routine with cues for the infant that it is time for sleep) and changing reinforcement for sleep-incompatible behaviours – they suggest that 'parental attention, and the warmth, comfort, nourishment, and entertainment it mediates, is a powerful natural reinforcer for children' (p.485) thus making staying awake a more positive experience than sleeping. They suggest that this may be an example of a 'coercive' family process that is mutually reinforcing.

A review by Jodi Mindell (1999) identified 41 studies with supportive data on treatment for bedtime refusal and night waking. Eight studies, including two single case studies and three studies with control groups, supported the use of extinction (child put to bed at a preset time and ignored until they quiet), and some evidence from a further seven studies supported graduated extinction. There was some evidence for the use of positive bedtime routines and for scheduled waking, but the latter was more difficult for parents to implement. A number of other behavioural studies were reviewed that showed beneficial effects but where there was an unclear approach or 'treatment fidelity' (how closely the programme was adhered to) was uncertain. This review indicated that the behavioural approaches reported seemed to have a good success rate but much of the literature was methodologically poor. A futher systematic review of the literature appeared in 2000 (Ramchandani *et al.* 2000) that also concluded that the weight of evidence supported behavioural approaches.

One RCT reported on the use of bibliotherapy (written advice on infant sleep) coupled with three sessions of advice on 'controlled crying' (Hiscock and Wake 2002). In the study 76 families of 6–12-month-old infants with parentally rated severe sleep problems were given the active intervention, with 76 randomized controls. At 2 months, significantly more of the intervention group were rated as resolved (53/76) compared to the controls (36/76), with a parallel improvement in Edinburgh Postnatal Depression Scale (EPDS) scores for the mothers. This finding held for mothers who were above the depression cut-off on the Edinburgh. By 4 months, however, although improvements in maternal depression ratings were sustained, there was no continued difference in infant sleep pattern between the groups.

As postnatal depression has a strong effect on maternal sleep (Dørheim *et al.* 2009), and the effects are reciprocal (Gunlicks and Weissman 2008), the above findings could be extremely important for clinical intervention in this group.

A home-based project assessed the effects of planned ignoring on disruptive night-time behaviour in a group of four children with developmental disorders, one of whom, a 6.5-year-old boy, had a diagnosis of ASD (Didden *et al.* 2002). Treatment resulted in normalization of night-time behaviour that was maintained over a 5-month follow-up period.

Moore, Meltzer and Mindell (2008) reviewed behavioural interventions for bedtime problems and night waking in children. Their general conclusion was that there was empirical support for a number of approaches: extinction; graduated extinction; positive routines and faded bedtime routines; scheduled awakening; parent education and prevention, and interventions to reduce night-time fears. They also suggested that these approaches improved family functioning in addition to the effects they had on sleep per se.

One early study (Giebenhain and O'Dell 1984) described the treatment of six 3–11-year-old children who presented with fear of the dark. The treatment described was administered through the use of a parent's manual that explained desensitization (gradually reducing bedroom lighting levels), positive reinforcement (rewarding non-fearful behaviour) and verbal self-control statements (the children were encouraged to say things such as 'I am brave and I can take care of myself when I'm alone or when I'm in the dark' to themselves). The results were presented as three matched pairs where treatment was staggered to begin at different times – in all cases, improvements occurred when the treatment was introduced.

A further early study (King, Cranstoun and Josephs 1989) used emotive imagery for systematic desensitization – gradually helping the three children, aged 6, 8 and 11, to get used to the images and feelings associated with being in the dark. This was carried out as a multiple baseline design, beginning treatment at different times and demonstrating that improvements paralleled treatment. The children were rated by checking their responses to being put into a darkened room at home on alternate days during treatment.

Ramchandani *et al.* (2000) carried out a systematic review of published studies of treatments for settling and night waking problems in children under 5 years old. They concluded that both behavioural treatments and medication had good evidence for short-term benefit but only behavioural interventions had been shown to produce lasting improvement.

A small study evaluated the effects of a social story approach with four normal 2–7-year-old children with bedtime resistance, two of whom also exhibited frequent night waking. Parental diaries indicate a 78 per cent drop in disruptive bedtime behaviours and a complete resolution in night waking. At 3-month follow-up, there was a further 7 per cent drop in disruptive bedtime behaviours with no recurrence of night waking issues (Burke *et al.* 2004).

HOW LIKELY ARE THEY TO RESPOND TO TREATMENT?

There is good evidence for the effectiveness and practicality of planned ignoring (both extinction and graduated extinction), and of positive bedtime routines (improved sleep hygiene) for settling and night waking problems. The literature suggests that these treatments are effective in around 70 per cent of cases; however, good RCTs are lacking (Gordon *et al.* 2007).

Settling and night waking issues appear to be around five times more prevalent in the ASD population. There is no published evidence on relative effectiveness of these approaches with ASD.

Table E.1 provides a representative selection from the extensive literature on treatment of settling and night waking problems. (For systematic reviews of studies in this area, see Ivanenko and Patwari 2009; Mindell 1999; Montgomery and Dunne 2007).

TABLE E.1 SETTLING AND NIGHT WAKING STUDIES

Approach	Reported population	Outcome	Follow-up	Issues	Source references
Withdrawal of reinforcement for problem behaviour	19 under 5-year-olds	17/19 improved, 16/19 maintained at follow-up	6/12		Jones and Verduyn 1983
Alimemazine tartrate	18/50 1–3-year-olds	Reduced waking, longer sleep	Not reported	Cardiac instability, respiratory depression	Simonoff and Stores 1987
'Systematic ignoring'	Infants and toddlers, 6–54 months 11 systematic ignoring (SI) 11 scheduled waking (SW) 11 non-intervention control	SI=SW> Control	3 and 6 weeks		Rickert and Johnson 1988
Faded bedtime with response cost protocol	Four children, LD, self-injury + ASD	Improve-ments in all	Variable from 1 month to 1 year		Piazza and Fisher 1991
Faded bedtime with response cost protocol	Develop-mentally normal 2-year-old toddler	Improvement	1 month		Ashbaugh and Peck 1998
Standard ignoring (SI) and graduated ignoring (GI)	16–48-month-olds 16 standard ignoring; 17 graduated ignoring; 16 list control	SI=GI-> Control	2 months		Reid, Walter and O'Leary 1999
Written information and 'controlled crying'	76 6–12-month-olds and 76 controls	53 vs 36/76 improved at 2 months but not sustained	2 and 4 months		Hiscock and Wake 2002
Social stories	Four normal 2–7-year-olds	Night waking resolved in all, better night-time behaviour	3 months		Burke, Kuhn and Peterson 2004

Insomnia

'He can't seem to get to sleep – we hear him up at all hours.'

> 'Peter' is a 12-year-old boy who has a diagnosis of Asperger syndrome. His parents say that he has always seemed to need less sleep than the rest of his family. He sleeps in the same room as his brother Alan. His brother, who is 14, is always asleep by 11.00 on school nights while Peter is usually still awake well after 1.00. Sometimes he is tired in the mornings, but he usually seems to get up without any difficulty at 7.15, the same time as his brother.

WHAT IS INSOMNIA?

Insomnia is usually defined as a difficulty in getting to sleep or in staying asleep (see Sarris and Byrne 2010). Typically by the time help is sought the presentation will be of chronic insomnia – the symptoms will have been present for a month or more.

A general overview of insomnia covering its definition, prevalence, aetiology and consequences can be found in Roth (2007).

In adults, insomnia has been found to be associated with anxiety, depression and persecutory ideation. This finding holds both in individuals with a clinical diagnosis of schizophrenia and in the general population (Freeman *et al.* 2009).

HOW COMMON IS IT?

The epidemiology of insomnia in children with ASD has recently been reviewed (Miano and Ferri 2010; Silvia and Raffaele 2010). Their conclusions were that insomnia is the predominant sleep concern in ASD, is multifactorial in origin, and results from a number of neurochemical, psychiatric and behavioural factors.

Insomnia has been reported as a frequent problem in Asperger syndrome (Allik, Larsson and Smedje 2006a; Tani *et al.* 2003, 2004). Studies have reported difference prevalence rates, in part at least because of the variation across the methods and definitions that have been used.

A study of Chinese sleep patterns and problems in children (Liu *et al.* 2000) reported that 16.9 per cent of the adolescents aged 12–18 years described insomnia symptoms, and a later comparative study of Chinese and US children produced similar figures (Liu *et al.* 2005). Johnson *et al.* (2006) reported a prevalence of DSM-IV defined insomnia in adolescents aged 13–16 of 9 per cent compared to a lifetime prevalence of 11 per cent.

The variation in prevalence reported is largely attributable to differences in the measures used for assessment. This has been highlighted in longitudinal studies that have used multiple assessment tools and data sources (see, e.g. Fricke-Oerkermann *et al.* 2007).

DOES IT TEND TO GET BETTER IN ANY EVENT?

The natural history of insomnia shows that without intervention to address the issue, the likelihood that it will improve is low, once it has become a chronic presentation (see reviews in Matteson-Rusby *et al.* 2010; Morin *et al.* 2009). As noted by Johnson *et al.* (2006) rates appear to increase from adolescence into adulthood.

WHAT CAN BE DONE TO TREAT IT?

An early behavioural study focused on frequent night waking in a group of seven infants aged 8–20 months (France and Hudson 1990). The approach used was a 4-week programme of extinction (not responding at night to the child other than to check on them silently if concerned) coupled with stimulus control (establishing a clear bedtime routine). Improvement was seen in all cases and maintained at 3- and 24-month follow-up.

A recent study of manualized distance treatment in three autistic children aged 8–9 (two males, one female) used weekly telephone contact with a therapist and a treatment handbook to enable parents to implement a behavioural programme which used a faded bedtime, response cost and positive reinforcement approach (Moon, Corkum and Smith 2011). In all three, time getting to sleep reduced and this was maintained in two and variable in the third at 12-week follow-up.

There have been a number of studies on the use of CBT in the treatment of insomnia (see the following reviews: Espie 1993; Espie and Kyle 2009; Manber and Harvey 2005; Morin 2006; Morin *et al.* 2006). From these reviews, it is clear that CBT has an evidence base demonstrating it to be as effective as medication in the treatment of insomnia with a significantly lower relapse rate on follow-up (see Riemann and Perlis 2009).

This having been said, often CBT can be complemented by the use of medication once benefits have been optimized as medication can often lengthen overall sleep time beyond what can be achieved with CBT alone. Although longer-term outcome data are lacking, this is reasonably well established in adults (Vallieres, Morin and Guay 2005), but the evidence base is weak for work with children and adolescents.

With the exception of melatonin, the pharmacological management of insomnia currently lacks a robust evidence base in children and adolescents (see Mindell *et al.* 2006), and further research particularly on ADHD and ASD is needed. A recent review of prescribing for paediatric insomnia in child psychiatric practice in the USA demonstrated marked variations in practice (Owens *et al.* 2010).

A review of clinical cases in which melatonin had been used to treat children with ASD and insomnia detailed experiences with 107 children aged 2–18 (Andersen *et al.* 2008): 27 (25%) were reported as cured, 64 (60%) as improved but with ongoing sleep issues, 14 (13%) were unchanged, one child's sleep deteriorated and one was undetermined. Three children had mild side-effects (including morning sleepiness and bedwetting). Most of the children were on psychotropic medication. There was no exacerbation of seizures.

In a small placebo-controlled randomized crossover trial of melatonin in 7 of an initial group of 11 ASD children, melatonin significantly extended length of sleep and reduced night-time wakening (Garstang and Wallis 2006).

A randomized crossover trial studied 22 children aged 3–16 who had ASD and whose sleep difficulties had proved resistant to behaviour management advice (Wright *et al.* 2010). The trial consisted of 3 months of placebo/active melatonin, a 1-month washout period, then a further 3 months of active melatonin/placebo. The study demonstrated a significant beneficial effect of melatonin on both sleep latency (the children falling asleep on average 47 minutes earlier) and on length of sleep (sleeping on average for 52 minutes longer).

An open trial of low-dose melatonin in Angelman syndrome elevated serum levels, reduced motor activity during sleep and promoted sleep (Zhdanova, Wurtman and Wagstaff 1999). Following on from this, a RCT in eight children with Asperger syndrome showed a significant improvement in how quickly they got to sleep, the length of time spent asleep and in the number of night wakings. As in the earlier paper, these positive changes were paralleled by increased salivary melatonin levels (Braam *et al.* 2008).

HOW LIKELY IS INSOMNIA TO RESPOND TO TREATMENT?

A number of psychological treatments have been demonstrated to produce significant benefits. Stimulus control, relaxation training, sleep restriction, CBT (both with and without relaxation) and paradoxical intention have been demonstrated to be of benefit, primarily when compared to waiting list or placebo controls. Overall 70–80 per cent of those with insomnia improve through using behavioural and cognitive-behavioural therapies. Only a small percentage will achieve full remission, however, and medication is often used to build on improvements.

With regard to medication, barbiturates have fallen out of use due to their high levels of side effects. There is evidence for short-term benefit from benzodiazepines; however, tolerance, lethargy on waking and a lack of maintenance of benefits are issues. Melatonin supplementation and melatonin receptor agonists have promising preliminary data but do not as yet have a robust evidence base.

Short night-time sleep (hyposomnia)

'Why doesn't she sleep?'

'Fiona', who is 16 years old, has never seemed to need much sleep. She is a large girl for her age and is preoccupied with her weight and diet. Her parents were exhausted with her as a baby when they seemed to be lucky if she would nod off for 20 minutes before waking and demanding attention. When she was 9, because of concerns about her lack of friends and social anxiety she was assessed, and diagnosed with Asperger syndrome. Her sleep pattern has improved in that she will now sleep for 6 hours more-or-less without a break, but this continues to be far less than other girls of the same age. She is revising for her exams and is becoming increasingly worried that she will perform poorly because of her difficulties with sleep which tend to get worse when she is anxious.

WHAT IS SHORT NIGHT-TIME SLEEP?

Short night-time sleep (also known as hyposomnia) is defined as a significant lack of sleep – sleeping for a shorter period than desired on a regular basis. I have discriminated here between hyposomnia and insomnia. In insomnia the sleep pattern is often broken and the diagnosis is based on the presence of these difficulties for a month or more. In hyposomnia the sleep pattern is normal but the length of sleep is truncated.

This is an issue that is defined relative to what is normal for the population and is thus based on a statistical rather than a qualitative difference from the rest of the population. Many individuals who have a limited need for sleep do not want or need help with this, although it can be an issue that troubles their bed-partners.

One paper reports on hyposomnia resulting from a brainstem lesion sustained in a road traffic accident. This 32-year-old caucasian male made a good physical recovery but developed a chronic hyposomnia. Most noteworthy is his report that he does not need more than 2 or 3 hours of sleep each night, in marked contrast to his recollection of sleeping 7.5–8.5 hours prior to the accident. However, 'His wife complained about his sleep habits: he wakes up in the middle of the night and is unable to go back to sleep. However, the patient himself does not complain of insomnia or sleepiness during the day, and he is perfectly able to perform with small amounts of sleep' (Guilleminault, Cathala and Castaigne 1973, p.178).

HOW COMMON IS IT?

Although there are rare cases that are traumatic in origin, in general hyposomnia would be defined in terms of a statistical cutoff, usually as someone typically being more than two standard deviations below the typical length of sleep for the population. Using this statistical yardstick, we can say that hyposomnia affects 2.14 per cent of that population.

The studies that have looked at sleep duration have found differences by age, sex and population. This has been discussed above in Section A in 'What do we know about the normal range of sleep in childhood?'.

Short sleep duration in infancy is a risk factor for becoming overweight in childhood. 'Project Viva' was a follow-up study of 915 US children examined any association between maternally reported sleep pattern at 6 months, 1 and 2 years and the children's body proportions at 3 years of age, controlling for a range of other factors. Their main finding was that children who were reported to sleep for less than 12 hours per day in infancy were more than twice as likely to be overweight when followed up at 3 (OR 2.04) (Taveras *et al.* 2008).

Earlier in the book the data on normal sleep patterns were discussed. For ease of reference, from the Zurich cohort longitudinal studies (e.g. Iglowstein *et al.* 2003), typical total sleep at early ages was approximately as follows:

	Typical amount of sleep in a 24-hour period
At 6 months	14.5 hours, varying between 11 and 17.5 (+/- 2 SD)
At 1 year	13.5 hours, varying from 11–16.5 (+/- 2 SD)
By 2 years	12.75 hours, varying between 11 and 14.75 (+/- 2 SD)

The effects on weight that were reported by Taveras *et al.* would seem to be having an effect within the range of sleep patterns that are reported as being normal from epidemiological research rather than being seen in a distinct pathological subgroup.

One large international study in 17,465 young adults (Steptoe, Peacey and Wardle 2006) demonstrated a significant association between short sleep and self-rated poor health.

DOES IT TEND TO GET BETTER IN ANY EVENT?

This is a difficult question to answer, as there are no good longitudinal data. There will always be a bottom 2.14 per cent of the population and what we do not know at this point is whether this is the same 2.14 per cent at different ages and whether the extent to which this subgroup differs from the rest of the population changes over time.

WHAT CAN BE DONE TO TREAT IT?

A number of studies have been published on approaches to extending sleep duration.

One case analysis (O'Reilly 1995) found that sleep deprivation was a consequence of aggressive behaviour in a 31-year-old man with severe developmental disabilities whose aggression was being negatively reinforced (his aggressive behaviour allowed him to escape from social demands that he was uncomfortable with). Recording also showed that restricted sleep also increased the number of subsequent aggressive episodes so the two behaviours seemed to be mutually reinforcing. Changing the social demands across settings resulted in reduced aggression and improved sleep that was maintained over a 7-month follow-up period.

A study of four children (two girls aged 3 and 19 and two boys aged 4 and 13) all of whom were referred with self-injurious behaviour, learning difficulties and insomnia (Piazza and Fisher 1991) presented a novel approach to treatment. The authors used a 'faded bedtime with response cost protocol' to treat shortened sleep and frequent night waking. From baseline recording, each child was initially set a bedtime close to their baseline time of getting to sleep and then the bedtime was gradually made earlier by 30 minutes each night ('faded bedtime'). If they did not get to sleep within 15 minutes, they were removed from bed and kept awake for 1 hour ('response cost') after which the process was repeated. All four showed improvement over the period of treatment that was maintained over the variable periods of reported follow-up.

HOW LIKELY IS IT TO RESPOND TO TREATMENT?

The evidence base is too limited to draw any firm conclusions here. As only a few papers have reported on this issue and all are studies on small numbers with no controls, all that can be said is that the treatments used to date were feasible and the cases that have been reported showed clinical benefits.

Excessive night-time sleep (hypersomnia)

'Sometimes we start to think he won't wake up.'

'Thomas' is 11 years old and has always slept for longer than anyone else his family has known – as a baby he often slept continuously for 14 hours at a time and his parents were convinced there was something seriously wrong with him. The family have nicknamed him 'Rip van Winkle' because he is always first to bed and first to sleep at night, but is the last to wake in the morning.

He has undergone various investigations but so far nothing has shown up and they have always been told that there is nothing physically wrong with him.

WHAT IS EXCESSIVE NIGHT-TIME SLEEP?

Excessive sleep (also known as hypersomnia) is a dyssomnia that can be defined as typically sleeping for significantly longer than would be normal for a child of the same age.

The best-known condition that has so far been linked to ASD is Kleine-Levin syndrome (KLS) (see Aitken 2010a, Chapter 45). A subgroup of girls with KLS appears to have a form that is cyclical and linked to their menstrual period (Billiard, Guilleminault and Dement 1975). This is a rare condition within the overall hypersomnia group that does not significantly alter the overall prevalence of hypersomnia.

A 17-year period of periodic hypersomnia has been described in association with another unusual genetic anomaly (premature centromere division) in a 45-year-old woman (Hasegawa, Morishita and Suzumura 1998).

Hypersomnia can also result from environmental factors such as traumatic brain injury (PTS or post-traumatic hypersomnia), particularly if there has been damage to the ascending reticular activating system (ARAS).

The majority of cases of hypersomnia, however, have no known biological basis, and it may be that they are just the upper tail of a normal distribution of sleep patterns within the general population.

HOW COMMON IS IT?

As with short sleep, the definition of excessive sleep is by comparison to the normal range of sleep duration for any given age. As this is a statistical cutoff rather than an absolute value, the percentage of children who qualify for the diagnosis will be consistent, again as being more than two standard deviations away from the average length of sleep for any given population. On this basis, hypersomnia could also be said to affect 2.14 per cent of that population. Clinically it has been suggested that around 0.3 per cent of the population have a sleep pattern that would qualify for a diagnosis of idiopathic hypersomnia (Ohayon 2008b). In adults, there is some evidence to suggest that the condition is more common at younger ages and that it is not easily identified using techniques such as the multiple sleep latency test (MSLT) (Vernet and Arnulf 2009).

DOES IT TEND TO GET BETTER IN ANY EVENT?

As children get older their sleep pattern becomes more settled and tends to follow the circadian pattern of the geographical area into which they have been born. In addition, with increasing age the tendency is for the amount of sleep in a 24-hour period to shorten gradually.

WHAT CAN BE DONE TO TREAT IT?

Most successful attempts to treat hypersomnia to date have used medications and other treatments that increase wakefulness and vigilance, such as methylphenidate and modafinil. In adults both approaches demonstrate a reasonable level of success, with one review of a series of clinical cases finding improvement or remission in 38/40 cases maintained on methylphenidate and 22/25 maintained on modafinil (Ali *et al.* 2009).

In a study of sleep disorders after traumatic brain injury, one of the two cases of post-traumatic hypersomnia reported showed clinical resolution from the use of modafinil (Castriotta *et al.* 2009).

HOW LIKELY IS IT TO RESPOND TO TREATMENT?

The studies to date may be on good responders and controlled data are required to substantiate the results of Ali *et al.* (2009). If replicated, their findings suggest that there is a high degree of success from the use of either methylphenidate or modafinil and that both produce clinical benefit in the majority of cases.

Excessive daytime sleepiness/tiredness

'He seems to be tired all the time.'

'Philip' is a 9-year-old boy who attends a school for children with complex learning problems and ASD. Sometimes he naps in class and his teachers find him difficult to wake and his concentration is poor. His parents have had numerous letters sent home because of his extreme tiredness in school, asking them to try to get him to bed early and keep him from doing things that are overly energetic out of school. They are worried that there could be something physically wrong with him, as he seems equally tired when he is with them over weekends and during the holidays.

WHAT IS EXCESSIVE DAYTIME SLEEPINESS?

Recognition of excessive daytime sleepiness as a clinical condition has only developed over the past decade. The reasons for hypersomnia and its prevalence have only recently come to attention (Mignot 2008a).

Excessive daytime sleepiness (EDS) or tiredness (EDT) is essentially a strong and excessive daytime compulsion to sleep which is outside the normal daily pattern for the person's age and sex, resulting in an inability to stay awake and alert during the major waking episodes of the day with unintended lapses into drowsiness or sleep. The clinical criterion for diagnosis is that the above pattern has been present on most days for a period of at least 3 months.

A number of links have recently been made between EDS and abnormalities of certain clock genes.

It has been discovered that the orexin2-hypocretin2 gene receptor can be mutated in people with EDS who also have the movement disorder known as Tourette's syndrome (Thompson *et al.* 2004).

Decreased levels of hypocretin-1 are found in patients with myotonic dystrophy in association with excessive daytime sleepiness (Martínez-Rodríguez *et al.* 2003). This may be important here because myotonic dystrophy is associated with ASD and in other cases of ASD individuals with excessive daytime sleepiness an association has so far only been reported in association with hypocretin-2.

When part of a more complex presentation including cataplexy, hypnagogic hallucinations and sleep paralysis, and disturbed night-time sleep, EDS can form part of the condition known as narcolepsy (see below).

Research in adults is highlighting a number of predictors for EDS. One study (Bixler *et al.* 2005), of 1741 20–100-year-old individuals presenting with EDS, linked depression, body mass index, age, sleep duration, diabetes, smoking and sleep apnoea to EDS (in decreasing order of association) as risk factors. Prevalence of EDS decreased with age, and depression was more likely in younger people in this sample. Based on a detailed study of 1106 consecutive patients (741 men and 365 women) with possible sleep apnoea, in males lack of regular exercise, depression and obesity are all associated with a higher risk, while in women the major predictor appears to be poorer apnoea-hypopnoea scores (Basta *et al.* 2008).

A useful discussion of some of the issues around difficulties in diagnosis, aetiology and comorbidity can be found in Ohayon (2008a).

In adults one of the best measures for assessment of daytime sleepiness is the Epworth Sleepiness Scale (ESS) (see Johns 1991, 1992, 1993, 2000). The ESS can be used in adolescence. Currently the best equivalent for assessment in children is the Pediatric Daytime Sleepiness Scale (PDSS) (Drake *et al.* 2003). This scale is a 13 item self-report measure that has been standardized on a sample of 450 11–15-year-old mainstream schoolchildren in Ohio.

It is helpful to discuss the results of any standardized assessments with a clinician who is familiar with their use. There are now a large number of assessments available to monitor EDS (see Weaver 2001). Many Internet resources provide copies of scales such as the Epworth Sleepiness Scale, but often with no accompanying information or with information that is incomplete or inaccurate (see Avidan and Chervin 2002).

HOW COMMON IS IT?

Excessive daytime sleepiness is a common feature in adolescents, with almost a quarter of all students scoring at the extreme end of the ESS and around 14 per cent judging themselves to be extremely sleepy during school hours in two surveys that were carried out on a total of 3235 Canadian adolescents (Gibson *et al.* 2006).

There are limited data on adult populations. One early study, the US National Institute of Mental Health Epidemiologic Catchment Area study, collected data from 7954 people from the general adult population and reported a rate of 3.4 per cent (Ford and Kamerow 1989).

In a screening assessment of 2612 adults, 67 per cent had a concurrent medical disorder. The risk of EDS was elevated. In particular, a significantly increased risk of EDS (based on an ESS score of more than 10) was reported in association with ulcers (reported in 9.3%), migraine (16%) and depression (16%) (Stroe *et al.* 2010). In addition, EDS occurs more commonly in individuals with a number of medical conditions, and the effect was additive – the more complex the clinical picture, the greater was the likelihood of EDS.

Given the variation in reported rates, there is clearly a need for more systematic epidemiological research to establish how common EDS is at different ages.

DOES IT TEND TO GET BETTER IN ANY EVENT?

There are no good longitudinal data on this issue that clearly answers this question.

Most adult studies quote a rate of around 5 per cent of individuals as reporting EDS. If the Canadian figure of 14 per cent in adolescence is replicable in other populations, this suggests that around 2/3 people who have EDS in their school years may improve as they get older. There is no useful prospective data on this issue.

Variations in the criteria used and the paucity of epidemiological data, particularly the lack of longitudinal data, make it impossible to give a clear picture of prognosis (see discussion in Ohayon 2008b).

WHAT CAN BE DONE TO TREAT IT?

A range of methods is available for initial assessment of the child who presents with EDS.

The PDSS (Drake *et al.* 2003) and the BEARS Sleep Screening Tool (see Owens and Dalzell 2005) can be useful in assessment. Details of both measures are given in the appendices.

A brief overview of treatment is provided in Kothare and Kaleyias (2008b). As in all of the other conditions discussed here, it is helpful to get a confirmed diagnosis and a clear baseline before commencing any form of management or treatment.

A recent review (O'Malley in Black *et al.* 2007) suggests that improvement to sleep hygiene; treatment of sleep-disordered breathing; the use of bright-light therapy to reset the circadian rhythm and wake-promoting medications are of particular benefit. Another review gives further detail on medications that have been reported as being helpful (psychostimulants; modafinil; sodium oxybate; tricyclic antidepressants and selective serotonin reuptake inhibitors all have some support from studies in the clinical literature (Kothare and Kaleyias 2008a)).

One paper details a behavioural intervention for 'Robert', a 13-year-old boy with EDS, ASD and learning difficulties (Friedman and Luiselli 2008). Three strategies were employed as a package. These were implemented using an ABAB design:

1. Stimuli related to sleeping were removed (a soft floor mat and beanbag chair on which he usually slept in school).

2. When staff observed behaviour that usually led to sleep, this pattern was interrupted and he was redirected into other activities.

3. He was praised for engaging in activities other than sleeping.

This approach eliminated daytime sleep in school and the improvement was maintained over a 6-month follow-up period.

A review of medication in the treatment of EDS can be found in Banerjee, Vitiello and Grunstein (2004). The medications that have been most commonly used in practice are psychostimulants such as methylphenidate.

There has been increasing use of modafinil; this is a medication with an uncertain mode of action that has been reported to have a better side-effect profile than psychostimulants and a lower addiction risk. Modafinil has shown considerable benefit in improving daytime alertness in adult cases and it appears to be safe and well tolerated in children. In a chart review study of its use in a clinical group, ten children with narcolepsy and three with idiopathic EDT were followed up for a mean duration of 15.6 months. Beneficial effects on EDS were reported in 90 per cent of cases (Ivanenko, Tauman and Gozal 2003). In two children with pre-existing conditions, these issues (one had seizures and the other psychotic symptoms) were both worsened. The authors noted a trend towards reduction in REM sleep when modafinil was used.

EDS is a commonly reported issue in Prader-Willi syndrome (PWS) (see, e.g. Wagner and Berry 2007). PWS is a genetic disorder that is overrepresented in the ASD population (see Aitken 2010b, Chapter 61). Unlike the other sleep issues in this condition, such as obstructive sleep apnoea (OSA), from the evidence to date, EDS does not seem to be helped by weight reduction. In a preliminary report on three PWS clinical cases, two were treated in a placebo-controlled crossover design, suggesting that modafinil can be of significant benefit in improving EDS (Heussler *et al.* 2008).

HOW LIKELY IS IT TO RESPOND TO TREATMENT?

Montgomery and Dunne (2007) in their review of treatments for sleep disorders were unable to find evidence of any specific treatment trials for EDS.

There has been a trial of modafinil in the treatment of EDS (Ivanenko *et al.* 2003). The trial involved 13 children, 10 who had narcolepsy and 3 with idiopathic EDS. All showed beneficial effects on their length of sleep but there was a trend towards REM sleep reduction and in two cases worsening of seizures and psychotic symptoms.

A useful supportive review on the potential role of modafinil that discussed its role in daytime sleepiness appeared in 2008 (Schwartz 2008).

Recent changes (22 July 2010) to the regulation of modafinil introduced by the European Medicines Agency currently restricts its use across Europe, including the UK.

Nightmares

> Stage direction for Antigonus
> in William Shakespeare's *The Winter's Tale*, Act III,
> scene iii Bohemia.
> A desert country near the sea.
> *'Exit, pursued by a bear.'*

'Charlotte', who is 4 years old, often wakens everyone in the house by screaming hysterically in the middle of the night. When her parents go in to her room, she is usually awake and talks about what has frightened her – something which she usually describes as being chased through a dark forest by a bear and trying to escape.

WHAT ARE NIGHTMARES?

The currently accepted definition of nightmares is as follows:

> recurrent episodes of awakening from sleep with recall of intensely disturbing dream mentation, usually involving fear or anxiety, but also anger, sadness, disgust, and other dysphoric emotions. There is generally full alertness upon awakening immediately after a nightmare, and intact

recall of the dream experience. Additionally, there may be delayed return to sleep after the episodes. (International Classification of Sleep Disorders-2, American Academy of Sleep Medicine 2005)

As with other types of dreams, nightmares are thought to occur primarily when someone wakes from REM sleep (Hasler and Germain 2009).

In many people with ASD, because of communication difficulties it can often be difficult to discriminate between nightmares and other conditions that can result in night-time distress such as night terrors, nocturnal seizures and REM sleep behaviour disorder.

One recent model describes nightmares as an 'affective network dysfunction' (Nielsen and Levin 2007). This is defined as a problem in the functioning of the neural system that is involved in processing and extinction of fear imagery.

HOW COMMON ARE THEY?

For an apparently common and distressing problem, studies on the prevalence of nightmares are surprisingly rare. One study has suggested that bad dreams/nightmares affect around 13.5 per cent of nursery school-age children (Muris et al. 2000), and another that nightmares frequently affect some 41 per cent of 6–10-year-olds (Salzarulo and Chevalier 1983).

The first prospective study of bad dreams in the preschool period collected data on 1434 Canadian infants followed from 29 months to 6 years at five separate time points (Simard et al. 2008). Maternally reported rates were lower than predicted, with the percentage of children being reported as often or always having bad dreams being 2.4 per cent at 29 months; 3.9 per cent at 41 months; 2.2 per cent at 50 months; 2.6 per cent at 5 years and 1.5 per cent at 6 years.

Nightmares are more commonly reported in females than males at all ages (see, e.g. Nielsen, Stenstrom and Levin 2006).

Retrospective assessments of frequency are unreliable, so it is important to collect a prospective baseline before thinking about intervention (see Lancee et al. 2008b).

DO THEY TEND TO GET BETTER IN ANY EVENT?

The study by Simard et al. (2008) shows that, although there is a peak at around 41 months, a high proportion of those who present with bad dreams at 29 months are still reported as having the same pattern at 6 years of age. Without help the pattern seems to be robust and not typically to improve much over time. On this basis, those who have early onset nightmares seem likely to persist, while those whose nightmares start at around 2–3 years, during a particularly active period of brain development, seem more likely to improve spontaneously.

WHAT CAN BE DONE TO TREAT THEM?

A review of best-practice treatment for nightmares in adults has recently appeared (Aurora *et al.* 2010).

The current treatment of choice for nightmares is CBT, particularly using a technique known as imagery rehearsal (see Spoormaker and Montgomery 2008). This is only likely to be effective in someone with ASD who has a reasonable level of language use and the ability to use it metacognitively (to share thoughts, feelings and ideas).

One early study (Graziano and Mooney 1982) provided 2.5–3-year follow-up data on the use of a 3-week relaxation training intervention to provide a self-control strategy for night-time fears; 39/40 children were rated as improved at the end of the 3-week period. At follow-up, 31/34 families who could be located reported that there had been no recurrence of problems.

Another early study used relaxation, reinforcement and cognitive self-instruction with six children who had severe night-time fears (Friedman and Ollendick 1989). Significant improvements were reported in five of the six children; however, improvements preceded active treatment, suggesting that improvements resulted from non-specific aspects of the interventions.

Other approaches with supportive evidence are relaxation, exposure/ desensitization and the medication prazosin.

Almost all of the literature is concerned with adults whose nightmares had become problematic after some sort of trauma, and one research group in Albuquerque has generated a large proportion of this literature.

There is a stronger evidence base for imagery rehearsal; however, in the only direct comparison to exposure/desensitization the researchers failed to show differences in outcome (Kellner *et al.* 1991).

Imagery rehearsal (Marks 1978) is a method in which the person who has experienced the nightmare first records their experience in detail, usually as a written record, and then substitutes a new ending. This is a technique that can be employed individually and has had some limited success when implemented as a self-treatment approach sent out to patients by correspondence (Burgess, Gill and Marks 1998; Burgess, Marks and Gill 1994).

Only one of the studies to date (Krakow, Sandoval *et al.* 2001b) has involved the use of imagery rehearsal with younger subjects, and focused on treatment of nightmares in adolescent girls in a residential facility, most of whom had nightmares that appeared to have been related to sexual assault or abuse. The approach was successful; all the girls (nine treatment and ten controls) were experiencing approximately 20 nightmares per month at baseline. Imagery rehearsal resulted in a 71 per cent drop in nightmares per month with no significant change reported by the controls. In this study the programme used was presented in three parts. The first, 'facts about nightmares', was an information-giving session about nightmares and how they can affect sleep. The second, 'practising pleasant imagery', practised pleasant imagery and seven basic techniques – thought stopping, breathing, grounding, talking, writing, acknowledging and choosing. The third section, 'imagery rehearsal treatment of nightmares', used a three step process – 'select a nightmare', 'change it any way you wish' and 'rehearse the images for this new dream while awake'. Initially the girls were encouraged to write the nightmares and new dreams down, but could move on to doing this mentally if they felt confident to do this.

A helpful overview of the cognitive principles underlying imagery rehearsal can be found in Spoormaker (2008).

Imagery rehearsal has been used successfully in the treatment of chronic nightmares (Burgess et al. 1998; Krakow et al. 1995). It has also been used in the treatment of nightmares resulting from various conditions such as post-traumatic stress disorder (PTSD) resulting from combat trauma (Forbes, Phelps and McHugh 2001; Forbes et al. 2003; Nappi et al. 2010) and from sexual assault (Krakow, Hollifield et al. 2001a; Krakow, Sandoval et al. 2001b).

A similar approach, called 'dream reorganization', has been reported as successfully treating a 10-year-old boy (Palace and Johnston 1989). This is a two component approach using systematic desensitization to help the child cope with imagining frightening dream content while using progressive relaxation to keep calm, and guided rehearsal of mastery endings to dream content – practising thinking through the dream to a positive ending.

Lancee et al. (2008a) carried out a systematic review of the research on CBT treatments for nightmares. They identified a total of nine RCTs that were described in a total of 12 papers. Overall, the results demonstrated both exposure and imagery rehearsal produced benefits, but the quality of the research to date was variable and further independent research comparing approaches was advocated.

Relaxation training alone has also been reported to have some success in the treatment of nightmares, but to be less effective than desensitization, in a group of 32 adults with chronic nightmares allocated to the two approaches (Miller and DiPilato 1983).

It has been found that the treatment of other sleep problems such as sleep disordered breathing can often resolve a problem with nightmares without any direct intervention over the nightmares themselves (Krakow et al. 2000).

Most of the literature on the use of medication has had poor or inconclusive results and has largely focused on nightmares subsequent to post-traumatic stress (van Liempt et al. 2006). The exception is the use of the alpha-1 agonist prazosin. There are three small RCT studies that have described its use in the treatment of nightmares with good success. The effects of prazosin appear only while on active medication and there is a reversion to nightmares when medication is stopped.

HOW LIKELY ARE THEY TO RESPOND TO TREATMENT?

There is limited research to date on the treatment of nightmares in ASD or in children. Imagery rehearsal, desensitization, relaxation and prazosin all have some empirical evidence to support their use, mainly with acute onset nightmares triggered by trauma.

There is limited evidence on treatment of children and none on treatment in ASD.

The outcome results so far obtained on PTSD-related nightmares are promising but may be found to differ from results with chronic idiopathic nightmares.

Night terrors

'He just seems to wake up, scream and scream and scream.'

'Simon', who is 5 years old, often wakes his parents by moving around his room, usually a couple of hours after he has been put to bed. He will normally be crying loudly or screaming, and appears to be frightened, not wanting cuddles or reassurance. He is usually sitting up in bed, flushed and sweating. He resists physical contact, pushing anyone away who tries to settle him. He usually appears distant, as if he is still half-asleep. Often he will seem to quieten and return to sleep after a few minutes.

Simon's parents have been told that this is a normal phase and he will grow out of it but find these episodes difficult to understand and are worried that he may be having seizures or that there is something else wrong with him that has been missed.

WHAT ARE NIGHT TERRORS?

Night terrors (also known as *pavor nocturnes)* are parasomnias in which the person wakes from slow-wave non-REM sleep usually in a highly distressed state. In night terrors the person exhibits distress but is unable to give a reason for this, unlike nightmares in which the person can usually describe a frightening dream.

Some cases presenting with night-time distress are epileptic in origin (Lombroso 2000), but the large majority are not.

HOW COMMON ARE THEY?

Night terrors are most common in the 2–6-year age range when approximately 15 per cent of children are reported to have such episodes.

DO THEY TEND TO GET BETTER IN ANY EVENT?

A telephone survey of 4972 adults found a reported rate of 2.2 per cent for night terrors (Ohayon, Guilleminault and Priest 1999). Given the prevalence in preschoolers it seems that spontaneous improvement can be expected in around 85 per cent of cases. What is unclear is the time course and we do not know how many cases will show persisting problems through childhood and adolescence.

One study of night terrors in twins looked at 161 monozygotic (identical) and 229 dizygotic (non-identical) twin pairs at 18 and 30 months of age (Nguyen *et al.* 2008). At 18 months, 36.9 per cent fulfilled criteria for night terrors and at 30 months 19.7 per cent. Although this is a 50 per cent drop in prevalence, the reported rates at both times are extremely high.

WHAT CAN BE DONE TO TREAT THEM?

In a number of early studies, benzodiazepine medications such as midazolam were shown to suppress stage 3 sleep and reduce the frequency of night terrors (Fisher *et al.* 1973; Popoviciu and Corfariu 1983). In the study by Popoviciu and Corfariu midazolam was well tolerated in a group of 15 6–15-year-old children, eliminating night terrors in all but one case, and with improvements in patient-reported sleep quality.

A paper by Bryan Lask from Great Ormond Street (1988) reported on the treatment of 19 children aged 5–13 who were referred for sleep terrors with no comorbid problems. After keeping a baseline record, parents were asked to rouse the child 10–15 minutes prior to the typical time at which, from their sleep diaries, they normally woke. In all cases the problem resolved within a week of starting this routine. In three cases the problem recurred but resolved again on reinstituting the same approach.

Jan *et al.* (2004) reported on the treatment of night terrors and sleepwalking in a 12-year-old boy with Asperger syndrome. Therapy involved the use of melatonin to correct sleep-phase onset delay and resulted in the resolution of both problems within 2 days of beginning treatment.

HOW LIKELY ARE THEY TO RESPOND TO TREATMENT?

Night terrors are a common problem in preschoolers that tend to resolve spontaneously in most cases. The limited published data show that management by night waking and resettling, benzodiazepines or melatonin have all been successful in resolving persistent night terrors. To date, however, the evidence base is small and no RCTs have been reported.

The waking and resettling approach advocated by Lask is minimally invasive, has no obvious side-effects, and could be used with all ability levels so would seem a sensible initial strategy.

Night-time eating disorders

'It's as if he can't stop eating and he just ignores us when we ask him why.'

'Tom' is a 13-year-old boy with ASD. His parents are concerned because they have noticed that he has a habit of getting up during the night and binge eating. This pattern has been noticeable for some months and since starting to do this he has put on a considerable amount of weight. As there is a family history of heart problems his parents are concerned about the longer-term effects of this pattern were it to continue.

A recent clinical assessment resulted in Tom being diagnosed as having a comorbid diagnosis of 'sleep-related eating disorder' or SRED. In one way his parents were relieved to be given a diagnosis but could find little information on the condition or what it meant.

'Julie' is an 11-year-old girl with a diagnosis of Asperger syndrome. She has always had a healthy appetite but over the past 18 months she has steadily increased her snacking at night while watching television with her parents, eating chocolate and biscuits.

Julie's mother Sandra has recently been diagnosed with type-2 diabetes and her father is overweight. Both Julie's parents are concerned that Julie is turning out to have similar problems and are worried in case she develops diabetes – they think she would find it very difficult to manage the treatment.

A recent review with the school doctor found that she had gained significantly more weight than expected and she is starting to have difficulties keeping up with her classmates in PE and swimming, both of which she used to enjoy but now she is starting to complain about becoming breathless and tries to opt out whenever she can. The doctor mentioned that she might have 'night eating syndrome' (NES), and has made a referral to an eating disorders clinic for further investigations.

WHAT ARE NIGHT-TIME EATING DISORDERS?

There are several useful reviews of work in this area (see Auger 2006; Howell *et al.* 2009; Schenck *et al.* 1991).

Currently two distinct types of night-time eating problems are recognized – night eating syndrome (NES), and sleep-related eating disorder (SRED).

In NES the person eats to excess between their main evening meal and bedtime and/or wakes to eat through the night to eat. People with NES rarely engage in pica (swallowing inedible material). Onset has not been linked to the use of any specific medication.

The evidence to date is limited; however, it appears that NES is frequently familial (Lundgren, Allison and Stunkard 2006). In those affected there is a high prevalence of associated mood disorders such as depression (see, e.g. Vetrugno *et al.* 2006).

In sleep-related eating disorder (SRED) sleep-related nocturnal eating occurs either during sleep or when not fully aroused from sleep. SRED commonly involves ingestion of unpalatable or inedible substances (pica). It is seen in association with a number of sleep disorders such as sleepwalking, restless legs syndrome (RLS) and obstructive sleep apnoea (OSA). Onset has been reported after the use of a number of sedative hypnotics. Zolpidem, triazolam, olanzapine and risperidone have all been reported as triggering the problem (reported as a selective reaction to sedative hypnotics: see Morgenthaler and Silber 2002; Schenck *et al.* 2005).

Where sleep EEG recordings have been available it seems that SRED takes place in an unusual state of arousal and should be classified as a form of parasomnia, similar to nightmares and sleepwalking.

Daytime eating disorders are also prevalent in people with sleep problems. In an adult series of 60 patients with narcolepsy-cataplexy, 23.3 per cent fulfilled criteria for an eating disorder, as compared to none of 120 matched controls (Droogleever Fortuyn *et al.* 2008). There is a clinical overlap as obesity is also more likely in individuals with a diagnosis of NES, with most patients claiming that the obesity antedated the onset of NES; however, the picture is not entirely clear (Colles, Dixon and O'Brien 2007).

HOW COMMON ARE THEY?

In adults a prevalence rate of 1.5 per cent for NES has been reported (Rand, Macgregor and Stunkard 1997; Striegel-Moore *et al.* 2005). A population prevalence survey of 6-year-old children in a German urban population gave a rate of 1.1 per cent for night-time eating (Lamerz *et al.* 2005).

To date, no prevalence figures for SRED have been published.

DO THEY TEND TO GET BETTER IN ANY EVENT?

There is no longitudinal data on how NES and SRED evolve over time in the individual. The limited cross-sectional information on NES suggests that the prevalence is greater in adulthood than childhood and that the condition may be fairly stable over time. There is no data on SRED prevalence at different ages.

WHAT CAN BE DONE TO TREAT THEM?

In NES sertraline has been reported to produce clinical benefits (O'Reardon, Stunkard and Allison 2004; Stunkard *et al.* 2006).

In SRED the problem behaviour occurs when the person is not fully aware of their actions. The association with pica suggests that it is important to check for possible lead toxicity, as it would be if the behaviour happened while the person was awake. Several best practice statements recommend that blood lead levels should be tested in autistic children who engage in pica (Advisory Committee on Childhood Lead Poisoning Prevention 2000; Filipek *et al.* 1999).

A number of medications including dopaminergics, topiramate and benzodiazepines have been reported to be of benefit in SRED (topiramate seems most effective in controlling the problem, but has a high rate of unacceptable side-effects; see Schenck and Mahowald 2006).

HOW LIKELY ARE THEY TO RESPOND TO TREATMENT?

The recent RCT of sertraline in NES produced beneficial effects in 12/17 cases (71%), with improvements being recorded in 3/17 placebo controls (18%). Other treatments have either not been evaluated at this time (as is the case with non-pharmacological approaches), or have shown lack of benefit, or deleterious effects, such as increasing night-time eating, as with zolpidem (Morgenthaler and Silber 2002).

SRED often improves with the treatment of comorbid sleep problems such as RLS or OSA. In cases where the problem is either the only presenting issue or is comorbid with sleepwalking, treatment has so far largely been ineffective (see review in Howell *et al.* 2009).

Nocturnal seizures

> 'He gets hot and sweaty, shakes in his sleep and usually wets the bed.
> We can always tell when one is coming.'

'Hector', a 7-year-old boy with autism and mild learning difficulties, has always been a restless sleeper, so much so that his parents tend to take him in to bed with them so he does not disturb his brothers. He has a history of febrile convulsions, having had a number of fits when he was smaller that were brought on by high temperatures when he had ear infections. Recently there have been a number of episodes when his parents have awoken to find him convulsing in his sleep. The episodes have been quite brief, lasting at most 30 seconds or so, and a couple of times he has wet the bed.

WHAT ARE NOCTURNAL SEIZURES?

Nocturnal seizures are epileptic fits that occur during sleep. A useful review of nocturnal seizures can be found in Bazil (2004).

They can be made worse by the presence of a different underlying sleep disorder such as OSA and may improve when this has been brought under control (e.g. Hollinger *et al.* 2006). In a recent study 14.2 per cent of 127 child OSA cases had paroxysmal activity on EEG (Miano *et al.* 2009).

A range of unusual presentations of nocturnal seizures can be seen including stridor (a high-pitched wheezing breath) (Wyder-Westh *et al.* 2005); a form of sleepwalking known as episodic nocturnal wandering (Jiménez-Genchi *et al.* 2007) and choking (Davis *et al.* 2008; Elkay *et al.* 2010).

Some seizures that can present during sleep are benign (Panayiotopoulos *et al.* 2008; Stores, Zaiwalla and Bergel 1991). As the prognosis for such epilepsies is good without treatment, management should be on a case-by-case basis, recognizing the possible side-effects from treatment of current symptoms (Oguni 2011).

Epilepsy is a complex topic and the evidence base on what is best practice is changing rapidly. It is important that this is diagnosed/excluded by a clinician with expertise in the area – typically this will be a neurologist or 'epileptologist'.

There is a high possibility that someone with an ASD will show EEG abnormalities. One study reported on 889 patients with ASDs collected by a Chicago clinic over a 9-year period (Chez *et al.* 2006). None of these had a diagnosis of epilepsy, a known genetic condition, or an identified clinical malformation. Overall, over 60 per cent showed evidence of epileptiform activity on ambulatory EEG recording. In the majority, the clinical activity was over the right temporal lobe. In 7 per cent of these cases the abnormality was recorded during sleep, but none showed the continuous spike and wave activity seen in Landau-Kleffner syndrome (a regressive, hard to control form of seizure disorder that often presents with ASD-like behavioural regression). None of those with abnormal sleep EEGs presented with behavioural regression.

Giannotti *et al.* (2008) compared EEGs in 34 regressive and 70 non-regressive ASD cases. In contrast to the findings of Chez *et al.* this group found a higher rate of EEG abnormalities in the regressed ASD group.

Abnormal EEGs were found in the non-autistic non-epileptic siblings of 12 of the Chez autistic and epileptic series described above (Chez *et al.* 2004). The abnormalities were of types commonly seen in childhood and do not suggest a common pathogenesis with the problems seen in their affected siblings.

Conditions that cause epilepsy are overrepresented in the ASD population. The most common conditions identified to date are 15q11–q13 duplication; 22q13 deletion syndrome; adenylosuccinate lyase (ADSL) deficiency; Angelman syndrome; ARX gene mutations; CATCH 22; juvenile dentatorubral-pallidoluysian atrophy; Down's syndrome; Dravet's syndrome; Fragile-X syndrome; GAMT deficiency; HEADD syndrome; neurofibromatosis type 1; NAPDD; Orstavik 1997 syndrome; phenylketonuria; Rett syndrome and Rett syndrome (Hanefeld variant); Schindler disease; Sotos syndrome and tuberous sclerosis. All of these conditions are discussed in some detail in Aitken (2010a).

Rarely, non-epileptic seizures where there is behavioural evidence of fitting but no EEG abnormality occur during sleep. One review identified a small number of such cases using EEG videotelemetry (Orbach, Ritaccio and Devinsky 2003), but they constituted less than 1 per cent of a sample of over 2000 people investigated.

HOW COMMON ARE THEY?

Nocturnal seizures are not common; however, the extent to which sleep disorders and epilepsy actually overlap is unclear and has rarely been investigated (Manni and Terzaghi 2010) and there is no systematic data. The exact prevalence of nocturnal seizures is currently unclear.

What is clear, however, is that in many cases treatment of a seizure disorder can result in improvement in comorbid sleep problems (Tachibana *et al.* 1996; Touchon *et al.* 1987). It is also the case that some medications used in the management of epilepsy have a significant risk of causing iatrogenic sleep disorders (see Bazil 2003).

That there is an interaction between circadian rhythms and epilepsy is also clear; however, the nature and extent of this association is poorly understood and there are large gaps in our current knowledge (Hofstra and de Weerd 2009).

DO THEY TEND TO GET BETTER IN ANY EVENT?

Benign seizures, by definition, improve over time.

The risk of progression to daytime seizures in epilepsies in people who initially present only with seizure during sleep is reported as being between 0 per cent and 19 per cent (D'Alessandro *et al.* 2004; Gibberd and Bateson 1974; Park *et al.* 1998) so, based on the literature at present, there is a better than 4 in 5 chance that someone who presents with nocturnal seizures will not develop epilepsy.

WHAT CAN BE DONE TO TREAT THEM?

The treatments of choice and the likelihood of benefit depend on the type of nocturnal seizure identified and management should be under the supervision of a competent, appropriately accredited doctor.

A number of different types of epilepsy can present with nocturnal seizures. Benign Rolandic epilepsy, nocturnal frontal lobe epilepsy (NFLE) and generalized tonic-clonic seizures would seem to constitute the bulk of cases. Nocturnal tonic seizures are characteristic of Lennox-Gastaut syndrome. These typically occur during NREM sleep and are usually difficult to control (see discussion in Camfield and Camfield 2002).

An interesting parallel between some forms of seizure and some types of sleep disorders is the association with low endogenous melatonin levels and improvement with the use of melatonin supplementation that can be seen in some seizure disorders (Bazil *et al.* 2000; Fauteck *et al.* 1999).

Certain sorts of sleep problem are significantly more common in people with epilepsy. Obstructive sleep apnoea (OSA) is seen in 20 per cent of children with epilepsy (Kaleyias *et al.* 2008) and seizure control can improve with appropriate treatment of the OSA.

In Rolandic epilepsy, no treatment is usually required.

In generalized tonic-clonic seizures, outcome tends to be poorer (Rantala and Putkonen 1999); however, some positive responses to ketogenic diet have been reported (Calandre, Martinez-Martin and Campos-Castellano 1978; Prats Vinas, Madoz and Martin 1976).

HOW LIKELY ARE THEY TO RESPOND TO TREATMENT?

As with choice of treatment, outcome is dependent on the type of seizure involved.

In Rolandic epilepsy, most cases improve spontaneously during puberty and the person outgrows the disorder. Although there has been some debate in the literature, most neurologists would seem to agree that in the vast majority of cases a good outcome is predictable without treatment and it is acceptable not to use antiepileptic medication in such cases (Peters, Camfield and Camfield 2001).

In NFLE, around 70 per cent of cases are well controlled on antiepileptic medication with improvements in seizures and sleep and a good developmental outcome. Good control has been reported in drug-resistant cases with surgical resection of the affected tissue (Nobili *et al.* 2007), but no long-term follow-up of a surgical series has yet been reported.

In generalized tonic-clonic seizures, based on the current literature, seizures are more difficult to control and outcome tends to be poorer (Rantala and Putkonen 1999).

Sleep-related rhythmic movement disorder

'Why on earth does he keep doing that?'

'James' is an 8-year-old boy with a diagnosis of Asperger syndrome. He is a bright boy but has difficulty concentrating in school and is being assessed for ADHD because his teachers feel that he is 'underachieving' academically. He has always been a restless sleeper but, recently, since his parents have been checking on his younger brother who has started sharing a room with him, they have become concerned when they have observed unusual jerking movements of his legs when he is asleep and are worried that he may be taking fits during his sleep. He has become more tired recently and complains about having 'sore muscles'.

Movement disorders during sleep are often thought to be epileptic in origin. There are now guidelines to help in discriminating between epileptic and non-epileptic movement disorders in sleep (Tinuper *et al.* 2007). Recordings of brainwave activity coupled with video recording of behaviour are the best way to discriminate between the two. If such video-EEG recording is not readily available, then features such as the age of onset, and the number, timing and duration of events can often help to differentiate between them.

Current classifications discriminate between sleep-related rhythmic movement disorder (SRMD) and restless legs syndrome (RLS). There is a significant degree of clinical overlap and the genetic research shows a heightened risk of either diagnosis in children of a parent with a diagnosis of RLS (see Picchietti *et al.* 2009). The two diagnoses have been treated separately here, as the literature tends to cover these as separate conditions.

WHAT IS SLEEP-RELATED RHYTHMIC MOVEMENT DISORDER?

SRMD is a condition where the person affected has stereotyped repetitive rhythmic movements of large muscles, typically of the head and neck, that occur either while going to sleep or once asleep. It typically takes the form of head banging (which is sometimes called *jactatio capitis nocturna*), head rolling or body rocking.

The term periodic limb movement disorder (PLMD) of sleep has also been used to describe the same clinical features (Crabtree *et al.* 2003). There is a reported association between PLMD and ADHD in a high proportion of cases, with around 45 per cent of PLMD cases being comorbid.

In some cases, the pattern may be complex and involve several stereotyped movements (Su *et al.* 2009). These movements can look like seizures but do not have a concurrent epileptic EEG. It is classified as a sleep-related movement disorder on the ICSD-2.

HOW COMMON IS IT?

In infancy such movements are common and have been reported to affect as many as 59 per cent of infants, dropping to around 5 per cent by age 5 (see discussion in Mayer, Wilde-Frenz and Kurella 2007). The persistence of SRMD into older ages is typically associated with the presence of either ASD or learning disability (see Newell *et al.* 1999).

DOES IT TEND TO GET BETTER IN ANY EVENT?

The majority of SRMD presentations will remit in early childhood, typically before school entry. In those cases where this is not the case, the problem can be chronic and is likely to require treatment. A study that classified a series of clinical SRMD cases found 20/24 to be male, and that only two cases had a family history of the condition (Mayer *et al.* 2007). A link between persistence of SRMD and the presence of comorbid ADHD has been suggested (Stepanova, Nevsimalova and Hanusova 2005).

WHAT CAN BE DONE TO TREAT IT?

In cases where SRMD is associated with sleep apnoea, improvements are often seen in the movement problem when the sleep apnoea is brought under control (Chirakalwasan *et al.* 2009).

A systematic review of the evidence on treatments up to 2003 (Hoban 2003) concluded that there were only a few single case reports of pharmacotherapy, some claiming symptomatic control with low-dose clonazepam (Chisholm and Morehouse 1996; Manni and Tartara 1997).

A recent review (Picchietti and Picchietti 2008) recommends initially reviewing sleep hygiene, and suggests using a strategy they call the 'Peds RLS NEWREST' algorithm as an *aide memoire* (reproduced here with permission from Table 5, p.95 of Picchietti and Picchietti 2008).

The Peds RLS NEWREST chart: tips for better sleep

N Nutritional needs. A healthy age-appropriate diet should be adopted. Any foods containing caffeine, such as chocolate, and drinks such as soda, energy drinks, iced tea and coffee should be restricted, especially in the late afternoon and evening. Current dietary iron intake and the need for iron supplementation should be assessed.

E Environment for sleeping. The bedroom should be relaxing, quiet and only for sleeping. Find another room for studying, loud music, TV and 'timeout'.

W Watch for and report restlessness, uncomfortable leg sensations and disturbed sleep, especially when these affect daytime function.

R Regular sleep schedule with a routine bedtime and wake up time even at weekends.

E Exercise daily. Physical activity can reduce RLS sensations and increases deep sleep.

S Stop substance use that interferes with good sleep such as tobacco, alcohol and recreational drugs.

T Take prescribed medicine and/or approved iron supplements consistently.

There is evidence that symptoms of SRMD are associated with low normal levels of serum ferritin and that these can improve with supplementation (Simakajornboon *et al.* 2003, 2006). Low serum ferritin is reported in a high proportion of autistic cases (Dosman *et al.* 2006) and supplementation has been shown, in general, to be helpful in the management of sleep disorders (Dosman *et al.* 2007).

It is possible that this is a consequence of the need for iron as an essential co-factor for tyrosine hydroxylase. Tyrosine hydroxylase is a rate-limiting enzyme in the production of dopamine, one of the main neurotransmitter systems in the brain (Earley *et al.* 2000).

There has been little research on the use of medication for SRMD. The limited evidence base to date is consistent with the ferritin findings above. Dopamine agonists (drugs that increase dopamine or dopaminergic activity) such as ropinirole have been reported to be of benefit (see Erichsen, Ferri and Gozal 2010). There is currently very limited information on the use, benefit or side-effects of using dopamine agonists in the management of SRMD.

HOW LIKELY IS IT TO RESPOND TO TREATMENT?

A helpful recent overview of outcome can be found in Bonnet *et al.* (2010).

Despite the lack of a validated treatment, the majority of cases remit in childhood. Even in those cases where the sleep movements do not improve, there appears to be no significant effect on IQ or overall development (Mayer *et al.* 2007).

In some cases symptoms persist into adulthood (Chisholm and Morehouse 1996; Stepanova *et al.* 2005) typically with headbanging and/or body rolling.

Where video telemetry has been used in persistent cases unusual epileptiform EEG patterns at 0.5–2.0 Hz can often be seen during the sleep behaviours (Manni and Terzaghi 2005). This suggests, in contrast to much current opinion, either a comorbidity with seizure activity or an epileptic basis to the movements themselves.

Sleep bruxism (tooth grinding while asleep)

'We can hear her through the whole house; it's like someone is using a drill next door.'

'Fiona' is a 10-year-old girl with autism and communication difficulties. She often appears to be highly anxious and chews at her sleeves when she is told off or gets upset. While asleep, she has a longstanding habit of grinding her teeth noisily together. This can go on for lengthy periods, and her brothers find it difficult to sleep through the noise. When the bruxism has been particularly noticeable, she often says that her jaw is sore the following day.

WHAT IS SLEEP BRUXISM?

Sleep bruxism, or tooth clenching and grinding during sleep, is a problem that has been known of at least since early Babylonian times.

Here is a translation of one of the earliest suggested treatments:

If a man grinds (or, 'grates') his teeth in his sleep, you will take a human skull, wash and anoint it with oil, and for seven days it shall be kept in place at the head of his bed. Before he lies down he shall kiss it seven times and lick it seven times so he will recover. (Babylonisch-Assyrian medicine, c. 1900–1600 BC cited in Kinnier Wilson 1996, p.137)

The success of this treatment is not documented, and it has fallen from popularity in recent millennia as a way of treating this common sleep difficulty.

Sleep bruxism is classified as a simple, stereotypic, repetitive and localized sleep-related movement disorder.

HOW COMMON IS IT?

Tooth grinding during sleep typically starts at around 1 year of age, soon after the first incisor teeth erupt. Its prevalence in children ranges from 14 per cent to 20 per cent (Abe and Shimakawa 1966; Widmalm, Christiansen and Gunn 1995). The reported prevalence by adolescence is around 13 per cent (Strausz *et al.* 2010) and it continues to drop, reaching around 3 per cent in old age (Lavigne and Montplaisir 1994).

Tooth grinding when awake is associated with a number of psychosocial stressors being linked to high stress sensitivity, anxiety and depression; however, there is no evidence to suggest any such link for sleep bruxism (Manfredini and Lobbenzoo 2009), and it is thought that day and night bruxism may represent two different conditions with different aetiologies (see Kato, Dal-Fabbro and Lavigne 2003).

It has been suggested that sleep bruxism is an inherited condition (Abe and Shimakawa 1966), and there is a significant level of twin concordance (Hublin *et al.* 1998). To date there has been little systematic research on the genetic or biological basis to this often-troubling disorder.

DOES IT TEND TO GET BETTER IN ANY EVENT?

If we assume that the various cross-sectional studies at different ages reflect the change in bruxism over time, it appears that fewer people present with bruxism as they get older and that there is a reasonable chance that at some stage someone will 'grow out of it'. As adult rates are around 8 per cent and rates in the over 60s some 3 per cent, some half of all children with bruxism are likely to persist in this habit well into adult life. The only longitudinal study of this phenomenon was a 9-year follow-up of a Finnish population cohort from age 14 to age 23 (Strausz *et al.* 2010). Self-report of tooth grinding increased in this population from 13.7 to 21.7 per cent over the period from adolescence into young adulthood.

One factor that significantly increases the rate of bruxism is the use of stimulant medications such as methylphenidate, and there is evidence to suggest that the rate of sleep bruxism is increased in stimulant treated ADHD (see Gau and Chiang 2009). The chronology is important, therefore, if the onset of the sleep bruxism seems to have coincided with the use of specific medication.

There are a number of case reports of bruxism in association with ASD (Barnoy *et al.* 2009; Muthu and Prathibha 2008).

WHAT CAN BE DONE TO TREAT IT?

A variety of treatment approaches have been advocated including various physical devices to prevent tooth grinding (occlusal and palatal splinting, nociceptive trigeminal inhibition (NTI) splints, mandibular advancement device (MAD)), transcutaneous electric nerve stimulation (TENS), behavioural therapies and pharmacological strategies (Blount *et al.* 1982; Lang *et al.* 2009; Lavigne and Manzine 2000).

A recent review (Kato and Lavigne 2010) summarizes the principal treatment approaches.

A range of *orodental strategies* has been used in attempts to treat sleep bruxism. These have included occlusal splints (see Macedo *et al.* 2007), mouth guards, NTI splints and MADs. The effects of these various appliances have been studied extensively but there is no definitive evidence of benefit from any at the present time. In people with OSA, there is also some evidence that occlusal splinting may interfere with breathing during sleep (Gagnon *et al.* 2004).

Two major *behavioural strategies* have been advocated to date:

1. Lifestyle instruction, relaxation and improved sleep hygiene (where possible minimizing the known risk factors for sleep bruxism such as stress, alcohol, smoking and irregular sleep pattern). No outcome studies have looked at the effectiveness of these behavioural strategies alone.

2. Biofeedback, focusing on EMG feedback of tension in the jaw muscles reduces sleep bruxism; however, as with much other biofeedback it fails to show functional carryover once treatment is stopped (Cassisi, McGlynn and Belles 1987; Pierce and Gale 1988).

3. One study combined CBT with nocturnal biofeedback over a 3-month period (Ommerborn *et al.* 2007). Results were no better than occlusal splinting and benefits had not persisted when followed up at 6 months.

A number of *pharmacological strategies* have been evaluated for possible beneficial effects on sleep bruxism: amitriptyline, bromocriptine, clonidine, clonazepam, L-dopa, propranolol and tryptophan have all been evaluated in published treatment trials. To date only clonidine has shown good results but it also has a significant level of side-effects.

One paper on the treatment of sleep problems in children with epilepsy found that successful treatment of the epilepsy also produced significant benefit to bruxism in those patients who exhibited both problems (Elkhayat *et al.* 2010).

HOW LIKELY IS IT TO RESPOND TO TREATMENT?

Currently, there is no well-validated treatment that appears to have a high probability of success without significant side effects.

Two papers have attempted a comparative evaluation based on NNT (number needed to treat) and effect size analyses (Huynh *et al.* 2006, 2007). These studies concluded that the mandibular advancement device (MAD) and clonidine were the most successful treatments. Both treatments were, however, associated with high rates of side-effects, physical discomfort for the MAD and suppression of REM sleep and low morning blood pressure for clonidine.

As there would appear to be a reasonable rate of spontaneous remission, sleep bruxism does not have major problems associated with it and the treatments to date are not without their own problems; intervention is only warranted where the condition interferes with other aspects of the person's daily life or their relationships.

Obstructive sleep apnoea (OSA)

'He could snore for England.'

> 'Gordon' is a 7-year-old boy with ASD who snores loudly in his sleep. When his mother has sat with him at night, sometimes she has also become worried that he often seems to stop breathing for a few seconds at a time. Gordon is slightly overweight for his age and gets easily tired when taking part in sports at school. PE lessons are voluntary and Gordon typically 'opts out'.
>
> He has been seen by a clinical geneticist and has been found to have a Fragile-X 'CGG expansion', while his mum and one of her sisters have a 'pre-mutational' expansion. His maternal granddad has recently developed a hand tremor and is being investigated for something called 'FRAXTAS'.
>
> The family are worried that there could be something seriously wrong medically with Gordon and that he could come to harm when he stops breathing.

WHAT IS OSA?

OSA is a form of sleep apnoea (apnoea is when breathing briefly stops and there is no discernible muscle movement). It is a common paediatric presentation that is typically linked to obesity (Katz and D'Ambrosio 2010). Loud snoring is common, interspersed with periods of up to 10 seconds when breathing seems to stop altogether. People troubled with OSA typically have raised blood pressure, are overweight and are troubled by daytime sleepiness.

ASD conditions in which OSA is more likely to present are those associated with obesity such as Biedl-Bardet syndrome (Middela *et al.* 2009), Cohen syndrome (see de Sousa *et al.* 2008), Fragile-X syndrome (Reynolds 2004), Prader-Willi syndrome (see Nixon and Brouillette 2002) and Rubinstein-Taybi syndrome (Zucconi *et al.* 1993). For overviews of the main genetic obesity syndromes, see Goldstone and Beales (2008) and Aitken (2010a).

There is no specific literature on OSA in ASD, but the treatment approaches in someone with ASD who had an OSA would be identical to the treatment of OSA in other groups (for a review, see Gozal 2008).

If it is left untreated OSA can have significant effects on both daytime cognitive functioning and on behaviour (Beebe and Gozal 2002). From a large cohort study in Tucson of 6–11-year-old children there is evidence to suggest an association between sleep-disordered breathing, somatic complaints, oppositional and aggressive behaviours and social problems (Zhao *et al.* 2008). Some issues such as social withdrawal seem to be related more to obesity per se, could affect treatments targeted at these other issues and should ideally be addressed in tandem when they are present (see Mulvaney *et al.* 2006).

HOW COMMON IS IT?

There is a surprising variation in the reported prevalence of paediatric OSA depending on the definition and the data collection method employed, with rates from 0.9 per cent to 13 per cent being cited (see Lumeng and Chervin 2008).

DOES IT TEND TO GET BETTER IN ANY EVENT?

> We have begun to understand that sleep disorders in general, and more particularly, sleep-disordered breathing, can lead to substantial morbidities affecting the central nervous system (CNS), the cardiovascular and metabolic systems, and somatic growth, ultimately leading to reduced quality of life.
>
> Capdevila *et al.* 2008, p.274

In children and adolescents who have both OSA and problems with obesity, the presentation tends to be more pronounced and the outcome is poorer. Both paediatric OSA and obesity are significant predictors of development of metabolic syndrome (the combination of insulin resistant diabetes, dyslipidemia, hypertension and obesity) in adulthood, the presence of OSA making someone at six times greater risk (Redline *et al.* 2007).

The diagnosis of OSA is itself often preceded by an earlier diagnosis of cardiovascular issues or hypertension (see Smith *et al.* 2002).

WHAT CAN BE DONE TO TREAT IT?

A range of treatment alternatives are available in the management of OSA (see Capdevila *et al.* 2008; Halbower, McGinley and Smith 2008).

Treatment of severe OSA can require one of several approaches:

- behavioural intervention
- use of prosthetic devices to maintain an open airway by positioning the jaw or limiting movement of the tongue
- use of mechanical devices to maintain airway pressure during sleep such as CPAP (typically a face mask connected to a machine)
- in extreme cases that have proven unresponsive to other approaches, surgical intervention (maxillomandibular advancement).

In children who are significantly overweight, increased exercise has been shown to improve OSA symptoms. In one study of 7–11-year-old overweight children, both 20 minutes per day (N = 36) and 40 minutes per day (N = 37) aerobic exercise groups improved significantly on the Pediatric Sleep Questionnaire (PSQ) (Chervin *et al.* 2000) compared to a no-additional exercise control group (N = 27) (Davis *et al.* 2006).

It may be necessary to work on behavioural issues in tandem with management of OSA in children (Owens *et al.* 1998). A study that looked at behavioural sleep difficulties and daytime problems in 100 children with OSA found additional behavioural sleep difficulties were present in almost one in four (22%), and the principal comorbid problem was bedtime refusal. The children who had both OSA and behavioural sleep issues were more likely to have daytime externalizing behaviour difficulties and sleepiness.

As was discussed earlier, obese people tend to sleep less not more, so a focus on sleep hygiene and improving bedtime routines may be an important adjunct to OSA targeted approaches.

There is some evidence that improvements in cognitive functioning are seen in parallel with improvements in aerobic fitness (Davis *et al.* 2007).

Most cases of severe OSA are associated with enlarged tonsils and adenoids. Successful and sustained improvement in OSA is achieved in approximately 85 per cent of cases through surgical removal (Lipton and Gozal 2003).

In the 15 per cent of cases where surgery to remove the tonsils and adenoids is not indicated or where it has been carried out but has proven unsuccessful, CPAP (nasal continuous positive airway pressure) is usually advocated as the treatment of choice (see, e.g. Massa *et al.* 2002; Palombini, Pelayo and Guilleminault 2004).

Other types of surgery are sometimes used – uvulopalatopharyngoplasty (also known as UPPP or UP3). This tends to have a low success rate except using the 'Stanford Protocol' which claims to have a complete cure rate of 50–70 per cent with significant improvements in a high percentage of cases (Li *et al.* 2000; Wietske *et al.* 2007).

Application of corticosteroids by nasal spray has been reported to have some success in alleviating symptoms of OSA (Berlucchi *et al.* 2007).

Orthopaedic devices, worn during sleep to keep the airway open, are reported as being helpful to some (Carvalho *et al.* 2007), but the evidence of significant benefit is disputed (Fox 2007).

An issue for many with OSA is excessive daytime tiredness, which again may require to be treated in tandem with the OSA. This was discussed under Excessive daytime sleepiness above.

HOW LIKELY IS IT TO RESPOND TO TREATMENT?

OSA can typically be successfully controlled through one or more of the strategies briefly outlined above. Weight control and improved exercise tolerance should be the first strategy. If implementing a diet and exercise regime at home is not producing any benefit, help with implementing these may be required through an appropriate paediatric service, which could involve occupational therapy and dietetics.

Differences in definitions and outcome criteria across the studies to date, and the lack of any good medium- to long-term outcome studies, make precise estimation of treatment response difficult to gauge. The results of the published studies carried out to date suggest that there is a high likelihood of improvement or remission with active treatment; however, there is no good longer-term information on compliance or relapse rates.

In addition to the apnoea itself, there is some evidence to suggest that neurobehavioural issues such as excessive daytime sleepiness, hyperactivity and inattention can improve when the condition is effectively treated (Chervin *et al.* 2006).

In one 5-year-old girl with autism, appropriate treatment of her OSA resulted in an improvement in her daytime behaviour and of her ASD severity as rated on the Autism Diagnostic Observation Schedule (Malow, McGrew *et al.* 2006).

Narcolepsy

> 'Everything is going along fine, then a balloon pops and we find him in a heap on the floor.'

'Greig' who is 14 has always had a problem with getting to sleep at night. He will often fall asleep while in the middle of things that would hold his friends' interest – at the cinema, on the bus, or while waiting to take his turn when bowling. He complains that he is a poor sleeper at night, and sometimes that he feels 'stuck to the bed' when he wakes up, as if he is paralysed.

Something else his parents are worried by is that he can slump to the ground if he is startled by a sudden noise. This can happen if he hears a car backfire, a starting pistol at a race, or if someone pops a balloon or bursts a crisp packet at a party.

WHAT IS NARCOLEPSY?

Narcolepsy is a condition with two key features – excessive daytime sleepiness and cataplexy (where there is a sudden loss of muscle tone, usually in response to laughing or being tickled, but sometimes in response to loud noises or other sudden shocks) (Challamel *et al.* 1994; Dahl, Holttum and Trubnick 1994). In addition, there is often disruption to night-time sleep and REM sleep can occur at or near sleep onset and can sometimes result in what are known as hypnagogic hallucinations (American Academy of Sleep Medicine 2005); a part of the condition can also be sleep paralysis – where the person feels unable to move during the transitional period from being asleep to becoming fully awake (see Cheyne and Girard 2009).

Narcolepsy was first described in 1880 by the French neurologist J.B.E. Gelineau (Gelineau 1880) and is sometimes referred to in the literature as 'Gelineau's syndrome'. A useful overview of narcolepsy in children can be found in Stores (1999).

In around 1/3, the onset is in childhood, with 4.5 per cent of cases being identified before age 5 and 16 per cent before age 10 (Challamel *et al.* 1994).

Assessment and diagnosis typically relies on an assessment called the multiple sleep latency test (MSLT) (Carskadon *et al.* 1986). For a MSLT, an overnight EEG recording is made together with assessments of sleep latency on several daytime naps. This is not always sufficiently clear to provide a definitive diagnosis (Moscovitch, Partinen and Guilleminault 1993).

In nine out of ten cases where the structure of the brain has been studied, there is poor development of lateral neurons in an area called the posterior hypothalamus (see, e.g. Blouin *et al.* 2005). A partial loss of cells in this area is seen in 'narcolepsy without cataplexy' (Thannickal, Nienhuis and Siegel 2009) and there is reduced production of a type of neurochemical called hypocretin (orexin) (Zeitzer, Nishino and Mignot 2006). Hypocretins are recently discovered neuropeptides that are highly conserved in evolutionary terms. They have been found to be involved in a number of body processes including pituitary and cardiovascular regulation and in the control of the sleep–wake cycle (Martynska *et al.* 2005).

In one case of early-onset narcolepsy, a mutation of the hypocretin gene (HCRT) on chromosome 17q21 has been reported (Peyron *et al.* 2000). A number of other genetic differences have been reported in association with narcolepsy (4p13-q21; 14q11.2; 21q11.2; 21q22.3; 22q13) and with variation at the HLA locus on 6p21. Most cases are sporadic, with the HLA haplotype but without any of the specific gene markers so far reported. Identical twins are both affected in 25–31 per cent suggesting a significant level of genetic susceptibility (Mignot 1998).

Low levels of hypocretin-1 in cerebrospinal fluid (CSF) are seen in 88.5 per cent of cases of narcolepsy with cataplexy with a specificity of 99.1 per cent (Dauvilliers *et al.* 2003). It is a potentially useful component of the clinical assessment in cases where things such as an MSLT do not provide clear answers (Mignot *et al.* 2002). Drawing off CSF is an invasive physical assessment with not insignificant clinical risks so should not be undertaken without clear medical indications.

Cataplexy is almost invariably associated (in around 95% of cases). It is seen in a number of rare conditions including Coffin-Lowry syndrome (Crow *et al.* 1998), and Prader-Willi syndrome (Stephenson 1990), conditions that have been reported in association with ASD (see Aitken 2010b) and is also reported in Niemann-Pick type C (Kandt *et al.* 1982; Oyama *et al.* 2006).

HOW COMMON IS IT?

Narcolepsy is a rare condition with an overall prevalence though to be around 1 in 2000–5000. There are wide reported variations in prevalence, however, from 1 in 600 in Japan (Honda 1988) to 1 in 500,000 in Israel (Lavie and Peled 1987).

Narcoleptic patients may receive a wide range of alternative diagnoses before the nature of their clinical condition has been clarified (see Kryger, Walld and Manfreda 2002).

DOES IT TEND TO GET BETTER IN ANY EVENT?

Narcolepsy is a lifelong condition but fortunately it is non-progressive – the features do not tend to worsen as the person gets older. There is, however, an increased risk of being involved in car accidents. This is thought to result from poorer attention.

People suffering from narcolepsy have been found to show poorer performance on tests of vigilance carried out under controlled conditions (Findley *et al.* 1995).

WHAT CAN BE DONE TO TREAT IT?

Various treatments have been advocated for narcolepsy (see Aran *et al.* 2010; Billiard *et al.* 2006; Kothare and Kaleyias 2008a).

The general treatment approach that has been most strongly advocated involves improved sleep hygiene, including the incorporation of daytime naps (see Vendrame *et al.* 2008), in conjunction with pharmacotherapy.

A range of medications have been advocated:

- Modafinil significantly improves alertness (Littner *et al.* 2001; Moldofsky, Broughton and Hill 2000).

- Sodium oxybate has also been found to improve the symptoms of narcolepsy (Mamelak *et al.* 2004) and to reduce daytime sleepiness in narcoleptic patients (Black and Houghton 2006).

- Venlafaxine, an SNRI (serotonin-norepinephrine reuptake inhibitor), has been shown to be of benefit. It is the third most used medication currently for paediatric narcolepsy after modafinil and sodium oxybate (Aran *et al.* 2010).

- Methylphenidate, amphetamines and other psychostimulants have been shown to be of some benefit (Morgenthaler *et al.* 2007; Wise and Lynch 2001).

- SSRIs have been advocated, but the reported benefits are non-specific and there is a significant rate of reported side-effects (Langdon *et al.* 1986).

- One research letter describes the successful treatment of two boys aged 15 and 17 by the use of hypnosis (Weidong *et al.* 2009).

For general reviews of narcolepsy treatment, see Stores (1999) and Wise *et al.* (2007).

HOW LIKELY IS IT TO RESPOND TO TREATMENT?

The studies published to date suggest that a high proportion of those with narcolepsy can be successfully controlled with modafinil, sodium oxybate or venlafaxine in conjunction with behavioural interventions. The cumulative data suggest that the use of these strategies is likely to result in a significant level of improvement in symptoms in well over 2/3 of cases.

Nocturnal enuresis (bedwetting)

> 'His bed is always saturated and he refuses to wear anything at night. We're sure he does it just to annoy us.'

'Roberto' is a 9-year-old boy who has a diagnosis of ASD. He has additional motor problems and a diagnosis of 'Becker-type' muscular dystrophy. He attends a school for children with moderate learning problems.

He shares a room with his 6-year-old younger brother Tony who has recently started teasing him about being 'smelly' and being a big boy who still wets his bed. Tony's teasing began not long after he became dry at night about a year ago. Their parents had made a big fuss over Tony becoming dry and hoped it would encourage his brother. If anything he became resentful of Tony and tried to boss him around whenever he had the opportunity. 'Roberto' is now fully continent during the day but is self-conscious about his problem at night and won't sleep over with other children if they invite him or have them to stay. The problem is made more difficult as he refuses to wear a pad at night and the bedding is usually soaking.

Although he appears to relate well to his peers in school his parents are worried that he is getting progressively more isolated outside as the issues around his night-time wetting continue and feel he could get teased about it or get bullied.

WHAT IS ENURESIS?

Enuresis is the term used for losing voluntary bladder control and involuntarily passing urine. Nocturnal enuresis is where the person wets themselves during sleep – urinating in the nappy (diaper)/incontinence pad, or wetting the bed if the person no longer sleeps with such protection – but they are typically dry while awake.

There is nothing to suggest that nocturnal enuresis is a deliberate pattern of behaviour but it is often viewed as such and can be a source of stress between children and parents. Where it persists, it can often cause the child to become self-conscious, being reluctant to accept invitations to sleep overnight at friends, to invite friends to sleep over or to go on school trips that involve overnight stays. Any form of incontinence can lead to teasing and stigmatization by peers and it is not uncommon for children to move schools because of these 'secondary problems'.

HOW COMMON IS IT?

The majority of children of both sexes have achieved night-time urinary continence and are dry through the night by the time they enter full-time education; however, there is no 'normal' pattern and there is a wide range of individual variation both between people from the same population and across cultures.

Taking the typical definition, that the individual wets the bed twice or more per week, through childhood the rates of nocturnal enuresis remain fairly high but gradually reduce with age. At age 5 it affects approximately 15 per cent of children, with around 15 per cent of this group showing spontaneous improvement each year (Mammen and Ferrer 2004). The problem is reported to be approximately twice as common in boys compared to girls.

The ALSPAC cohort study followed 13,971 children who were born in the same area of southwest England between 1991 and 1992. By 7.5 years, approximately 15.5 per cent of children were reported to have night-time wetting of any frequency, with only 1 per cent wetting almost every night and 0.2 per cent wetting once or more per night (Butler *et al.* 2005). This last group, and children who are still wetting by age 10, are unlikely to show spontaneous resolution of their problems.

DOES IT TEND TO GET BETTER IN ANY EVENT?

In an Italian study of adolescents with persistent nocturnal enuresis, 22 per cent had failed to respond to desmopressin, 23 per cent had had poor compliance to any therapies offered when they were younger, while 40 per cent had not been offered any form of therapy when they were younger (Nappo *et al.* 2002). In 80 per cent of the cases they reported the problem was severe. In this group of 107 cases, around 60 per cent were males, most (82%) had a family history of bedwetting and most (74%) were primary enuretics – they had never had a period of night-time bladder control.

Not surprisingly, children who show a pattern of nocturnal-only enuresis typically respond more successfully to treatment than children who have diurnal enuresis (both daytime and night-time difficulties) (Fielding 1980).

A large-scale survey of a random sample of women enrolled with a large health maintenance organization screened 2109 women aged 40–69 for current and childhood urinary symptomology (Fitzgerald *et al.* 2006). Of this group 8 per cent reported childhood nocturnal enuresis and 10 per cent reported that nocturia (the need to urinate frequently at night) had been a problem during childhood.

Childhood nocturnal enuresis predicted adult urge incontinence (OR 2.7), and childhood nocturia predicted adult nocturia (OR 2.3).

Further research is required to discover the proportion of childhood enuretics that persist (the above studies only state for those who do what their problems are, not what proportion of children persist); however, for those that do their problems tend to be severe, and can have major psychosocial consequences.

WHAT CAN BE DONE TO TREAT IT?

A wide range of treatment approaches has been advocated for night-time enuresis through the ages. There have been a variety of reviews of the various treatments that have been used (see, e.g. Caldwell *et al.* 2005; Evans 2001a, 2001b; Lyon and Schnall 2010; Wright 2008).

MEDICATIONS

Two principal types of medication, tricyclics and desmopressin, have been used in the treatment of night-time enuresis.

Tricyclics

A variety of tricyclic medications such as imipramine have been prescribed extensively for the treatment of nocturnal eneuresis, with over 58 published randomized studies in the literature. Most of these trials (those using imipramine, amitriptyline, viloxazine, nortriptyline, clomipramine and desipramine) show some limited improvement while on active medication which typically relapses on cessation. Trials using mianserin have shown no significant benefits, and movement problems have been reported as a side-effect (Aggarwal 2010).

What are they? Tricyclic medications contain bioactive compounds that have two six-carbon benzene rings attached on either side of a seven-carbon ring as a common feature. Their main mode of action is through enhancing the function of monoamine neurotransmitters such as serotonin, dopamine and noradrenalin.

Are there any side-effects or complications? A range of minor side-effects is common while taking tricyclics (these include low blood pressure, dry mouth, constipation, perspiration, increased heart rate and insomnia). In addition, overdose can result in both heart and liver damage (see Glazener, Evans and Peto 2003a).

Desmopressin acetate (DDAVP)

DDAVP is a synthetic compound that mimics the action of the hormone vasopressin. Vasopressin has the action of reducing urine production by the kidneys. As a consequence, wetting is reduced because there is less urine being made and the bladder does not get so full during sleep.

A 12-centre study of 114 primary childhood night-time and daytime enuretics randomly assigned cases to DDAVP (for night-time enuresis) (N = 66), to oxybutinin or combination treatment with both medications for day and night wetting. The study design was to have a 2-week baseline period, 6 weeks of active treatment and a 2-week follow-up period off active medication. Of those with night-time wetting alone, 79 per cent showed a good or intermediate clinical improvement on DDAVP alone. Of those with diurnal (daytime and night-time) wetting 71 per cent showed comparable improvement on the combined treatment while 54 per cent improved on oxybutinin alone (Caione *et al.* 1997).

A number of reviews of the role of DDAVP in the treatment of nocturnal enuresis have appeared. Glazener and Evans (2002) reviewed the treatment literature on children, concluding that it is not a long-term treatment, only improving wetting on the nights that it is used.

Enuresis alarm treatments are slower to take effects but have a lower relapse rate, and DDAVP can cause problems if fluid restriction is not adhered to by the child. Alloussi *et al.* (2010) reviewed the 99 studies published to date, concluding that the evidence for DDAVP is stronger in the management of monosymptomatic enuresis and as an adjunct to other therapies, and that structured withdrawal rather than acute cessation improves outcome with a lower likelihood of symptom relapse.

Two safety reviews (Van de Walle *et al.* 2007; Van de Walle, Van Herzeele and Raes 2010) have concluded that the overall safety profile of DDAVP is good. Both reviews highlight concerns over hyponatremia – low sodium levels in body fluids, but noted that these reports were largely in the elderly. They suggest that this is also a possible issue at younger ages if the dose used was excessive and inadequate fluid restriction implemented. The importance of night-time fluid restriction while on DDAVP was emphasized.

Other medications

A wide range of other medications has been evaluated as possible treatments, the best known being oxybutinin chloride.

One small randomized comparative study found that pseudoephedrine (N = 1) was significantly better than either oxybutynin (N = 9) or indomethacin (N = 9) in the treatment of night-time enuresis and that oxybutinin had the highest level of reported side-effects of the three (Varan *et al.* 1996).

In one study (Tahmaz *et al.* 2000) the combination of imipramine and oxybutynin was shown to be effective and well tolerated in a consecutive open case series of 77 childhood enuretic cases.

For a review of the extensive literature on alternative pharmacotherapies for night-time enuresis, see Glazener, Evans and Peto (2003b).

Behavioural interventions

There have been two Cochrane reviews of behavioural interventions for nocturnal enuresis. The first dealt with simple behavioural and physical approaches (Glazener and Evans 2004) and the second with more complex behavioural and educational interventions (Glazener, Evans and Peto 2004).

In their review of simple behavioural treatments such as reward charts; fluid restriction; regular waking and lifting, Glazener and Evans identified 13 trials (Glazener and Evans 2004). The general conclusion they reached was that these approaches were better than non-intervention controls but performed less well overall than either enuresis alarms or medication. The authors point out that there is a benefit of trying these types of behavioural intervention first despite their lower success rate because they are less demanding, have a reasonable chance of producing benefit and do not have any significant risk of side-effects.

In reviewing more complex behavioural treatment interventions, Glazener *et al.* (2004) identified 18 trials in which a multi-component intervention was used, typically involving dry bed training coupled with an enuresis alarm. Their conclusion was that the evidence base was insufficient to draw any firm conclusion concerning additional benefit, but that there was some evidence for a reduced level of relapse after stopping use of an alarm when both approaches had been used, without the potential side-effects from use of adjunctive medication.

Retention control training (also known as 'stream interruption', 'start-stop' and 'bladder drill training')

Retention control training has shown success in improving functional bladder capacity, as do medications such as oxybutynin. One early controlled trial of retention control training showed an increase in bladder capacity in 18 enuretic children but there was no apparent effect on the rate of bedwetting (Harris and Purohit 1977). In a small proportion of cases, however, improvements in capacity and awareness can be sufficient to resolve enuresis, normally by enabling the child to recognize bladder fullness, waken and use the toilet at night (see De Wachter *et al.* 2002).

Comparison of rentention control training to the use of an enuresis alarm either separately or in combination suggests that both singly and in combination the enuresis alarm contributes significantly more to the management outcome and has a greater chance of achieving success.

Dry bed training (DBT) (Bollard and Nettlebeck 1982)

DBT is an approach in which an initial baseline is used to establish the night-time pattern to the child's wetting. This is followed by a period of regular waking and toileting, timed to ensure that the child achieves a dry bed. Once this pattern has been established the time between lifts is gradually extended until the child is able to stay dry throughout the night.

This is a very demanding approach for those carrying out the programme and should not be tried unless it can be properly implemented. This can often require in-patient admission for the early stages or families to arrange the time to carry out a home-based programme during holidays or over a long weekend break.

Enuresis alarms

There have been a large number of clinical trials of enuresis alarms (for a detailed review, see Glazener, Evans and Peto 2005). The enuresis alarm, typically referred to as the 'bell and pad' (Figure E.7), has the most robust evidence base of any biofeedback treatment for a sleep-related problem, and does demonstrate sustained benefits from treatment. Its use can be dated back to Mowrer and Mowrer's classic work, first published in 1938. A useful review of the development of the use of enuresis alarms can be found in Forsythe and Butler (1989).

The Mowrers hypothesized that 'if some arrangement could be provided so that the sleeping child would be awakened just after the onset of urination, and only at that time, the resulting association of bladder distension and response of awakening and inhibiting further urination should provide precisely the form of training which would seem to be most specifically appropriate' (Mowrer and Mowrer 1938).

This was a simple device operating on a simple principle that is the same for the various alarms in current use: by wetting the bed, or in some devices by wetting a strip containing two electrodes that is worn within trainer pants or a diaper, the child's urine completes an electrical circuit thus setting off an alarm that should rouse them from sleep.

The point of this process is for the child to come to associate the act of voiding (wetting) with being woken by the bell, and subsequently learning to avoid being aroused by the bell by either waking and going to the toilet or by holding on and not voiding. This is similar to the simple stimulus response associative learning pattern in Pavlovian conditioning, although the fact that the child wetting triggers the bell means that the stimulus occurs after the child has wet rather than before.

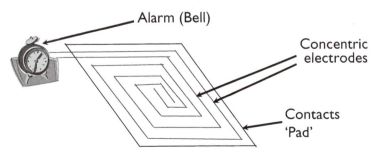

Figure E.7 The 'bell and pad' alarm

When 14 consecutive dry nights was taken as treatment success, in studies that compared the use of an alarm to no-treatment controls (14 studies, 304 on active treatment compared to 248 controls), the use of an alarm was successful in 68 per cent of cases while similar improvements in wetting were reported in 4 per cent of non-intervention controls. The approach is as effective as desmopressin and there is no additional advantage from using both in combination (see Kiddoo 2007).

This illustrates the success rate from use of an alarm to be around 2 out of 3 cases. It also highlights that improvements unrelated to treatment are likely to be seen in 1 in 25 cases.

Alarms that wake the child seem to work best, sound emitting alarms are best, and there is no difference in outcome between alarms that are fitted to the bed compared to those that are worn (usually in modified pants/nappies).

When compared to behavioural treatments, alarms are more effective in reducing wet nights but no better overall than stream interruption ('stop-start'), and dry bed training and alarm treatment are reported as being equally effective. Alarm treatment alone is as effective as the combined use of alarm and behavioural intervention.

Compared to tricyclic medication, treatment with an alarm appears to be slightly more effective and has a lower relapse rate. There is no evidence of any greater benefit from combining the two approaches.

When the use of an alarm is compared to desmopressin, medication appears to act more quickly but improvements are less sustained and the relapse rate is higher. On follow-up, combined desmopressin plus alarm treatment appears to have a poorer outcome than either alone. One study compared the combination of giving desmopressin first followed by its use combined with an enuresis alarm (N = 16) to the initial use of an alarm followed by its use in combination with desmopressin (N = 14) (Vogt et al. 2010): 22/30 children (73%) were successfully treated with combination therapy but there was no significant difference in outcome between the two groups.

In the past there have some safety concerns, and cases have been reported where alarms have caused electrical burns to children who slept through their alarm being triggered (Greaves 1969; Hursthouse 1973). This should not be a problem with any current commercially available alarms, but if you plan to use a commercially bought alarm check with the manufacturer if you have any concerns.

A list of alarms and where these can be obtained is provided in the Resources section, p.175.

Alternative and complementary treatments

A Cochrane review (Glazener, Evans and Cheuk 2005) looked at the evidence for a range of complementary and alternative treatments for night-time enuresis.

Their general conclusions were as follows:

Hypnosis – There has only been one report on the use of hypnosis to treat childhood enuresis (Edwards and van der Spuy 1985). The authors suggested that the use of trances and/or hypnotic suggestion produced a better outcome than was seen in waiting list controls. Unfortunately the sample size was not large enough to draw any strong conclusions and the severity of wetting in the two groups differed significantly at baseline.

Chiropractics – There is only one small study that supports the use of chiropractic treatment for nocturnal enuresis (Reed *et al.* 1994), and a further small study that is inadequate to draw any clear conclusions on how effective it might be (Leboeuf *et al.* 1991).

Dietary interventions – These can be indicated in specific conditions – for example, a low calcium diet has been reported to be of help in some children whose enuresis results from hypercalcuria (see Valenti *et al.* 2002).

Herbal remedies – A number of traditional herbal remedies have some empirical support in the treatment of night-time enuresis.

The Chinese remedy Yi Niao Ling Fang has been reported as an effective treatment for childhood nocturnal enuresis (Yu-lian, Xiao-yun and Chun-hua 2002). A cohort of 96 children aged 5–13 who had been referred for night-time enuresis and had a median of 1.28 episodes of wetting per night were documented. Fifty were treated with Yi Niao Ling Fang and their treatment response was compared against 46 whose problem was treated with imipramine: 98 per cent of those on Yi Niao Ling Fang showed clinical improvement, compared to 73 per cent of the imipramine group. The group allocation of cases was unclear as was the extent to which both groups were followed up. The paper reports on follow-up to 2 years for the treatment responders.

Several Japanese Kampo treatments are widely used but currently lack a clinical evidence base. The most commonly used treatments for night-time enuresis are Chibaku-Jiohu-Gan, Hachimi-Jiohu-Gan and Keishi-Ka-Ryukotsu-Borei.

In southern Africa, Buchu is commonly used for the treatment of night-time enuresis, but again an evidence base is currently lacking.

HOW LIKELY IS IT TO RESPOND TO TREATMENT?

Based on the extensive material reviewed above, there is good evidence that night-time enuresis can be successfully treated in the majority of cases. Mild night-time enuresis (when there are wet beds on two or fewer nights per week) has a high likelihood of resolving without any intervention. Chronic nightly enuresis is unlikely to resolve without specific treatment (Wright 2008). The likelihood of spontaneous resolution is very low where the problem occurs nightly and particularly where it persists after the age of 10 (Yeung *et al.* 2006). Intervention is particularly important where the problem is chronic and high frequency.

A subgroup of cases appears to gain little benefit from clinical treatment. These treatment-resistant cases are typically males with longstanding primary nocturnal enuresis (see Nappo *et al.* 2002). This subgroup would be a useful focus for future research on intervention.

REM sleep behaviour disorder (RSBD)

'The boy who fights with his dreams.'

'Tom' was 13 and had always been a restless sleeper. His parents were used to often finding his duvet in a heap across the room and Tom shivering, fast asleep, on the edge of his bed. He was often heard thrashing about as if he was fighting with something and he told them stories about his dreams in which he was usually being chased by wild animals through a dark forest.

WHAT IS REM SLEEP BEHAVIOUR DISORDER?

REM sleep behaviour disorder (RSBD) is a condition where the normal loss of muscle control seen during REM sleep does not occur and the affected individual exhibits complex motor behaviour while dreaming, acting as if the dream were real (see Boeve 2010; Olson, Boeve and Silber 2000; Paparrigopoulos 2005; Schenck and Mahowald 2002).

RSBD is typically a condition that affects elderly males; however, it has also been reported as affecting children with autism (Thirumalai, Shubin and Robinson 2002). These authors describe the characteristic features of RSBD in 5 of 12 patients assessed on polysomnography because of sleep disruption and nocturnal awakening. RSBD is often missed in clinical practice unless specific questions are asked about the nature of behavioural events during sleep (Frauscher *et al.* 2010).

The current diagnostic criteria require:

1. The presence of REM sleep without atonia on polysomnography (REM sleep on the EEG without loss of muscular control)

together with at least one of the following:

2. a) Sleep-related injurious, potentially injurious or disruptive behaviours elicited by history (consistent with acting out dream content)

or

   b) abnormal behaviour documented during REM sleep on polysomnography

and

3. a lack of epileptiform activity during REM sleep (unless RBD can be clearly distinguished from any concurrent REM sleep-related seizure disorder).

In addition

4. the problem cannot be better explained as another type of sleep disorder, a separate medical, neurological or mental disorder, an effect of medication or by a substance use disorder.

A number of helpful case examples describe the features of the condition in adults. A useful clinical description of the typical features of RSBD is given by Mattewal, Casturi and Subramanian (2010).

A clear adult case example is given in the paper 'The man who fought in sleep' (Budhiraja 2007). This paper describes a 60-year-old man with RSBD who could clearly describe having dreams in which he was fighting with animals or monsters. These episodes occurred during polysomnography corroborated REM sleep, and his concurrent behaviour consisted of kicking, punching and shouting at his partner.

RSBD has been well described in the literature as a consequence of damage to two specific brain areas – the pontine tegmentum and the medial medulla (see Iranzo and Aparicio 2009).

There is a clinical overlap between RSBD and narcolepsy. Around 50 per cent of narcoleptic cases show the same pattern of REM sleep muscle activity as is seen in RSBD (Dauvilliers *et al.* 2007).

HOW COMMON IS IT?

The prevalence of RSBD is unclear. The majority of cases reported to date are in the elderly, and most are male. The report of Thirumalai *et al.* (2002) suggests that the prevalence of RSBD in ASD children with disturbed sleep may be greater than had been previously realized.

DOES IT TEND TO GET BETTER IN ANY EVENT?

As until recently this condition had only been described in the elderly, the evolution of this condition with younger onset has not so far been described. The natural history of RSBD in such cases is currently unclear.

WHAT CAN BE DONE TO TREAT IT?

A best practice guide on treatment of REM sleep behaviour disorder has recently been published by the American Academy of Sleep Medicine (Aurora *et al.* 2010), and a review of pharmacological management appeared in 2006 (Gagnon, Postuma and Montplaisir 2006).

A wide range of conventional medications (acetylcholinesterase inhibitors such as zopiclone, rivastigmine, and donepezil; various benzodiazepines; carbamazepine; clozapine; desipramine; L-DOPA and sodium oxybate) and one Chinese herbal formula (Yi-Gan San) have been reported to be of benefit in small numbers of cases; however, the evidence base for these is limited. This is true for all except four: melatonin, clonazepam, pramipexole and paroxetine.

Melatonin

Melatonin has resulted in improvements in RSBD symptoms in over 81 per cent of cases. This is based on data on 38 cases across four trials, all in adults.

Clonazepam

Clonazepam has resulted in improvements in RSBD in over 91 per cent of cases, based on data on 339 cases across 22 trials, all in adults.

In one series of 57 adult cases treated with clonazepam from a consecutive series of 70 diagnosed with REM sleep behaviour disorder, a success rate of 89.5 per cent was claimed (Schenck and Mahowald 1990).

Pramipexole

Pramipexole, a dopamine agonist used in the treatment of Parkinson's disease, has resulted in improvements in RSBD in over 80 per cent of cases based on data on 29 cases across three trials, all in adults.

It has been recommended that medications that increase serotonergic activity, including some antidepressants, should be used cautiously (see Winkelman and James 2004). These can exacerbate movement during REM sleep and could cause a worsening of RSBD symptoms.

HOW LIKELY IS IT TO RESPOND TO TREATMENT?

No treatment trials on RSBD in children or in ASD have yet been published. A review of the effects of treatment, largely of effects in older adult cases, can be found in Boeve (2010).

Restless legs syndrome and periodic limb movements in sleep

'Fidgety Philip.'

'Oliver' is a 10-year-old boy who has a longstanding problem – he has always been described by his family as a restless sleeper. He is often found with his duvet in a pile on the floor in the morning. His parents have on several occasions gone into his room and found him with his legs jerking repeatedly in an odd way and have been worrying that he may have been in an epileptic fit. A recent sleep EEG managed to record while one of these episodes happened and there was no evidence of seizure activity.

WHAT ARE RESTLESS LEGS SYNDROME AND PERIODIC LIMB MOVEMENTS IN SLEEP?

Restless legs syndrome (RLS) and periodic limb movement disorder in sleep (PLMD) are differentiated conditions that are both characterized by abnormal leg movements that occur during sleep. In RLS the movements are said to be accompanied by disagreeable sensations, while in PLMD the characteristic pattern is of repetitive involuntary contractions of the lower limbs with no reported discomfort. The evidence from recent research is that the two conditions are closely related and the high prevalence of RLS in parents of children and adolescents with RLS or PLMD suggests that there may be a common underlying genetic basis (Picchietti *et al.* 2009).

A standardized scale, the Pediatric Restless Legs Syndrome Severity Scale (P-RLS-SS)©, has recently been developed for 6–18-year-olds, to capture a clear clinical picture of RLS (Arbuckle *et al.* 2010). A parallel parent questionnaire has been developed. It is intended as a clinically relevant research tool but could also be used for monitoring in individual cases.

Descriptions consistent with RLS can be dated back to Thomas Willis in 1672, but the credit for its description is usually given to Ekbom who published a well-articulated clinical description in 1945.

Both RLS and PLMD are described as being different from SRMD (see above). The extent to which these differences are clinically meaningful and result from different causes, or are merely differences in severity or presentation of the same clinical condition remains to be clearly established.

HOW COMMON ARE THEY?

In the general population, RLS has been reported to have a prevalence of 5.5 per cent and PLMD 3.9 per cent. This is based on a population survey across five European countries of a large sample of 18,980 subjects (Ohayon and Roth 2002). A large US–UK screening survey of over 10,000 children and adolescents with RLS reported lower rates with RLS in 1.9 per cent of 8–11-year-olds and 2 per cent in 12–17-year-olds (Picchietti *et al.* 2007). The US–UK survey used fairly conservative diagnostic criteria.

DO THEY TEND TO GET BETTER IN ANY EVENT?

The natural history of untreated RLS is that it is a lifelong disorder that can worsen with age but can also go through periods of complete remission. Adult cases report a 40 per cent rate of similar symptomology to those reported in childhood (Picchietti and Stevens 2008). No prospective studies on rate of remission have been published.

There is currently no information on the natural history of untreated PLMD.

WHAT CAN BE DONE TO TREAT THEM?

RLS tends to worsen when the person is sleep deprived. A first obvious step is to ensure that the person has a good sleep routine and that the factors discussed under sleep hygiene have been reviewed and made as good as possible.

A range of behavioural strategies has been recommended. These include avoidance of substances and medications that tend to exacerbate symptoms (these are primarily nicotine, caffeine and alcohol), engaging in mental alerting activities (computer games; crosswords, etc.), and using cognitive-behavioural strategies that are the same as those used in insomnia (Pigeon and Yurcheshen 2009; Silber *et al.* 2004). There is limited evidence at present to support the second and third of these as a research base is lacking.

PLMD can worsen when there is low serum ferritin, and can be exacerbated by both antidepressants and antihistamines. Iron levels should be checked and supplemented to achieve good normal levels if required.

One widely cited group (Simakajornboon *et al.* 2006) has reported consistently good effects in PLMD from supplementation with 3mg of elemental iron per day in children with <50mg per ml of iron, and that these improvements are maintained at least at 2-year follow-up.

Ropinirole is a dopamine agonist that gained generic status in 2008 when its patent expired. It is widely available and is approved by the FDA for the treatment of RLS. A recent systematic review (Erichsen *et al.* 2010) concluded that there is a substantial body of evidence supporting its safe and effective use in the management of both RLS and PLMD.

Other dopamine agonists such as rotigotine are being reported as producing good results in RLS (see e.g. Högl *et al.* 2010), strengthening the hypothesis that the primary problem is to do with dopaminergic function. Rotigotine has not been researched on people below the age of 18, but is showing good results in older groups (see Merlino *et al.* 2009).

The lack of a biological marker, and until recently the lack of clear agreed criteria for assessing dopamine augmentation, has hampered developments in this area (see Allen and Earley 1996; Garcia-Borreguero and Williams 2010).

In a small clinical series of seven cases, the use of dopamine agonists such as pergolide and the naturally occurring dopamine precursor L-DOPA (used in the medication Levopdopa) have been shown to be clinically beneficial in paediatric cases with RLS/PLMD who have comorbid ADHD and have responded poorly to stimulant medication (Walters *et al.* 2000).

Systematic reviews of pharmacological treatments of RLS have been produced (Pelayo and Dubik 2008; Trenkwalder *et al.* 2008): these papers review published studies up to 2006. Studies supportive of the use of levodopa, ropinirole, pramipexole, cabergoline, pergolide and gabapentin were identified.

A report on a 12-week RCT with 28 patients found that in contrast to the reports on its beneficial effects in PLMD, ferrous sulphate was ineffective in the management of RLS symptoms (Davis *et al.* 2000).

HOW LIKELY ARE THEY TO RESPOND TO TREATMENT?

Studies to date have been from a small number of centres and differences in efficacy are reported which may not be treatment specific. A large number of treatments, principally affecting the dopamine system, have some level of empirical support for their use. Some have good reported results with good long-term outcome, as with Simakajornboon *et al.*'s 2006 paper on 2-year follow-up on elemental iron in RLS.

There is a need for more systematic research on the role of non-pharmacological approaches other than iron supplementation and for clearer understanding of the mechanism/s underpinning RLS/PLMD.

In general, RLS and PLMD are lifelong conditions, which if untreated can have periods of remission but tends to worsen gradually over time. Current therapies can control the symptoms in most cases.

Conclusion

I hope that this book has provided an overview of many of the issues and complexities that need to be considered in understanding and sorting sleep difficulties for someone with an ASD.

Some sleep problems are simple, some are complex, some are common to ASD while others are not and there is a wide range of options and outcomes, some of which will require clinical help and supervision.

Some issues, such as poor sleep hygiene, respond to general interventions that are likely to be helpful in many cases. Many of the approaches we have discussed will help only for specific problems, and it is important to be clear about what problem needs to be addressed. This is why I have repeatedly stressed the importance of getting baseline information, being clear about the nature of interventions and monitoring outcome.

Sleep difficulties in ASD are problems for which the evidence base is growing rapidly and what is best practice can alter based on changing information. I hope that this short volume provides an up-to-date summary of best practice in late 2011, and will help people who need to work with these often confusing and perplexing problems.

Tables can be found in the appendices that summarize the various treatment approaches covered and their evidence base.

A table summarizing treatments of choice for each condition, overall success rate and any potential issues can be found on p.183–184.

Tables dealing with the principal sleep medications, uses and potential issues can be found on p.183–187.

Resources

Useful web material

Dement William C. (September 2008)
'TechTalk' lecture to Google, 'The Role of Sleep in Achieving Happiness at Google.' Available at www.sleepquest.com/sq_dement.shtml, accessed September 2011.

Associations and web resources

A large number of national and international associations are in existence. Contact details for some of the main groups are provided below.

World Sleep Federation: World Federation of Sleep Research and Sleep Medicine Societies
Website: www.wfsrsms.org/index.aspx

American Sleep Apnea Association
6856 Eastern Avenue, NW
Suite 203
Washington, DC 20012
USA
Tel: (202) 293-3650
Fax: (202) 293-3656
Website: www.sleepapnea.org

American Sleep Association
Website: www.sleepassociation.org/index.php

American Sleep Disorders Association (ASDA)
6301 Bandel Road
Suite 101
Rochester, MN 55901
USA
Tel: (507) 287-6006
Fax: (507) 287-6008
Email: asda@asda.org
Website: www.asda.org

Associated Professional Sleep Societies, LLC
2510 North Frontage Road
Darien, IL 60561
USA
Tel: (630) 737-9700
Fax: (630) 737-9789
Website: www.apss.org/default.aspx

British Sleep Society
PO Box 247
Colne
Huntingdon PE28 3UZ
UK
Email: enquiries@sleeping.org.uk
Website: www.neuronic.com/british.htm

British Snoring and Sleep Apnoea Association
Castle Court
41 London Road
Reigate
Surrey RH2 9RJ
UK
Tel: 01737 245638
Email: info@britishsnoring.co.uk
Website: www.britishsnoring.co.uk

Edinburgh Sleep Centre
13 Heriot Row
Edinburgh EH3 6HP
UK
Fax: 0131 524 9730
Website: www.edinburghsleepcentre.com

London Sleep Centre
137 Harley Street
London W1G 6BF
UK
Tel: 020 7725 0523
Email: info@londonsleepcentre.com
Website: www.londonsleepcentre.com

Enuresis Resource and Information Centre (ERIC)
34 Old School House
Britannia Road
Kingswood
Bristol BS15 8DB
UK
Helpline: 0845 370 8008 (10 am–4 pm weekdays)
Tel: 0845 370 8008
Email: info@eric.org.uk
Website: www.eric.org.uk

Kidzzzsleep
Pediatric Sleep Disorders Program
Rhode Island Hospital
593 Eddy Street
Providence, RI 02903
USA
Tel: (401) 444-1614
Fax: (401) 444-6218
Website: www.kidzzzsleep.org

Narcolepsy Association UK (UKAN)
PO Box 13842
Penicuik EH26 8WX
UK
Tel: 0845 4500 394
Email: info@narcolepsy.org.uk
Website: www.narcolepsy.org.uk

National Center on Sleep Disorders Research
National Heart, Lung, and Blood Institute, NIH
6701 Rockledge Drive
Bethesda, MD 20892
USA
Tel: (301) 435-0199
Fax: (301) 480-3451
Website: http://rover.nhlbi.nih.gov/about/ncsdr

National Foundation for Sleep and Related Disorders in Children (NFSRDC)
4200 W. Peterson
Suite 109
Chicago, IL 60646
Tel: (708) 971-1086
Fax: (312) 434-5311

National Sleep Foundation
1522 K Street, NW
Suite 500
Washington, DC 20005
Tel: (202) 347-3471
Fax: (202) 347-3472
Email: nsf@sleepfoundation.org
Website: www.sleepfoundation.org

Narcolepsy Network
110 Ripple Lane
North Kingstown, RI 02852
USA
Toll-Free: (888) 292-6522
Tel: (401) 667-2523
Fax: (401) 633-6567
Website: www.narcolepsynetwork.org

Restless Legs Syndrome Foundation
1610 14th St NW Rochester
Suite 300
Rochester, MN 55902
Tel: (507) 287-6465
Email: rlsfoundation@rls.org
Website: www.rls.org

Sleep Apnoea Trust
12A Bakers Place
Kingston
Oxfordshire OX39 4SW
UK
Tel: 0845 6060 685
Website: www.sleep-apnoea-trust.org

Sleep Matters Helpline
PO Box 3087
London W4 4ZP
UK
Tel: 020 8994 9874 (6 pm–8 pm daily)
Email: info@medicaladvisoryservice.org.uk
Website: www.medicaladvisoryservice.org.uk

Sleep Research Society
2510 North Frontage Road
Darien, IL 60561
USA
Tel: (630) 737-9702
Website: www.sleepresearchsociety.org

Sleep Scotland
8 Hope Park Square
Edinburgh EH8 9NW
UK
Tel: 0131 651 1392
Fax: 0131 651 1391
Website: www.sleepscotland.org

Stanford Sleep and Dreams
Website: www.end-your-sleep-deprivation.com/sleep-and-dreams.html

TEST AND TREATMENT MATERIALS

Melatonin testing

Testing for circadian differences in melatonin levels is not a routine part of clinical investigation in the UK or in many US clinics. Salivary testing is the easiest and least invasive method of assessment and can be obtained from Genova Diagnostics in Europe and North America.

Genova Diagnostics
63 Zillicoa Street
Asheville, NC 28801
USA
Tel: (800) 522-4762

Genova Diagnostics Europe Headquarters
Parkgate House
356 West Barnes Lane
New Malden
Surrey KT3 6NB
UK
Tel: 020 8336 7750

General products to aid with sleep

Light Therapy Products
5865 Neal Avenue North
Suite 153
Stillwater MN, Maryland 55082
USA
Website: www.lighttherapyproducts.com

This company markets a range of lighting products, and in addition it markets a variety of other products including sleep CDs, hypoallergenic bedding and blackout kits.

Devices to treat obstructive sleep apnoea

Various devices are available to keep the airway open during sleep and reduce/eliminate snoring. A representative range of companies offering such devices is as follows:

Ripsnore
PO Box 16283
City East, Brisbane
Q 4002
Australia
Tel: (0410) 843-498

PO Box 225065
San Francisco, CA 94122
USA
Tel: (415) 699-0264

PO Box 40025
Ottawa, ON K1V 0W8
Canada
Tel: (613) 355-6496

PO Box 64965
London SW19 9BL
UK
Tel: (779) 4489044

Website: www.ripsnore.com

SleepPro
MEDiTAS Ltd
PO Box 567
Winchester
Hampshire SO23 2HJ
UK
Tel: 01962 761 831
Website: www.sleeppro.com

Snorban
Snoring Relief Labs, Inc.
4007 Pretense Ct
Fair Oaks, CA 95628
USA
Tel: (916) 966-5026
Website: www.snorban.com

Snoremender
Sleep Well Enjoy Life Ltd
12 Station Road
Eckington
Sheffield S21 4FX
UK

TheraSnore
Distar UK Ltd
Manor Farm House
Main Street
Gamston
Nottingham NG2 6NN
UK
Tel: 0115 969 64 29
Website: www.thera-snore.co.uk

Enuresis alarms

Enuresis alarms are widely available and can be purchased for home use. A wide range of such alarms is now available.

Europe
Astric
Astric Medical
148 Lewes Road
Brighton
Sussex BN2 3LG
UK
Tel: 01273 608 319
Email: astricmed@aol.com

Drinite, Drinite Vibrawake, Rodger Wireless Bedwetting Alarm System
Dri-Nites
199 Aston Clinton Road
Aylesbury
Bucks HP22 5AD
UK
Tel: 01296 631118
Website: www.dri-nites.co.uk

Enurad
UK Electronic
Bultgatan 13B
S-442 40 KUNGALV
Sweden
Tel: (0)303 58400
Website: www.enurad.com

Malem
Malem Medical
10 Willow Holt
Lowdham
Nottingham NG14 7EJ
UK
Tel: 0115 966 4440
Website: www.malem.co.uk

Noppy Bed-Wetting Enuresis Alarm
Rehan Electronics Ltd
Brunswick Row
Aughrim Road
Carnew
County Wicklow
Eire
Tel: 3 53 9426742
Website: www.rehanelectronics.com

Petit Enuresis Alarm
Nottingham Rehab Supplies (NRS)
Clinitron House
Excelsior Road
Ashby de la Zouch
Leicestershire LE65 1JG
UK
Tel: 0845 121 8111
Website: www.nre-uk.co.uk/Products/3135/petit-enuresis-alarm.html

Various models are available from:
Living Made Easy
Disabled Living Foundation
380–384 Harrow Road
London W9 2HU
Tel: 0845 130 9177

North America
www.wetbuster.com/alarms.htm

DRI Sleeper
AMG Medical
8505 Dalton
Montreal, QC H4T 1V5
Canada
Tel: (514) 737-5251
Website: www.amgmedical.com

DryTime
Health Sense International Inc.
657 Newmark Avenue
PO Box 293
Coos Bay, OR 97420
USA
Tel: (800) 9422-3858

Nature Calls
Nature Calls Marketing Corp.
Box 7335
Saskatoon, SK S7K 4J2
Canada
Tel: 1-877-379-6377
Website: www.naturecalls.sk.ca

NiteTrain-r
Koregon Enterprises Inc.
9735 SW Sunshine Court
Suite 100
Beaverton, OR 97005
USA
Tel: (800) 544-4240
Website: www.nytone.com

Nytone
Nytone Inc.
2424 S. 900 W
S.L.C.
UT 84119
USA
Tel: (801) 973 4090
Website: www.nytone.com

Palco Wet-Stop3
Palco Laboratories
8030 Soquel Avenue
Santa Cruz, CA 95062
USA
Tel: (831) 476-0790
Website: www.wetstop.com

Potty Pager
Ideas for Living Inc.
1285 N. Cedarbrook Road
Boulder, CO 80394
USA
Tel: (800) 497-6573
Website: www.pottypager.com

Sleep Dry Alarm
Starchild Labs
PO Box 3497
57 Tierra Cielo Lane
Santa Barbara, CA 93105
USA
Tel: (805) 564-7194
Website: www.sleepdryalarm.com

Other areas

DRI Sleeper
Anzacare Ltd
120 Princess Drive
Nelson
New Zealand
Tel (US): (877) 331 2768
Tel (NZ): 64-3-5489655
Website: www.dri-sleeper.com

PandaWill Infant Bed-wetting Alarm
PandaWill
Room 405
Eastwing
Huamei Building
ZhenXing Road
518000
Shenzhen
Guandong
China
Tel: 0086 755 83650148
Website: www.pandawill.com/bed-wetting-enuresis-toddler-baby-urine-sensor-alarm-red-color_p34127.html

Epilepsy sensors

Night-time seizures are not uncommon and a number of commercial systems are now available, typically triggered by changes in movement or respiration that monitor nocturnal seizure activity.

Bedsior Monitor (P154); Advanced Bedside Monitor (P139)
Alert It
iTs Designs (Alert-it Alarms)
Atherstone House
Merry Lees Industrial Estate
Desford LE9 9FE

UK
Tel: 0845 217 9951
Website: www.alert-it.co.uk

Emfit Nocturnal Tonic-Clonic Seizure Monitor

In Europe
Emfit Ltd
Konttisentie 8 B
Vaajakoski Finland
FI-40800
Tel: 358 14 332 9000
Website: www.emfit.com

In the USA
Emfit Corp.
PO Box 342394
Austin, TX 78734
USA
Tel: (512) 266-6950
Website: www.emfit.com

MedPage (various models)
Easylink UK
3 Melbourne House
Corby Gate Business Park
Priors Haw Road
Corby
Northants NN17 5JG
UK
Tel: 01536 264869
Website: www.easylinkuk.co.uk

The Sensalert EP200 Epilepsy Monitor
Sensorium Ltd
9 Netherton Broad Street
Dunfermline
Fife KY12 7DS
UK
Tel: 01383 720600
Website: www.sensorium.co.uk

MEDICATIONS USED IN SLEEP DISORDERS

This appendix provides information on the medications that are most commonly reported as being or having been prescribed in the management of sleep disorders. Recommendations on the use of medication can change over time and vary from country to country.

Appropriate advice on prescription medication should always be sought from a suitably qualified medical practitioner.

Medications have been extensively used in the management of sleep problems at least since the reported use of juniper berries, cyprus and beer to treat bedwetting by physicians in the Akkadian Empire over 4000 years ago. This early practice was noted in the Ebers papyrus around 1550 BC. Opium was reportedly used to aid sleep in Egypt around 1300 BC.

In more recent times a wide range of medications has been used in the management of sleep disturbances (Table App 1.1) (for general reviews, see Pagel and Parnes 2001; Reed and Findling 2002; Siriwardena *et al.* 2008; for ASD, see Attarian 2010; Johnson and Malow 2008c). The British Association of Psychopharmacology recently released a consensus statement on evidence-based treatment for sleep problems (Wilson *et al.* 2010).

TABLE APP 1.1 SUMMARY TABLE OF APPROACHES TO SPECFIC SLEEP DISORDERS

SLEEP DISORDER	Treatments of choice	Key evidence	Reported success rate for treatment	Possible issues
Difficulty settling to sleep and frequent night waking	Behavioural	Multiple studies, see: Moore, Meltzer and Mindell 2008; Ivanenko and Patwari 2009	70%	None
Insomnia	Behavioural and cognitive – behavioural and medication	Espie and Kyle 2009	70%+	None
Short night-time sleep	Behavioural	O'Reilly 1995; Piazza and Fisher 1991	Evidence base too small to compute	None
Excessive night-time sleep	Modafinil	Ali et al. 2009	88% (one study only)	Recent restrictions on use
Excessive daytime sleepiness/ tiredness	Modafinil	Ivanenko 2003	Modest benefits in all (one small study)	Exacerbation of seizures and psychotic symptoms Recent restrictions on use
Nightmares	Imagery rehearsal; desensitization; relaxation and prazosin	Krakow et al. (2001a,b); Lancee et al. 2008a	Most studies with traumatic onset nightmares	Lack of maintained improvement with prazosin alone
Night terrors	Night waking and resettling; benzodiazepines; melatonin	Lask 1988; Popoviciu and Corfariu 1983; Jan et al. 2004	High spontaneous resolution rate; no RCTs	Uncertain due to limited evidence base
Night-time eating disorders	Sertraline; topiramate	O'Reardon et al. 2006; Stunkard et al. 2006	71%	Topiramate most effective but with a high rate of side effects
Nocturnal seizures	Medication – type dependent on diagnosis	Bazil 2003	No reliable data	Dependent on medication of choice
Sleep-related rhythmic movement disorder		Picchietti and Picchietti 2008	Self-remitting in most cases	No relevant safety data on ropinirole
Sleep bruxism	Orodental; behavioural; clonidine	Huynh et al. 2006; Huynh et al. 2007	Unclear	MADs can cause physical discomfort; clonidine can cause REM suppression and low morning BP

TABLE APP 1.1 CONT.

SLEEP DISORDER	Treatments of choice	Key evidence	Reported success rate for treatment	Possible issues
Obstructive sleep apnoea	Weight reduction; improved fitness; CPAP	Capdevila et al. 2008; Halbower 2008	80%+	Discomfort from CPAP and prostheses; general risks from surgery
Narcolepsy	Improved sleep hygiene coupled with medication (modafinil, sodium oxybate, venlafaxine or psychostimulants)	Kothare and Kaleyis 2008; Aran et al. 2010	70%	SSRIs have significant side-effects but are not first choice for management
Nocturnal enuresis	DDAVP; enuresis alarm; behavioural	Evans 2001a, 2001b; Wright 2008; Lyon and Schnall 2010	79%	Results with DDAVP do not generalize
REM sleep behaviour disorder	Melatonin; clonazepam; pramipexole; Yi-Gan San	Gagnon et al. 2006; Aurora et al. 2010	No studies in relevant populations	Variable dependent on treatment of choice; see reviews
Restless legs syndrome and periodic limb movements in sleep	Improved sleep hygiene; iron supplementation	Trenkwalder et al. 2008	There are no long-term outcome data on RLS or PLMD	As for SRMD: no relevant safety data on ropinirole

Appendix 1.1 provides a brief summary of the evidence on approaches to specific sleep problems, their likely success rate and any possible issues with the best-choice strategy.

TABLE APP 1.2 THE MAIN MEDICATIONS USED IN SLEEP PROBLEMS AND THEIR US AND UK PRODUCT NAMES

Medication	US product name/s	UK product name/s
Alimemazine tartrate aka trimeprazine tartrate		Vallergan; Vallergan-Forte
Aripiprazole	Abilify; Abilify discmelt	Abilify
Clonidine hydrochloride	Catapres; Dixarit	Catapres; Dixarit
Chloral hydrate		Welldorm
Desmopressin acetate	DDAVP; Stimate; Minurin	DDAVP; DDAVPMelt; DesmoMelt; Desmospray; Desmotabs; Octim
Diphenhydramine	Benadryl, Tylenol PM	Benadryl, Nytol

TABLE APP 1.2 CONT.

Medication	US product name/s	UK product name/s
Fluoxetine	Prozac	Prozac
Hydroxyzine	Vistaril	Atarax; Ucerax
Melatonin	Generic (multiple brands)	Circadin
Mianserin	Bolvidon; Depnon; Norval; Tolvon	Bolvidon; Norval; Tolvon
Modafinil	Provigil	Provigil
Prazosin	Minipress; Vasoflex; Pressin; Hypovase	Hypovase
Ramelteon	Rozerem	
Risperidone	Risperdal	Risperdal
Sodium oxybate		Xyrem
Triclofos		Discontinued May 2010

TABLE APP 1.3 THE MAIN MEDICATIONS WITH THEIR PRIMARY USES, KEY REFERENCES AND POSSIBLE ISSUES

Medication	Primary use in sleep problems	General studies on its use	Possible issues
Alimemazine tartrate aka trimeprazine tartrate	Night waking	Simonoff and Stores 1987	Cardiac instability; respiratory depression
Aripiprazole	To induce tiredness	Greenaway and Elbe 2009	Weight gain, extrapyramidal symptoms, akathisia, sedation, headache, nausea
Clonidine hydrochloride	To induce tiredness	Ming, Gordon *et al.* 2008	Clonidine can have effects on blood pressure being capable of causing both hypotension and hypertension
Chloral hydrate	To induce tiredness	Gauillard *et al.* 2002	Digestive problems, cardiac arrythmias, dermatologic reactions, withdrawal, hallucinations, delusions, dependency, visual disturbances
Desmopressin acetate	For bedwetting	Van de Walle *et al.* 2010	Hyponatraemia
Diphenhydramine	To induce tiredness	Use for sleep problems is off-label and there are no published studies on its use	Can have paradoxical effects in infants from excitation to seizures and death

TABLE APP 1.3 CONT.

Medication	Primary use in sleep problems	General studies on its use	Possible issues
Fluoxetine	Has been used to treat isolated sleep paralysis. More commonly a cause of sleep problems	Olivier *et al.* 2011; Hoque and Chesson 2010	Cessation can induce RLS and PLMS
Hydroxyzine	Insomnia	Primarily used for control of anxiety and as an antihistamine. Use for sleep problems is off-label and there are no published studies on its use	Daytime drowsiness; paradoxical hyperactivity; cardiac toxicity in excess
Melatonin	Improves getting to sleep	Turk 2003; Buscemi *et al.* 2006; Wirojanan *et al.* 2009	Few reported side-effects (Buscemi *et al.* 2006)
Mianserin (replaced clinically by mirtazapine)	Night-time enuresis	Smellie *et al.* 1996	Poorer response than alternatives such as desmopressin
Modafinil	Narcolepsy; EDS and associated memory and attentional problems	Schwartz *et al.* 2003; Baranski *et al.* 2004; Muller *et al.* 2004	Concerns raised over child and adolescent use by the Federal Drug Administration's Psychopharmacologic Drugs Advisory Committee because of case reports of Stevens-Johnson syndrome
Prazosin	Nightmares and other sleep effects of PTSD	Raskind *et al.* 2003; Krystal and Davidson 2007; Raskind *et al.* 2007; Taylor *et al.* 2008	Currently used only for hypertension in children – lowers blood pressure
Ramelteon	As for melatonin	Stigler, Posey and McDougle 2006	Hyperprolactinaemia
Risperidone	To induce tiredness	FDA approved for treatment of irritability in ASD. Use for sleep problems is off-label and there are no published studies on its use	Tiredness and weight gain are the main reasons for discontinuing
Sodium oxybate	Treatment of narcolepsy	FDA approved for the management of narcolepsy-cataplexy	Physical dependence; psychosis, seizures and suicidal ideation on withdrawal
Triclofos	No longer in use	No longer in use	Headache, confusion, nightmares, GI problems

TABLE APP 1.4 EVIDENCE SUMMARY TABLE OF NON-PHARMACOLOGICAL APPROACHES

Approach	Strength of evidence base	Used for	Availability	Contraindications
Acupuncture	Weak	No specific studies on use for sleep. Some reported improvements in people treated for other issues. There is one child study on use in cerebral palsy	Variable	None reported
Aromatherapy	Weak	One good feasibility study on its use. Nothing on clinical benefit	Widely available	Pregnancy, hypertension, thrombosis
Behavioural approaches	Good	See information on specific sleep problems	Widely available	None reported
Biofeedback	Good for nocturnal enuresis; limited for other conditions	Nocturnal enuresis; nocturnal seizures; insomnia	Limited	None reported
Buchu	Anecdotal	Nocturnal enuresis	Limited	Unclear
Chinese herbal	No RCT evidence	Insomnia, nocturnal enuresis, night terrors	Widely available	See information on specific herbs and sleep problems
Chiropractics	Limited	Single case studies on 'sleep problems'. One clinical trial on nocturnal enuresis. One single case study in ASD	Widely available	None reported
Cognitive-behavioural approaches	Good	Insomnia	Widely available	None reported
Dietary interventions	Weak	Secondary evidence of beneficial effects in treatment for other reasons – ADHD, ASD	Widely available	See: Aitken 2008

TABLE APP 1.4 CONT.

Approach	Strength of evidence base	Used for	Availability	Contraindications
Exercise	Limited	Insomnia RCT (adult), snoring RCT (child)	Widely	None reported
Homeopathy	Limited – one RCT	Insomnia	Widely available	Pregnancy
Hypnosis	Fair but no RCT data	Insomnia and parasomnias	Variable	Psychosis, schizophrenia, epilepsy, depression
Japanese Kampo herbal medicine	Limited	Nocturnal enuresis, insomnia, night sweats	Limited outside of Japan	See information on specific herbs and combinations
Light therapy	Good	Sleep phase syndromes	Variable	None reported
Massage	Fair	Settling to sleep	Widely available	None
Meditation	Limited	Difficulty with getting to sleep	Widely available	None reported
Traditional Mexican herbal treatments	Anecdotal	'Sleep problems'	Limited outside North America	Not known
Prescription medications	Good	See information above and sections on specific sleep problems	Widely available	Varies dependent on medication
Psychotherapy (analytic)	Limited	Unclear	Limited	Not used for this purpose
Relaxation	Fair	Insomnia and as part of a combined approach for most other sleep difficulties	Widely available	None reported
'Western' herbal treatments	Variable	Better evidence for stimulant herbs on tiredness than sedative herbs for insomnia but some support for both	Widely available: largely unregulated	See information on specific herbs
Yoga	Limited	Improved sleep quality	Widely available	None

In one survey of sleep problems in 59 children with ASD (Souders *et al.* 2009) 37.3 per cent of the sample (22) were on sleep medications. Most (18) were taking a single sleep medication. The treatments in use, in order of prevalence, were as follows (numbers of cases in brackets): melatonin (15); risperidone (4); catapres (3); aripiprazole (2); hydroxyzine (1); fluoxetine (1).

WHAT ARE THESE MEDICATIONS AND HOW DO THEY WORK?
Alimemazine tartrate

Alimemazine tartrate is an antihistamine. It is normally used for the treatment of allergies. A well-reported side-effect of its use with allergies was that it caused drowsiness. This effect has been capitalized on by some clinicians working with sleep disorders. It has been extensively used in paediatric sleep disorders for many years.

There is no systematic research on its use in ASD.

Aripiprazole

Aripiprazole is not commonly used in the treatment of sleep problems. It is an atypical antipsychotic and antidepressant medication used in the treatment of a number of conditions such as schizophrenia, depression and bipolar disorder.

It has been shown to have some benefit in the management of irritability in autism (see Marcus *et al.* 2009; Owen *et al.* 2009). In the US it was approved in November 2009 specifically for this use in autism in 6–17-year-olds.

It is sometimes used in the management of insomnia because of its common effect of inducing drowsiness; however, there are concerns over the high rate of side-effects such as pyramidal movement problems (seen in over 20% of reported cases to date) and weight gain (typically c. 1.5kg) in adults.

There is some evidence of poorer general treatment response to aripiprazole for sleep problems in ASD (Valicenti-McDermott and Demb 2006). Recent preliminary research suggests that this medication may be useful in addressing irritability in ASD (see Erickson *et al.* 2010).

Catapres (clonidine hydrochloride)

Catapres is an alpha-2 adrenergic agonist. It reduces blood pressure and slows heart rate. In animal models it has been shown to reduce ADHD symptomology. It is used by some clinicians in the treatment of a variety of conditions including ADHD (for which it is an 'off-label' use).

In one open trial with 19 children aged 4–16 with ASD the results showed improvements in 'sleep initiation latency and night awakening' with lesser effects on 'attention deficits, hyperactivity, mood instability and aggressiveness' (Ming, Gordon *et al.* 2008).

Chloral hydrate

Chloral hydrate is a sedative hypnotic that was first synthesized in the early nineteenth century. The first report of its use for sedation was in 1869 (Liebreich 1869).

It has a range of side-effects, one of which is that it is relatively easy to overdose on. Consequently it has largely fallen out of use (see Gauillard *et al.* 2002).

There is no systematic research on its use in ASD.

Clomipramine

Clomipramine is a tricyclic (the term indicates that it is a heterocyclic compound that includes three interconnected rings of atoms). It has been used for the treatment of nocturnal enuresis. In a study of 29 boys aged 5–14 allocated to imipramine, clomipramine or alarm treatment, changes in nights wet over 15 days were as follows from baseline to follow-up (weeks 6–8 of treatment): imipramine 9.1 > 4.1; clomipramine 11.2 > 6.6; alarm treatment 10.9 > 2.8 (Motavalli *et al.* 1994). Clomipramine was the least successful of the three approaches, but all three showed significant improvements.

No specific clomipramine treatment trials with sleep disorders in ASD have so far been published.

There appears to be a relatively high rate of side-effects experienced by individuals with ASD who have been treated with clomipramine for other indications. One double-blinded RCT study compared haloperidol to clomipramine in the treatment of stereotypy (Remington *et al.* 2001). Of the 36 ASD subjects in the trial (aged 10–36, mean age 16.3 years) only 37.5 per cent of the clomipramine group were able to complete the trial due to unacceptable levels of side-effects from medication, as compared to 69.7 per cent of the haloperidol group.

Desipramine

Desipramine is a tricyclic that has been used for the treatment of nocturnal enuresis. An early double-blinded RCT (Liederman, Wasserman and Liederman 1969) of desipramine with 38 females and 71 males aged 6 to 22 years found that 12/53 were dry on active treatment compared to 3/47 controls when followed up at 2 months.

No specific desipramine treatment trials with sleep disorders in ASD have so far been published.

Desmopressin acetate

Desmopressin is used as a short-term treatment approach with bedwetting. It has a direct action on kidney function, acting to reduce the volume of urine produced.

Desmopressin is a synthetic molecule that is very similar in structure and mode of action to vasopressin. Vasopressin is a diuretic hormone that naturally controls the reabsorption of compounds by the tubules of the kidney, controlling the output of urine.

It is also used in the treatment of diabetes insipidus (overproduction of urine), in the management of certain blood disorders including mild or moderate haemophilia, and to help rebalance physiology after surgical removal of the pituitary gland.

A useful recent review of safety issues with desmopressin can be found in Van de Walle *et al.* (2007). It has been found that desmopressin can cause hypernatraemia in the elderly but it seems largely well tolerated as a short-term treatment for persistent nocturnal enuresis in the paediatric age range.

There is no systematic research on the use of desmopressin in the management of night-time enuresis in ASD.

Diphenhydramine

Diphenhydramine was one of the earliest antihistamines (medications that block the binding of histamines – nitrogen-based compounds that are involved in inflammatory allergic responses) to be identified. It is primarily used in the treatment of allergies. Because it also acts as a powerful hypnotic, it has been used as a sleep medication. This medication is not widely used today because of its side-effect profile.

Diphenhydramine is addictive and has been taken as a drug of abuse (Thomas *et al.* 2009). Extreme paradoxical reactions, including fatality, have been reported in infants (Baker *et al.* 2003).

There is no systematic research on the use of diphenhydramine in the management of insomnia in ASD.

Fluoxetine

Fluoxetine is a selective serotonin reuptake inhibitor (SSRI) (it inhibits the reabsorption of serotonin by a neuron that has fired, released serotonin into the post synaptic cleft, freeing more serotonin to be taken up by the next nerve in the pathway).

Fluoxetine has a limited evidence base for its use in sleep disorders. It has been used as a treatment for a number of sleep issues including obstructive sleep apnoea (Hanzel, Proia and Hudgel 1991) and sleep-related eating disorders (Schenck *et al.* 1993). In one small study of its effects on sleep in adult depression, it was shown to have a worsening effect on sleep pattern – reducing REM sleep and increasing night wakenings (Armitage *et al.* 1997).

It has been used in two RCTs in the treatment of autism. A recent Cochrane review concluded as follows: 'There is no evidence of effect of SSRIs in children and emerging evidence of harm' (Williams *et al.* 2010, p.2).

There is no basis on which to conclude that it might be selectively beneficial in people with ASD.

Hydroxyzine

Hydroxyzine is an antihistamine first developed in the mid-1950s. It is used in the treatment of depression, neuroses, anxiety and insomnia.

There have been no specific studies on its use in the treatment of sleep problems in ASD.

Imipramine

Imipramine has been the most widely used tricyclic in the treatment of nocturnal enuresis. Imipramine is associated with around twice the rate of adverse reactions when compared to other tricyclics and sudden cardiac arrest is a recognized serious adverse reaction (Müller, Roehr and Eggert 2004).

One study reported on the use of imipramine in a group of 49 treatment resistant cases that had failed to respond to demopressin, anticholinergic treatments or alarms. 31 (64.6%) showed clinical improvement and 22 (45%) became completely dry (Gepertz and Nevéus 2004). Ten of the children experienced minor side-effects such as nausea.

A recent study (Zadeh, Moslemi and Zadeh 2010) carried out a randomized prospective trial of imipramine compared against imipramine plus pseudoephedrine in 100 5–12-year-old children with uncomplicated night-time enuresis. One month after cessation of treatment, 52 per cent of the imipramine alone group and 74 per cent of the combined group were classified as improved. Only limited conclusions can be drawn as enrolment was on the basis of >2 wet beds per week and improvement was <2 wet beds per week.

Taken in excess, normally a young child ingesting a bottle of tablets, imipramine can cause convulsions, damage to the heart muscle, and in extreme cases death. Parkin and Fraser described 31 paediatric deaths from overdose between 1962 and 1969 (Parkin and Fraser 1972).

There has been only one open-label study that has reported on the effects of imipramine in ASD (Campbell et al. 1971). An 'open-label' study is one in which all parties are aware of the treatment being given as the study is going on. As this may affect the results, it is a less stringent assessment than a blinded study in which no one is aware of who is given the active treatment being trialled until after the study has finished. This was not a study on effects on sleep but an exploratory study because imipramine shows 'a mixture of stimulating, tranquilizing and disorganizing effects'. The paper reported that three improved markedly, three improved slightly and five deteriorated.

There have been no specific studies on its use in the treatment of night-time enuretic problems in ASD.

Melatonin

Melatonin is a chronobiotic compound naturally produced in the human pineal gland. It plays a number of important roles in biological development (Davis 1997).

Normally a large amount of melatonin is released into the circulation shortly before sleep, typically as light levels diminish (Lewy 2007). Chemically it is the same compound as the skin pigment melanin. In tablet form it can be taken orally and has been extensively studied in improving sleep quality in adult shift workers and in the treatment of jet lag. There is a limited literature on its use in the treatment of sleep problems in ASD; however, the published literature to date suggests that it is effective and well tolerated in both children and adults (Carr *et al.* 2007; Galli-Carminati, Deriaz and Bertschy 2009; Wirojanan *et al.* 2009).

There can be individuals in whom abnormalities of the liver cytochrome P450 enzyme CYP1A2 results in loss of response to exogenous melatonin treatment. In these cases, clearance testing should be carried out and lower dose supplementation considered if initial response has been favourable (Braam, van Geijlswijk *et al.* 2010).

There is some evidence to suggest that in young adults with sleep problems, learning disability and challenging behaviour, improvements in sleep through the use of melatonin leads to improvements in daytime challenging behaviour (Braam, Didden *et al.* 2010).

A recent meta-analysis of the literature on efficacy of melatonin in management of sleep problems in individuals with learning disability reviewed 9 trials on 183 individuals in all (Braam *et al.* 2009). The review found that sleep latency decreased by an average of 24 minutes, total sleep duration increased by an average of 50 minutes and that there was a significant reduction in the number of night-time wakenings.

Melatonin is widely used as an over-the-counter supplement in the USA, taken primarily for sleep problems such as those caused by jet lag and shift work. In a US survey of over 31,000 adults, 5.2 per cent were found to use melatonin (Bliwise and Ansari 2007).

There is a limited literature on its use in the treatment of sleep problems in ASD; however, the published literature to date suggests that it is effective and well tolerated in both children and adults (Galli-Carminati *et al.* 2009; Paavonen *et al.* 2003; Wirojanan *et al.* 2009).

One open-label trial of controlled-release melatonin in 25 autistic children aged 2.6 to 9.6 years reported good results that were maintained at 1–2-year follow-up with no reports of significant side-effects (Giannotti *et al.* 2008).

In a recent RCT in behaviour management resistant sleep problems in ASD, for the 17 who completed the trial, both sleep latency and sleep duration were significantly better during melatonin administration than during the placebo phase of the trial (Wright *et al.* 2010). Significant questions remain, particularly around safety of longer-term melatonin use (Guenole and Baleyte 2010), and around metabolic differences that can lead to attenuating treatment response (Braam, van Geijlswijk *et al.* 2010).

There has been a recent large-scale RCT of melatonin in the treatment of sleep disorder in neurodevelopmental disorders at Alder Hey Hospital under Dr Peter Appleton that completed data collection in November 2010 (International Standard Randomised Controlled Trial Number Register N05534585). The results of this study are not available at the time of writing.

Mianserin

Mianserin is a quadricyclic that has been used in the treatment of nocturnal enuresis.

In one early double-blinded randomized comparison trial in 80 5–13-year-old enuretics, 65 boys and 15 girls, imipramine was compared against mianserin and placebo (Smellie *et al.* 1996). Over an 8-week trial, imipramine produced clinical improvement in 88 per cent (22/25), mianserin in 58 per cent (15/26), while 38 per cent (11/29) of the placebo group also improved. The authors concluded that 'Mianserin would not be a satisfactory alternative treatment for nocturnal enuresis' (p.62).

There have been no specific studies on its use in the treatment of night-time enuretic problems in ASD.

Modafinil

Modafinil is a CNS stimulant. Modafinil and its mirror isomer or enantiomer (a non-identical mirror opposite molecule) armodafinil are approved in the US by the Food and Drug Administration (FDA) for the treatment of a number of sleep disorders: narcolepsy, shift work sleep disorder and EDS associated with OSA. In Europe modafinil is currently approved for the treatment of narcolepsy. Detailed reviews of the evidence base for its use can be found in Schwartz (2008) and Kumar (2008).

Its precise mode of action remains unclear. Although it has been shown to have positive effects in ADHD (Biederman and Pliszka 2008), it has not been FDA approved for this use due to a number of reported cases of Stevens-Johnson syndrome (a toxic and potentially fatal skin reaction) (12 cases were reported out of 933 treated with modafinil across 12 trials).

In a detailed research trial, Baranski *et al.* (2004) demonstrated improvements in fatigue, motivation, reaction time and vigilance in a group of 18 healthy adults. Muller *et al.* (2004) studied effects on working memory in 16 healthy adults, finding that modafinil significantly reduced error rates on working-memory-intensive numerical tasks.

A number of studies have demonstrated that modafinil combined with CPAP, when this is used to control OSA, significantly reduces daytime sleepiness compared to CPAP used alone (see, e.g. Pack *et al.* 2001; Schwartz *et al.* 2003).

In the treatment of excessive daytime sleepiness in children, Ivanenko, Tauman and Gozal (2003) carried out a chart review of 13 children where it was used as the sole treatment for EDS in association with narcolepsy or idiopathic hypersomnia. One child failed to show improvement and two were switched to other medications due to limited improvement; the other ten showed significant improvements in EDS symptoms. At the time of review the mean duration of modafinil use was 15.6 months. The authors' conclusion was that 'Modafinil has a modest, yet significant effect on EDS in children and appears to be safe and well tolerated' (p.79).

A recent RCT showed good results in the treatment of ADHD symptomology in a group of 46 children aged 6–15 years followed up for 42 days (Kahbazi *et al.* 2009).

As sleep problems are a common issue resulting from the use of stimulant medication in the ASD population to treat ADHD symptomology (Nickels *et al.* 2008), treatments which have a positive impact on both may prove to be of greater selective benefit in this population.

In a further recent prospective RCT, it was shown to be effective in the management of EDT but not fatigue caused by traumatic brain injury in a group of 20 adult cases (Kaiser *et al.* 2010).

Nortriptyline

Nortriptyline is a tricyclic that has been used in the treatment of nocturnal enuresis but is no longer widely used.

The only controlled trial that has compared imipramine to nortriptyline or placebo studied 253 boys with primary enuresis. This study found no difference in outcome between the imipramine and nortriptyline groups (Forsythe and Merrett 1969).

There have been no published trials or case series on the use of nortriptyline in the treatment of sleep problems in ASD.

Prazosin

Prazosin is an alpha-1 receptor adrenergic blocking agent that is used primarily to control blood pressure.

It has been found to be effective in the management of nightmares brought on in PTSD (Krystal and Davidson 2007; Raskind *et al.* 2003, 2007).

In non-combat PTSD in adults, it has been shown that in addition to reducing nightmares, it affects a range of other sleep parameters including increasing duration of both overall and REM sleep (Taylor *et al.* 2008).

There have been no published trials or case series on its use in the treatment of sleep problems either in children or in ASD.

Ramelteon

Ramelteon is a synthetic melatonin analogue that binds to melatonin receptors in the suprachiasmatic nucleus thus promoting sleep onset. It received FDA approval for use in primary insomnia in 2005.

To date there is only a single study on its use in ASD. This study, on two cases, reported beneficial effects. This was a report on two boys aged 7 and 18 with autism and significant difficulties with sleep onset and night waking (Stigler *et al.* 2006). In both cases, sleep onset was earlier, night waking reduced and there was no evidence of daytime drowsiness.

Risperidone

Risperidone is an atypical antipsychotic that has effects on both dopamine D2 receptor pathways and several of the serotonin receptor systems. It has been approved for use in the USA in the management of persistent irritability and challenging behaviour since 2006. There is an emerging literature on its use in related conditions such as Tourette syndrome (Arana-Lechuga *et al.* 2008).

In ASD, risperidone is typically used in the management of aggression, impulsivity and stereotypies, and increasing tiredness and weight gain are the principal reasons for discontinuation (Lemmon, Gregas and Jeste 2010).

Risperidone is sometimes used to induce tiredness in children with ASD who have persistent sleep difficulties. In one study of 23 children with ASD and Down's syndrome, 88 per cent of the 16 with pre-existing sleep problems showed significant improvement in their sleeping pattern after treatment with risperidone (Capone *et al.* 2008).

Secretin

Secretin is an endogenous polypeptide that triggers pancreatic function and digestion in the lower bowel (for discussion, see Aitken 2008).

One open study reported that secretin reduced night-time waking in ASD (SARC 2001).

There has been only one RCT (Honomichl *et al.* 2002b) using the Child Sleep Habits Questionnaire with accompanying sleep diaries or time-lapse video-recording of sleep, the subjects being enrolled from two separate ongoing trials. This study examined the effect of secretin on sleep pattern in children with ASD, but failed to demonstrate any effect from treatment.

Sodium oxybate

Sodium oxybate (also known as gamma hydroxybutyric acid (GHB)) is a medication recently licensed in Europe for the treatment of narcolepsy, and is the only medication that shows positive effects on a range of narcoleptic symptomology. It has been used 'off-label' (prescribing of medicine that is not FDA approved for such use) for childhood narcolepsy-cataplexy in the USA (Murali and Kotagal 2006) and appears to be as effective in paediatric as in adult cases (Aran *et al.* 2010).

Sodium oxybate has been submitted for FDA approval in the US for the treatment of fibromyalgia.

Some concerns have been voiced over suicidal ideation, and there has been a recent clinical report on a 53-year-old man (Ortega-Albás *et al.* 2010). Acute withdrawal has been reported to result in psychotic symptoms with aggression and physical complications (see, e.g. Veerman, Dijkstra and Liefting-Kluft 2010; Wojtowicz, Yarema and Wax 2008). Sodium oxybate has been a drug of abuse in the USA since around 1990, and has been reported to induce coma and seizures and to foster physical dependency (Galloway *et al.* 1997).

There have been no specific studies on the use of sodium oxybate in the treatment of sleep problems in ASD.

Triclofos

Triclofos is a medication that was used in the treatment of resistant insomnia. It was withdrawn in May 2010 because of various problems including dependency and the fact that persistent use could lead to liver damage.

There have been no published studies on its use in the treatment of sleep problems in ASD.

Viloxazine

This is a tricyclic that has been used for the treatment of nocturnal enuresis.

A double-blind RCT compared viloxazine against imipramine and placebo in 22 girls and 11 boys aged 5 to 13 (Attenburrow, Stanley and Holland 1984). At follow-up, the mean number of dry nights per week was 4.1, 2.8 and 1.3 in the three groups indicating that viloxazine appeared more successful than imipramine. It also produced significantly fewer reported side-effects.

One further RCT of 37 boys aged over 6 compared viloxazine against imipramine but reported no significant difference in outcome (Yurdakok *et al.* 1987).

There have been no specific studies on the use of viloxazine in the treatment of night-time enuresis in ASD.

In the USA a high proportion of those presenting with paediatric sleeping difficulties are given prescription medication. Much is 'off-label' (see Stojanovski *et al.* 2007).

A number of medications are in development as treatments for sleep disorders:

- *Gaboxadol* is a direct GABA-A agonist (Wafford and Ebert 2006) that is anxiolytic and enhances slow-wave sleep.

- *Pregabalin*, another GABA agonist (Dworkin and Kirkpatrick 2005), is an anticonvulsant that modifies calcium channel activity. It has been found to have significant effects on the sleep–wake cycle. In contrast to benzodiazepines, it seems to enhance slow-wave sleep, and could be particularly useful where there is a comorbid problem with anxiety (Hindmarch, Dawson and Stanley 2005).

FURTHER GENERAL SOURCES OF INFORMATION ON MEDICATION

MedlinePlus
www.nlm.nih.gov/medlineplus/druginformation.html

Drugs.com
www.drugs.com

WebMD USA
www.webmd.com/drugs

WebMD UK
http://drugs.webmd.boots.com/drugs

emc+
www.medicines.org.uk/emc

COMPLEMENTARY AND ALTERNATIVE TREATMENT APPROACHES

A wide range of approaches, that have come to be known as complementary and alternative treatments (or CAMs), are frequently advocated for sleep problems. The evidence base for the approaches discussed here is extremely variable. Various forms of acupuncture; aromatherapy; chiropractics; dietary interventions; exercise and herbal supplements have all been recommended.

Reviews of this area can be found in Oken 2004 (see, in particular: Chapter. 22 by Ernst on CAMs for insomnia; Chapter 23 by Meoli on snoring and OSA; and Chapter 24 by Nickel on CAM use by families whose children have disabilities).

For general information on CAM treatments, see:

The National Center for Complementary and Alternative Medicine
http://nccam.nih.gov

ACUPUNCTURE

There is a limited literature on acupuncture which has looked at its use as a treatment for sleep disorders. A Cochrane review of the evidence for acupuncture in insomnia concluded that it was largely ineffective (Cheuk *et al.* 2007).

In published reviews of the effects of acupuncture, however, beneficial effects on sleep have been noted in a number of client reports (Gold *et al.* 2009). In one small study on the effects of osteopathy and acupuncture in the treatment of children with cerebral palsy, improved sleep was reported in 10/19 receiving acupuncture alone (53%), 9/23 (39%) receiving osteopathy, 2/7 (29%) receiving both treatments, but in 0/17 (0%) of controls (Duncan *et al.* 2004).

In a survey of adult patients receiving acupuncture in the London Borough of Lambeth over a 5-month period, from a potential sample of 210, of whom 205 agreed to take part, 116 completed questionnaires after their seventh visit, and 78 returned a 6-month follow-up questionnaire (Paterson, Unwin and Joire 2010). Of those responding at follow-up, 14 per cent reported improved sleep as a beneficial effect from treatment. As a high proportion of those who had agreed to take part defaulted from follow-up it is difficult to assess the extent to which this is representative of the likelihood of gaining benefit.

There have been no published studies on the use of acupuncture in the treatment of sleep problems in ASD.

To locate an acupuncturist, see:
In the USA
www.medicalacupuncture.org
www.acufinder.com

In the UK
www.acupuncture.org.uk/index.php

AROMATHERAPY

There is a single preliminary study on the effects of aromatherapy on sleep in a group of 12 autistic children (10 male, 2 female, age range 12 years 2 months to 15 years 7 months) (Williams 2006). All children attended a residential school and had severe learning difficulties. In this study, using a within-subject, repeated measures design, the effects of 3 nights of massage with lavender oil were compared to 14 nights without massage in an ABABAB format. The study did not demonstrate any difference between nights when massage was used and nights when it was not.

This study did demonstrate that the use of aromatherapy was feasible and acceptable and no deleterious effects were reported with this client group. As the subjects who took part were sleeping an average of approximately 8 hours per night, their sleep pattern without aromatherapy was essentially normal for their age group, and continued to be so when aromatherapy was used. Unless one was to hypothesize that aromatherapy is specifically soporific and should lead to longer periods of sleep than normal, no further specific conclusions can be drawn from this research. Further research with autistic children with a sleep disorder would need to be carried out before conclusions as to efficacy could be drawn.

To locate an aromatherapist, see:
In the USA
Alliance of International Aromatherapists
Suite 323, 9956
W. Remington Place – Unit A10
Littleton, CO 80128
USA
Email: info@alliance-aromatherapists.org
Website: www.alliance-aromatherapists.org

National Association for Holistic Aromatherapy
PO Box 1868
Banner Elk, NC 28604
USA
Tel: (828) 898-6161
Fax: (828) 898-1965
Email: info@naha.org
Website: www.naha.org

In the UK
The Aromatherapy and Allied Practitioners Association (AAPA)
PO Box 36248
London SE19 3YD
UK
Tel: 0208 653 9152
Website: www.aapa.org.uk

CHIROPRACTICS

Chiropractics is a technique largely focused on physical manipulation of the spine. The approach was pioneered by Daniel David Palmer who founded the Palmer College of Chiropractic in Davenport, Iowa, in 1895. It has been used to treat a wide variety of neuromuscular conditions and more recently disorders which are hypothesized by its practitioners to be linked such as night-time enuresis and insomnia.

There is a literature of single-case studies on the use of chiropractic manipulation to help with sleep problems. Alcantara and Anderson (2008), for example, give a detailed account of work with a 3-month-old baby who was experiencing reflux and sleep difficulties. These resolved after 3 months of spinal and cranio-sacral manipulation. Miller (2007) reviews the role of chiropractic help with poor sleep in infancy and Miller and Klemsdal (2008) present a pilot prospective cohort series of 117 infants presenting with poor sleep, and significant improvements in settling were reported in 2/3 of cases.

Van Poecke and Cunliffe (2009) record a case series of 33 consecutive children with primary night-time enuresis aged 3–18. Treatment was with counselling, star charts and chiropractic manipulation. At baseline bedwetting was virtually incessant in all cases. Clinical improvement was reported in 22 cases with the number of wet beds per fortnight going from 13.73 at baseline to 0.13 at 1-year follow-up.

It is acknowledged in the chiropractic literature that there is a limited evidence base. One review of the chiropractic literature on insomnia (Kingston *et al.* 2010) states: 'Some studies have noted improvement in insomnia following manual therapy; however, based on clinical trials, there is minimal evidence of support for chiropractic in insomnia. Further studies with high methodological scores need to be conducted.'

This is clearly absence of adequate evidence rather than evidence of a lack of effect (the evidence so far is suggestive but not adequate).

For a review that covers chiropractic treatments for non-muscular issues and that discusses sleep problems in infancy, see Ferrance and Miller (2010).

One case study has described work with a 5-year-old autistic girl with significant sleep problems (Amalu 1998). She had a complex medical picture including asthma, allergies, left sided strabismus and irritable bowel syndrome and would wake at least twice nightly in distress, often screaming for 1–1.5 hours before being settled back to sleep. Her first night of good sleep in parental memory occurred after her first session of spinal manipulation. By the end of the first month of therapy she was reportedly sleeping through the night perfectly and continued to be undisturbed at 8-month follow-up.

Finding a chiropractor
In the USA
www.acatoday.org/patients/index.cfm

In the UK
www.chiropractic-uk.co.uk/advancedsearch.aspx

DIETARY INTERVENTION

A recently published RCT in a group of 3.8–8.5 year old children with ADHD compared a group using an elimination diet (N = 13) to a non-intervention control group (N = 11) (Pelsser *et al.* 2010). The study found significant benefits from the diet on reported rates of headaches, bellyaches, excessive thirst and unusual breathing patterns and in the frequency of sleep complaints. In both of the groups five children were initially reported as having sleep problems; in the control group all five continued while in the diet group only one continued to have poor sleep. The diet employed in this study was essentially the 'few foods diet' advocated by Peter Hill and Eric Taylor (Hill and Taylor 2001).

A wide range of dietary approaches has been advocated in helping those with ASD (see Aitken 2008). Some of these dietary approaches have been reported as having beneficial effects on sleep problems. This could be, in part, a consequence of improvements in factors such as brain electrical activity. Ketogenic diets, for example, have been found to have beneficial effects in both the management of seizure activity in epilepsy (Gaby 2007) and in improving symptomology in people with ASD (Evangeliou *et al.* 2003).

Finding a dietician with specific knowledge of ASD and sleep disorders:
In the UK it should be possible to get a referral to a local NHS dietician through your general practitioner.
To locate a private dietician: www.dietitiansunlimited.co.uk

The British Dietetic Association have a Dietitians' Autistic Spectrum Interest Group
(DASIG)
5th Floor, Charles House
148/9 Great Charles Street
Queensway
Birmingham B3 3HT
Tel: 0121 200 8080
Fax: 0121 200 8081
Website: www.bda.uk.com/index.html

In the USA, appropriately qualified and registered dieticians can be found through the
American Dietetic Association:
120 South Riverside Plaza
Suite 2000
Chicago, IL 60606
Tel: (800) 877-1600 or (312) 899-0040
Website: www.eatright.org/public/fard.aspx

Further general information can be found in Aitken (2008) and on the NutritionNutrition
website: www.nutritionnutrition.com/index.html.

EXERCISE

A recent paper reported on 17 older sedentary people (55+ years) with insomnia in an
RCT of aerobic exercise + improved sleep hygiene compared to non-physical activity
+ improved sleep hygiene who were followed over 4 months (Reid *et al.* 2010). The
study found that the aerobic group reported significantly greater improvements across
all scales of the Pittsburg Sleep Quality Index (PSQI) (Buysse *et al.* 1989) with less
daytime tiredness and improved vitality.

A randomized controlled study was carried out with 100 healthy 7–11-year-old
children, with body mass indices at or above the 85th centile, to look at the effect of
aerobic exercise on snoring (Davis *et al.* 2006). No exercise controls (N = 27) were
compared to 'low-dose' (20 minutes per day) (N = 36) and 'high-dose' (40 minutes per
day) (N = 37) aerobic exercise with heart-rates increased to an average of 164 BPM.
The results demonstrated a 'dose-related' effect on snoring – the more aerobic exercise
the greater the benefit. There was no effect of exercise on either sleepiness or body
mass index.

Appropriate exercise programmes for anyone depend on their basic fitness level
and capabilities. Any medical contraindications would need to be identified before
commencing on a fitness regime – factors such as obesity, cardiovascular difficulties
and possible seizure activity are important.

There have been no published studies on the use of exercise in the treatment of sleep problems in ASD.

Before embarking on an exercise regime, fitness level should also be assessed by an appropriately qualified fitness instructor/personal trainer with appropriate advice on the best exercise program.

Homeopathy

A randomized, placebo-controlled crossover trial with 34 volunteers (La Pine *et al.* 2006) investigated the effects of a homeopathic treatment, 'No-Shift-Lag', on the effects of circadian dysrhythmia due to night shift working. The study used a computer based vigilance task, the scanning visual vigilance test (Lieberman, Coffey and Kobrick 1998), and subjective questionnaires on fatigue, work performance and quality of off-duty time. No beneficial or statistically significant effects could be demonstrated.

A randomized double-blind placebo-controlled trial compared homeopathic simillimum (prepared in lactose powder with ethanol) to placebo sachets containing lactose powder with ethanol alone in 30 patients with chronic primary insomnia (Naudé, Couchman and Maharaj 2010). Diary sleep records and the Sleep Impairment Index (SII) (Morin 1993; and see Bastien *et al.* 2004) were used as outcome measures. Simillimum was found to have a significantly greater beneficial effect than placebo. In this study placebo treatment also produced an initial but unsustained benefit.

One study has related EEG parameters to the effects of homeopathic medication for sleep difficulties triggered by caffeine (Bell *et al.* 2011). Two treatments were used: either Nux Vomica or Coffea Cruda. In a double-blinded design, 54 subjects had eight at-home EEG sleep recordings on one of which (the third recording) they received placebo, and on another (the seventh) they received the homeopathic treatment. No differences were seen on actigraphy or self-rating on the Pittsburg Sleep Quality Index (PSQI) (Buysse *et al.* 1989). On the homeopathic treatment compared to placebo there was more sleep recorded and the amount of non-REM sleep was increased, there were more night wakings and there were more stage changes during sleep. The data in the paper do not allow further analysis, but one clear criticism of the design is that there could have been an order effect – subjects might just have slept better on later sessions, because, for example, they had become used to the recording process which required the subject to wear six EEG and two ECG leads while asleep.

There have been no specific clinical or research trials on the use of homeopathic treatments in the management of sleep disorders in ASD.

To find out more:

In the USA
The American Institute of Homeopathy
101 S. Whiting Street
Suite 16
Alexandria, VA 22304
USA
Tel: (888) 445-9988
Website: www.homeopathyusa.org

In the UK
The Society of Homeopaths
11 Brookfield, Duncan Close
Moulton Park
Northampton NN3 6WL
Tel: 0845 450 6611
Fax: 0845 450 6622
Website: www.homeopathy-soh.org/about-homeopathy/find-a-homeopath

British Homeopathic Association
Hahnemann House
29 Park Street West
Luton LU1 3BE
Tel: 01582 408675
Fax: 01582 723032
Website: www.britishhomeopathic.org

HYPNOSIS

> Most of the literature is limited to case reports or studies with
> such a small sample that at times it is very difficult to interpret
> the results. There is a major placebo effect, so uncontrolled trials
> are of limited value.
>
> Ng and Lee (2008)

Hypnosis/hypnotherapy is an approach that has been used with a variety of sleep disorders including insomnia, nightmares, nocturnal enuresis, and parasomnias such as rocking and sleepwalking.

A retrospective review presented data on 84 child and adolescent cases (aged 7–17) referred for hypnotherapy to help with insomnia (Anbar and Slothower 2006). Of the

70 who could be followed up, 90 per cent reported improved sleep onset, typically from the first session. If we assume that the reporting is accurate, that those not followed up had been unresponsive, and that these findings were representative, this suggests a positive response to hypnotherapy in just over 52 per cent of cases.

In a 1995 meta-analytic review, Kirsch, Montgomery and Sapirstein concluded that the use of hypnosis as an adjunct to cognitive behavioural therapy substantially improved treatment outcome for a range of problems including insomnia.

Subsequent publications have strengthened the conclusion that this can be a useful combined treatment approach in those who are able to comply with the verbal demands of these approaches.

One study has detailed the long-term follow-up of the use of a single or at most two sessions of hypnosis in the treatment of a group of 36 patients with parasomnias (11 with sleepwalking, 10 nightmares, 6 sleep terrors, 4 epic dreaming, 2 sleep-related eating disorder, and 1 each with sleep-related groaning, sleep-related hallucinations and severe sleep talking) (Hauri, Silber and Boeve 2007). The mean age of the group was 32.7 years but four were children aged 6–16 years. In total, 45.4 per cent of the group reported that they were symptom free or substantially improved at 1-month follow-up, and 40.5 per cent at 5-year follow-up. Sleepwalking and nightmares seemed to be the most likely to benefit, with 2/3 cases reporting maintained benefits at 5-year follow-up, while sleep terrors seemed least likely to show a beneficial response. As the sample size is small and the study is of self-selected cases, it is difficult to draw strong conclusions from this study alone.

One recent paper has shown that CBT and hypnotic relaxation were successful in treating stress-related sleep difficulties in a 14-year-old girl with type-1 diabetes (Perfect and Elkins 2010).

From their review of the literature, Ng and Lee (2008) conclude that in individual cases hypnotherapy has proven beneficial for a range of sleep issues including chronic insomnia, nightmares, sleep terrors, rocking, bedwetting and sleepwalking. They acknowledge the difficulty in developing an adequate evidence base given the problems in conducting RCTs where the cooperation and rapport between the therapist and client are key features for the approach to be effective.

There have been no specific clinical or research trials on the use of hypnosis in the management of sleep disorders in ASD.

To find out more:

In the USA
American Society of Clinical Hypnosis
140 N. Bloomingdale Rd
Bloomingdale, IL 60108
USA
Website: www.asch.net

In the UK

Hypnosis and Hypnotherapy in the UK

www.hypnosis.me.uk/pages/find.html

The Hypnotherapy Association

14 Crown Street

Chorley

Lancashire PR7 1DX

Tel: and fax: 01257 262124

www.thehypnotherapyassociation.co.uk/index.htm

MASSAGE THERAPY

Field *et al.* (1997) studied the effects of a simple 15-minute massage programme administered by a volunteer student, or of a control play intervention period of the same duration. The subjects were 22 autistic children attending a preschool facility in Miami who were around 4.5 years old. As assessed on the Autism Behavior Checklist (ABC) and the Early Social Communication Scales (ESCS), comparing the two interventions, the massage group showed greater improvements in orienting and a greater reduction in stereotypies.

A subsequent study by the same group used a home-based parent-administered massage programme with 20 3–6-year-old autistic children randomly allocated to the same 15-minute massage programme used in the 1997 study but this time carried out by a parent, or to an attention control group ('Dr Seuss' story reading) for 15 minutes before bedtime over a 1-month trial. On completion of the study, the control group were also taught the massage intervention (Escalona *et al.* 2001). From sleep diaries completed by parents, fussing and restlessness, crying, self-stimulating behaviours and the number of times the child attempted to leave the bed significantly reduced in the massage group after 1 month of treatment.

As previously discussed, there is a study on the acceptability of aromatherapy massage in a residential unit for ASD (Williams 2006); however, this did not look at sleep outcomes.

A 2-month RCT compared the use of sensory integration (SI) to SI together with Thai traditional massage (Piravej *et al.* 2009). The study looked at 60 children aged 3 to 10 years of age. In both groups there were improvements across conduct problems, hyperactivity, inattention and sleeping problems. The addition of Thai massage produced greater improvements in anxiety, conduct problems and stereotypies than SI alone.

A qualitative study of the effects of a massage therapy course on parental perceptions of their child with ASD showed a strong positive effect of participation on the parent–child relationship (Cullen and Barlow 2002).

To find out more:

In the USA
The Touch Research Institute
Dept. of Pediatrics (D820)
University of Miami School of Medicine
PO Box 016820
Miami, FL 33101
USA
Website: www6.miami.edu/touch-research/about.html

In the UK
Infant massage
The International Association for Infant Massage
IAIM UK Chapter
Unit 10
Marlborough Business Centre
96 George Lane
South Woodford
London E18 1AD
Tel: 020 8989 9597
Website: www.iaim.org.uk/index.htm

Adult massage
General Council for Massage Therapies
27 Old Gloucester Street
London WC1N 3XX
Tel: 0870 850 4452
Website: www.gcmt.org.uk/home.aspx

MEDITATION

Various forms of meditation have been assessed from the point of view of their effects on sleep. Banquet and Sailhan (1974), for example, reported on EEG assessments carried out during 'Transcendental Meditation'. They reported increased levels of alpha activity in what were then reported as stage 3 and 4 sleep (now both identified as stage 3 sleep).

There is evidence of increased melatonin levels in meditators on nights following various forms of meditation (e.g. Harinath *et al.* 2004; Solberg *et al.* 2004; Tooley *et al.* 2000).

A number of publications provides more detailed overviews of the physiological effects of meditation (see Cahn and Polich 2006; Jevning, Wallace and Beidebach 1992).

Some work indicates that regular meditation strengthens functional connectivity in those areas of the posterior cingulate and medial prefrontal cortex known as the default mode network (DMN) (Jang *et al.* 2011). This effect can be demonstrated when the person is in a resting state. As these are areas that show increased activation during attention to internal states, it suggests that regular meditation can have effects on brain activity that are persistent. As there are demonstrable deficits in connectivity in the DMN in ASD (Assaf *et al.* 2010), the possibility that meditation could correct this to some extent in individuals who were capable of using such techniques should be explored further.

There has been no systematic research on effects of meditation in people who have sleep disorders or of its use in ASD.

For further information:
There is a worldwide directory of meditation groups that provides links to a range of schools and groups: http://meditation.org.au/questionaire_display.asp.

PSYCHOTHERAPY

I use the term psychotherapy here specifically to stand for therapeutic approaches that are based on psychoanalytic principles. Although there are differences between the various psychoanalytic models and approaches, as there is no evidence for the effectiveness of any of these in the treatment of sleep disorders and none on their use in such work with ASD, I will refrain from providing any detailed descriptions here.

There have been attempts made by proponents of the psychoanalytic view to reconcile psychoanalytic models with the developments in our biological understanding of sleep and dreaming, and to highlight the lack of focus in other approaches on the importance of emotional aspects of functioning (see, in particular Solms 2000, 2004). Journals such as *Neuropsychoanalysis* (www.neuro-psa.org.uk) are devoted to discussion of how these approaches can be mutually beneficial in advancing our understanding of brain function. A recent lecture, 'From Mirror Neurons to Embodied Simulation' (Gallese 2010), highlights how these models are beginning to coalesce.

Psychoanalytic approaches have been practised for over a century, and they developed largely before the era of brain science that has informed our more recent approaches.

There have been no published trials on the use of analytic psychotherapies in general in the treatment of sleep disorders, and there is no published literature on their use with sleep problems in ASD. This may seem surprising; however, as dream recall is a core component of therapy, attempts to modify or abolish dream content would not perhaps be seen by its practitioners as a useful therapeutic aim.

The lack of an evidence base makes it impossible to recommend the use of such analytic approaches in the treatment of sleep disorders in general or in the treatment of sleep problems in ASD at the present time.

RELAXATION

Most relaxation work that has been tried as part of the treatment offered for sleep disorders is based on the progressive muscle relaxation approach developed by Douglas Bernstein and Thomas Borkovec (see Bernstein and Borkovec 1973). In sleep disorders, relaxation training has been most widely used with individuals who present with insomnia, but in general it is likely to be helpful in individuals who have anxiety or overarousal as a component of their presenting problem.

Relaxation training approaches have been adapted for a range of populations and approaches have been developed that can be used with adults and children with significant learning disabilities, often using 'cue-controlled' techniques (see, e.g. Kiesel, Lutzker and Campbell 1989; Lindsay *et al.* 1994).

Relaxation training is often proposed as a treatment approach for sleep-related issues, usually as a component of a package also involving improved sleep hygiene and/or cognitive behavioural work.

A number of studies with different populations have shown that relaxation training as a monotherapy is better than no therapy at all in matched patients with geriatric insomnia (waiting list controls) (Rybarczyk *et al.* 2002); compared to no-treatment controls during active weaning off from of sleep medication (Lichstein *et al.* 1999); as a primary treatment for insomnia (Edinger *et al.* 2001; Means *et al.* 2000) and compared to sleep hygiene education (Waters *et al.* 2003). There have been no published studies on relaxation training as a primary treatment for sleep disorders in children or adolescents.

From the adult literature, there is evidence that relaxation training is better than improving sleep hygiene alone for sleep initiation in insomnia (Chambless and Hollon 1998), that it is better than no treatment controls (Lichstein *et al.* 1999; Means *et al.* 2000; Rybarczyk *et al.* 2002); and is better than placebo (Edinger *et al.* 2001; Lichstein *et al.* 2001). In direct comparisons, CBT was shown to produce greater benefits on sleep (Edinger *et al.* 2001; Lichstein *et al.* 2001; Rybarczyk *et al.* 2002).

Clinical psychologists or other therapists trained in the use of behavioural techniques most frequently teach relaxation training.

For further information, see the associations listed under Behavioural and cognitive-behavioural treatments.

LIGHT THERAPY

Light therapy, also known as phototherapy or heliotherapy, is the term for controlled exposure to full or restricted spectrum bright light. This has been validated for the treatment of certain skin disorders such as acne vulgaris (Papageorgiou, Katsambas and Chu 2000) and conditions such as seasonal affective disorder (Eastman *et al.* 1998), Parkinson's disease and dementia (see Terman 2007).

A good recent review of the rationale, uses of and research evidence on light therapy, including its use in the treatment of sleep disorders, can be found in Shirani and St Louis (2009).

The use of light therapy is empirically supported for a number of sleep problems such as advanced and delayed sleep phase syndromes (ASPS and DSPS) (see Chesson *et al.* 1999).

There has been no systematic research on effects of light therapy with people who have sleep disorders in the context of ASD.

The availability of light therapy in this context (rather than for its use in the treatment of seasonal affective disorder) tends to be restricted to specialist sleep clinics.

BIOFEEDBACK

A general definition of biofeedback is the use of methods (often the detection and display of electrical activity of the muscles or nervous system) to inform the person of bodily processes of which they are not normally aware. This conscious awareness of processes that are normally involuntary or under the control of the autonomic nervous system can in some cases allow a degree of voluntary control to be developed.

Several types of biofeedback device have been used in the treatment of sleep problems. An early paper (Bell 1979) described the successful treatment of sleep onset insomnia over 11 sessions of theta rhythm (4–7 Hertz activity) EEG biofeedback in a 42-year-old woman. The treatment was associated with sustained improvement over a 3-month follow-up period after sessions were finished.

Some devices are claimed to enhance EEG rhythms that are conducive to sleep. Devices aimed at providing electrodermal activity (EDA) feedback (previously known as GSR or galvanic skin response) have also been claimed to be beneficial.

If we assume that there is a positive treatment response, a frequent difficulty with EEG feedback, as with its other uses, is generalization of the improvement. In the home environment without the sustained use of feedback equipment, it is often difficult to maintain effects. This has proven to be a problem when increasing sensorimotor rhythm to reduce seizure activity in epileptics – the treatment effect is not maintained unless the person continues to use an EEG feedback device. The biofeedback device is a prosthesis rather than a way of establishing a normal response, as is also true for CPAP treatment in OSA or use of a MAD for snoring.

The best-known biofeedback device relevant to sleep issues does not address EEG activity; it is the 'bell and pad' used in the treatment of bedwetting. For discussion on the use of enuresis alarms see the earlier section on nocturnal enuresis.

There has been no systematic research on biofeedback approaches with people who have sleep disorders in the context of ASD.

To find out more:

In the USA
Association of Applied Psychophysiology and Biofeedback
10200 West 44th Avenue
Suite 304
Wheat Ridge, CO 80033
USA
Tel: (800) 477-8892 or (303) 422-8436
Website: www.aapb.org/home.html

In Europe
Biofeedback Foundation of Europe
Po Box 555
3800 AN Amersfoort
The Netherlands
Tel/fax: (+31) 84 83 84 696
Website: www.bfe.org/index.html

BEHAVIOURAL AND COGNITIVE-BEHAVIOURAL TREATMENTS

For overviews of such approaches, see Espie 2006; Ospina *et al.* 2008; Sadeh 2005.

The development of behavioural and cognitive-behavioural methodologies has resulted in detailed approaches to case analysis and the development of individualized therapies based on the pattern of presentation in the individual. Commonalities in treatment approach are important but so are individual differences in presentation. This is a very different view of the science of therapy when compared to the 'one size fits all' approach used in the RCT. There has been an ongoing debate in the literature since these differences first became clear about how, if at all, it is possible to reconcile the two (see, e.g. Evans 1996; Keenan and Dillenburger 2011). It is important to grasp this critical difference when RCTs are being held as the 'gold standard' for evidence that given approaches are effective – if individual differences are critical to outcome, randomizing cases to different approaches becomes a meaningless exercise. Where this is the case, a series of well-described single cases with good clinical results may be far more important than an RCT with equivocal results.

There is a large amount of single case and small group case series work published on behavioural approaches to specific sleep problems. One paper systematically reviewed the various approaches published up to 2003 (Kuhn and Elliott 2003). The conclusion was that to that time behavioural approaches for bedtime refusal and night waking were well supported. Treatment for night terrors and sleepwalking had some empirical support, but treatments for circadian rhythm disorders, nightmares and rhythmic movement disorder lacked sufficient empirical evidence to support their use. Many of the studies have been discussed when we came on to consider different approaches in the sections on specific sleep difficulties.

A more recent review of behavioural treatment of sleep problems in developmental disorders (Richdale and Wiggs 2005) states that 'The impact of sleep problems and successful treatment is largely unexplored, while professional awareness regarding sleep problems and their treatment appears poor' (p.165). There is still a long way to go in arriving at a clear picture of what approaches work best, where, when and with whom, however, the evidence base is growing and clarity is gradually emerging. A range of approaches with some evidence for benefit is available for most sleep problems and agreed methods of assessing what can work are now fairly routine.

When considering these types of approach, it is important to try to establish that a therapist is both competent in the approach being suggested and that they are familiar with and have used it to treat the type of problem for which you are trying to get help. How competence is established and how specific the training is a matter of debate (for a general discussion of these issues, see Davidson and Scott 2009). It should at least be possible to establish that the person is appropriately qualified, that they are registered with a regulatory body and that they are qualified to work with the particular client group.

Behavioural and cognitive-behavioural approaches have many overlapping components. Both approaches rely on collecting detailed information on processes in the individual problem situation, deriving hypotheses about why the problem is being maintained and testing out changes which should bring about improvement assuming that the hypothesis is correct. This is called a hypothetico-deductive approach.

Relaxation training (discussed separately above) is often included as a component of both behavioural and CBT approaches.

Behavioural approaches are essentially approaches to the management of problems in which the environmental antecedents (the things leading up to the problem) or its consequences (the things that follow on from it) are identified and systematically altered in some way.

Behavioural approaches can be highly structured and formulated in specific detail or may be presented as a small number of clear rules. In either event, the principles employed are essentially the same.

The basic model has been well described for many years. I would recommend two core books on behavioural approaches – Martin Herbert's classic *Behavioural Treatment of Children with Problems: A Practice Manual* (1987) is simple, clear and well written, giving the basics of behavioural analysis and intervention. Alan Repp's (1983) book *Teaching the Mentally Retarded* goes into greater technical detail on behavioural practice and is helpful if you are grappling with some of the terminology and finding parts of the relevant literature difficult to grasp. The importance of individually targeted case formulation on CBT is highlighted in Bruch and Bond (1998).

Behavioural approaches

The most common and most widely used approaches to the treatment of sleep problems in ASD are behavioural techniques (see Kodak and Piazza 2008).

Several behavioural strategies can be taught to parents as preventative measures, usually working in the early months providing information on potentially successful strategies. A Cochrane review of parent group training for a range of issues including sleep in the 0–3-year age group can be found in Barlow *et al.* (2010). A number of studies have demonstrated benefit from such educational approaches for sleep issues in general population samples:

> Wolfson *et al.* (1992) demonstrated better sleep on parental diary measures at 6–9-week follow-up in an intervention group of 30 first-time parents who received two ante- and two postnatal training sessions compared to 30 randomly allocated controls.

> Adair *et al.* (1992) compared an intervention group of 164 infants presenting at 4-month well baby follow-up who were provided with educational advice to 128 historical controls from the same population. At 20-week follow-up, the rate of night waking, again on parent diary measures, was halved in the intervention group compared to the controls.

> Kerr, Jowett and Smith (1996) randomly assigned 169 families to receiving written and verbal information and behaviour management advice about sleep issues or to a control group and followed up at 9 months with a parental interview. The intervention group reported significantly fewer sleep problems than the placebo group.

Once sleep problems have developed, a number of simple steps form the starting point for working behaviourally:

1. *Assess the problem* – It is important to have some sort of baseline assessment in order to tell whether anything put in place to try to help is making any difference. Use something like the Child's Sleep Habits Questionnaire (CSHQ) (Owens, Spirito ad McGuinn 2000; Owens *et al.* 2000) to give an idea of the type of difficulties being experienced. See Appendix 4 for the CSHQ proforma.

2. *Collect a 'baseline'* – Armed with this framework – the information you think is most likely to be helpful, information on the problem that seems relevant and that you would hope to improve on, things such as how often a problem occurs, how bad it can be…construct some sort of day-to-day recording to give an indication of sleep pattern (see Appendix 4 for examples of sleep diary layout – these may need to be adapted to capture the right information depending on the specifics of the problem).

Typically the best format for recording this type of information will be in the form of a sleep diary, but some problems may be more amenable to other ways of recording – self-ratings of tiredness for example.

3. *Try to work out 'why' the problem is happening* – Having collected your initial baseline, the next stage is to see what the record shows and to work out why the problem is likely to be being maintained – was your initial idea of what might be causing the difficulties borne out by your recording? Here the aim is to develop a working hypothesis to account for the problem. This will often focus on factors such as increased attention that could reinforce or strengthen the problem.

4. *Change the antecedents, the behaviour itself or its consequences* – If there seems to be a clear pattern, for example, your child is very late going to sleep but is usually active when you check on them, playing with toys, say, you might decide to change the consequences by seeing whether removing access to their toys from the time you are asking them to go to bed makes any difference.

After functional analysis and baseline recording, behavioural approaches can be most easily described under general headings that attempt to modify the pattern leading up to the behaviour; the behaviour itself; or its effects.

As the specifics of a behavioural programme will differ depending on the results of the assessment and the nature of the problem, refer to the relevant section of the book dealing with specific sleep issues for more detail on typical behavioural interventions.

5. *Monitor* – Remember to continue noting sleep pattern after making a change so that you can see whether it is having an effect.

6. *Adjust* – You need to make sure that you have left enough time for your strategy to work, remembering that there may be an initial 'extinction burst'. Assuming your change has been beneficial but has not sorted the problem completely, you may need to adjust this a little; in the above example maybe removing access to toys for the last 15 minutes before bedtime would allow time for settling.

7. *Review* – Having sorted out the problem, you need to review things periodically to make sure that the problem is not returning – maybe checking the sleep pattern every few weeks.

In some cases the basis to behavioural intervention can be clarified by physical assessments such as overnight EEG recording and actimetry (automated recording of movement during sleep). These would normally be recommended, when required, by your medical practitioner who would have responsibility for helping with these aspects of your child's care.

Overall, behavioural interventions have a good evidence base and have been demonstrated to be effective in a significant proportion of cases of sleep disorder both in the general population (Owens, Palermo and Rosen 2002), and in those with ASD (see, e.g. Glazener and Evans 2004; O'Reilly 1995; Piazza and Fisher 1991; Weiskop, Richdale and Matthews 2005).

Cognitive-behavioural therapy approaches

Cognitive-behavioural therapy (CBT) approaches combine behavioural management strategies with a focus on changing the thoughts and feelings the person has that are associated with the problem.

CBT has been advocated for a range of child parasomnias; however, to date, the evidence base for this is limited (see discussion in Sadeh 2005; Tikotzky and Sadeh 2010). The use of CBT methods is more difficult in younger or less cognitively able children (Grave and Blissett 2004), and would need to be carried out by a therapist with good developmental understanding and CBT training with an appropriate client group.

CBT approaches have been successfully used in the treatment of insomnia in young and middle-aged adults and compared favourably to the effects of medication in an RCT (Jacobs *et al.* 2004).

CBT can be difficult to implement with individuals who have an ASD as a consequence of the language problems that can often complicate understanding and make implementation more difficult. This having been said, CBT has been successfully implemented in working with both adults and adolescents with high-functioning autism and with Asperger syndrome (Beebe and Risi 2003; Gaus 2007). There has been some work on using CBT with adult and adolescent sleep problems in Asperger syndrome, but nothing reported to date with younger children.

There are no controlled trials on the use of CBT with sleep problems in an ASD population.

To find out more:

International
Association for Behavior Analysis International (ABAI)
550 W. Centre Ave.
Portage, MI 49024-5364
USA
Tel: (269) 492-9310
Fax: (269) 492-9316
Email: mail@abainternational.org
Website: www.abainternational.org

In the USA

The National Association of Cognitive-Behavioral Therapists (NACBT)
203 Three Springs Drive
Suite 4
Weirton, WV 26062
USA
Tel: (800) 853-1135
Website: www.nacbt.org/

Association for Behavioral and Cognitive Therapies
305 7th Avenue
16th Fl.
New York, NY 10001
USA
Tel: (212) 647-1890
Fax: (212) 647-1865
Website: www.abct.org/home/?m=mhomeandfa=dhome

In the UK

The British Association for Behavioural and Cognitive Psychotherapy (BABCP)
Imperial House
Hornby Street
Bury BL9 5BN
UK
Tel: 0161 705 4304
Fax: 0161 705 4306
Website: www.babcp.com

For a broad range of European societies that support and/or regulate behavioural and CBT therapists, see www.cbtarena.com/resources/societies.

YOGA

There are various forms of yoga, but in general terms yoga combines breathing exercises, gentle movements, poses and meditation techniques that are said to reduce arousal.

One preliminary study reported on the effects of a 6-week course of Kundalini yoga, after a 2-week baseline period, with a group of 34 adult patients experiencing chronic insomnia. For the 20 who completed the intervention there were significant improvements across a range of parameters: sleep efficiency; total sleeping time; total time awake; sleep onset latency and time to waking from the onset of sleep (Khalsa 2004).

A more recent study has examined physiological effects in 16 Sivananda yoga practitioners (who had been regularly using yoga for 3 years or more) and 10 non-yoga practising controls (Vera *et al.* 2009). The study used the Pittsburg Sleep Quality Index (PSQI) (Buysse *et al.* 1989) for a subjective measure of sleep and blood measures of adrenocorticotropic hormone (ACTH), cortisol and dehydroepiandrosterone sulphate (DHEA-S). All blood samples were drawn at 9.00 into EDTA and cooled to −70°C. Unfortunately it is not clear how this corresponded to the timing of yoga classes or any other activities that may have affected the physiological measurements. The yoga subjects obtained better scores on the PSQI and higher cortisol levels than the controls. Decreased cortisol has been reported as being correlated with poorer sleep and reduced ability to cope with experimentally induced stress (Wright *et al.* 2007).

A helpful review on the use of yoga as a complementary therapy with children and adolescents can be found in Kayley-Isley *et al.* 2010.

There has been no systematic research on effects of yoga with people who have sleep disorders in the context of ASD.

To find out more:

Worldwide listing of members of the International Yoga Federation:
Website: www.internationalyogafederation.net/fiyorganizations.html

In the UK
UK Yoga Centres and Associations
Website: www.yogauk.com/links/organisations.htm

The Iyengar Yoga Association
IYA (UK)
PO Box 4730
Sheffield S8 2HE
UK
Tel: 07510 326997
Email: admin@iyengaryoga.org.uk
Website: www.iyengaryoga.org.uk

In the USA
International Association of Yoga Therapists
PO Box 12890
Prescott, Arizona
AZ 86304
USA
Tel: (928) 541-0004
Website: www.iayt.org

Professional Yoga Therapy
Website: https://www.professionalyogatherapy.org

APPENDIX 3

HERBAL TREATMENTS

A range of herbal approaches, principally covered under the headings of Western, Chinese and Japanese herbal treatments, all have their advocates.

The use of such approaches is common in Western societies. Their use is typically associated with adherence to other health-promoting behaviours, and in families with a higher level of education (Sánchez-Ortuño *et al.* 2009).

Many herbal approaches have been advocated historically and many continue to be advocated for the treatment of sleep problems. A number, such as caffeine, ephedra and kava kava can have significant adverse cardiovascular effects (Cohen and Ernst 2010). A high proportion of families use or have used such approaches with children who have ASD. Many are taken by adolescents (Guyda 2005) and are recommended by healthcare professionals (Gardiner and Kemper 2002).

Currently few clinicians seem to be sufficiently aware of the extent to which non-prescription products are used, especially in ASD. Use tends to be focused on perceived problems and sleep is an important concern for many families. A 2003 US survey of 284 children with ASD found that approximately 30 per cent were taking some form of complementary or alternative medicine (CAM) (Levy *et al.* 2003). In one affluent US group, CAMs were being used with some 92 per cent of autistic children (Harrington *et al.* 2006). A further survey of 479 families found a wide range of CAM treatments were being employed (Goin-Kochel, Myers and Mackintosh 2007).

It is important when considering herbal treatments to be aware that natural does not necessarily mean safe, and that the treatment may interact with other treatments that the person may be taking. A useful discussion of herbs as medication and possibilities of adverse reactions can be found in Aithal (2005). In anyone who is taking prescription medication it is important to check with the prescriber about possible interactions and contraindications both if the person is taking non-prescription treatments before starting or is considering taking non-prescription treatments and is already on medication.

A number of these treatments can interact with more 'conventional' pharmaceutical approaches. The potentials for negative interactions with conventional medication are often unrecognized but can be very important to avoid. Useful introductions to the issues around possible toxic effects of herbal treatments can be found in Myers and Cheras (2004) and Tovar and Petzel (2009), and reviews of uses and interactions in psychiatry in Werneke, Turner and Priebe (2006). An earlier review more specifically on herbal product use with children is provided in Snodgrass (2001).

The literature on herbal treatments is complex as many of the constituents are often unclear, particularly in products made from multiple ingredients, or where the Chinese, Korean or Japanese names are unfamiliar, and interactions with conventional treatments are often not known or may be poorly understood. An excellent review of the biochemical actions, interactions with conventional medications and safety issues in many herbal medicines can be found in Corns (2003).

The regulation of dietary supplements to ensure safety is a complex and difficult area. One recent UK review (Petroczi, Taylor and Naughton 2010) provides a survey of products investigated through the European Union's Rapid Alert System for Food and Feed (RASFF) over the period 2003–10. Of the dietary supplements reviewed, 21 per cent were contaminated; 6 per cent had poor quality control; 6 per cent had unlicensed additives and 2 per cent had unlicensed steroids.

As herbal treatments are widely used as over-the-counter methods of addressing sleep problems, I have tried to provide an overview of the available information in this area. This overview is largely restricted to the literature available in English language journals.

A basic introduction to the role of herbal treatments can be found in Vickers, Zollman and Lee (1999), and a brief review of common adverse reactions in Ko (1999).

'WESTERN' HERBAL TREATMENTS

A variety of herbal treatments that derive mainly from medieval Western medical practice have been advocated for sleep problems (for a brief overview, see Gyllenhaal *et al.* 2000) and their use is widespread (Sánchez-Ortuño *et al.* 2009). I have included under this heading some herbal treatments such as the Californian poppy and skullcap that have been incorporated by European settlers from Native American pharmacopoeia.

A wide range of herbal treatments have been used of which caffeine, Californian poppy, chamomile, hops, ginseng, kava kava, lemon balm, passionflower, skullcap, St John's wort and valerian are the best-known traditional treatments used in Western herbal medicine for sleep problems, mainly as soporifics, but some as stimulants. Many are also used for their anxiolytic properties (Abascal and Yarnell 2004).

There have been no specific clinical or research trials on the use of Western herbal treatments in the management of sleep disorders in ASD.

For further general information, see:

MedlinePlus
www.nlm.nih.gov/medlineplus/druginformation.html

Table App 3.1 summarizes information on herbal approaches.

TABLE APP 3.1 THE MAIN HERBS IN WESTERN HERBAL MEDICINE WITH THEIR PRIMARY USES, KEY REFERENCES AND POSSIBLE ISSUES

Herb/extract	Primary use in sleep problems	General studies on its use	Possible issues
Sedative herbs/extracts			
Californian poppy	Used in combination with other herbs to reduce anxiety/agitation	Rolland *et al.* 2001	Limited data
Chamomile	Insomnia	Viola, Wasowski and Levi de Stein 1995	Idiosyncratic reactions (rare) (e.g. Thien 2001)
Ginseng	Reduce response to stress	Coon and Ernst 2002	Bizarre manic behaviour (rare)
Hops	?mildly sedative – supporting evidence lacking	Cornu *et al.* 2010	No evidence of physiological effect
Kava kava		Emser and Bartylla 1991	Some concerns over liver toxicity (rare)
Lemon balm	Mildly calming and sedative	Muller and Klement 2006	None of note
Immature oat seeds	Mildly sedative	Blumenthal *et al.* 1998	No evidence of any significant positive or negative effects
Passionflower	Treatment of insomnia	Deng *et al.* 2010; Krenn 2002	Generally considered safe
Skullcap	Mildly sedative	Wolfson and Hoffmann 2003 (adults only)	Limited data
St John's wort	General calming and antidepressant	Hubner and Kirste 2001	Overall problem rate similar to placebo but some cases reported of agitated psychotic behaviour (rare)
Valerian	General disturbance of sleep and insomnia	Taibi *et al.* 2007	Safe but limited data on efficacy
Stimulant herbs/extracts			
Caffeine	Improves vigilance and concentration	Ghanizadeh 2010 (adequate research currently lacking)	Psychotic and cardiovascular reactions and some fatalities at high doses
Ephedra	Stimulant	See Shakelle *et al.* 2003	Seizures. Currently banned in the USA and now prescription only in the UK
Yohimbine	Increases attention and activity level	Gentili *et al.* 1996	Nausea, vomiting, abdominal pain

The herbs used with sleep problems in general can be divided into those with purported sedative and those with purported stimulant effects.

Sedative herbs and extracts

Californian poppy, chamomile, hops, kava kava, lemon balm, passionflower, skullcap, St John's wort and valerian are the best-known herbal treatments with supposed sedative effects.

For a helpful recent systematic review dealing with the published studies on passionflower, kava kava and St John's wort in adults, see Lakhan and Vieira (2010).

CALIFORNIAN POPPY (*ESCHSCHOLZIA CALIFORNICA*)

The Californian poppy is a herb that is known to have anxiolytic effects at lower doses and sedative effects at higher doses (Rolland *et al.* 1991, 2001). It is used in traditional Native American medicine, typically in combination with other nervine herbs to help with sleep, anxiety or pain control (see discussion in Abascal and Yarnell 2004).

CHAMOMILE (*MATRICARIA RECUTITA*)

Chamomile has been widely advocated and used in the treatment of insomnia. It is a biologically complex substance from which four main active compounds – matrizine, chamazulene, apigenin and bisabolol – have been isolated. In addition, over 35 other compounds have been identified, and they appear in different proportions in chamomile extracts from different countries (Orav, Raal and Arak 2010).

Chamomile flowers contain apigenin, a compound that binds to benzodiazepine receptors (Viola *et al.* 1995), and accounts for its calming effects.

GINSENG (*PANAX GINSENG OR PANAX QUINQUEFOLIUS*)

Several different types of ginseng are commonly available. The most widely sold is *Panax ginseng*, also known as red or Asiatic ginseng. The others that are commonly available are *Panax quinquefolius* or American ginseng and *Eleutherococcus senticosus* or Siberian ginseng.

There is no systematic evidence base on the use of any form of ginseng in the treatment of sleep disorders; however, there is widespread anecdotal mention of its use.

A systematic review published in 2002 concluded from the available data that *Panax ginseng* was well tolerated by most users and that the majority of reported side-effects were mild and reversible (Coon and Ernst 2002). There have however been several case reports of bizarre manic behaviour consequent to taking ginseng supplements both in combination with psychotropic medication and on its own (see Joshi and Faubion 2005).

HOPS (*HUMULUS LUPULUS*)

One study to date has demonstrated specific sedating effects of hop extracts in an animal model (Schiller *et al.* 2006).

A number of studies, including RCTs, have reported on the effects of an extract of valerian root and Hops 'ZE 91019' (marketed in Europe as ReDormin and the USA as Alluna) (e.g. Dimpfel and Suter 2008; Koetter *et al.* 2007).

One recent RCT on the use of a hop extract together with polyunsaturated fatty acids failed to demonstrate any effects on physiological parameters such as melatonin metabolism, the sleep–wake cycle or self-ratings on the Leeds Sleep Evaluation Questionnaire, comparing 51 active to 50 placebo intervention (Cornu *et al.* 2010).

There is no other systematic evidence base on the use of any form of hop extract alone in the treatment of sleep disorders, and none on specific use in ASD. There is widespread anecdotal mention of its use and it is included in a number of over-the-counter preparations aimed at improving sleep.

KAVA KAVA (*PIPER METHYSTICUM*)

Kava kava is a plant indigenous to the Western Pacific. The roots are used in traditional medicines from this area as it has mildly sedative properties. Kava lactones have been shown to be useful in the treatment of tension and anxiety (Cairney, Maruff and Clough 2002) and as an adjunct to standard pharmacotherapy (Malsch and Kieser 2001).

There has been only one small placebo-controlled study of the effects of 300mg of kava kava root extract in a group of 12 healthy adult volunteers. This study reported improvements on the active supplement in both subjective and objective measures of sleep (Emser and Bartylla 1991).

There have been concerns about severe liver damage reported from the use of some supplements, and its use has been restricted; however, most problems have been from products using leaf and bark in addition to root extracts and no toxicity has been reported from root extracts alone (see Gruenwald and Skrabal 2003).

For a recent evaluation of the evidence on the use and safety of kava kava, see Ernst (2007).

LEMON BALM (*MELISSA OFFICINALIS*)

Lemon balm is a herb indigenous to southern Europe that has a variety of both medicinal and culinary uses, as a leaf extract or made into a tea it appears to have mild anxiolytic properties and to be mildly sedative (Kennedy, Little and Scholey 2004).

One placebo-controlled double-blind multicentre study of a combined valerian/lemon balm sleeping aid in healthy adult volunteers with 2:1 randomization, 66 receiving active treatment (360mg of valerian and 240mg of lemon balm per day) and 32 receiving a visually matched placebo, examined the effects of treatment over a 30-day period (Cerny and Schmid 1999). No serious adverse events were reported. Neither group showed any changes in blood chemistry, haematology blood pressure or pulse rate. In the control group there were no significant changes in perceived quality of sleep, while in the active treatment group 33 per cent reported a significantly higher quality of sleep.

There has been only one study reported on the use of lemon balm in the treatment of childhood sleep problems (Muller and Klement 2006). This was an open trial of a combined lemon balm + valerian treatment (Euvegal®forte) on a large sample of 918 children aged under 12. It found the medication to be well tolerated with no adverse effects reported and improvements in sleeping (80.9% improved) and restlessness (70.4% improved) in most cases, while improvements in around a third of other presenting sleep problems were seen.

IMMATURE OAT SEEDS (*AVENA SATIVA*)

The green 'tops' or grains of the immature oat have a long history as a herbal remedy for anxiety and insomnia.

A review of the evidence on efficacy carried out by the German 'Commission E' (Blumenthal *et al.* 1998) was unable to find adequate research that the ingestion of any form of supplement produced from immature oat seeds has any significant effect on conditions for which it has been claimed to be of benefit. Claims had been made for effects on conditions such as acute and chronic anxiety, stress, excitability, neurasthenic and pseudoneurasthenic syndromes, skin diseases, connective tissue deficiencies and weakness of the bladder (see discussion in Abascal and Yarnell 2004).

PASSIONFLOWER (*PASSIFLORA INCARNATA*)

Extracts made from the flower, leaves and stem of the passionflower have a long history of being used in the herbal treatment of tension, anxiety, restlessness, irritability, insomnia and addiction. It is thought to exert its primary action through increasing levels of CNS GABA activity.

As with the Californian poppy, passionflower has an anxiolytic effect at lower doses and is sedative at higher doses (for a recent animal study and literature review of this topic see Deng *et al.* 2010).

For a useful review of passionflower uses including its clinical applications, pharmacology and toxicology, see Dhawan, Dhawan and Sharma (2004).

There is an extensive clinical literature on the sedative effects of passionflower, typically used in combination with other herbs in the treatment of difficulties in sleeping linked to restlessness (see Krenn 2002).

SKULLCAP (*SCUTELLARIA LATERIFLORA*)

Skullcap (also known as blue skullcap) is a North American herb that has been traditionally used for its supposed anxiolytic properties. There are over 350 different species with different constituents and there is limited peer-reviewed research on its use.

In one RCT in 19 healthy adult volunteers, three different preparations of freeze-dried skullcap were compared to placebo control capsules, all showing positive effects on anxiety, cognition and energy levels on Likert self-ratings (Wolfson and Hoffmann 2003).

ST JOHN'S WORT (*HYPERICUM PERFORATUM*)

St John's wort is a perennial herb with a yellow flower, which has a long history of use as a herbal treatment. The best-known use for St John's wort is in the treatment of depression, for which there is some evidence (see Linde, Berner and Kriston 2008).

There is limited research on tolerability and effectiveness of St John's wort in children. There is one German 35-centre post-marketing surveillance study of 101 children aged less than 12 years who were assessed by parents and clinicians over a 6-week period and who had been prescribed St John's wort for depression and 'psychovegetative disturbances'. In this series sleep disturbances were recorded in 75 of the children at baseline and reported as cured in over 90 per cent of cases at follow-up (Hubner and Kirste 2001).

There have been a number of case reports of agitated psychotic symptomology and relapse after taking St John's wort supplements both in combination with psychotropic medication and on its own (see Joshi and Faubion 2005).

VALERIAN (*VALERIANA OFFICINALIS*)

Valerian is typically used as an oil. It is extracted from the dried root and rhizome of the plant *Valeriana officinalis*. Hippocrates recommended valerian as a remedy for insomnia. The root and rhizome contains approximately 1 per cent oil which is a complex biological product containing valerianic acid, isovalerianic acid, valerenone, valerenal, hydroxyvaleric acid, citronellyl isovalerate, borneol, pinene, camphene, methyl-2-pyrrole ketone and assorted sesquiterpenes. The preparation also contains various other compounds such as epoxy iridoid esters, which rapidly degrade during storage, glycoside (valerosidatum), volatile pyridine alkaloids (valerine, valerianine, actinidine, chatinine), choline, flavonoids, sterols, phenolic acids, sugars, fixed oil, resin and gum.

In the general population some research has shown good positive results in double-blinded trials (e.g. Lindahl and Lindwall 1989), and one large trial has shown modest positive effects (Oxman *et al.* 2007). A systematic review (Taibi *et al.* 2007) of 29 controlled and 8 open-label trials, however, concluded that although valerian was safe in the management of insomnia with few reported adverse events, there was limited evidence of benefit.

One study of 23 admissions with apparent adverse reactions to an over-the-counter preparation containing hyocine, cyproheptadine and valerian found four to be asymptomatic and the others to present with a range of signs of CNS effects from drowsiness and dilated pupils to confusional states and visual hallucinations (Chan, Tang and Critchley 1995).

An adult open-label trial (Waldschutz and Klein 2008) compared valerian at normal recommended doses (N = 164) to a homeopathic preparation ('Neurexan' N = 156) in the treatment of adult insomnia. Both treatments were reported to increase length of sleep significantly, with Neurexan having a larger effect on reported daytime fatigue.

Valerian is one of the most widely used over-the-counter herbal supplements taken for sleep problems. In a US survey of over 31,000 adults, 5.9 per cent were found to use valerian as an aid to sleeping (Bliwise and Ansari 2007).

Stimulant herbs and extracts

A range of stimulants is also employed in the treatment of drowsiness or excessive sleepiness. Caffeine, ginseng, ephedra and yohimbine are the best known and most widely used of these.

CAFFEINE (*COFFEA ARABICA*)

The compound caffeine is found in a variety of plants including *Coffea arabica*, which is its principal source. It is a psychostimulant xanthine alkaloid that has been used, at least since the fifteenth century in Yemen where its consumption was first noted, for its stimulant effects, and today is consumed by most people around the world.

The biological effects and safety of caffeine have been extensively reviewed (Heckman, Weil and de Mejia 2010). At low doses, in randomized controlled research, compared to controls, it improves concentration and academic performance and increases self-reported anxiety (Smith, Sturgess and Gallagher 1999).

Caffeine interacts with a range of pharmaceutical products (Durrant 2002), and high levels of caffeine ingestion can result in life-threatening intoxication (Kromhout *et al.* 2008).

Historically, caffeine consumption was largely restricted to adults. There has been rapidly increasing marketing to and consumption of caffeinated drinks by children and adolescents in recent years, beginning in the 1960s (Harnack and Stang 1999). Despite a worrying lack of information on possible effects (see, e.g. Castellanos and Rapoport 2002), this marketing is now targetted at children as young as 4 (Temple 2009).

When taken by rats, caffeine increases wakefulness and reduces the amount of all sleep stages in a dose-response fashion (Yanik, Glaum and Radulovacki 1987).

Many people avoid taking caffeine before bed on the basis that it has a disruptive effect on their sleep. There is some evidence that for many people this is indeed the case. In normal control subjects, caffeine taken before bed has a disruptive effect on sleep, delaying onset, reducing overall sleep time and reducing the amount of stage 2 sleep (Paterson *et al.* 2009).

Caffeine is an adenosine receptor antagonist (Ribeiero and Sebastiao 2010; Scharf *et al.* 2008) and affects dopaminergic transmission (see Ferre 2010).

Factors affecting the effects of caffeine consumption have not been extensively studied. From the research to date, genetic factors are relevant to caffeine-induced anxiety and sleep disturbance, and there is a specifically increased risk of heart attack linked to carrying a cytochrome P450 polymorphism (Yang, Palmer and de Wit 2010).

There has been speculation, but to date no systematic research, on the possible therapeutic use of caffeine in ASD (Ghanizadeh 2010). From the research to date in the general population, there is evidence that caffeine could be used systematically to increase daytime alertness in individuals with excessive daytime tiredness.

Recent data from the Norwegian Mother and Child Cohort Study (MoBa) indicates that higher consumption of caffeinated soft drinks in the middle stages of pregnancy (recorded for the 17th and 13th weeks) increased the likelihood of infant overactivity at 18 months (Bekkhus *et al.* 2010).

There are some reported cases of psychotic reactions to caffeine ingestion (see Hedges, Woon and Hoopes 2009). Fatalities from caffeine can occur, typically through ingesting excessive numbers of caffeine stimulant tablets (see, e.g. Thelander *et al.* 2010). Although advised against in childhood, these are often taken by adolescents to aid attention during revision and as noted above, when taken later at night this is likely to compromise the quality of subsequent sleep.

In a review of 65 incidents in which seizures were possibly triggered by dietary supplements (Haller, Meier and Olson 2005), 15 of the 33 cases in which it was concluded that supplementation was related involved the use of herbal caffeine-containing supplements. How many individuals regularly consume such supplements is not clear so the relative risk is unknown. In most reported cases the supplements involved also contained ephedra, so the evidence on caffeine supplements without ephedra is less clear.

There are increasing concerns over emerging links between the prevalence of problem behaviour in adolescents (Miller 2008) and the rapid increase in consumption of caffeinated energy drinks (Reissig, Strain and Griffiths 2009).

EPHEDRA (*EPHEDRA SINICA*)

Ephedra is an extract from the plant *Ephedra sinica* and has been extensively used in traditional Chinese herbal medicine in the treatment of asthma and hay fever. It is also found in the Chinese herbal tea Ma Huang. Ephedra is a stimulant that increases metabolism, brain activity and heart rate.

Extensive use of ephedra by athletes was linked to two high profile US fatalities: Korey Stringer, an offensive player in the US National Football League for the Minnesota Vikings in 2001, and Steve Bechler, a major league baseball pitcher for the Baltimore Orioles in 2003. A range of concerns has been raised concerning its use both as a supplement (Haller and Benowitz 2000) and in athletic training (Powers 2001).

The FDA banned the use of ephedra-containing supplements in April 2004. It is now a restricted substance in the USA and available by prescription only in the UK.

There is ongoing controversy over the best ways to monitor possible side effects of dietary supplements. A useful review of some of the issues, highlighting the problems with ephedra, can be found in Schulman (2003). A commissioned meta-analysis of research on ephedra was instrumental in the FDA ban (Shakelle *et al.* 2003).

In a review of 65 incidents in which seizures were possibly triggered by dietary supplements (Haller *et al.* 2005), 27 of the 33 cases in which it was concluded that supplementation was related involved the use of ephedra-containing supplements, primarily for weight loss or sports performance enhancement. It is unclear how many of these cases had seizure problems prior to the event that was reported.

There have been no studies published on the use of ephedra or ephedra-containing supplements in ASD or in the treatment of sleep problems in children or adolescents.

YOHIMBINE (*PAUSINYSTALIA YOHIMBE* / *RAUWOLFIA SERPENTINA*)

Yohimbine is an alkaloid stimulant found in *Pausinystalia yohimbe* and *Rauwolfia serpentina*. Yohimbine hydrochloride is available on prescription in the US under various names (Actibine; Aphrodyne; Baron-X; Dayto Himbin; PMS-Yohimbine; Prohim; Thybine; Yocon; Yohimar; Yohimex; Yoman; Yovital).

Yohimbine is an alpha-2 adrenoreceptor antagonist. In primate studies it has been shown to induce hyperactivity when injected directly into the prefrontal cortex inducing alpha-2 adrenoreceptor blockade (Ma, Arnsten and Li 2005).

Anxiety symptoms and panic attacks have been reported from taking yohimbine and it can induce rapid heart rate and high blood pressure when taken with medications such as modafinil. Yohimbine is also reported to counteract the effects of sodium oxybate.

Combination herbal treatments

A variety of products are available that use a combination of herbal or herbal and non-herbal ingredients.

No peer-reviewed research has been carried out on the use of most such combined products that have individually been shown to affect sleep. As effects of combining these products could be additive, synergistic or antagonistic, it is difficult to assess the likely efficacy of such products.

'Sleep factors', for example, is a supplement available in the USA that combines valerian, blue skullcap, chamomile, hops, passionflower extract, wild lettuce leaf extract, California poppy, Jamaican dogwood, L-theanine and jujube fruit extract with melatonin, 5-HTP, GABA, calcium and magnesium. Many of these have been shown individually to have some effects on reported sleep problems.

'SleepCycle' contains the herbal ingredients Tang-Kuei root, hops, lemon balm, passionflower, polygala, valerian, jujube and wullinshen together with L-theanine, melatonin and 5-HTP and is marketed as a supplement aimed at improving sleep. Again the ingredients have been shown to be effective individually but there is no research on their use in this combination.

To find out more:

In the UK
National Institute of Medical Herbalists
Elm House
54 Mary Arches Street
Exeter
Devon EX4 3BA
UK
Tel: 01392 426022
Fax: 01392 498963
Email: nimh@ukexeter.freeserve.co.uk
Website: www.nimh.org.uk

In the USA
American Herbalists Guild
PO Box 230741
Boston, MA 02123
Tel: (857) 350-3128
Website: www.americanherbalistsguild.com
A useful website is Henriette's Herbal Homepage, maintained by a German-Finnish herbalist: www.henriettesherbal.com.

CHINESE HERBAL TREATMENTS

Chinese herbalism can be dated back reliably to 200–300 BC but some have argued it developed as early as 2852 BC in the reign of Emperor Fu Xi (Cheng 1984).

A wide range of Chinese herbal medicines is advocated and used in the treatment of insomnia. Baijianggen, Baiziren, Banxia, Chaihu, Chuanxiong, Danggui, Danshen, Dazao, Fuling, Fuxiaomai, Ganjiang, Hehuanpi, Lingzhi, Longyanrou, Shouwuteng, Suanzaoren, Wuweizei and Zhusha are amongst the more common. Many are used in combination or incorporated in preparations such as drinks and soups (for discussion, see Wing 2001).

Many herbs in use in the Chinese pharmacopoeia have strong biological activity and the biochemical basis to these processes is only just becoming better understood within a Western frame of reference (see Ehrman, Barlow and Hylands 2007a, 2007b).

Although randomized placebo-controlled trials are beginning to be used in the evaluation of Chinese herbal treatments both in mainland China and elsewhere, the quality of many of the studies to date is poor in comparison to the standards expected of Western research (Zhong *et al.* 2010). There are moves to ensure that, with the increasing popularity of Chinese herbal treatments, manufacture, labelling and safety monitoring conform to expected standards (see discussion by Ko 2004).

A 2009 paper collated the various Cochrane reviews of Chinese herbal treatments up until then. The paper found that in 22 of the 42 specific reviews of herbal medicine there was insufficient evidence of adequate quality to draw any conclusions concerning the efficacy of the treatments reviewed (Manheimer *et al.* 2009). None of the Cochrane reviews examined treatment of sleep difficulties.

Chinese herbal treatments are outside of my area of training and expertise and much of the literature remains untranslated and is not easily accessible. As these approaches have a long history, an accepted evidence base, and are widely accessible in Europe and North America they are covered here to the best of my ability, for information as best as I can ascertain on their usage and to provide information on potential issues and benefits where knowledge of these is available. It can be seen that many of the ingredients have close parallels to the Western herbal tradition. For many of the Chinese herbal supplements in use (see Table App 3.2), however, this information is not available or easily accessible to a non-Chinese-reading audience.

There have been no clinical or research trials on the use of Chinese herbal treatments in the management of sleep disorders in ASD.

TABLE APP 3.2 THE MAIN CHINESE HERBS WITH THEIR PRIMARY USES, KEY REFERENCES AND POSSIBLE ISSUES

Herb/Extract	Primary use in sleep problems	General studies on its use	Possible issues
Baijianggen	Difficulty sleeping – insomnia	As for valerian	See valerian in Table App 3.1
Baiziren	Insomnia, motor restlessness, night sweats	Wing 2001	Variation in constituents of different types
Banxia	Insomnia	Wing 2001	Contains ephedrine
Chaihu	Insomnia (usually in combination – see Da-Chai-Hu-Tang and Xiao-Chai-Hu-Tang under Chinese herbal formulae)	Shimizu 2000 (as a constituent of Xiao-Chai-Hu-Tang)	No safety information used singly. Some concerns over liver toxicity from Da-Chai-Hu-Tang and Xiao-Chai-Hu-Tang
Chuanxiong	Insomnia	Relaxes smooth muscle inducing reduction in blood pressure in animal models (see Chan *et al.* 2006). Human research is limited	None noted. Overdose can induce vomiting and dizziness
Danggui	Insomnia	Kupfersztain *et al.* 2003	Only evaluation in treatment of menopausal sleep problems

TABLE APP 3.2 CONT.

Herb/Extract	Primary use in sleep problems	General studies on its use	Possible issues
Danshen	Problems sleeping due to overarousal	Two studies claim good results in adult insomnia cases but no randomization or placebo controls. Li 2000; Wu and Han 1999	Counteracts blood thinning medications such as warfarin. Interferes with cytochrome P3A4 activity
Dazao	Insomnia	Mode of action is uncertain	A rare reaction is 'Dazao-induced angioneurotic oedema'
Ephedra	As a stimulant	See Shakelle et al. 2003	Currently banned in the USA and prescription only in the UK
Fuling	Insomnia, disturbed dreams	Wing 2001	No known side-effects
Fuxiaomai	Insomnia	Wing 2001	None unless coeliac or otherwise sensitive to gluten
Ganjiang	Insomnia	Wing 2001	Rare – mild heartburn and GI upset
Hehuanpi	Insomnia, disturbed dreams, overarousal	Wing 2001	Exacerbation of asthma has been reported
Hong Hwa	Insomnia	Chen et al. 2009	Can elevate levels of liver enzymes and white blood cells
Lingzhi	Insomnia	Sanodiya et al. 2009	Minor – most commonly dry throat, nosebleeds. Can lower both blood pressure and blood sugar level. Liver damage (rare)
Longyanrou	Restless sleep, minor insomnia	Wing 2001	Unclear
Sang Piao Xiao	Night-time enuresis	Helmer 2007	Unclear
Shouwuteng	Insomnia	Wing 2001	None reported
Wuweizi	Insomnia, disturbed dreams, overarousal, night-time enuresis	Helmer 2007	Abdominal upset, decreased appetite and skin rash
Zhusha (cinnabar)	Night terrors	Liu and Yang 2000	As for methyl mercury, but substantially less toxic

Specific Chinese medicinal herbs
used for sleep problems

BAIJIANGGEN

The dried root and rhizome of the plant *Patrinia scabiosaefolia,* Baijianggen is a relative of *Valeriana officinalis,* much used in Western herbal medicine, and is overlapping in its constituent compounds and actions (see Houghton 1988). Baijianggen is used as a powder or oil extract that contains triterpenoid saponins, patrinene, isopatrinene and isovaleric acid.

BAIZIREN

The dried kernel of the seed of *Platycladus orientalis*, in Chinese herbal medicine Baiziren is used to treat insomnia where there is motor agitation, night sweating and dream-disturbed sleep. This plant is extensively grown across mainland China for use in herbal medicine. A recent study of samples from 16 different areas identified significant regional variations in the chemical composition and four chemotypes (based on analysis of leaf compounds by gas chromatography and gas chromatography-mass spectrometry) (Lei *et al.* 2010). This suggests that there may be considerable variation in the constitution of medicines based on the different forms of Baiziren available.

BANXIA

The dried tuber of *Pinellia ternata*, Banxia contains glutamic acid, arginine, aminotubyric acid, choline, ß-sitosterol and homogentisic acid. It is used in traditional pinella and millet soup in the treatment of insomnia. Banxia is thought to contain ephedrine (see Simone 2004).

CHAIHU

Chaihu is the dried root of herbs of the *Bupleurum* genus. *Bupleurum chinensis*, *Bupleurum scorzonerifolium* and *Bupleurum marginatum* are the most commonly used of over 20 species that have been said to have medicinal properties. The powdered root contains saikosaponin, adonitol, a-spinasterol and volatile oils, and extracts have been shown to have effects on hepatic and immune function and on both GABA and 5-HT receptors. See Xiao-Chai-Hu-Tang under Chinese herbal formulae below.

CHUANXIONG

Chuanxiong is the dried rhizome of *Ligusticum chuanxiong* and contains butylidenephthalide, butylphthalide, tetramethylpyrazine and indole. Extracts have been shown to have effects on both GABA and 5-HT receptor function.

DANGGUI

The dried root of *Angelica sinensis*, Danggui contains monoterpenoids, sesquiterpenoids, ß-sitosterol, ferulic acid and succinic acid. It has been shown to have effects on both GABA and 5-HT receptor function. Danggui is a common ingredient in Chinese insomnia treatments.

Danggui has been found to be helpful in the treatment of sleep disorders and fatigue in menopausal women (Kupfersztain *et al.* 2003) but has not been tested in other groups.

DANSHEN

Danshen is the dried root of *Salvia miltiorrhiza* or *Salvia przewalskii*. It has been shown to contain tanshinone, cryptotanshinone, isotanshinone, miltirone and danshenxinkun. Miltirone has been shown to be a partial central benzodiazepine receptor agonist with tranquillizing effects when given orally (Lee *et al.* 1991).

Two studies in Chinese, cited by Wing 2001, claim good results in insomnia. In the first study (a series of 48 cases) (Wu and Han 1999), Danshen combined with Wuweizi produced improvements in 92 per cent of cases in the second series of 80 cases (Li 2000) Danshen with Huangqi (*Radix astragali*) produced improvement in 93 per cent. Huangqi is not a constituent of other traditional Chinese treatments used for sleep problems.

There is recent mouse research supporting the effects of Danshen on sleep – hastening sleep onset and lengthening sleeping time (Fang *et al.* 2010), but no good human studies of Danshen alone have yet appeared.

DAZAO

The dried fruit of *Zizyphus jujuba*, Dazao is a traditional Chinese herbal treatment for insomnia, usually taken in the form of liquorice, wheat and jujuba soup. The active ingredients are not clear.

EPHEDRA

An extract from *Ephedra sinica*, called Ma Huang in Chinese medicine, is a stimulant, which increases heart rate, blood pressure and body temperature (often termed as thermogenic because it cause the body to heat up). Use of ephedra was banned in the USA from 2004 because of reported cases of cardiac death, disability and insomnia.

FULING

Fuling is the dried encysted threads or hyphae of the fungus *Tuckahoe/Poria cocos*. It is known to contain a number of active constituents including triterpenic acids, histidine, adenine, choline, ß-pachymanase, lecithin, ergosterol and porin.

FUXIAOMAI

Fuxiaomail or *Triticum aestivum*, is wheat grain. It contains saccharides, sitosterol, vitamins and enzymes and is a key ingredient in medicinal soups such as liquorice, wheat and jujuba.

GANJIANG

Ganjiang, known in the West as ginger, is the dried rhizome of *Zingiber officinale*; it contains zingiberol, zingiberene, bisabolene and farnesene and has been noted to prolong sleeping time in animal studies.

HEHUANPI

The dried stem bark of *Albizzia julibrissin durazz*, Hehuanpi is used in the treatment of insomnia and has been noted to contain a number of saponins including julibroside J6, acacigenin B and tannin.

HONG HWA (SAFFLOWER)

Hong Hwa, *Carthamus tinctorius,* is extensively used in the Taiwanese population as a treatment for insomnia (Chen *et al.* 2009).

LINGZHI

Lingzhi is the dried fruiting bodies from either of two fungi: *Ganoderma lucidum* or *Ganoderma sinense*. It contains a number of active ingredients including ganoderic acid, lucidenic acid and ganolucidic acid and has a number of suggested medicinal uses including treatment of insomnia.

Liver damage has been reported in two cases (one resulting in fatal fulminant hepatitis) (Wanmuang *et al.* 2007).

LONGYANROU

The dried fruit of the longan (*Euphoria longan*), Longyanrou, contains sugars and vitamins. It is commonly taken to combat insomnia in Chinese medicine but there are no published clinical studies.

SANG PIAO XIAO

Sang Piao Xiao is made from the egg case of the praying mantis, which is a high source of protein. It is a traditional Chinese remedy used for a variety of urinary problems including bedwetting. There are no published clinical studies.

SHOUWUTENG

Shouwuteng is made from the dried stems of *Polygonum multiflorum*. The active chemical compounds appear to be anthroquinones, which have a sedative-hypnotic effect. In animal studies it proportionally increases stage 1 and reduces REM sleep.

WUWEIZI

Wuweizi is the dried ripened fruit of *Schisandra chinensis* or *Schisandra sphenanthera*. The name translates as 'Five-Flavoured seed'. It is the dried fruit of the orange magnolia vine. Wuweizi is used in the treatment of night sweating. It is biochemically complex, and reported to contain Deoxyschisandrin, kadsuranin, schisanhenol, schisanhenol acetate, gomisin, schisandrin, isoschisandrin, schisandrol, angeloylgomisin, tiggoylgomisin, benzoylgomisin, rubschisandrin, epigomisin, schisantherin, andeloylgomisin, tigloylgomisin, binankadsurin, angeloylbinankadsurin, isobutyroylibinankadsurin, benzoylbinankadsurin, rubschisantherin.

There have been no published studies in the Western peer-reviewed literature on its use in ASD, in children and adolescents, or in the treatment of sleep disorders.

ZHUSHA

Zhusha is a cinnabar mineral that contains mercuric sulphide and other minerals. It has antiseptic properties. It has a risk of causing toxic side effects. The toxicity profile of cinnabar is markedly lower than for other mercurials and it is around 1000 times less toxic than methyl mercury; however,there is limited justification from a clinical evidence base for its widespread use in traditional Chinese medicine (Liu *et al.* 2008).

In animal models, the use of cinnabar reduces brain levels of serotonin, which results in reduced anxiety (Wang *et al.* 2007). The neurochemical mode of action of orally administered cinnabar is beginning to be clarified through animal models (Huang, Liu and Lin-Shiau 2007).

In one Chinese study, cinnabar as a topical application was reported as a treatment for night terrors (Liu and Yang 2000 (study in Chinese, cited in Wing 2001)). Zhusha was applied to the skin rather than being used orally because of the reduced risk of mercury toxicity.

Chinese herbal formulae

The following section deals with combinations of Chinese herbal product, normally referred to as formulae. Often herbs are combined in Chinese classic formulae that are said by practitioners to be more effective than the components taken individually. For the treatment of sleep problems, some of the better known of these herbal formulae are discussed below.

ANMIAN PIAN (PEACEFUL SLEEP PILLS)

These contain *Ziziphus jujuba* seed, *Polygala tenuifolia* root, *Poria cocos* fungus, *Gardenia jasminoides* fruit, *Massa fermenta* and *Glycyrrhiza uralensis* root.

There have been no studies reported on its use in the treatment of children or in individuals with ASD.

ANSHUI WAN (CALM SLEEP PILLS)

These contain *Polygonum multiflorum* vine, *Triticum aestivum* seed, *Polygala tenuifolia* root, *Rehmannia glutinosa* root-prep, *Biota orientalis* seed, *Citrus reticulata* peel, *Ziziphus spinosa* seed, *Dioscorea opposita* rhizome, *Poria cocos* fungus, *Codonopsis pilosula* root, *Platycodon grandiflorum* root, *Angelica sinensis* root, *Scrophularia ningpoensis* root, *Ophiopogon japonicus* tuber, *Atractylodes macrocephala* rhizome, *Glycyrrhiza uralensis* root, *Acorus gramineus* rhizome and *Schisandra chinensis* fruit.

There have been no studies reported on its use in the treatment of children or in individuals with ASD.

CHAI HU JIA LONG GU MU LI TANG (SAIKO-KA-RYUKOTSU-BOREI-TO)

This is recommended for neurotic insomnia (Fruehauf 1995). It contains Chaihu (*Radix bupleuri*), Huang Qin (*Radix scutellariae baicalensis*), Da Huang (*Rhizoma rhei*), Banxia, Sheng Jiang (*Rhizoma zingiberis officinalis recens*), Ren Shen (*Radix ginseng*), Da Zao (*Fructus zizyphi jujubae*), Gui Zhi (*Ramulus cinnamomi cassiae*), Fu Ling (*Sclerotium poriae cocos*), Long Gu (*Os draconis*) and Mu Li (*Concha ostreae*).

There have been no studies reported on its use in the treatment of children or in individuals with ASD.

DA-CHAI-HU-TANG (DAI-SAIKO-TO)

This is widely used as a treatment for hypertension and insomnia. It is made from a combination of bupleurum root, peony root, scutellaria root, jujube, pinellia tuber, rhubarb, ginger and immature bitter orange. It has been reported as causing autoimmune hepatitis (Kamiyama *et al.* 1997).

There have been no studies reported on its use in the treatment of children or in individuals with ASD.

DANZHI ANSHEN (QUALITY SLEEP PILLS)

This contains wild jujube seed, cnidium, anemarrhena, dwarf lilyturf tuber, prepared tuber fleeceflower root, schizandra fruit, red sage root and poria.

There have been no studies reported on its use in the treatment of children or in individuals with ASD.

JIA-WEY-SHIAU-YAU-SAN

This contains *Angelica sinensis*, *Atractylodes macrocephala*, *Paeonia lactiflora*, *Bupleurum chinense* and *Poria coco*.

There have been no studies reported on its use in the treatment of children or in individuals with ASD.

SUAN-ZAO-REN-TANG

This is a combined medication made from the dried ripened seeds of sour jujube seed (*Ziziphus acidojujuba*), together with Fu-Ling *(Sclerotium poriae cocos)* and liquorice *(Glycyrrhiza glabra)*. It is the most commonly used Chinese herbal treatment for insomnia (Chung and Lee 2002). Active constituents include jujuboside A and B, betulic acid, betulin spinosin, and feruloyl spinosin. Studies on its biochemical mode of action indicate that it affects both tryptophan and gamma-aminobutyric acid metabolism (see Chuang *et al.* 2009; Yi *et al.* 2007).

In one early placebo-controlled study of 60 adult patients with sleep disorders significant improvements in sleep quality and wellbeing were reported during active treatment (Chen and Hsieh 1985).

There have been no studies reported on its use in the treatment of children or in individuals with ASD.

XIAO-CHAI-HU-TANG (SHO-SAIKO-TO)

This is widely used as a treatment for both liver problems and fatigue (Shimizu 2000). It consists of a mixture of seven herbal extracts: bupleurum root, pinellia tuber, scutellaria root, jujube fruit, ginseng root, glycyrrhiza root and ginger rhizome, all of which we have discussed above. A number of adult cases of liver damage have now been reported through the use of this treatment (Hsu *et al.* 2006; Itoh *et al.* 1995).

YI-GAN SAN

This is made from *Atractylodis lanceae* rhizoma, hoelen, *Cnidii rhizoma*, *Angelicae radix*, *Bupleuri radix*, *Glycyrrhizae radix* and *Uncariae ramulus et uncus*. This has been reported as a treatment for REM sleep behaviour disorder in a series of three adult cases (Shinno *et al.* 2008).

YI NIAO LING FANG

This is made from fresh Bai Guo (*Semen ginkgonis bilobae*), Mu Li (*Concha ostreae*), Sang Ji Sheng (*Ramulus loranthi seu visci*), Sang Piao Xiao (*Ootheca mantidis*), Wu Bei Zi (*Galla rhois*), Wu Wei Zi (*Fructose schisandrae chinensis*), Yi Zhi Ren (*Fructus alpiniae oxyphyllae*), Shan Zhu Yu (*Fructus corni officinalis*), Shu Di Huang (*cooked Radix rehmanniae*) and Suan Zao Ren (*Semen zizyphi spinosae*), Shan Yao (*Radix dioscoreae oppositae*) and Jiu Cai Zi (*Semen alli tuberosi*).

It has recently been reported as an effective treatment for nocturnal enuresis in children (Yu-lian *et al.* 2002). A cohort of 96 children aged 5–13 who had been referred for night-time enuresis and had a median of 1.28 episodes of wetting per night were reported on. Fifty cases were treated with Yi Niao Ling Fang and treatment response was compared against 46 cases treated with imipramine: 98 per cent of those on Yi Niao Ling Fang showed clinical improvement, compared to 73 per cent of the imipramine group. Case allocation and follow-up were unclear; however, follow-up to 2 years on treatment responders is reported in the paper.

There have been no specific clinical or research trials reported on the use of CHM in the treatment of children or in individuals with ASD.

For further information on traditional Chinese Herbal Medicine:
The Association of Traditional Chinese Medicine (UK)
5A Grosvenor House
1 High Street
Edgware
London HA8 7TA
UK
Tel: 020 8951 3030
Fax: 020 8951 3030
Email: info@atcm.co.uk
Website: www.atcm.co.uk/index.htm

JAPANESE KAMPO HERBAL TREATMENTS

Kampo means 'method from the Han period of Ancient China', an approach that was first practised and taught in Japan by Korean physicians in the early seventh century. The approach is based on tailoring the treatment to symptoms elicited by examination of the patient and in this respect is similar to more traditional Western medicine.

Japanese herbal treatments are typically given in combinations which can have physiological effects sometimes not observed when administered singly. Assessment of the biological activities of and interactions between the components of these preparations is only starting to be addressed (see, e.g. Borchers *et al.* 2000; Kiyohara, Matsumoto and Yamada 2004). Currently, 148 different preparations are commonly available in Japan, but the evidence base on their uses and efficacy has only just begun to receive scientific attention. Some 37 RCTs of Kampo treatments for a variety of conditions are available in English (see Watanabe *et al.* 2011).

There have been no specific clinical or research trials on the use of Kampo treatments in the management of sleep disorders in ASD.

Some of the Kampo treatments used in the treatment of sleep or sleep-related conditions are discussed below.

CHIBAKU-JIOHU-GAN

This is a herbal medicine used for the control of nocturnal enuresis.

HACHIMI-JIOHU-GAN (BA-WEI-WAN)

This has a beneficial effect on renal function in animal models (Yamabe and Yokozawa 2006) and is a common traditional Japanese treatment for nocturnal enuresis. This formula has eight herbal ingredients: rehmannia root (Shu di huang); cornus fruit (Shan zhu yu); dioscorea rhizome (Shan yao); alisma rhizome (Ze xie); moutan bark (Mu dan pi); cinnamon bark (Gui pi); Hoelen (Fu ling) and processed lateral root of aconite (Fu zi).

HOCHU-EKKI-TO

This is a traditional Kampo herbal medicine. It combines ten hot-water extracted herbal essences (of *Ginseng radix*, *Atractylodis rhizoma*, *Astragali radix*, *Angelicae radix*, *Zizyphi fructus*, *Bupleuri radix*, *Glycyrrhizae radix*, *Zingiberis rhizoma*, *Cimicifugae rhizoma* and *Aurantii nobilis pericarpium*) and is used to correct Kikyo or 'delicate constitution'. The only randomized placebo-controlled trial to date assessed its adjunctive effects in the treatment of atopic dermatitis, and demonstrated that as an adjunct its use significantly improved response to conventional therapy (Kobayashi *et al.* 2010).

KEISHI-KA-RYUKOTSU-BOREI

This is a combination of seven hot-water extracted herbal essences (*Cinnamomi cortex*, *Paeoniae radix*, *Zizyphi fructus*, *Ostreae testa*, *Fossilia ossis mastodi*, *Glycyrrhizae radix* and *Zingiberis rhizoma*). It is used for night sweating, insomnia and nocturnal enuresis.

NINJIN-YOUEI-TO

This combines 12 hot-water extracted herbal essences (*Angelicae radix*, *Rehmanniae radix*, *Ginseng radix*, *Atractylodis rhizoma*, hoelen, *Cinnamoni cortex*, *Aurantii nobilis pericarpium*, *Paeoniae radix*, *Polygalae radix*, *Astragali radix*, *Schisandrae fructus* and *Glycyrrhizae radix*).

Further information:
A useful website with information on Kampo is maintained by the Keio University Medical School in Tokyo: www.keio-kampo.jp/index_en.html
Center for Kampo Medicine
Keio University School of Medicine
Shinomachi 35
Shinjuku-Ku
Tokyo
Japan 160-8582
Tel: (+81) 93-3353-1211

OTHER HERBAL TREATMENTS

Herbal medicines are widely used in many other countries and cultures (see, for general examples, Patwardhan *et al.* 2005 on Ayurvedic medicine and Oshikoya *et al.* 2008 on Nigerian herbal medicine). Many of the herbs that are used are the same either botanically or in their mode of action; however, an evidence base on efficacy and safety in much of this practice is limited or lacking.

BUCHU

Buchu (*Agathosma betulina*) is a shrub native to South Africa. The name derives from the Hottentot word for the plant, 'bookoo/buku/bucku/bucco' (Moolla and Viljoen 2008).

The leaves can be used to make an essential oil. Analysis shows the oil to contain limonene, isomenthone, diosphenol (buchu camphor), terpinen-4-ol and several minor sulphur-containing compounds. Preparations from the leaf of this plant have been suggested as being helpful for a range of medical conditions including urinary tract infections and bedwetting (Simpson 1998).

There are no studies on the use of buchu in the treatment of sleep disorders that would allow any conclusions concerning its safety or efficacy.

MEXICAN HERBAL TREATMENTS

To take one further example, Mexican herbal medicine is complex but has as yet received little systematic research (Rodriguez-Fragoso *et al.* 2008). Many of the herbs in use are used in other herbal approaches, but some such as nopal (*Opuntia ficus indica*), chapparal (*Larrea divaricata*) and mullein (*Verbascum densiflorum*) are not used in the Western or Asian pharmacopoeia. Chaparral has been reported to cause toxic hepatitis (Gordon *et al.* 1995). Mullein is extensively used in Mexican herbal medicine including its use as a treatment for sleep problems. This herb has a complex chemistry (Turker and Camper 2002), but the only published research to date concerns its use in the treatment of otitis media (Gagnier *et al.* 2006).

There have been no specific clinical or research trials on the use of Mexican herbal treatments in the management of sleep disorders in ASD.

APPENDIX 4

—— ❊ ——

ASSESSMENT TOOLS FOR SLEEP PROBLEMS

A wide range of measures of sleep in children and adolescents is currently available. A recent review discusses 21 separate measures that are currently in use (Lewandowski, Toliver-Sokol and Palermo 2011). Table App 4.1 shows some of the main measures and their uses. All are referred to in the text, and the key references are given to allow comparison with normative and clinical data.

TABLE APP 4.1 MEASURES OF SLEEP IN CHILDREN AND ADOLESCENTS

Measure	Key paper/s	Uses
Sleep diary	Generic – a variety of forms are available	Baseline in all types of sleep problem to track changes
Brief Infant Sleep Questionnaire (BISQ)	Sadeh 2004	Screen correlated well with actigraphy and sleep diary measures
Children's Sleep Hygiene Scale (CSHS)	Harsh *et al.* 2002	Parent-report assessment of sleep hygiene in 2–8-year-olds
Adolescent Sleep Hygiene Scale (ASHS)	LeBourgeois *et al.* 2004, 2005	Assessment of sleep hygiene in 12–17-year-olds
Adolescent Sleep–Wake Scale (ASWS)	LeBourgeois *et al.* 2005	Assesses sleep initiation, maintenance and quality in 12–18-year-olds
Children's Sleep Habits Questionnaire (CSHQ)	Goodlin-Jones *et al.* 2008; Owens, Spirito and McGuinn 2000; Owens *et al.* 2000	Screening assessment for 4–10-year-old sleep problems, covering eight key domains
Pediatric Daytime Sleepiness Scale (PDSS)	Drake *et al.* 2003	A self-report scale for 11–15-year-olds to assess EDS
Pediatric Sleep Questionnaire (PSQ)	Chervin *et al.* 2000	Parent questionnaire for 2–18-year-olds reliably assesses sleep-related behaviour disorders, snoring, sleepiness and daytime behavioural issues

TABLE APP 4.1 CONT.

Measure	Key paper/s	Uses
Epworth Sleepiness Scale Revised for children (ESS-RC)	Melendres *et al.* 2004; Moore *et al.* 2009	Assesses EDS in children and adolescents
Pittsburgh Sleep Quality Index (PSQI)	Buysse *et al.* 1989	An adult scale with data on good sleepers, sleep disordered patients and depressed patients
Children's ChronoType Questionnaire (CCTQ)	Werner *et al.* 2009	Parent report measures 4–11-year-olds – discriminates three chronotypes and correlated with discrimination on actigraphy
Flinders Fatigue Scale (FFS)	Gradisar *et al.* 2007; Hudson *et al.* 2009	Originally an adult measure. Recently used as a measure of recent fatigue to characterize sleep features of an anxious group in a 7–12-year-old population
BEARS screening instrument	Owens and Dalzell 2005	A simple five-item screening tool to identify sleep problems in 2–12-year-olds
Behavioral Evaluation of Disorders of Sleep Scale (BEDSS)	Schreck 1997/1998; Schreck *et al.* 2003	Systematic assessment of main sleep problems – data from 307 families of 5–12-year-olds
Bedtime Routines Questionnaire	Henderson and Jordan 2010	Questionnaire for parents of 2–8-year-olds

A number of useful sleep measures are downloadable from the KIDZZZSLEEP website at http://kidzzzsleep.org; these include alternative sleep diary formats to the one I have given.

SLEEP DIARY

Name _____   Person recording information _____

Date _____

Medication _____

Sleep event	Location	Behaviour	Setting events

Sleep event: time sleep began and time awakened

Location: where the person slept

Behaviour: any significant behaviours (snoring; speech; crying out; sweating…)

Setting events: any relevant events (background noise; awoken by…; etc.; room unusually hot/cold, etc.)

This is a list of sources for the scales outlined in Table App 4.1.

1. The Brief Infant Sleep Questionnaire (BISQ) (Sadeh 2004)

The BISQ is a brief, nine-item, multiple choice scale and is an appendix to the Sadeh 2004 paper. The paper gives data on 43 sleep disturbed and 57 control BISQ ratings, and an internet survey which obtained data from a further 1028 families. The BISQ can be downloaded from: www.sleep.tau.ac.il/BISQ%20-%20Pediatrics%202004.pdf.

2. The Child Sleep Hygiene Scale (Harsh et al. 2002)

This is a 25-item scale, with each item scored on a 6-point scale from 'Never' to 'Always'. It was developed by the Sleep Research Laboratory of the University of Southern Mississippi as a parent report measure for sleep hygiene in 2–8-year-olds. In the original paper, which presented data on 246 US children, the mean score on the scale in children without sleep issues was 57.2 (maximum possible score = 150).

Refer to the original paper for further details; the scale is reproduced below:

		1.	2	3	4	5	6
1.	Naps within 4 hours of bedtime						
2.	Caffeine within 4 hours of bedtime						
3.	Does things that are relaxing before bedtime						
4.	Drinks a lot of liquids before bedtime						
5.	Plays rough before bedtime						
6.	Does things that are alerting before bedtime						
7.	Goes to bed about the same time every day						
8.	Complains of being hungry at bedtime						
9.	Does things in bed that keep them awake						
10.	Goes to bed in the same place						
11.	Goes to bed feeling upset						
12.	Goes to bed with worries						
13.	Sleeps in a darkened room						
14.	Sleeps in a room that is too hot or too cold						
15.	Sleeps in a room where there are loud noises						
16.	Sleeps alone (in their own bed)						
17.	Sleeps in a room that is stuffy						
18.	Sleeps all or part of the night with someone else						
19.	Sleeps in a bed that is comfortable						
20.	Sleeps in a home where someone smokes						
21.	Has a calming bedtime routine						
22.	Uses bed for things other than sleep						

		1	2	3	4	5	6
23.	Put to bed after falling asleep						
24.	Stays up past usual bedtime						
25.	Gets out of bed about same time in morning						

1: Never; 2: Occasional; 3: Sometimes; 4: Typical; 5: Frequent; 6: Always

3. The Adolescent Sleep Hygiene Scale (ASHS) (LeBourgeois et al. 2004, 2005)

This is a 28-item scale, with each item scored on a 6-point scale from 'Never' to 'Always'. Questions are clustered to cover nine specific topics: physiological, cognitive, emotional, sleep environment, daytime sleep, substance use, bedtime routine, sleep stability and bed/bedroom sharing. It has been standardized on samples of 12–17-year-old adolescents both from the USA (N = 552) and Italy (N = 776).

The ASHS appears as an appendix to the LeBourgeois *et al.* (2005) article, downloadable from http://pediatrics.aappublications.org/content/115/Supplement _1/257.full.

4. The Adolescent Sleep–Wake Scale AS-WS) (LeBourgeois et al. 2005)

This is a 28-item scale, with each item scored on a 6-point scale from 'Never' to 'Always'. Separate groups of items deal with going to bed; falling asleep; maintaining sleep; reinitiating sleep and returning to wakefulness.

The AS-WS also appears as an appendix to the LeBourgeois *et al.* (2005) article, downloadable from: http://pediatrics.aappublications.org/content/115/ Supplement_1/257.full.

5. The Children's Sleep Habits Questionnaire (CSHQ) (Preschool and School-Age) (Owens Spirito and McGuinn 2000; Owens et al. 2000)

This is a 51-item scale. All items are scored as 'usually', 'sometimes' or 'rarely' and scored for whether or not the item is seen as a problem. Items are clustered as 'night-time', 'sleep behaviour', 'waking during the night' and 'morning waking'. It was originally standardized on 469 normal 4–10-year-old children and a sample of 154 children attending a paediatric sleep disorder clinic.

The abbreviated 22-item version of the CSHQ and a scoring document can be downloaded from: http://kidzzzsleep.org/research/intruments.

6. Pediatric Daytime Sleepiness Scale (PDSS) (Drake et al. 2003)

The PDSS is a well-established 8 item scale initially validated on a sample of 450 11-15 year olds, with an additional reported sample aged 5-13y. It is a reliable scale for this age range. The PDSS can be downloaded from the Iowa Sleep Disorders Center website at www.iowasleep.com/pdfs/Pediatric%20Daytime%20Sleepiness%20Scale.pdf

7. The Pediatric Sleep Questionnaire (PSQ) (Chervin et al. 2000)

This 22-item scale was standardized on a sample of 54 children (age range 2–18) with polysomnographically confirmed sleep disordered breathing, and 108 children who were attending general paediatric clinics.

This scale would need to be obtained from the source paper or by contacting the lead author, Dr Chervin. At the time of writing Dr Chervin is based at the Mayo School of Graduate Medical Education in Rochester, Maryland, USA.

8. The Epworth Sleepiness Scale (ESS) (Johns 1991)

The ESS is a well-validated scale for daytime sleepiness in adults. A paediatric version, the ESS-R C (Epworth Sleepiness Scale- Revised for Children) has been developed for 2–18 year olds (Melendres et al. 2004; Moore et al. 2009). This 8-item four-point scale can be completed by either the child or a caregiver, and a good correlation is reported between the two ratings. The ESS-RC can be found as an appendix to the Melendres et al. paper and can be downloaded from http://pediatrics.aappublications.org/content/114/3/768.full.html. The original version of the ESS is available for personal use from the author's website (http://epworthsleepinessscale.com). A commercial licence needs to be obtained for non-personal use and an annual licence fee is payable. A licence application can be made through http://epworthsleepinessscale.com/licence-registration.

9. The Pittsburgh Sleep Quality Index (PSQI) (Buysse et al. 1989)

The PQSI is an adult scale which could be a useful adjunct for assessing parental sleep pattern in some cases. This scale can be accessed through the University of Pittsburgh Sleep Medicine Institute website at http://www.sleep.pitt.edu/content.asp?id=1484. Copyright is owned by the University and permission for use needs to be obtained from the first author.

10. The Children's ChronoType Questionnaire (CCTQ) (Werner et al. 2009)

This is a 27-item scale for assessment of the typical sleep pattern in a child presenting with erratic sleep. This scale has been standardized on 152 children (77 boys, 75 girls) aged 4–11 (mean 6.7 years +1.5 years).

This scale is an appendix to the source paper. This is an NIH public access manuscript and can be downloaded from www.ncbi.nlm.nih.gov/pmc/articles/PMC2988284.

11. The Flinders Fatigue Scale (FFS) (Gradisar et al. 2007; Hudson et al. 2009)

This is a simple 7-item scale for rating daytime fatigue associated with insomnia. It uses a 5-point rating on 6 of the items and a 7-period rating for times of peak tiredness. Clinical use of the scale is based on an initial online validation study; a study of sensitivity to change in a 5-week CBT programme for insomnia; and a study that used the scale in assessment of sleep patterns in 7–12-year-old children with clinical anxiety.

This scale is an appendix to the first source paper. The paper is a PubMed Central open access document and can be downloaded from www.ncbi.nlm.nih.gov/pmc/articles/PMC2556916.

12. The BEARS screening instrument (adolescent questions) (Owens and Dalzell 2005)

This is a brief screening scale consisting of five core questions and four supplementary ones. It is not a standardized scale and is recommended for use by clinicians familiar both with the symptoms and risk factors for adolescent sleep problems.

Refer to the source paper for further information. The Acronym BEARS stands for key questions about: Bedtime problems; Excessive daytime sleepiness; Awakenings during the night; Regularity and duration of sleep and Sleep-disordered breathing. The supplementary questions are about daytime napping, exercise, stimulants (caffeine, tea and cola) and alcohol intake.

13. The Behavioral Evaluation of Disorders of Sleep Scale (BEDSS) (Schreck 1997/1998; Schreck et al. 2003)

The BEDSS is a systematic assessment of sleep problems that has been validated on a sample of 307 families of 5–12 year old children with sleep problems. Data using this scale have been published on 1361 5–12-year-old children. Factor analysis identified five different types of sleep issues: Expressive Sleep Disturbances; Sensitivity to the Environment; Disoriented Awakening; Requiring Sleep Facilitators (medication/pacifier) and Apnoea/Bruxism.

This scale was developed by Dr Kimberley Schreck who at the time of writing is Associate Professor of Psychology at Penn State University in Harrisburg, Pennsylvania, USA. Further information, including a list of publications, can be found at http://harrisburg.psu.edu/faculty-and-staff/kimberly-schreck-phd.

14. The Bedtime Routines Questionnaire (Henderson and Jordan 2010)

This is a recent scale developed by Jill Henderson and Sara Jordan at the University of Mississippi in Harrisburg. It is a 31-item questionnaire with a 5-point rating on each item. The scale has four subscales, and covers weekday and weekend bedtime routines; reactivity to changes in routine and activities before bedtime. The scale is reproduced in their paper.

FURTHER READING

Basic books on sleep and sleep disorders

Carranza, C. (2004) *Banishing Night Terrors and Nightmares*. London: Kensington Books.

Daymond, K. (2001) *The 'Parentalk' Guide to Sleep*. London: Hodder & Stoughton Ltd.

Douglas, J. and Richman, N. (1988) *My Child Won't Sleep*. Harmondsworth: Penguin.

Durand, M.V. (1997) *Sleep Better!: Guide to Improving Sleep for Children with Special Needs*. Baltimore, MD: Paul H. Brookes.

Durand, M.V. (2008a) *When Children Don't Sleep Well: Interventions for Pediatric Sleep Disorders Therapist Guide (Treatments that Work)*. Oxford: Oxford University Press.

Durand, M.V. (2008b) *When Children Don't Sleep Well: Interventions for Pediatric Sleep Disorders Parent Workbook (Treatments that Work)*. Oxford: Oxford University Press.

Epstein, L. and Mardon, S. (2006) *The Harvard Medical School Guide to a Good Night's Sleep*. New York, NY: McGraw-Hill.

Espie, C.A. (2006) *Overcoming Insomnia and Sleep Problems: A Self-Help Guide Using Cognitive Behavioral Techniques*. London: Constable and Robinson.

Ferber, R. (1985) *Solve Your Child's Sleep Problems*. New York, NY: Simon and Schuster.

Haslam, D. (1992) *Sleepless Children: A Handbook for Parents*. London: Piatkus Books.

Hirshkowitz, M. and Smith, P.B. (2004) *Sleep Disorders for Dummies*. Hoboken:, NJ Wiley Publishing Co.

Hobson, J.A. (1988) *The Dreaming Brain*. New York, NY: Basic Books.

Horne, J. (2006) *Sleepfaring: A Journey through the Science of Sleep*. Oxford: Oxford University Press.

Hollyer, B. (2002) *Sleep: The Easy Way to Peaceful Nights*. London: Cassell.

Jouvet, M. (2001) *The Paradox of Sleep: The Story of Dreaming*. Cambridge, MA: MIT Press.

Jouvet, M. (2008) *The Paradox of Sleep: The Castle of Dreams*. Cambridge, MA: MIT Press.

Margo, S. (2008) *The Good Sleep Guide*. London: Vermillion.

Martin, P. (2002) *Counting Sheep: The Science and Pleasures of Sleep and Dreams*. London: HarperCollins.

Morrisroe, P. (2010) *Wide Awake*. New York, NY: Spiegel & Grau.

Oswald, I. (1966) *Sleep*. Harmondsworth: Penguin.

Pantley, E. (2002) *The No-Cry Sleep Solution: Gentle Ways to Help Your Baby Sleep through the Night*. Chicago, IL: McGraw-Hill.

Stores, G. (2009a) *The Facts: Sleep Problems in Children and Adolescents*. Oxford: Oxford University Press.

Stores, G. (2009b) *Insomnia and other Adult Sleep Problems: The Facts*. Oxford: Oxford University Press.

Wiedman, J. (1998) *Desperately Seeking Snoozing: The Insomnia Cure from Awake to Zzzz*. Wisconsin: University of Wisconsin Press.

Wiley, T.S. and Formby, B. (2000) *Lights Out: Sleep Sugar and Survival*. New York, NY: Simon & Schuster Inc.

Wilson, S. and Nutt, D. (2008) *Sleep Disorders* (Oxford Psychiatry Library). Oxford: Oxford University Press.

Textbooks on Sleep and Related Issues

Barkoukis, T.J. and Avidan, A.Y. (2007) *Review of Sleep Medicine*. New York, NY: Butterworth-Heinemann.

Collop, N.A. (2007) *Medical Disorders and Sleep* (Sleep Medicine Clinics: 2 (The Clinics: Internal Medicine)). New York, NY: Saunders.

Durand, M.V. (2008) *When Children Don't Sleep Well: Therapist Guide: Interventions for Pediatric Sleep Disorders (Treatments that Work)*. New York, NY: Oxford University Press.

Kryger, M.H., Roth, T. and Dement, W.C. (eds) (2005) *Principles and Practice of Sleep Medicine*, 4th edn. Philadelphia, PA: Elsevier/Saunders.

Lee-Chiong, T.L. (ed.) (2006) *Sleep: A Comprehensive Handbook*. Hoboken, NJ: Wiley.

Lee-Chiong, T. (2008) *Sleep Medicine: Essentials and Review*. New York, NY: Oxford University Press.

McNamara, P., Barton, R.A. and Nunn, C.L. (eds) (2010) *Evolution of Sleep: Phylogenetic and Functional Perspectives*. Cambridge: Cambridge University Press.

Pandi-Perumal, S.R. and Kramer, M. (eds) (2010) *Sleep and Mental Illness*. Cambridge: Cambridge Medicine.

Refinetti, R. (2006) *Circadian Physiology*. Boca Raton, FL: CRC Press.

Steriade, M. (2003) *Neuronal Substrates of Sleep and Epilepsy*. Cambridge: Cambridge University Press.

Stickgold, M. and Walker, M.P. (2009) *The Neuroscience of Sleep*. London: Academic Press.

Thorpy, M.J. and Billiard, M. (eds) (2011) *Sleepiness: Causes, Consequences and Treatment*. Cambridge: Cambridge University Press.

GLOSSARY

I have not included medications or herbal treatments in this glossary as the relevant ones are indexed and have been explained in the appendices.

Acetylserotonin methyltransferase (ASMT)	The enzyme that catalyses the reaction that converts n-acetylserotonin into melatonin.
Actigraphy	An automated method of recording movement during sleep, usually through a wrist recorder that registers change in position.
Adenosine	Adenosine is a nucleic acid component of DNA and RNA. It can also function as a neurotransmitter. It is composed of adenine and d-ribose.
Adenosine triphosphate (ATP)	ATP is an adenine nucleotide with three phosphate groups that is involved in mitochondrial energy production. In addition it has functions as a neurotransmitter and is involved in muscle activity through myosins which are ATP dependent.
Adrenocorticotropic hormone (ACTH)	A hormone secreted by the pituitary gland that affects the production of cortical steroids by the adrenal glands.
Agonist	A compound that acts to increases the available levels of a biologically active substance.
Alveolar hypoventilation	A build-up of carbon dioxide in the bloodstream resulting from a decreased rate of breathing.
Amygdala	An almond-shaped brain structure in the frontal part of the temporal lobes. It is a part of the limbic system and is involved in the processing of emotion.
Anopnthalmia	Failure of the eyes to develop.
Anterior cingulated cortex	A deep part of the frontal cortex, surrounding the corpus callosum. It is involved in various aspects of autonomic regulation such as heart rate, breathing and blood pressure, and in decision-making and processing of emotion.
Apnoea	A brief period when someone stops breathing.
Apoptosis	Selective programmed cell death as a means of refining brain function.
Applied Behaviour Analysis (ABA)	The application of learning theory principles to the modification of behaviour.
Aromatic amino acid l-carboxylase (AADC)	The lyase enzyme (AKA 5-hydroxytryptophan decarboxylase) that converts 5-HTP to serotonin.

Ascending reticular activating system (ARAS)	The ARAS is a midbrain system that regulates our state of arousal.
Astrocyte	The largest and most prolific glial cells in the nervous system. They have projections in all directions, hence the name, derived from the Greek word ástron meaning star.
Atonia	Sleep paralysis, a condition where the person is awake and aware but unable to perform voluntary movements.
B6	One of the B vitamins, AKA pyridoxal. The active form, pyridoxal phosphate (P-5-P) is involved in many aspects of amino acid metabolism including the production of serotonin.
B12	A B vitamin, aka cobalamin, is a cobalt-based compound with a structure not unlike haemoglobin. It is involved in a wide range of bodily processes from DNA synthesis, fatty acid and blood production to brain function.
BH4	see: THBP4 (tetrahydrobiopterin).
Body mass index (BMI)	The BMI is a number (given by computing a person's weight divided by the square of their height; this is sometimes called the Quetelet index after the mathematician who devised the scheme, which is used as a proxy figure for body fat compared to the general population).
Bruxism	Tooth-grinding – habitual involuntary grinding or clenching of the teeth.
CAP	The CAP is a fluctuating pattern seen in the unstable phases of NREM sleep which are composed of arousal and rebound phases of between 20 and 40 seconds.
Cardiotocography	A system for recording the foetal heart rate and uterine contractions in the third trimester of pregnancy, typically with ultrasonic sensors.
CAT scan	A computerized axial tomography (or CAT) scan is a method that enables information from an X-ray source rotated around an object to be built up to give a cross-sectional image. In brain imaging, this was the first technique that allowed imaging of brain structures *in situ*.
Cataplexy	A sudden loss of muscle tone and voluntary control brought on by a strong emotion such as fear or shock or an unexpected noise or movement.
Catathrenia	Sleep-related groaning.
Coeliac	An allergic reaction to gluten that can be tested for (people with coeliac disease have antiendomesial and anti-gliadin antibodies).
Centromere	The centromere is a section of DNA where the two halves of the chromosome are closest during metaphase, and the point at which the two halves of each chromosome separate prior to cell division.
Chronobiology	The study of biological processes that typically follow an ultradian, circadian or monthly cycle.
Chronotype	This term is used to classify people according to their daily rhythms – typically into groups who are at their best in the morning or evening.
Circadian	Processes that typically follow a 24-hour cycle.
Clock genes	Genes whose expression varies through the day dependent on other circadian processes.

CNS	The central nervous system.
Co-factor	A co-factor is an additional compound that is required for a metabolic process to work effectively.
Colostrum	This is the early milk produced by the mother around the time of childbirth. It is higher in protein, salt and vitamin A and has lower levels of fats, carbohydrates and potassium than later breastmilk. It is also rich in antibodies and helps to establish the newborn's immune system.
Conservation	A gene is conserved if it is unchanged across a range of species. It is assumed that lack of change is an indication that the gene specifies a process that is biologically important and the wider the range (say a gene was the same in all species from amoebae to man), the greater its significance and the earlier it evolved.
Cortisol	A steroid hormone produced by the adrenal glands which is increased in response to stress. Cortisol increases blood sugar levels.
CPAP (continuous positive airway pressure)	This is a method of treating obstructive sleep apnoea by wearing a device (typically a face mask connected to a machine) that delivers compressed air to the person while they are sleeping. The increased air pressure keeps the airways open, making breathing easier and typically reducing or eliminating snoring.
Cycling alternating pattern	see: CAP.
Dendritic arborization	The growth of dendrites occurring as a network is strengthened through use.
Dendritic pruning	The reduction in dendrites resulting from lack of use.
Diastolic blood pressure	The minimum blood pressure during a heartbeat.
Dream sleep	see: REM sleep.
Drosophila melanogaster	The fruit fly – a common creature used in genetic research; its small size and fast rate of breeding make it a good subject.
DTI (diffusion tensor imaging)	A form of MRI imaging that extracts information on interrelationships across different structures in the nervous system based on fractional anisotropy.
Dyslipidaemia	A term for abnormally low or high levels of lipids in the bloodstream. Typically used to mean elevated levels.
Dysmorphogenesis	Where there is a difference in the development of physical structures resulting from a difference in genetic programming/ontology.
Dyssomnias	Sleep disorders that make getting to sleep and/or staying asleep more difficult than normal.
EBM (evidence-based medicine)	Making systematic use of the best available published evidence to optimize clinical practice through improving the basis for decision-making.
EEG (electro-encephalogram)	This is a means of making a recording of electrical activity from the brain by using pairs of surface electrodes that are attached to the scalp. Occasionally, this can involve sphenoidal electrodes attached below the skin if detailed recording from deeper temporal lobe structures is required. This enables the different stages of sleep to be monitored and identified and could also identify some types of epileptic activity as they occur.

Effect size	A measure of the strength of an association between two variables in any given population.
EMG (electro-myography)	Recording of muscular activity from surface electrodes.
EOG (electro-oculography)	Recording of movements of the eye muscles which can be useful in identifying periods of REM sleep.
Empathy	The ability to recognize and relate to the feelings of others.
Enuresis	Involuntary urination beyond the age when bladder control is typically achieved.
Encopresis	Involuntary bowel movements in inappropriate places beyond the age when bowel control is typically achieved.
Epiphenomenon	An association that occurs consistently but which does not have causal or biological significance.
Extinction	A means of reducing a learned response to a cue that was previously paired with an undesired situation. In this context, the child who has been used to parent attention for noisy behaviour on being put to bed (the learnt response) is ignored until quiet and rewarded once settled (pairing the desired behaviour with the expected outcome).
Ferritin	A protein complex found throughout the body that stores and releases iron.
fMRI	Functional magnetic resonance imaging is a technique for imaging metabolic activity by using the proxy measure of changes in blood flow.
Fractional anisotropy	An imaging technique that allows fibre tracts in the brain to be traced through the direction of water movement in these systems.
FRAXTAS	Fragile-X Associated Tremor-Ataxia syndrome is a recently recognized late-onset motor conditon first reported in the maternal grandfathers of boys with Fragile-X syndrome.
GABA (gamma-aminobutyric acid)	GABA is an inhibitory neurotransmitter that regulates muscle tone.
GERD (gastro-oesophageal reflux disease)	A condition where gastric juices from the stomach are brought up the oesophagus resulting in irritation and inflammation of the lining of the throat.
Ghrelin neuropeptide	A recently identified sleep and appetite controlling hormone produced primarily by the stomach with receptors in the pituitary and hypothalamus.
Glia	A class of non-neuronal cells that are part of the nervous system.
Gluten	A protein derived mainly from wheat, barley, rye and other related grains.
Glycogen	A polysaccharide which constitutes the major carbohydrate energy reserve of the body, stored primarily in liver and muscle tissue.
Graduated extinction	As for extinction, except that bedtime tantrums are ignored for gradually extended periods of time.
Growth hormone	A pituitary peptide hormone involved in a range of processes affecting cell growth and differentiation that is secreted primarily during stage 3 sleep.
Head-banging	Self-injurious behaviour typically involving hitting the head off the headboard, the wall or into the pillow.

Hemifacial microsomia	A condition in which one side of the face has grown to a lesser extent than the other. Goldenhaar's syndrome is the best known example.
Hertz	A measure of the number of times a pattern repeats every second; in this context it is a measure of the speed of the electrical activity recorded from the brain by an electroencephalogram.
Hypercalcuria	Elevated urinary calcium levels.
Hypertension	Elevated blood pressure.
Hypnagogic hallucination	A vivid dream-like hallucination said to occur as someone is falling asleep.
Hypocretin	see: Orexin.
Hyponatraemia	Low body levels of sodium.
Hypopnoea	A transient period of shallow breathing occurring for 10 seconds or more that occurs while asleep.
Hyposomnia	Where someone sleeps at night for significantly shorter amounts of time than normal.
Hypothalamic-pituitary-adrenal (HPA) axis	The HPA axis is a closely integrated system that is involved in various processes including adaptation to stress, sleep, digestion and immune function.
Hypothalamus	A deep midbrain structure, lying below the thalamus that is the main centre for control of the autonomic nervous system.
Infradian	Processes that typically follow a cycle, repeating over more than a day.
Insomnia	When a person or their caregiver complains about their sleep resulting from problems getting to sleep; frequent night waking and problems getting back to sleep; early morning waking or feeling unrested on wakening.
Insulin	A large pancreatic hormone that regulates glucose metabolism.
Intergeniculate leaflet	An anatomically and functionally distinct part of the lateral geniculate complex. The intergeniculate leaflet produces neuropeptide Y and projects to the suprachiasmatic nucleus.
Interneurons	Nerve cells whose axon and dendrites lie completely within the central nervous system, often linking afferent and efferent systems.
ITGB3	A gene for the ß3 subunit of the platelet membrane adhesive protein receptor complex that has recently been shown to be involved in control of male serotonin levels.
Jactatio capitis nocturna	Headbanging that occurs during sleep.
K-complexes	The largest electrical component seen on EEG, these are observed in stage 2 sleep particularly during early sleep cycles.
Kampo	Traditional Japanese herbal medicine derived originally from Chinese herbal treatment, first taught in Japan in 602 AD by a Korean physician by order of Empress Suiko.
Ketogenic diet	A low-carbohydrate high-fat diet designed to encourage lipid digestion as a primary energy source. It results in ketone excretion as a by-product of lipid breakdown.

Ketone	Ketones are a group of compounds in which a carbonyl group is bonded to two others. Acetone is the best known. In the current context, ketones are compounds excreted when triglyceride fats are broken down to provide energy.
Landau-Kleffner syndrome	A form of regressive epilepsy with early onset which is often mistaken for ASD. It affects language areas of the brain.
Leptin	A hormone involved in regulation of energy metabolism that is mainly synthesized from white adipose tissue with a circadian release pattern.
Locus coeruleus	A brainstem nucleus involved in modulation of stress. Abnormalities have been noted in Rett syndrome and speculated about in ASD.
MAD (mandibular advancement device)	A device to hold the lower jaw and the tongue forward in an attempt to make breathing easier and reduce snoring.
Manualized	Converted into a format that uses a written manual to convey information rather than face-to-face contact.
Magnocellular neurosecretory cells	Large cells found mainly in the hypothalamus, in the supraoptic and paraventricular nuclei primarily involved in circadian production of melatonin or vasopressin.
Melatonin	An endocrine hormone released in a circadian pattern by the pineal gland. It is involved in initiation of sleep.
Metabolic syndrome	A pattern of features associated with increased risks of cardiovascular diseases and type-2 diabetes. A number of diagnostic criteria are in use; common features are usually taken as central obesity, dyslipidaemia and raised blood pressure.
MRI (magnetic fields resonance imaging)	A method of imaging that uses strong magnetic fields to align atoms in lower molecular weight molecules, aligning the magnetization using radio frequency. In human imaging this process allows clear imaging of softer tissues that are high in lower weight molecules such as water.
rhythm	An EEG pattern with fluctuations in the 8–12 Hertz band. The pattern normally disappears when watching someone else's actions.
MSLT (multiple sleep latency test)	A standardized test, normally involving an overnight sleep study and the following day, four or five daytime scheduled daytime sleep opportunities, usually over a period of around 7 hours during which a number of things are monitored including EEG, muscle activity and eye movements.
Myotonic dystrophy	A common form of muscular dystrophy, usually developing in adults, but with a milder type of the DM1 form (aka Steinert's dystrophy/disease) which has been reported in association with ASD developing in childhood.
N-acetylserotonin	The intermediate molecule produced in the production of melatonin from serotonin.
Narcolepsy	A condition which is characterized by sudden uncontrollable compulsion to sleep at odd times.
Neuropeptide Y	A hypothalamic peptide neurotransmitter involved in a range of functions including energy balance, food intake and circadian rhythm.
Nightmares	Dreams with frightening, horrible or distressing content that are recalled on waking.
Night sweats	Excessive sweating that occurs at night.

Night terrors (aka sleep terrors; *pavor nocturnus*)	Extreme fear and agitation when waking from non-REM sleep not associated with dream recall.
NNT	'Number needed to treat'. This is an estimate of the number of people who would have to receive a particular treatment for one person to improve.
Nociceptive trigeminal inhibition (NTI) splint	A device that alters the movement of the lower jaw, redirecting it forwards and twisting. This is an uncomfortable movement which should deter bruxism.
Nocturnal enuresis	Urinating during sleep – typically presenting as bedwetting.
Nocturia	The need to urinate frequently at night.
Nocturnal seizures	Epileptic seizures that occur during sleep.
NREM	Non-rapid eye movement phases of sleep.
Obstructive sleep apnoea (OSA)	A breathing problem that results in snoring during sleep, often associated with obesity.
Occlusal splint	A moulded cover for the upper or lower teeth that prevents tooth grinding.
Odds Ratio (OR)	This is a measure of the level of increased risk of one type of outcome based on the presence of another. An OR of 1.00 implies that there is no increased or decreased risk, the larger the OR, the greater the risk – an OR of 5.3 would imply that you would be 5.3 times more likely to have one condition given the presence of the other while an OR of 0.5 would indicate that your risk was halved.
Optogenetic deconstruction	Methods that allow the stimulation of populations of particular neuronal subtypes in specific physical locations within the brain using microbial opsin-based neuromodulation tools.
Orexin	A strongly conserved pair of neuropeptide hormones, also called hypocretins. They have been found to play a major role in the control of wakefulness.
Otitis media	Ear infection due to inflammation around the eustachian tubes in the middle ear.
Oxytocin	A peptide hormone produced by the hypothalamus which is involved in social behaviour.
Paradoxical sleep	see: REM sleep.
Parietal cortex	The brain area involved in integration of sensory, motor and social information forming the upper surface of the rear portion of the cortex.
Parasomnias	Sleep disorders in which there are unusual movements, emotions, behaviours, perceptions or reported dreams.
Pedunculopontine nucleus	A principal component of the reticular activating system.
Peroxiredoxins	A group of ubiquitous antioxidant enzymes. They are found at high levels in red blood cells. They demonstrate preserved and currently unexplained circadian patterns in the absence of other biological cues and are important in protecting against oxidative stress.
PET	Positron Emission Tomography, the first useful method of *in vivo* functional neuroimaging.

Phasic REM	The phasic stages of REM sleep coincide with higher levels of eye movement and dream recall. The arousal threshold is similar to that seen in stage 3 sleep.
Photoentrainment	Where physiological and/or behavioural functions change in a circadian pattern, in time with the light–dark cycle resulting from planetary motion.
Pineal gland	A tiny endocrine structure situated between the thalamic nuclei at the base of the brain which releases melatonin in a circadian pattern affected by retinal input on ambient light levels.
Pituitary adenylate cyclase activating peptide (PACAP)	PACAP acts as a hormone, neurotransmitter and neuromodulator with a similar mode of action to vasoactive intestinal peptide (VIP). It interacts with both secretin and VIP receptors. It acts primarily in the central nervous system and the gastrointestinal system.
Plasma	The yellowish liquid which is the fluid component of human blood and carries red blood cells.
Polysomnography	An assessment of various functions during sleep including EEG, eye movements, heart and respiratory rate, pulse oximetry and skeletal muscle activity.
Ponderal index	A measure of body proportions calculated as the relationship between mass and length.
Pontine tegmentum	A part of the pons, an area at the base of the brain, adjacent to the lower parts of the ventricular system that is involved in REM sleep initiation.
Positive reinforcement	Systematic reward that increases the probability of recurrence of behaviour that preceded it.
Prolactin	A circadian peptide hormone released by the pituitary gland with levels correlated with amount of REM sleep. Typically associated with its role in stimulating breastmilk production after birth.
Pyridoxal phosphate (P5P)	The biologically active form of vitamin B6.
RCT (randomized controlled trial)	A type of research where matched subjects are allocated at random to different groups to examine the effects of specific differences in treatment on outcome.
REM sleep	Rapid eye movement/paradoxical sleep is a specific sleep stage during which most dreams appear to be recalled. Characterised by intense waking-like cortical activation with a lack of muscular movement apart from the eyes.
S-adenosyl methionine (SAM)	A compound, primarily active in liver, with a variety of metabolic functions one of which is to catalyse the conversion of N-acetylserotonin to melatonin.
S-adenosyl-l-homocysteine (SAH)	SAH is produced from SAM in the production of melatonin.
Scaffolding proteins	These proteins are involved in cofactor binding during gene transcription.
Scheduled awakening	An approach to night-time waking in which the child is gently and deliberately wakened and resettled.
SCFAs (short-chain fatty acids)	Fatty acids with aliphatic tails of less than six carbons. They are directly absorbed through the hepatic portal vein into the liver and are produced by digestion of dietary fibre.

Scotopic-photopic changes	Changes in retinal function when adapting to differences between low and high light levels.
SDB (sleep-disordered breathing)	A range of changes in breathing pattern which can be associated with disorders such as snoring and OSA.
Sensori-motor rhythm (SMR)	An oscillating EEG pattern typically of 12–14 Hertz that can be recorded during stage 2 sleep.
Serotonin	A key neurotransmitter, derived from tryptophan, and a precursor of melatonin. Important in regulation of gastrointestinal motility, and important in mood, appetite, muscle contraction and sleep.
Serum	Blood plasma from which the coagulants have been removed.
Sleep spindles	Bursts of EEG activity generated by the thalamus during stage 2 sleep that correspond to muscle twitches.
Sleep stage X	A rare type of EEG profile seen during sleep in people who have defects in the pontine tegmentum usually due to spinocerebellar degeneration. The pontine tegmentum is a part of the brain structure called the pons. In most mammals this structure emits PGO (pontogeniculooccipital) spikes prior to the start of REM sleep. When damaged, as in spinocerebellar degeneration, REM sleep can be abolished.
Sleepwalking	Movements during deep sleep that can include walking and other activities that would normally be performed while fully awake.
Snoring	Noises made by vibration of the soft palate caused by breathing during sleep, more commonly associated with obesity.
SNRI (serotonin-norepinephrine reuptake inhibitor)	A class of medications that increase the circulating levels of the neurotransmitters serotonin and norepinephrine. Most frequently used in clinical practice as antidepressants.
Somniloquy	Talking during sleep.
SPECT (Single-Photon Emission Computerized Tomography)	SPECT is an imaging technique that relies on detection of an injected radionucleotide (typically with a tagged form of oxygen). It is similar to PET scanning. SPECT provides lower resolution information but the approach is easier to develop as it uses isotopes 99mTc-HMPAO that do not require access to a local cyclotron and processing facility.
Spinocerebellar degeneration	A group of progressive genetic conditions resulting in problems with coordination.
SSRI (selective serotonin reuptake inhibitor)	A class of medications that increase the circulating levels of the serotonin by reducing reabsorption of serotonin from the post-synaptic cleft after a serotonergic nerve cell has fired. Frequently used in clinical practice as antidepressants.
Stridor	A high pitched wheezing sound made when someone is breathing in.
Superior temporal gyrus	The upper surface of the temporal lobe of the brain, containing the primary auditory cortex. It contains Wernicke's area, a key area that enables us to process the spoken language of others.
Suprachiasmatic nucleus	A small area of the brain directly above the optic chiasm (where the nerve tracts from the retinas join). It is a key structure in the neural and neurochemical control of circadian rhythms.

Systolic blood pressure	The maximum blood pressure during a heartbeat.
Taurine	This is a sulphur-containing amino acid that is derived from cysteine. It is found in the digestive system in bile. The name comes from the Greek word for bull because it was first identified in an extract from ox bile.
Testosterone	An androgen steroid hormone primarily secreted by the testes in males and ovaries in females. It shows a strong circadian pattern in men.
THBP4 (tetrahydro-biopterin)	An important co-factor in the degradation of phenylalanine and the production of a range of neurotransmitters.
Thyroid stimulating hormone	A circadian pituitary peptide hormone that controls thyroid function.
Tonic REM	This term is used to classify the periods of REM sleep that occur between phasic bursts of rapid eye movements. The arousal threshold during tonic REM is similar to that during Stage 2 sleep.
Tooth-grinding	see: Bruxism.
Transitional objects	Physical objects (typically blankets, soothers and soft toys) used by infants to help them to cope, typically at times when primary caregiver contact is not possible.
Tryptophan	An essential amino acid critical for the production of serotonin and melatonin.
Tryptophan hydroxylase	An enzyme which catalyses the reaction by which THBP4 and oxygen converts tryptophan to 5HTP with iron as a cofactor.
Tympanostomy	Surgical insertion of a grommet (a small tube) into the ear canal to hold it open and improve hearing.
Tyrosine hydroxylase	This enzyme limits production of the neurotransmitter dopamine.
Ultradian	Processes that typically follow a cycle repeating within a day.
UP3	Uvulopalatopharyngoplasty is a complex surgical procedure to try to widen the back of the throat and make breathing easier. It is used with OSA. Only the more complex 'Stanford protocol' has been reported to have a high rate of success.
Vasoactive intestinal peptide (VIP)	A short-acting peptide produced in many organs including the suprachiasmatic nucleus of the hypothalamus. It is thought to be a key component of the endogenous circadian system.
Vasopressin	A peptide hormone, produced in the paraventricular and supraoptic nuclei in the pituitary gland. It is similar in structure to oxytocin. Vasopressin controls blood pressure and kidney function.
Vibroacoustic stimulation	Sound stimulation using lower base frequencies that transmit through different media more easily.
Videosomnography	Video recording of the person during sleep to monitor REM and body movement.
Videotelemetry	This is a method that combines video recording of behaviour with EEG recording of brain activity (an explanatory leaflet can be downloaded from www.brainandspine.org.uk).

Zebrafish	The zebrafish, *Danio rerio* is a common subject for genetic research. Its genome has been fully sequenced, a number of well-studied genetic mutants are available for study and it has a well-documented range of predictable behaviours.
Zeitgeber	An environmental factor that provides a cue for the regulation or initiation of a biological clock.

REFERENCES

Abascal, K. and Yarnell, E. (2004) 'Nervine herbs for treating anxiety.' *Alternative and Complementary Therapies 10*(6): 309–315.

Abe, K. and Shimakawa, M. (1966) 'Genetic and developmental aspects of sleeptalking and teeth-grinding.' *Acta Paedopsychiatrica 33*(11): 339–344.

Abizaid, A., Liu, Z. W., Andrews, Z.B., Shanabrough, M. *et al.* (2006) 'Ghrelin modulates the activity and synaptic input organization of midbrain dopamine neurons while promoting appetite.' *Journal of Clinical Investigation 116*(12): 3229–3239.

Adair, R., Zuckerman, B., Bauchner, H., Philipp, B. and Levenson, S. (1992) 'Reducing night waking in infancy: A primary care intervention.' *Pediatrics 89*: 585–588.

Adamantidis, A., Carter, M.C. and de Lecea, L. (2010) 'Optogenetic deconstruction of sleep–wake circuitry in the brain.' *Frontiers in Molecular Neuroscience 2*, Article 31, 1–9, doi: 10.3389/neuro.02.031.2009.

Adams, J.B. and Holloway, C. (2004) 'Pilot study of a moderate dose multivitamin/mineral supplement for children with autistic spectrum disorder.' *Journal of Alternative and Complementary Medicine 10*(6), 1033–1039.

Adams, L.A. and Rickert, V.I. (1989) 'Reducing bedtime tantrums: Comparison between positive routines and graduated extinction.' *Pediatrics 84*: 756–761.

Advisory Committee on Childhood Lead Poisoning Prevention (ACCLPP) (2000) 'Recommendations for blood lead screening of young children enrolled in Medicaid: Targeting a group at high risk.' *CDC MMWR 49*(RR-14): 1–14.

Aggarwal, A. (2010) 'Akathisia associated with mianserin.' *Journal of Clinical Psychopharmacology 30*(3): 338–339.

Aithal, G.P. (2005) 'When is a herb a drug?' *European Journal of Gastroenterology and Hepatology 17*: 391–393.

Aitken, K.J. (2008) *Dietary Interventions in Autism Spectrum Disorders, Why They Work when They Do, Why They Don't when They Don't.* London: Jessica Kingsley Publishers.

Aitken, K.J. (2010a) *An A–Z of the Genetic Factors in Autism: A Handbook for Parents and Carers.* London: Jessica Kingsley Publishers.

Aitken, K.J. (2010b) *An A–Z of the Genetic Factors in Autism: A Handbook for Professionals.* London: Jessica Kingsley Publishers.

Alcantara, J. and Anderson, R. (2008) 'Chiropractic care of a pediatric patient with symptoms associated with gastroesophageal reflux disease, fuss-cry-irritability with sleep disorder syndrome and irritable infant syndrome of musculoskeletal origin.' *Journal of the Canadian Chiropractic Association 52*(4): 248–255.

Alfano, C.A. and Gamble, A.L. (2009) 'The role of sleep in childhood psychiatric disorders.' *Child Youth Care Forum 38*(6): 327–340.

Alfano, C.A., Pina, A.A., Zerr, A.A. and Villalta, I.K. (2010) 'Pre-sleep arousal and sleep problems of anxiety-disordered youth.' *Child Psychiatry and Human Development 41*(2): 156–167.

Ali, M., Auger, R., Slocumb, N.L. and Morgenthaler, T.I. (2009) 'Idiopathic hypersomnia: Clinical features and response to treatment.' *Journal of Clinical Sleep Medicine 5*(6): 562–568.

Allada, R. and Siegel, J.M. (2008) 'Unearthing the phylogenetic roots of sleep review.' *Current Biology 18*: R670–R679.

Allen, R.P. and Earley, C.J. (1996) 'Augmentation of the restless legs syndrome with carbidopa/levodopa.' *Sleep 19*: 205–213.

Allik, H., Larsson, J.O. and Smedje, H. (2006a) 'Insomnia in school-age children with Asperger syndrome or high-functioning autism.' *BMC Psychiatry 28*(6): 18, doi: 10.1186/1471-244X-6-18.

Allik, H., Larsson, J. and Smedje, H. (2006b) 'Sleep patterns of school-age children with Asperger syndrome or high-functioning autism.' *Journal of Autism and Developmental Disorders 36*(5): 585–595.

Allik, H., Larsson, J. and Smedje, H. (2008) 'Sleep patterns in school-age children with Asperger syndrome or high-functioning autism: A follow-up study.' *Journal of Autism and Developmental Disorders 38*(9): 1625–1633.

Alloussi, S.H., Murtz, G., Lang, C., Madersbacher, H. *et al.* (2010) 'Desmopressin treatment regimens in monosymptomatic and nonmonosymptomatic enuresis: A review from a clinical perspective.' *Journal of Pediatric Urology 7*(2): 10–20.

Amalu, W.C. (1998) 'Autism, asthma, irritable bowel syndrome, strabismus, and illness susceptibility: A case study in chiropractic management.' *Today's Chiropractic 27*(5): 32–47.

American Academy of Sleep Medicine (2005) *International Classification of Sleep Disorders: Diagnostic and Coding Manual*, 2nd edn. Westchester, IL: ASDA.

AMI (2009) 'MicroMini MotionLogger Actigraph.' Ardsley, NY: Ambulatory Monitoring Inc. Available at www.ambulatory-monitoring.com/index.html, accessed 15 September 2011.

Anbar, R.D. and Slothower, M.P. (2006) 'Hypnosis for treatment of insomnia in school-age children: A retrospective chart review.' *BMC Pediatrics 6*: 23, doi:10.1186/1471-2431-6-23.

Andersen, I.M., Kaczmarska, J., McGrew, S.G. and Malow, B.A. (2008) 'Melatonin for insomnia in children with autism spectrum disorders.' *Journal of Child Neurology 23*(5): 482–485.

Anderson, B.M., Schnetz-Boutau, N.C., Bartlett, J., Wotawa, A.M. *et al.* (2009) 'Examination of association of genes in the serotonin system to autism.' *Neurogenetics 10*(3): 209–216.

Anderson, J.R. and Meno, P. (2003) 'Psychological influences on yawning in children.' *Current Psychology Letters 11*(2): 2–7.

Aran, A., Einen, M., Lin, L., Plazzi, G. *et al.* (2010) 'Clinical and therapeutic aspects of childhood narcolepsy-cataplexy: A retrospective study of 51 children.' *Sleep 33*(11): 1457–1464.

Arana-Lechuga, Y., Sanchez-Escandón, O., de Santiago-Treviño, N., Castillo-Montoya, C. *et al.* (2008) 'Risperidone treatment of sleep disturbances in Tourette's syndrome.' *Journal of Neuropsychiatry and Clinical Neuroscience 20*(3): 375–376.

Arbuckle, R., Abetz, L., Durmer, J.S., Ivanenko, A. *et al.* (2010) 'Development of the Pediatric Restless Legs Syndrome Severity Scale (P-RLS-SS)©: A patient-reported outcome measure of pediatric RLS symptoms and impact.' *Sleep Medicine 11*: 897–906.

Archer, S.N., Robilliard, D.L., Skene, D.J., Smits, M., *et al.* (2003) 'A length polymorphism in the circadian clock gene *Per3* is linked to delayed sleep phase syndrome and extreme diurnal preference.' *Sleep 26*(4): 413–415.

Ardura, J., Gutierrez, R., Andres, J. and Agapito, T. (2003) 'Emergence and evolution of the circadian rhythm of melatonin in children.' *Hormone Research 59*(2): 66–72.

Argiolas, A., Melis, M.R. and Gessa, G.L. (1989) 'Oxytocin: An extremely potent inducer of penile erection and yawning in male rats.' *European Journal of Pharmacology 130*: 265–272.

Argiolas, A., Melis, M.R., Stancampiano, R. and Gessa, G.L. (1986) 'Penile erection and yawning induced by oxytocin and related peptides: Structure-activity relationship.' *Peptides 10*: 559–563.

Aristotle (c. 350 BC) On Sleep and Sleeplessness, trans. J.I. Beare. Available at http://ebooks.adelaide.edu.au/a/aristotle/sleep, accessed 12 Setember 2011.

Armitage, R., Flynn, H., Hoffmann, R., Vazquez, D. *et al.* (2009) 'Early developmental changes in sleep in infants: The impact of maternal depression.' *Sleep 32*(5): 693–696.

Armitage, R., Yonkers, K., Cole, D. and Rush, A.J. (1997) 'A multicenter, double-blind comparison of the effects of nefazodone and fluoxetine on sleep architecture and quality of sleep in depressed outpatients.' *Journal of Clinical Psychopharmacology 17*(3): 161–168.

Armstrong, K.L., Quinn, R.A. and Dadds, M.R. (1994) 'The sleep patterns of normal children.' *Medical Journal of Australia 161*: 202–206.

Arnulf, I., Zeitzer, J.M., File, J., Farber, N. and Mignot, E. (2005) 'Kleine-Levin syndrome: A systematic review of 186 cases in the literature.' *Brain 128*: 2763–2776.

Aserinsky, E. (1996) 'The discovery of REM sleep.' *Journal of the History of Neuroscience 5*: 213–227.

Aserinsky, E. and Kleitman, N. (1953) 'Regularly occurring periods of eye motility, and concomitant phenomena, during sleep.' *Science 118*: 273–274.

Aserinsky, E. and Kleitman, N. (1955) 'Two types of ocular motility during sleep.' *Journal of Applied Physiology 8*(1): 1–10.

Ashbaugh, R. and Peck, S.M. (1998) 'Treatment of sleep problems in a toddler: A replication of the faded bedtime with response cost protocol.' *Journal of Applied Behavior Analysis 31*: 127–129.

Ashwood, P., Krakowiak, P., Hertz-Picciotto, I., Hansen, R. *et al.* (2010) 'Elevated plasma cytokines in autism spectrum disorders provide evidence 4 of immune dysfunction and are associated with impaired behavioral outcome.' *Brain, Behavior, and Immunity 25* (1): 40–45.

Assaf, M., Jagannathan, K., Calhoun, V.D., Miller, L. *et al.* (2010) 'Abnormal functional connectivity of default mode sub-networks in autism spectrum disorder patients.' *NeuroImage 53*: 247–256.

Atsumi, T., Fujisawa, S., Nakabayashi, Y., Kawai, T., Yasui, T. and Yonosaki, K. (2004) 'Pleasant feeling from watching a comical video enhances free radical scavenging capacity in human whole saliva.' *Journal of Psychosomatic Research 56*: 377–379.

Attarian, H. (2010) 'Treatment options for parasomnias.' *Neurologic Clinics 28*(4): 1089–1106.

Attenburrow, A.A., Stanley, T.V. and Holland, R.P. (1984) 'Nocturnal enuresis: A study.' *Practitioner 228*(1387): 99–102.

Auger, R.R. (2006) 'Sleep-related eating disorders.' *Psychiatry (Edgmont) 3*(11): 64–70.

Aurora, R.N., Zak, R.S., Auerbach, S.H., Casey, K.R. *et al.* (2010) 'Best practice guide for the treatment of nightmare disorder in adults.' *Journal of Clinical Sleep Medicine 6*(4): 389–401.

Avidan, A.Y. and Chervin, R.D. (2002) 'ESS dot com.' *Sleep Medicine 3*: 405–410.

Baglioni, C., Spiegelhalder, K., Lombardo, C. and Riemann, D. (2010) 'Sleep and emotions: A focus on insomnia.' *Sleep Medicine Reviews 14*: 227–238.

Baird, J., Hill, C.M., Kendrick, T., Inskip, H.M. and the SWS Study Group (2009) 'Infant sleep disturbance is associated with preconceptional psychological distress: Findings from the Southampton Women's Survey.' *Sleep 32*(4): 566–568.

Baker, A.M., Johnson, D.G., Levisky, J.A., Hearn, W.L. *et al.* (2003) 'Fatal diphenhydramine intoxication in infants.' *Journal of Forensic Science 48*(2): 425–428.

Balbo, M., Leproult, R. and Van Cauter, E. (2010) 'Impact of sleep and its disturbances on hypothalamo-pituitary-adrenal axis activity.' *International Journal of Endocrinology*, doi:10.1155/2010/759234.

Ball, H.L. (2003) 'Breastfeeding, bed-sharing, and infant sleep.' *Birth 30*(3): 181–188.

Bamne, M.N., Mansour, H., Monk, T.H., Buysse, D.J. and Nimgaonkar, V.L. (2010) 'Approaches to unravel the genetics of sleep.' *Sleep Medicine Reviews 14*(6): 397–404.

Banerjee, D., Vitiello, M.V. and Grunstein, R.R. (2004) 'Pharmacotherapy for excessive daytime sleepiness.' *Sleep Medicine Reviews 8*(5): 339–354.

Banquet, J.P. and Sailhan, M. (1974) ['EEG analysis of spontaneous and induced states of consciousness.'], *Revue d'Electroencephalographie et Neurophysiologie Clinique 4*: 445–453.

Banting, W. (1863) *Letter on Corpulence, Addressed to the Public.* London: Harrison.

Baranski, J.V., Pigeau, R., Dinich, P. and Jacobs, I. (2004) 'Effects of modafinil on cognitive and meta-cognitive performance.' *Human Psychopharmacology: Clinical and Experimental 19*(5): 323–332.

Barf, R.P., Meerlo, P. and Scheurink, A.J. (2010) 'Chronic sleep disturbance impairs glucose homeostasis in rats.' *International Journal of Endocrinology*, doi:10.1155/2010/819414.

Barion, A. and Zee, P.C. (2007) 'A clinical approach to circadian rhythm sleep disorders.' *Sleep Medicine 8*(6): 566–577.

Barlow, D.H., Nock, M.K. and Hersen, M. (2008) *Single Case Experimental Designs: Strategies for Studying Behavior Change*, 3rd edn. Boston, MA: Allyn & Bacon.

Barlow, J., Smailagic, N., Ferriter, M., Bennett, C. and Jones, H. (2010) 'Group-based parent-training programmes for improving emotional and behavioural adjustment in children from birth to three years old.' *Cochrane Database Systematic Reviews*, Mar 17 (3):CD003680.

Barlow, K., Thompson, E., Johnson, D. and Minns, R.A. (2004) 'The neurological outcome of non-accidental head injury.' *Pediatric Rehabilitation 7*(3): 195–203.

Barnard, A.R. and Nolan, P.M. (2008) 'When clocks go bad: Neurobehavioural consequences of disrupted circadian timing.' *PLoS Genetics 4*(5): e1000040, doi:10.1371/journal.pgen.1000040

Barnoy, E.L., Najdowski, A.C., Tarbox, J., Wilke, A.E. and Nollet, M.D. (2009) 'Evaluation of a multicomponent intervention for diurnal bruxism in a young child with autism.' *Journal of Applied Behavior Analysis 42*(4): 845–848.

Basheer, R., Strecker, R.E, Thakkar, M.M. and McCarley, R.W. (2004) 'Adenosine and sleep-wake regulation.' *Progress in Neurobiology 73*(6): 379–396.

Basta, M., Lin, H.M., Pejovic, S., Sarrigiannidis, A. *et al.* (2008) 'Lack of regular exercise, depression, and degree of apnea are predictors of excessive daytime sleepiness in patients with sleep apnea: Sex differences.' *Journal of Clinical Sleep Medicine 4*(1): 19–25.

Bastien, C.H., Lamoureux, C., Gagne, A. and Morin, C.M. (2004) 'Validation of the sleep impairment index for the assessment of insomnia severity.' *Sleep 21*: 98.

Bateson, G. (1979) *Mind and Nature: A Necessary Unity.* London: Wildwood House.

Batt, S. (2000) 'What light through window wreaks – circadian rhythms and breast cancer.' *Breast Cancer Action Newsletter 61* (Sept–Oct).

Baxter, P. (ed.)(2001) *Vitamin Responsive Conditions in Paediatric Neurology.* London: MacKeith Press.

Bazil, C.W. (2003) 'Epilepsy and sleep disturbance.' *Epilepsy & Behavior 4*: S39–S45.

Bazil, C.W. (2004) 'Nocturnal seizures.' *Seminars in Neurology 24*(3): 293–300.

Bazil, C.W., Short, D.W., Crispin, D. and Zheng, W. (2000) 'Patients with intractable epilepsy have low melatonin, which increases following seizures.' *Neurology 55*: 1746–1748.

Beebe, D.W. and Gozal, D. (2002) 'Obstructive sleep apnea and the prefrontal cortex: Towards a comprehensive model linking nocturnal upper airway obstruction to daytime cognitive and behavioral deficits.' *Journal of Sleep Research 11*(1): 1–16.

Beebe, D.W. and Risi, S. (2003) 'Treatment of Adolescents and Young Adults with High-functioning Autism or Asperger Syndrome.' In F.M. Datilio and M.A. Reinecke (eds) *Cognitive Therapy with Children and Adolescents: A Casebook for Clinical Practice.* New York, NY: Guilford Press.

Beenhakker, M.P. and Huguenard, J.R. (2009) 'Neurons that fire together also conspire together: Is normal sleep circuitry hijacked to generate epilepsy?' *Neuron 62*: 612–632.

Bekkhus, M., Skjothaug, T., Nordhagen, R. and Borge, A.I. (2011) 'Intrauterine exposure to caffeine and inattention/overactivity in children.' *Acta Paediatrica 99*(6): 925–928.

Bell, I.R., Howerter, A., Jackson, N., Aickin, M. *et al.* (2010) 'Effects of homeopathic medicines on polysomnographic sleep of young adults with histories of coffee-related insomnia.' *Sleep Medicine 12*(5): 505–511

Bell, J.S. (1979) 'The use of EEG theta biofeedback in the treatment of a patient with sleep-onset insomnia.' *Biofeedback and Self Regulation 4*(3): 229–236.

Benington, J.H. and Heller, H.C. (1995) 'Restoration of brain energy metabolism as the function of sleep.' *Progress in Neurobiology 45*: 347–360.

Berk, L.S., Felten, D.L., Tan, S.A., Bittman, B.B. and Westengard, J. (2001) 'Modulation of neuroimmune parameters during the eustress of humor-associated mirthful laughter.' *Alternative Therapy and Health Medicine 53*: 62–76.

Berilgen, M.S., Mungen, B., Ustundag, B. and Demira, C. (2006) 'Serum ghrelin levels are enhanced in patients with epilepsy.' *Seizure 15*: 106–111.

Berlucchi, M., Salsi, D., Valetti, L., Parrinello, G. and Nicolai, P. (2007) 'The role of mometasone furoate aqueous nasal spray in the treatment of adenoidal hypertrophy in the pediatric age group: Preliminary results of a prospective, randomized study.' *Pediatrics 119*: e1392–e1397.

Berman, S.M., Kuczenski, R., McCracken, J.T. and London, E.D. (2009) 'Potential adverse effects of amphetamine treatment on brain and behavior: A review.' *Molecular Psychiatry 14*(2): 123–142.

Bernal, J.F. (1973) 'Night waking in infants during the first 14 months.' *Developmental Medicine and Child Neurology 15*: 760–769.

Bernstein, D.A. and Borkovec, T.D. (1973) *Progressive Relaxation Training: A Manual for the Helping Professions.* Champaign, IL: Research Press.

Berthier, M.L., Santamaria, J., Encabo, H. and Tolosa, E.S. (1992) 'Recurrent hypersomnia in two adolescent males with Asperger's syndrome.' *Journal of the American Academy of Child & Adolescent Psychiatry 31*(4): 735–738.

Biederman, J. and Pliszka, S.R. (2008) 'Modafinil improves symptoms of attention-deficit/hyperactivity disorder across subtypes in children and adolescents.' *Journal of Pediatrics 152*(3): 394–399.

Billiard, M., Bassetti, C., Dauvilliers, Y., Dolenc-Groselj, L. *et al.* (2006) 'EFNS guidelines on management of narcolepsy.' *European Journal of Neurology 13*(10): 1035–1048.

Billiard, M., Guilleminault, C. and Dement, W.C. (1975) 'A menstruation-linked periodic hypersomnia: Kleine-Levin syndrome or new clinical entity?' *Neurology 25*: 436–443.

Biswal, B.B., Mennes, M., Zuo, X.N., Gohel, S., *et al.* (2010) 'Toward discovery science of human brain function.' *Proceedings of the National Academy of Science, USA 107*(10): 4734–4739.

Bixler, E.O., Vgontzas, A.N., Lin, H.M., Calhoun, S.L. et al. (2005) 'Excessive daytime sleepiness in a general population sample: The role of sleep apnea, age, obesity, diabetes, and depression.' *Journal of Clinical Endocrinology and Metabolism 90*(8): 4510–4515.

Bjorness, T.E. and Greene, R.W. (2009) 'Adenosine and sleep.' *Current Neuropharmacology 7*: 238–245.

Bjorvatn, B., Sagen, I.M., Oyane, N., Waage, S. *et al.* (2007) 'The association between sleep duration, body mass index and metabolic measures in the Hordaland Health study.' *Journal of Sleep Research 16*: 66–76.

Black, J., Duntley, S.P., Bogan, R.K. and O'Malley, M.B. (eds) (2007) 'Recent advances in the treatment and management of excessive daytime sleepiness.' *CNS Spectrums 12*(suppl.2): 1–16.

Black, J. and Houghton, W.C. (2006) 'Sodium oxybate improves excessive daytime sleepiness in narcolepsy.' *Sleep 29*(7): 939–946.

Blampied, N.M. and France, K.G. (1993) 'A behavioral model of infant sleep disturbance.' *Journal of Applied Behavioral Analysis 26*: 477–492.

Bliwise, D.L. and Ansari, F.P. (2007) 'Insomnia associated with valerian and melatonin usage in the 2002 National Health Interview Survey.' *Sleep 30*(7): 881–884.

Blouin, A.M., Thannickal, T.C., Worley, P.F., Baraban, J.M. *et al.* (2005) 'Narp immunostaining of human hypocretin (orexin) neurons: Loss in narcolepsy.' *Neurology 65*: 1189–1192.

Blount, R.L., Drabman, R.S., Wilson, N. and Stewart, D. (1982) 'Reducing severe diurnal bruxism in two profoundly retarded females.' *Journal of Applied Behavior Analysis 15*(4): 565–571.

Blumenthal, M., Busse, W.R., Goldberg, A., Gruenwald, J. *et al.* (eds) (1998) *The Complete German Commission E Monographs: Therapeutic Guide to Herbal Medicines.* Austin, TX: American Botanical Council.

Blunden, S., Lushington, K., Lorenzen, B., Ooi, T., Fung, F. and Kennedy, D. (2004) 'Are sleep problems under-recognised in general practice?' *Archives of Disease in Childhood 89*: 708–712.

Boergers, J., Hart, C., Owens, J.A., Streisand, R. and Spirito, A. (2007) 'Child sleep disorders: Associations with parental sleep duration and daytime sleepiness.' *Journal of Family Psychology 21*(1): 88–94.

Boeve, B.F. (2010) 'REM sleep behavior disorder: Updated review of the core features, the RBD-neurodegenerative disease association, evolving concepts, controversies, and future directions.' *Annals of the New York Academy of Science 1184*: 15–54.

Bollard, J. and Nettlebeck, T. (1982) 'A component analysis of dry-bed training for treatment of bedwetting.' *Behaviour Research and Therapy 20*: 383–390.

Bonnet, C., Roubertie, A., Doummar, D., Bahi-Buisson, N. *et al.* (2010) 'Developmental and benign movement disorders in childhood.' *Movement Disorders 25*(10): 1317–1334.

Borchers, A.T., Sakai, S., Henderson, G.L., Harkey, M.R. *et al.* (2000) 'Shosaiko-to and other Kampo (Japanese herbal) medicines: A review of their immunomodulatory activities.' *Journal of Ethnopharmacology 73*(1): 1–13.

Boudreau, E.A., Johnson, K.P., Jackman, A.R., Blancato, J. *et al.* (2009) 'Review of disrupted sleep patterns in Smith-Magenis syndrome and normal melatonin secretion in a patient with an atypical interstitial 17p11.2 deletion.' *American Journal of Medical Genetics A. 149A*(7): 1382–1391.

Bourgeron, T. (2007) 'The possible interplay of synaptic and clock genes in autism spectrum disorders.' *Cold Spring Harbor Symposia on Quantitative Biology 72*: 645–654.

Braam, W., Didden, R., Maas, A.P., Korzilius, H. *et al.* (2010) 'Melatonin decreases daytime challenging behaviour in persons with intellectual disability and chronic insomnia.' *Journal of Intellectual Disability Research 54*(1): 52–59.

Braam, W., Didden, R., Smits, M.G. and Curfs, L.M. (2008) 'Melatonin for chronic insomnia in Angelman syndrome: A randomized placebo-controlled trial.' *Journal of Child Neurology 23*(6): 649–654.

Braam, W., Smits, M.G., Didden, R., Korzilius, H. *et al.* (2009) 'Exogenous melatonin for sleep problems in individuals with intellectual disability: A meta-analysis.' *Developmental Medicine and Child Neurology 51*(5): 340–349.

Braam, W., van Geijlswijk, I., Keijzer, H., Smits, M.G. *et al.* (2010) 'Loss of response to melatonin treatment is associated with slow melatonin metabolism.' *Journal of Intellectual Disability Research 54*(6): 547–555.

Brabant, G., Prank, K., Ranft, U., Schuermeyer, T. *et al.* (1990) 'Physiological regulation of circadian and pulsatile thyrotropin secretion in normal man and woman.' *Journal of Clinical Endocrinology and Metabolism 70*(2): 403–409.

Braun, A.R., Balkin, T.J., Wesenten, N.J., Carson, R.E. *et al.* (1997) 'Regional cerebral blood flow throughout the sleep-wake cycle: An H2(15)O PET study.' *Brain 120*: 1173–1197.

Brown, A.M. (2004) 'Brain glycogen re-awakened.' *Journal of Neurochemistry 89*: 537–552.

Brown, C.M. and Austin, D.W. (2009) 'Commentary: Fatty acids, breastfeeding and autism spectrum disorder.' *Electronic Journal of Applied Psychology: Innovations in Autism 5*(1): 49–52.

Brown, D.W. (1996) 'Autism, Asperger's syndrome and the Crick-Mitchison Theory of the biological function of REM sleep.' *Medical Hypotheses 47*: 399–403.

Bruch, M. and Bond, F.W. (1998) *Beyond Diagnosis: Case Formulation Approaches in CBT.* Chichester: John Wiley.

Brun, L., Ngu, L.H., Keng, W.T., Ch'ng, G.S. *et al.* (2010) 'Clinical and biochemical features of aromatic L-amino acid decarboxylase deficiency.' *Neurology 75*: 64–71.

Bruni, O., Ferri, R., Vittori, E., Novelli, L. *et al.* (2007) 'Sleep architecture and NREM alterations in children and adolescents with Asperger syndrome.' *Sleep 30*(11): 1577–1585.

Bruni, O., Novelli, L., Miano, S., Parrino, L. *et al.* (2010) 'Cyclic alternating pattern: A window into pediatric sleep.' *Sleep Medicine 11*: 628–636.

Bruni, O., Ottaviano, S., Guidetti, V., Romoli, M. *et al.* (1996) 'The Sleep Disturbance Scale for Children (SDSC): Construction and validation of an instrument to evaluate sleep disturbances in childhood and adolescence.' *Journal of Sleep Research 5*(4): 251–261.

Bruni, O., Verrillo, E., Novelli, L. and Ferri, R. (2010) 'Prader-Willi syndrome: Sorting out the relationships between obesity, hypersomnia, and sleep apnea.' *Current Opinion in Pulmonary Medicine 16*(6): 568–573.

Buckley, A.W., Rodriguez, A.J., Jennison, K., Buckley, J. *et al.* (2010) 'Rapid eye movement sleep percentage in children with autism compared with children with developmental delay and typical development.' *Archives of Pediatric and Adolescent Medicine 164*(11): 1032–1037.

Budhiraja, R. (2007) 'The man who fought in sleep.' *Journal of Clinical Sleep Medicine 3*(4): 427–428.

Burgess, M., Gill, M. and Marks, I. (1998) 'Postal self-exposure treatment of recurrent nightmares. Randomised controlled trial.' *British Journal of Psychiatry 172*: 257–262.

Burgess, M., Marks, I.M. and Gill, M. (1994) 'Postal self-exposure treatment of recurrent nightmares.' *British Journal of Psychiatry 165*(3): 388–391.

Burke, R.V., Kuhn, B.R. and Peterson, J.L. (2004) 'Brief report: A "storybook" ending to children's bedtime problems – the use of a rewarding social story to reduce bedtime resistance and frequent night waking.' *Journal of Pediatric Psychology 29*(5): 389–396.

Burlina, A.B., Burlina, A.P., Hyland, K., Bonafe, L. and Blau, N. (2001) 'Autistic syndrome and aromatic L-amino acid decarboxylase deficiency.' *Journal of Inherited Metabolic Disease 24*(suppl.1): 34.

Burnham, M.M., Goodlin-Jones, B.L., Gaylor, E.E. and Anders, T.F. (2002) 'Use of sleep aids during the first year of life.' *Pediatrics 109*(4): 594–601.

Buscemi, N., Vandermeer, B., Hooton, N., Pandya, R. *et al.* (2006) 'Efficacy and safety of exogenous melatonin for secondary sleep disorders and sleep disorders accompanying sleep restriction: Meta-analysis.' *British Medical Journal 332*(7538): 385–393.

Butler, R.J., Golding, J., Northstone, K. and Study Team ALSPAC (2005) 'Nocturnal enuresis at 7.5 years old: Prevalence and analysis of clinical signs.' *British Journal of Urology International 96:* 404–410.

Buysse, D.J., Reynolds, C.F., Monk, T.H., Berman, S.R. and Kupfer, D.J. (1989) 'The Pittsburgh Sleep Quality Index (PSQI): A new instrument for psychiatric research and practice.' *Psychiatry Research 28*: 193–213.

Byars, A.W., Byars, K.C., Johnson, C.S., deGrauw, T.J. *et al.* (2008) 'The relationship between sleep problems and neuropsychological functioning in children with first recognized seizures.' *Epilepsy and Behavior 13*(4): 607–613.

Byerly, M.S. and Blackshaw, S. (2009) 'Vertebrate retina and hypothalamus development.' *Systems Biology and Medicine 1*(3): 380–389.

Cahn, B.R. and Polich, J. (2006) 'Meditation states and traits: EEG, ERP, and neuroimaging studies.' *Psychological Bulletin 132*(2): 180–211.

Cai, Z.J. (1991) 'The functions of sleep: Further analysis.' *Physiology & Behavior 50*: 53–60.

Cain, N. and Gradisar, M. (2010) 'Electronic media use and sleep in school-aged children and adolescents: A review.' *Sleep Medicine 11*: 735–742.

Caione, P., Arena, F., Biraghi, M., Cigna, R.M. *et al.* (1997) 'Nocturnal enuresis and daytime wetting: A multicentric trial with oxybutynin and desmopressin.' *European Urology 31*(4): 459–463.

Cairney, S., Maruff, P. and Clough, A.R. (2002) 'The neurobehavioural effects of kava.' *Australian and New Zealand Journal of Psychiatry 36*(5): 657–662.

Calandre, L., Martinez-Martin, P. and Campos-Castellano, J. (1978) 'Tratamiento del syndrome de Lennox con trigliceridos de cadena media.' *Anales Espanoles de Pediatria 11*: 189–194.

Caldwell, P.H.Y., Edgar, D., Hodson, E. and Craig, J.C. (2005) 'MJA Practice Essentials – Paediatrices, 4. Bedwetting and toileting problems in children.' *Medical Journal of Australia 182*: 190–195.

Camfield, P. and Camfield, C. (2002) 'Epileptic syndromes in childhood: Clinical features, outcomes, and treatment.' *Epilepsia 43*(suppl.3): 27–32.

Camfield, P., Gordon, K., Dooley, J. and Camfield, C. (1996) 'Melatonin appears ineffective in children with intellectual deficits and fragmented sleep: Six 'N of 1' trials. *Journal of Child Neurology 11*: 341–343.

Campbell, M., Fish, B., Shapiro, T. and Floyd, A. (1971) 'Imipramine in preschool autistic and schizophrenic children.' *Journal of Autism and Developmental Disorders 1*(3): 267–282.

Canitano, R. (2007) 'Epilepsy in autism spectrum disorders.' *European Journal of Child and Adolescent Psychiatry 16*(1): 61–66.

Capdevila, O.S., Kheirandish-Gozal, L., Dayyat, E. and Gozall, D. (2008) 'Pediatric obstructive sleep apnea complications, management, and long-term outcomes.' *Proceedings of the American Thoracic Society 5*: 274–282.

Capone, G.T., Goyal, P., Grados, M., Smith, B. and Kammann, H. (2008) 'Risperidone use in children with Down syndrome, severe intellectual disability, and comorbid autistic spectrum disorders: A naturalistic study.' *Journal of Developmental and Behavioral Pediatrics 29*(2): 106–116.

Carpenter, J.S. and Andrykowski, M.A. (1998) 'Psychometric evaluation of the Pittsburgh Sleep Quality Index.' *Journal of Psychosomatic Research 45*(1): 5–13.

Carr, R., Wasdell, M.B., Hamilton, D., Weiss, M.D. *et al.* (2007) 'Long-term effectiveness outcome of melatonin therapy in children with treatment-resistant circadian rhythm sleep disorders.' *Journal of Pineal Research 43*(4): 351–359.

Carskadon, M.A., Dement, W.C., Mittler, M.M., Roth, T. *et al.* (1986) 'Guidelines for the Multiple Sleep Latency Test (MSLT): A standard measure of sleepiness.' *Sleep 9*: 519–524.

Carvalho, F.R., Lentini-Oliveira, D., Machado, M.A., Prado, G.F., Prado, L.B. and Saconato, H. (2007) 'Oral appliances and functional orthopaedic appliances for obstructive sleep apnoea in children.' *Cochrane Database of Systematic Reviews 4*(2): CD005520.

Casella, E.B., Valente, M., Navarro, J.M. and Kok, F. (2005) 'Vitamin B12 deficiency in infancy as a cause of developmental regression.' *Brain and Development 27*(8): 592–594.

Casey, B.J., Duhoux, S. and Cohen, M.W. (2010) 'Adolescence: What do transmission, transition, and translation have to do with it?' *Neuron 67*: 749–760.

Cassisi, J.E., McGlynn, F.D. and Belles, D.R. (1987) 'EMG-activated feedback alarms for the treatment of nocturnal bruxism: Current status and future directions.' *Biofeedback and Self Regulation 12*(1): 13–30.

Castellanos, F.X. and Rapoport, J.L. (2002) 'Effects of caffeine on development and behavior in infancy and childhood: A review of the published literature.' *Food Chemistry and Toxicology 40*: 1235–1242.

Castriotta, R.J., Atanasov, S., Wilde, M.C., Masel, B.E. *et al.* (2009) 'Treatment of sleep disorders after traumatic brain injury.' *Journal of Clinical Sleep Medicine 5*(2): 137–144.

Caton, R. (1875) 'The electrical currents of the brain.' *British Medical Journal* II: 378.

Caton, R. (1877) 'Interim report on investigation of the electrical currents of the brain.' *British Medical Journal* suppl., I: 62–65.

Caton, R. (1887) 'Researches on electrical phenomena of cerebral gray matter.' *Ninth International Medical Congress 3*: 246–249.

Catrett, C.D. and Gaultney, J.F. (2009) 'Possible insomnia predicts some risky behaviours among adolescents when controlling for depressive symptoms.' *Journal of Genetic Psychology 170*(4): 287–309.

Cermakian, N. and Boivin, D.B. (2003) 'A molecular perspective of human circadian rhythm disorders.' *Brain Research Reviews 42*: 204–220.

Cerny, A. and Schmid, K. (1999) 'Tolerability and efficacy of valerian/lemon balm in healthy volunteers (a double-blind, placebo-controlled, multicentre study).' *Fitoterapia 70*: 221–228.

Chagoya de Sanchez, V. (1995) 'Circadian variations of adenosine and of its metabolism. Could adenosine be a molecular oscillator for circadian rhythms?' *Canadian Journal of Physiology and Pharmacology 73*(3): 339–355.

Challamel, M.J., Mazzola, M.E., Nevsimalova, S., Cannard, C. *et al.* (1994) 'Narcolepsy in children.' *Sleep 17*(8 suppl.): S17–20.

Chambless, D.L. and Hollon, S.D. (1998) 'Defining empirically supported therapies.' *Journal of Consulting and Clinical Psychology 66*(1): 7–18.

Chan, P., Huang, T.Y., Chen, Y.J., Huang, W.P. and Liu, Y.C. (1998) 'Randomized, double-blind, placebo-controlled study of the safety and efficacy of vitamin B complex in the treatment of nocturnal leg cramps in elderly patients with hypertension.' *Journal of Clinical Pharmacology 38:* 1151–1154.

Chan, S.S.-K., Choi, A.O.-K., Jones, R.L. and Lin, G. (2006) 'Mechanisms underlying the vasorelaxing effects of butylidenephthalide, an active constituent of Ligusticum chuanxiong, in rat isolated aorta.' *European Journal of Pharmacology 537*(1–3): 111–117.

Chan, T.Y., Tang, C.H. and Critchley, J.A. (1995) 'Poisoning due to an over-the-counter hypnotic, Sleep-Qik (hyoscine, cyproheptadine, valerian).' *Postgraduate Medical Journal 71*: 227–228.

Chaste, P., Clement, N., Mercati, O., Guillaume, J.L. *et al.* (2010) 'Identification of pathway-biased and deleterious melatonin receptor mutants in autism spectrum disorders and in the general population.' *PloS One 5*(7): e11495.

Chen, H.C. and Hsieh, M.T. (1985) 'Clinical trial of suanzaorentang in the treatment of insomnia.' *Clinical Therapeutics 7*(3): 334–337.

Chen, L.C., Chen, I.C., Wang, B.R. and Shao, C.H. (2009) 'Drug-use pattern of Chinese herbal medicines in insomnia: A 4-year survey in Taiwan.' *Journal of Clinical Pharmacy and Therapeutics 34*(5): 555–560.

Cheng, R. (1984) 'Chinese herbalism.' *Canadian Family Physician 30*: 119–122.

Chervin, R.D., Hedger, K., Dillon, J.E. and Pituch, K.J. (2000) 'Pediatric Sleep Questionnaire (PSQ): Validity and reliability of scales for sleep-disordered breathing, snoring, sleepiness, and behavioral problems.' *Sleep Medicine 1*: 21–32.

Chervin, R.D., Ruzicka, D.L., Giordani, B.J., Weatherly, R.A. *et al.* (2006) 'Sleep-disordered breathing, behavior, and cognition in children before and after adenotonsillectomy.' *Pediatrics 117*(4): e769–778.

Chesson, A.L., Littner, M., Davila, D., Anderson, W.M. *et al.* (1999) 'Practice parameters for the use of light therapy in the treatment of sleep disorders.' *Sleep 22*(5): 641–660.

Cheuk, D.K.L., Yeung, J., Chung, K.F. and Wong, V. (2009) 'Acupuncture for insomnia.' *The Cochrane Library 2*: 1–46.

Cheyne, J.A. and Girard, T.A. (2009) 'The body unbound: Vestibular-motor hallucinations and out-of-body experiences.' *Cortex 45*: 201–215.

Chez, M.G., Buchanan, T., Aimonovitch, M., Mrazek, S. *et al.* (2004) 'Frequency of EEG abnormalities in age-matched siblings of autistic children with abnormal sleep EEG patterns.' *Epilepsy and Behavior* 5: 159–162.

Chez, M.G., Chang, M., Krasne, V., Coughlan, C., Kominsky, M. and Schwartz, A. (2006) 'Frequency of epileptiform EEG abnormalities in a sequential screening of autistic patients with no known clinical epilepsy from 1996 to 2005.' *Epilepsy and Behavior 8*: 267–271.

Chirakalwasan, N., Hassan, F., Kaplish, N., Fetterolf, J. and Chervin, R.D. (2009) 'Near resolution of sleep related rhythmic movement disorder after CPAP for OSA.' *Sleep Medicine 10*: 497–500.

Chisholm, T. and Morehouse, R.L. (1996) 'Adult headbanging: Sleep studies and treatment.' *Sleep 19*: 343–346.

Chuang, G., Mao, S., Tam, W., Tam, G. and Tam, C. (2009) 'Survey of biological active molecule in the Chinese herbal formula Suan Zao Ren Tang in treating insomnia.' *FASEB Journal 23* (Meeting Abstract suppl.), 902.13.

Chung, K.F. and Lee, C.K.Y. (2002) 'Over-the-counter sleeping pills: A survey of use in Hong Kong and a review of their constituents.' *General Hospital Psychiatry 24*: 430–435.

Cicogna, P., Natale, V., Occhionero, M. and Bosinelli, M. (2000) 'Slow wave and REM sleep mentation.' *Sleep Research Online 3*(2): 67–72.

Cirelli, C. and Tononi, G. (2008) 'Is sleep essential?' *PloS Biology 6*(8): 1605–1611.

Clements, J., Wing, L. and Dunn, G. (1986) 'Sleep problems in handicapped children: A preliminary study.' *Journal of Child Psychology and Psychiatry 27*(3): 399–407.

Cohen, P.A. and Ernst, E. (2010) 'Safety of herbal supplements: A guide for cardiologists.' *Cardiovascular Therapeutics 28*(4): 246–253.

Colles, S.L., Dixon, J.B. and O'Brien, P.E. (2007) 'Night eating syndrome and nocturnal snacking: association with obesity, binge eating and psychological distress.' *International Journal of Obesity (Lond) 31*(11): 1722–1730.

Comasco, E., Nordquist, N., Gokturk, C., Aslund, C. *et al.* (2010) 'The clock gene PER2 and sleep problems: Association with alcohol consumption among Swedish adolescents.' *Upsala Journal of Medical Sciences 115*: 41–48.

Coogan, A.N. and Wyse, C.A. (2008) 'Neuroimmunology of the circadian clock.' *Brain Research 1232*: 104–112.

Coon, H., Dunn, D., Lainhart, J., Miller, J. *et al.* (2005) 'Possible association between autism and variants in the brain-expressed tryptophan hydroxylase gene (TPH2).' *American Journal of Medical Genetics B 135*(1): 42–46.

Coon, J.T. and Ernst, E. (2002) 'Panax ginseng: A systematic review of adverse effects and drug interactions.' *Drug Safety 25*(5): 323–344.

Corkum, P., Panton, R., Ironside, S., Macpherson, M. and Williams, T. (2008) 'Acute impact of immediate release methylphenidate administered three times a day on sleep in children with attention deficit/hyperactivity disorder.' *Journal of Pediatric Psychology 33*(4): 368–379.

Corns, C.M. (2003) 'Herbal remedies and clinical biochemistry.' *Annals of Clinical Biochemistry 40*: 489–507.

Cornu, C., Remontet, L., Noel-Baron, F., Nicolas, A. *et al.* (2010) 'A dietary supplement to improve the quality of sleep: A randomized placebo controlled trial.' *BMC Complementary and Alternative Medicine, 10*: 29. Available at www.biomedcentral.com/1472-6882/10/29, accessed 12 September 2011.

Cortese, S., Konofal, E. and Yateman, N. (2006) 'Sleep and alertness in children with attention deficit hyperactivity disorder: A systematic review of the literature.' *Sleep 29*: 504–511.

Cortesi, F., Giannotti, F., Ivanenko, A. and Johnson, K. (2010) 'Sleep in children with autistic spectrum disorder.' *Sleep Medicine 11*(7): 659–664.

Cotton, S. and Richdale, A. (2006) 'Brief report: Parental descriptions of sleep problems in children with autism, Down syndrome, and Prader-Willi syndrome.' *Research in Developmental Disabilities 27*(2): 151–161.

Cotton, S. and Richdale, A. (2010) 'Sleep patterns and behaviour in typically developing children and children with autism, Down syndrome, Prader-Willi syndrome and intellectual disability.' *Research in Autism Disorders 4*(3): 490–500.

Coutinho, A.M., Oliveira, G., Morgadinho, T., Fesel, C. *et al.* (2004) 'Variants of the serotonin transporter gene (SLC6A4) significantly contribute to hyperserotonemia in autism.' *Molecular Psychiatry 9*(3): 264–271.

Coutinho, A.M., Sousa, I., Martins, M., Correia, C. *et al.* (2007) 'Evidence for epistasis between SLC6A4 and ITGB3 in autism etiology and in the determination of platelet serotonin levels.' *Human Genetics 121*(2): 243–256.

Couturier, J.L., Speechley, K.N., Steele, M., Norman, R. *et al.* (2005) 'Parental perception of sleep problems in children of normal intelligence with pervasive developmental disorders: Prevalence, severity and pattern.' *Journal of the American Academy of Child and Adolescent Psychiatry 44*: 815–822.

Crabtree, V.McL., Ivanenko, A., O'Brien, L.M. and Gozal, D. (2003) 'Periodic limb movement disorder of sleep in children.' *Journal of Sleep Research 12*: 73–81.

Crabtree, V.McL. and Williams, N.A. (2009) 'Normal sleep in childen and adolescents.' *Child and Adolescent Psychiatric Clinics of North America 18*(4): 799–811.

Cremonini, F., Camilleri, M., Zinsmeister, A.R., Herrick, L.M. *et al.* (2009) 'Sleep disturbances are linked to both upper and lower gastrointestinal symptoms in the general population.' *Neurogastroenterology and Motility 21*(2): 128–135.

Crick, F. and Mitchison, G. (1983) 'The function of dream sleep.' *Nature 304*: 111–114.

Crnic, K.A. and Greenberg, M.T. (1990) 'Minor parenting stresses with young children.' *Child Development 61*: 1628–1637.

Croonenberghs, J., Bosmans, E., Deboutte, D., Kenis, G. and Maes, M. (2002) 'Activation of the inflammatory response system in autism.' *Neuropsychobiology 45*(1): 1–6.

Crow, Y.J., Zuberi, S.M., McWilliam, R., Tolmie, J.L. *et al.* (1998) '"Cataplexy" and muscle ultrasound abnormalities in Coffin-Lowry syndrome.' *Journal of Medical Genetics 35*: 94–98.

Cubero, J., Sánchez, C.L., Bravo, R., Sánchez, J. *et al.* (2009) 'Analysis of the antioxidant activity in human milk, day vs. night.' *Cell Membrane and Free Radical Research 1*(3): 100–101.

Cubero, J., Valero, V., Sanchez, J., Rivero, M. *et al.* (2005) 'The circadian rhythm of tryptophan in breast milk affects the rhythms of 6-sulfatoxymelatonin and sleep in newborn.' *Neuroendocrinology Letters 26*(6): 657–661.

Cullen, L. and Barlow, J. (2002) 'Kiss, cuddle, squeeze: The experiences and meaning of touch among parents of children with autism attending a Touch Therapy Programme.' *Journal of Child Health Care 6*(3): 171–181.

Czisch, M., Wehrle, R., Kaufmann, C., Wetter, T.C. *et al.* (2004) 'Functional MRI during sleep: BOLD signal decreases and their electrophysiological correlates.' *European Journal of Neuroscience 20*: 566–574.

Czisch, M., Wetter, T.C., Kaufmann, C., Pollmacher, T. *et al.* (2002) 'Altered processing of acoustic stimuli during sleep: Reduced auditory activation and visual deactivation detected by a combined fMRI/EEG study.' *Neuroimage 16*: 251–258.

Dahl, R.E. (1996) 'The impact of inadequate sleep on children's daytime cognitive function.' *Seminars in Pediatric Neurology 3*(2): 44–50.

Dahl, R.E., Bernhisel–Broadbent, J., Scanlon-Holdford, S., Sampson, H.A. and Lupo, M. (1995) 'Sleep disturbances in children with atopic dermatitis.' *Archives of Pediatric and Adolescent Medicine 149*(8): 856–860.

Dahl, R.E., Holttum, J. and Trubnick, L. (1994) 'A clinical picture of child and adolescent narcolepsy.' *Journal of the American Academy of Child and Adolescent Psychiatry 33*(6): 834–841.

Dai, H., Zhang, L., Cao, M., Song, F. et al. (2011) 'The role of polymorphisms in circadian pathway genes in breast tumorigenesis.' *Breast Cancer Research and Treatment 127*(2): 531–540.

D'Alessandro, R., Guarino, M., Greco, G., Leona Bassein, L. and Cstat, for the Emilia-Romagna Study Group on Clinical and Epidemiological Problems in Neurology (2004) 'Risk of seizures while awake in pure sleep epilepsies: A prospective study.' *Neurology 62*: 254–257.

Daley, M., Morin, C.M., LeBlanc, M., Grégoire, J.P. and Savard, J. (2009) 'The economic burden of insomnia: Direct and indirect costs for individuals with insomnia syndrome, insomnia symptoms, and good sleepers.' *Sleep 32*(1): 55–64.

Dang-Vu, T.T., McKinney, S.M., Buxton, O.M., Solet, J.M. *et al.* (2010) 'Spontaneous brain rhythms predict sleep stability in the face of noise.' *Current Biology 20*(15): R626–R627.

Daoust, A.M., Limoges, E., Bolduc, C., Mottron, L. and Godbout, R. (2004) 'EEG spectral analysis of wakefulness and REM sleep in high functioning autistic spectrum disorders.' *Clinical Neurophysiology 115*(6): 1368–1373.

Datta, S. and MacLean, R.R. (2007) 'Neurobiological mechanisms for the regulation of mammalian sleep-wake behavior: Reinterpretation of historical evidence and inclusion of contemporary cellular and molecular evidence.' *Neuroscience and Biobehavioral Reviews 31*(5): 775–824.

Dauvilliers, Y., Baumann, C.R., Carlander, B., Bischof, M. *et al.* (2003) 'CSF hypocretin-1 levels in narcolepsy, Kleine-Levin syndrome, and other hypersomnias and neurological conditions.' *Journal of Neurology, Neurosurgery and Psychiatry 74*: 1667–1673.

Dauvilliers, Y., Rompré, S., Gagnon, J.F. and Vendette, M. (2007) 'REM sleep characteristics in narcolepsy and REM sleep behavior disorder.' *Sleep 30*(7): 844–849.

Davé, S., Sherr, L., Senior, R. and Nazareth, I. (2009) 'Major paternal depression and child consultation for developmental and behavioural problems.' *British Journal of General Practice 59*: 180–185.

Davidson, K. and Scott, J. (2009) 'Does therapists' competence matter in delivering psychological therapy?' *The Psychiatrist 33*: 121–123.

Davis, B.J., Rajput, A., Rajput, M.L., Aul, E.A. and Eichorn, G.R. (2000) 'A randomized, double-blind placebo-controlled trial of iron in restless legs syndrome.' *European Neurology 43*: 70–75.

Davis, C.L., Tkacz, J., Gregoski, M., Boyle, C.A. and Lovrekovic, G. (2006) 'Aerobic exercise and snoring in overweight children: A randomized controlled trial.' *Obesity (Silver Spring) 14*(11): 1985–1991.

Davis, C.L., Tomporowski, P.D., Boyle, C.A. Waller, J.L. *et al.* (2007) 'Effects of aerobic exercise on overweight children's cognitive functioning: A randomized controlled trial.' *Research Quarterly in Exercise and Sport 78*(5): 510–519.

Davis, F.C. (1997) 'Melatonin: Role in development.' *Journal of Biological Rhythms 12*(6): 498–508.

Davis, K.A., Cantor, C., Maus, D. and Herman, S.T. (2008) 'A neurological cause of recurrent choking during sleep.' *Journal of Clinical Sleep Medicine 4*(6): 586–587.

DeCasper, A.J. and Fifer, W.P. (1980) 'Of human bonding: Newborns prefer their mothers' voices.' *Science 208*: 1174–1175.

DeCasper, A.J. and Spence, M.J. (1986) 'Prenatal maternal speech influences newborns' perception of speech sound.' *Infant Behavior and Development 9*: 133–150.

De Leersnyder, H., Claustrat, B., Munnich, A. and Verloes, A. (2006) 'Circadian rhythm disorder in a rare disease: Smith-Magenis syndrome.' *Molecular and Cellular Endocrinology 252*(1–2): 88–91.

Dement, W.C. (1958) 'The occurrence of low voltage, fast electroencephalogram patterns during behavioral sleep in the cat.' *Electroencephalography and Clinical Neurophysiology 10*: 291–296.

Dement, W. and Kleitman, N. (1957a) 'Cyclic variations in EEG during sleep and their relation to eye movements, body mobility and dreaming.' *Electroencephalography and Clinical Neurophysiology 9*(4): 673–690.

Dement, W. and Kleitman, N. (1957b) 'The relation of eye movements during sleep to dream activity: An objective method for the study of dreaming.' *Journal of Experimental Psychology 53*(5): 339–346.

DeMore, M., Cataldo, M., Tierney, E. and Slifer, K. (2009) 'Behavioral approaches to training developmentally disabled children for an overnight EEG procedure.' *Journal of Developmental and Physical Disability 21*(4): 245–251.

Deng, J., Zhou, Y., Bai, M., Li, H. and Li, L. (2010) 'Anxiolytic and sedative activities of *Passiflora edulis f. flavicarpa.*' *Journal of Ethnopharmacology 128*: 148–153.

de Sousa, A.G.P., Cercato, C., Mancini, M.C. and Halpern, A. (2008) 'Obesity and obstructive sleep apnea-hypopnea syndrome.' *Obesity Reviews 9*: 340–354.

De Wachter, S., Vernmandel, A., de Moerloose, K. and Wyndaele, J.J. (2002) 'Value of increase in bladder capacity in treatment of refractory monosymptomatic nocturnal enuresis in children.' *Urology 60*: 1090–1094.

Dhawan, K., Dhawan, S. and Sharma, A. (2004) '*Passiflora*: A review update.' *Journal of Ethnopharmacology 94*(1): 1–23.

Diano, S. and Horvath, T.L. (2008) 'Anticonvulsant effects of leptin in epilepsy.' *Journal of Clinical Investigation, 118*(1): 26–28.

Díaz-Morales, J.F. and Sorroche, M.G. (2008) 'Morningness-eveningness in adolescents.' *Spanish Journal of Psychology 11*(1): 201–206.

Didden, R., Curfs, L.M.G., Sikkema, S.P.E. and deMoor, J. (1998) 'Functional assessment and treatment of sleeping problems with developmentally disabled children: Six case studies.' *Journal of Behavior Therapy and Experimental Psychiatry 29*(1): 85–97.

Didden, R., Curfs, L.M., van Driel, S. and de Moor, J.M. (2002) 'Sleep problems in children and young adults with developmental disabilities: Home-based functional assessment and treatment.' *Journal of Behavior Therapy and Experimental Psychiatry 33*(1): 49–58.

Dimpfel, W. and Suter, A. (2008) 'Sleep improving effects of a single dose administration of a valerian/hops fluid extract – a double blind, randomized, placebo-controlled sleep-EEG study in a parallel design using electrohypnograms.' *European Journal of Medical Research 13*(5): 200–204.

Diomedi, M., Curatolo, P., Scalise, A., Placidi, F., Caretto, F. and Gigli, G.L. (1999) 'Sleep abnormalities in mentally retarded autistic subjects: Down's syndrome with mental retardation and normal subjects.' *Brain & Development 21*: 548–553.

Dixit, V.D. and Taub, D.D. (2005) 'Mini review. Ghrelin and immunity: A young player in an old field.' *Experimental Gerontology 40*: 900–910.

Doghramji, K. (2007) 'Melatonin and its receptors: A new class of sleep-promoting agents.' *Journal of Clinical Sleep Medicine 3*(5), suppl.: S17–S23.

Dominick, K., Davis, N.O., Lainhart, J., Tager-Flusberg, H. and Folstein, S. (2007) 'Atypical behaviors in children with autism and children with a history of language impairment.' *Research in Developmental Disabilities 28*(2): 145–162.

Donlea, J.M. and Shaw, P.J. (2009) 'Sleeping together: Using social interactions to understand the role of sleep in plasticity.' *Advances in Genetics 68*: 57–81.

Doo, S. and Wing, Y.K. (2006) 'Sleep problems of children with pervasive developmental disorders: Correlation with parental stress.' *Developmental Medicine and Child Neurology 48*: 650–655.

Dørheim, S.K., Bondevik, G.T., Eberhard-Gran, M. and Bjorvatn, B. (2009) 'Sleep and depression in postpartum women: A population-based study.' *Sleep 32*(7): 847–855.

Dorrian, J., Baulk, S.D. and Dawson, S.D. (2011) 'Work hours, workload, sleep and fatigue in Australian Rail Industry employees.' *Applied Ergonomics 42*(2): 202–209.

Dosman, C.F., Brian, J.A., Drmic, I.E., Senthilselvan, A. *et al.* (2007) 'Children with autism: Effect of iron supplementation on sleep and ferritin.' *Pediatric Neurology 36*: 152–158.

Dosman, C., Drmic, I., Brian, J., Senthilselvan, A. *et al.* (2006) 'Ferritin as an indicator of suspected iron deficiency in children with autism spectrum disorder: Prevalence of low serum ferritin concentration.' *Developmental Medicine and Child Neurology 48*:1008–1009.

Drake, C., Nickel, C., Burduvali, E., Roth, T., Jefferson, C. and Pietro, B. (2003) 'The Pediatric Daytime Sleepiness Scale (PDSS): Sleep habits and school outcomes in middle-school children.' *Sleep 26*(4): 455–458.

Droogleever Fortuyn, H.A., Swinkels, S., Buitelaar, J., Renier, W.O. *et al.* (2008) 'High prevalence of eating disorders in narcolepsy with cataplexy: A case-control study.' *Sleep 31*(3): 335–341.

Drummond, S.P., Brown, G.G., Stricker, J.L., Buxton, R.B. *et al.* (1999) 'Sleep deprivation-induced reduction in cortical functional response to serial subtraction.' *NeuroReport 10*(18): 3745–3748.

Duncan, B., Barton, L., Edmonds, D. and Blashill, B.M. (2004) 'Parental perceptions of the therapeutic effect from osteopathic manipulation or acupuncture in children with spastic cerebral palsy.' *Clinical Pediatrics 43*: 349–353.

Durand, M.V. (1997) *Sleep Better!: Guide to Improving Sleep for Children with Special Needs*. Baltimore, MD: Paul H. Brookes.

Durand, M.V. (2008a) *When Children Don't Sleep Well: Interventions for Pediatric Sleep Disorders Therapist Guide (Treatments that Work)*. Oxford: Oxford University Press.

Durand, M.V. (2008b) *When Children Don't Sleep Well: Interventions for Pediatric Sleep Disorders Parent Workbook (Treatments that Work)*. Oxford: Oxford University Press.

Durrant, K.L. (2002) 'Known and hidden sources of caffeine in drug, food, and natural products.' *Journal of the American Pharmaceutical Association (Washington) 42*(4): 625–637.

Dworkin, R.H. and Kirkpatrick, P. (2005) 'Pregabalin.' *Nature Reviews: Drug Discovery 4*: 455–456.

Dzaja, A., Dalal, M.A., Himmerich, H., Uhr, M. *et al.* (2004) 'Sleep enhances nocturnal plasma ghrelin levels in healthy subjects.' *American Journal of Physiology, Endocrinology and Metabolism 286*: E963–E967.

Earley, C.J., Allen, R.P., Beard, J.L. and Connor, J.R. (2000) 'Insight into the pathophysiology of restless legs syndrome.' *Journal of Neuroscience Research 62*: 623–628.

Eastman, C.I., Young, M.A., Fogg, L.F., Liu, L. and Meaden, P.M. (1998) 'Bright light treatment of winter depression: A placebo-controlled trial.' *Archives of General Psychiatry 55*(10): 883–889.

Ebisawa, T. (2007) 'Circadian rhythms in the CNS and peripheral clock disorders: Human sleep disorders and clock genes.' *Journal of Pharmacological Science 103*: 150–154.

Edinger, J.D., Wohlgemuth, W.K., Radtke, R.A., Marsh, G.R. and Quillian, R.E. (2001) 'Cognitive behavioral therapy for treatment of chronic primary insomnia: A randomized, controlled trial.' *Journal of the American Medical Association 285*: 1856–1864.

Edwards, S.D. and van der Spuy, H.I. (1985) 'Hypnotherapy as a treatment for enuresis.' *Journal of Child Psychology & Psychiatry & Allied Disciplines 26*(1): 161–170.

Ehrman, T.M., Barlow, D.J. and Hylands, P.J. (2007a) 'Phytochemical databases of Chinese herbal constituents and bioactive plant compounds with known target specificities.' *Journal of Chemical Information and Modelling 47*(2): 254–263.

Ehrman, T.M., Barlow, D.J. and Hylands, P.J. (2007b) 'Phytochemical informatics of Traditional Chinese Medicine and therapeutic relevance.' *Journal of Chemical Information and Modelling 47*(6): 2316–2334.

Eiser, A.S. (2005) 'Physiology and psychology of dreams.' *Seminars in Neurology 25*(1): 97–105.

Elgar, M.A., Pagel, M.D. and Harvey, P.H. (1988) 'Sleep in mammals.' *Animal Behaviour 36*: 1407–1419.

Elia, M., Ferri, R., Musumeci, S.A., Del Gracco, S. *et al.* (2000) 'Sleep in subjects with autistic disorder: A neurophysiological and psychological study.' *Brain and Development 22*(2): 88–92.

Elkay, M., Poduri, A., Prabhu, S.P., Bergin, A.M. and Kothare, S.V. (2010) 'Nocturnal choking episodes: Under-recognized and misdiagnosed.' *Pediatric Neurology 43*: 355–358.

Elkhayat, H.A., Hassanein, S.M., Tomoum, H.Y., Abd-Elhamid, I.A. *et al.* (2010) 'Melatonin and sleep-related problems in children with intractable epilepsy.' *Pediatric Neurology 42*(4): 249–254.

Ellenbogen, J.M. (2005) 'Cognitive benefits of sleep and their loss due to sleep deprivation.' *Neurology 64*(7): E25–E27.

Emser, W. and Bartylla, K. (1991) 'Verbesserung der Schlafqualität. Zur wirkung von Kava-Extrakt WS 1490 auf das Schlafmuster bei Gesunden.' *TW Neurologie Psychiatrie 5*: 636–642.

Erichsen, D., Ferri, R. and Gozal, D. (2010) 'Ropinirole in restless legs syndrome and periodic limb movement disorder.' *Therapeutics and Clinical Risk Management 6*: 173–182.

Erickson, C.A., Stigler, K.A., Posey, D.J. and McDougle, C.J. (2010) 'Aripiprazole in autism spectrum disorders and Fragile X syndrome.' *Neurotherapeutics 7*: 258–263.

Ernst, E. (2007) 'Commentary: A re-evaluation of kava (*Piper methysticum*).' *British Journal of Clinical Pharmacology 64*(4): 415–417.

Escalona, A., Field, T., Singer-Strunck, R., Cullen, C. and Hatshorn, K. (2001) 'Improvements in the behavior of children with autism following massage therapy.' *Journal of Autism and Developmental Disorders 31*: 513–516.

Espie, C.A. (1993) 'Practical management of insomnia: Behavioural and cognitive techniques.' *British Medical Journal 306*: 509–511.

Espie, C.A. (2006) *Overcoming Insomnia and Sleep Problems: A Self-Help Guide Using Cognitive Behavioral Techniques.* London: Constable and Robinson.

Espie, C.A. and Kyle, S.D. (2009) 'Primary insomnia: An overview of practical management using cognitive behavioral techniques.' *Sleep Medicine Clinics 4*: 559–569.

Evangeliou, A., Vlachonikolis, I., Mihailidou, H., Spilioti, M. *et al.* (2003) 'Application of a ketogenic diet in children with autistic behavior: Pilot study.' *Journal of Child Neurology 18*(2): 113–118.

Evans, I. (1996) 'Individualizing therapy, customizing clinical science.' *Journal of Behaviour Therapy and Experimental Psychiatry 27*(2): 99–105.

Evans, J.H.C. (2001a) 'Evidence based management of nocturnal enuresis.' *British Medical Journal 323*: 1167–1169.

Evans, J.H.C. (2001b) 'Evidence-based case reviews: Nocturnal enuresis.' *Western Journal of Medicine 175*(2): 108–111.

Fakier, N. and Wild, L.G. (2010) 'Associations among sleep problems, learning difficulties and substance use in adolescence.' *Journal of Adolescence 34*(4): 717–726.

Fang, X.Sh., Hao, J.F., Zhou, H.Y., Zhu, L.X. *et al.* (2010) 'Pharmacological studies on the sedative-hypnotic effect of Semen Ziziphi spinosae (Suanzaoren) and Radix et Rhizoma Salviae miltiorrhizae (Danshen) extracts and the synergistic effect of their combinations.' *Phytomedicine 17*(1): 75–80.

Farah, M.H., Edwards, R., Lindquist, M., Leon, C. and Shaw, D. (2000) 'International monitoring of adverse health effects associated with herbal medicines.' *Pharmacoepidemiology and Drug Safety 9*(2): 105–112.

Faraone, S.V., Glatt, S.J., Bukstein, O.G., Lopez, F.A. *et al.* (2009) 'Effects of once-daily oral and transdermal methylphenidate on sleep behavior of children with ADHD.' *Journal of Attention Disorders 12*(4):308–315.

Fass, R., Quan, S.F., O'Connor, G.T., Ervin, A. and Iber, C. (2005) 'Predictors of heartburn during sleep in a large prospective cohort study.' *Chest 127*(5): 1658–1666.

Fauteck, J.D., Schmidt, H., Lerchl, A., Kurlemann, G. and Wittkowski, W. (1999) 'Melatonin in epilepsy: First results of replacement therapy and first clinical results.' *Biological Signals and Receptors 8*: 105–110.

Feldman, R., Weller, A., Sirota, L. and Eidelman, A.I. (2002) 'Skin-to-skin contact (kangaroo care) promotes self-regulation in premature infants: Sleep-wake cyclicity, arousal modulation, and sustained exploration.' *Developmental Psychology 38*: 194–207.

Ferrance, R.J. and Miller, J. (2010) 'Chiropractic diagnosis and management of non-musculoskeletal conditions in children and adolescents.' *Chiropractic & Osteopathy 18*: 14. Available at www.chiroandosteo.com/content/18/1/14, accessed 13 September 2011.

Ferre, S. (2010) 'Role of the central ascending neurotransmitter systems in the psychostimulant effects of caffeine.' *Journal of Alzheimers Disease 20*(suppl.1): S35–S49.

Field, T., Diego, M. and Hernandez-Reif, M. (2009) 'Infants of depressed mothers are less responsive to faces and voices: A review.' *Infant Behavior and Development 32*(3): 239–244.

Field, T., Lasko, D., Mundy, P., Henteleff, T. *et al.* (1997) 'Brief report: Autistic children's attentiveness and responsivity improve after touch therapy.' *Journal of Autism and Developmental Disorders 27*(3): 333.

Fielding, D. (1980) 'The response of day and night wetting children and children who wet only at night to retention control training and the enuresis alarm.' *Behaviour Research and Therapy 18*: 305–317.

Filipek, P.A., Accardo, P.J., Baranek, G.T., Cook, E.H. Jr *et al.* (1999) 'The screening and diagnosis of autistic spectrum disorders.' *Journal of Autism and Developmental Disorders 29*(6): 439–484.

Findley, L., Unverzagt, M., Guchu, R., Fabrizio, M. *et al.* (1995) 'Vigilance and automobile accidents in patients with sleep apnea or narcolepsy.' *Chest 108*: 619–624.

Fisher, C., Kahn, E., Edwards, A. and Davis, D.M. (1973) 'A psychological study of nightmares and night terrors: The suppression of stage 4 night terrors with diazepam.' *Archives of General Psychiatry 28*: 252–259.

Fitzgerald, M.P., Thom, D.H., Wassel-Fyr, C., Subak, L. *et al.* (2006) 'Childhood urinary symptoms predict adult overactive bladder symptoms.' *Journal of Urology 175*(3 pt. 1): 989–993.

Forbes, D., Phelps, A. and McHugh, T. (2001) 'Brief report: Treatment of combat-related nightmares using imagery rehearsal: A pilot study.' *Journal of Traumatic Stress 14*(2): 433–442.

Forbes, D., Phelps, A.J., McHugh, A.F., Debenham, P. *et al.* (2003) 'Imagery rehearsal in the treatment of posttraumatic nightmares in Australian veterans with chronic combat-related PTSD: 12-month follow-up data.' *Journal of Traumatic Stress 16*(5): 509–513.

Forbes, E.E., Cohn, J.F., Allen, N.B. and Lewinsohn, P.M. (2004) 'Infant affect during parent-infant interaction at 3 and 6 months: Differences between mothers and fathers and influence of parent history of depression.' *Infancy 5*(1): 61–84.

Ford, D.E. and Kamerow, D.B. (1989) 'Epidemiologic study of sleep disturbances and psychiatric disorders. An opportunity for prevention?' *Journal of the American Medical Association 262*(11): 1479–1484.

Forness, S.R. (2005) 'The pursuit of evidence-based practice in special education for children with emotional or behavioral disorders.' *Behavioral Disorders 30*(4): 311–330.

Forsythe, W.I. and Butler, R.J. (1989) 'Fifty years of enuretic alarms.' *Archives of Disease in Childhood 64*: 879–885.

Forsythe, W.I. and Merrett, J.D. (1969) 'A controlled trial of imipramine ('Tofranil') and nortriptyline ('Allegron') in the treatment of enuresis.' *British Journal of Clinical Practice 23*(5): 210–215.

Foster, R. and Kreitzman, L. (2005) *Rhythms of Life: The Biological Clocks that Control the Daily Lives of Every Living Thing.* London: Profile Books.

Foulkes, D. (1962) 'Dream reports from different stages of sleep.' *Journal of Abnormal and Social Psychology 65*(1): 14–25.

Fox, N.A. (2007) 'Insufficient evidence to confirm effectiveness of oral appliances in treatment of obstructive sleep apnoea syndrome in children.' *Evidence Based Dentistry 8*(3): 84.

France, K.G. and Hudson, S.M. (1990) 'Behavioral management of infant sleep disturbance.' *Journal of Applied Behavior Analysis 23*: 91–98.

Frauscher, B., Gschliesser, V., Brandauer, E., Marti, I. *et al.* (2010) 'REM sleep behavior disorder in 703 sleep-disorder patients: The importance of eliciting a comprehensive sleep history.' *Sleep Medicine 11*: 167–171.

Freeman, D., Pugh, K., Vorontsova, K. and Southgate, L. (2009) 'Insomnia and paranoia.' *Schizophrenia Research 108*(1–3): 280–284.

Freud, S. (1900) *The Interpretation of Dreams.* Standard edition, 4 and 5.

Freud, S. (1913) *The Interpretation of Dreams*, trans. A.A. Brill. New York, NY: MacMillan. (First published as *Die Traumdeutung* in 1899.)

Frey, D.J., Fleshner, M. and Wright, K.P., Jr (2007) 'The effects of 40 hours of total sleep deprivation on inflammatory markers in healthy young adults.' *Brain, Behavior, and Immunity 21*: 1050–1057.

Fricke-Oerkermann, L., Plück, J., Schredl, M., Heinz, K. *et al.* (2007) 'Prevalence and course of sleep problems in childhood.' *Sleep 30*(10): 1371–1377.

Friedman, A. and Luiselli, J.K. (2008) 'Excessive daytime sleep: Behavioral assessment and intervention in a child with autism.' *Behavior Modification 32*(4): 548–555.

Friedman, A.G. and Ollendick, T.H. (1989) 'Treatment programs for severe night-time fears: A methodological note.' *Journal of Behavior Therapy and Experimental Psychiatry 20*(2): 171–178.

Friedman, N.P., Corley, R.P., Hewitt, J.K. and Wright, K.P., Jr (2009) 'Individual differences in childhood sleep problems predict later cognitive executive control.' *Sleep 32*(3): 323–333.

Friman, P.C., Hoff, K.E., Schnoes, C., Freeman, K.A. *et al.* (1999) 'The bedtime pass: An approach to bedtime crying and leaving the room.' *Archives of Pediatric and Adolescent Medicine 153*(10): 1027–1029.

Froy, O. (2007) 'The relationship between nutrition and circadian rhythms in mammals.' *Frontiers in Neuroendocrinology 28*: 61–71.

Fruehauf, H. (1995) 'Commonly used Chinese herb formulas for the treatment of mental disorders.' *Journal of Chinese Medicine 48*: 21–34.

Furst, P. and Stehle, P. (2004) 'What are the essential elements needed for the determination of amino acid requirements in humans?' *Journal of Nutrition 134*: 1558S–1565S.

Gaby, A.R. (2007) 'Natural approaches to epilepsy.' *Alternative Medicine Review 12*(1): 9–24.

Gagnier, J.J., DeMelo, J., Boon, H., Rochon, P. and Bombardier, C. (2006) 'Quality of reporting of randomized controlled trials of herbal medicine interventions.' *American Journal of Medicine 119*(1): 1–11.

Gagnon, J.F., Postuma, R.B. and Montplaisir, J. (2006) 'Update on the pharmacology of REM sleep behavior disorder.' *Neurology 67*: 742–747.

Gagnon, Y., Mayer, P., Morisson, F., Rompre, P.H. *et al.* (2004) 'Aggravation of respiratory disturbances by the use of an occlusal splint in apneic patients: A pilot study.' *International Journal of Prosthodontics 17*: 447–453.

Gallese, V. (2010) 'From Mirror Neurons to Embodied Simulation.' Lecture at the Arnold Pfeffer Center for Neuropsychoanalysis, 2 October, available at http://npsafoundation.org/page6/page15/page15. html, accessed 13 September 2011.

Galli-Carminati, G., Deriaz, N. and Bertschy, G. (2009) 'Melatonin in treatment of chronic sleep disorders in adults with autism: A retrospective study.' *Swiss Medical Weekly 139*(19–20): 293–296.

Galloway, G.P., Frederick, S.L., Staggers, F.E., Jr, Gonzales, M. *et al.* (1997) 'Gamma-hydroxybutyrate: An emerging drug of abuse that causes physical dependence.' *Addiction 92*(1): 89–96.

Ganguly-Fitzgerald, I., Donlea, J.M. and Shaw, P.J. (2006) 'Waking experience affects sleep need in *Drosophila.*' *Science 313*: 1775–1781.

Garcia-Borreguero, D. and Williams, A.M. (2010) 'Dopaminergic augmentation of restless legs syndrome.' *Sleep Medicine Reviews 14*(5): 339–346.

Garcia-Fernàndez, J. (2005) 'The genesis and evolution of homeobox gene clusters.' *Nature Reviews: Genetics 6*(12): 881–892.

Garcia-Rill, E., Charlesworth, A., Heister, D., Ye, M. and Hayar, A. (2008) 'The developmental decrease in REM sleep: The role of transmitters and electrical coupling.' *Sleep 31*(5): 673–690.

Gardiner, P. and Kemper, K.J. (2002) 'Insomnia: Herbal and dietary alternatives to counting sheep.' *Contemporary Pediatrics 19*(2): 69–87.

Garstang, J. and Wallis, M. (2006) 'Randomized controlled trial of melatonin for children with autistic spectrum disorders and sleep problems.' *Child Care Health and Development 32*(5): 585–589.

Gau, S.S.-F. and Chiang, H.-L. (2009) 'Sleep problems and disorders among adolescents with persistent and subthreshold attention-deficit/hyperactivity disorders.' *Sleep 32*(5): 671–679.

Gauillard, J., Cheref, S., Vacherontrystram, M.N. and Martin, J.C. (2002) 'L'hydrate de chloral, un hypnotique à oublier?' [Chloral hydrate: a hypnotic best forgotten?] *L'Encephale 28*(3:1): 200–204.

Gaus, V.L. (2007) *Cognitive-Behavioral Therapy for Adult Asperger Syndrome.* New York, NY: Guilford Press.

Gaylor, E.E., Burnham, M.M., Goodlin-Jones, B.L. and Anders, T.F. (2005) 'A longitudinal follow-up study of young children's sleep patterns using a developmental classification system.' *Behavioral Sleep Medicine 3*(1): 44–61.

Gelineau, J. (1880) 'De la narcolepsie.' *Gazette Hopital* (Paris) *53*: 626–628.

Gentili, A., Godschalk, M.F., Gheorghiu, D., Nelson, K. *et al.* (1996) 'Effect of clonidine and yohimbine on sleep in healthy men: A double-blind, randomized, controlled trial.' *European Journal of Clinical Pharmacology 50*(6): 463–465.

Gepertz, S. and Nevéus, T. (2004) 'Imipramine for therapy resistant enuresis: A retrospective evaluation.' *Journal of Urology 171*(6 pt 2): 2607–2610.

Geschwind, D.H. and Levitt, P. (2007) 'Autism spectrum disorders: Developmental disconnection syndromes.' *Current Opinion in Neurobiology 17*: 103–111.

Ghanizadeh, A. (2010) 'Possible role of caffeine in autism spectrum disorders, a new testable hypothesis.' *Journal of Food Science 75*(6): ix.

Giannotti, F., Cortesi, F., Cerquiglini A., Miraglia, D. *et al.* (2008) 'An investigation of sleep characteristics, EEG abnormalities and epilepsy in developmentally regressed and non-regressed children with autism.' *Journal of Autism and Developmental Disorders 38*: 1888–1897.

Gibberd, F.B. and Bateson, M.C. (1974) 'Sleep epilepsy: Its pattern and prognosis.' *British Medical Journal 2*: 403–405.

Gibertini, M., Graham, C. and Cook, M.R. (1999) 'Self-report of circadian type reflects the phase of the melatonin rhythm.' *Biological Psychology 50*(1): 19–33.

Gibson, E.S., Powles, A.C.P., Thabane, L., O'Brien, S. *et al.* (2006) '"Sleepiness" is serious in adolescence: Two surveys of 3235 Canadian students.' *BMC Public Health 6*: 116, doi:10.1186/1471-2458-6-116.

Giebenhain, J.E. and O'Dell, S.L. (1984) 'Evaluation of a parent-training manual for reducing children's fear of the dark.' *Journal of Applied Behavior Analysis 17*(1): 121–125.

Gillette, M.U. and Abbott, S.M. (2009) 'Biological timekeeping.' *Sleep Medicine Clinics 4*(2): 99–110.

Gimble, J.M. and Floyd, Z.E. (2009) 'Fat circadian biology.' *Journal of Applied Physiology 107*: 1629–1637.

Gingras, J.L., Mitchell, E.A. and Grattan, K.E. (2005) 'Fetal homologue of infant crying.' *Archives of Disease in Childhood: Fetal and Neonatal Edition 90*: F415–F418.

Gironell, A., de la Calzada, M.D., Sagales, T. and Barraquer-Bordas, L. (1995) 'Absence of REM sleep and altered non-REM sleep caused by a haematoma in the pontine tegmentum.' Letter to the Editor. *Journal of Neurology, Neurosurgery and Psychiatry 59*(2): 195–196.

Glaze, D.G., Rosen, C.L. and Owens, J.A. (2002) 'Toward a practical definition of pediatric insomnia.' *Current Therapeutic Research 63*(suppl.B): B4–B17.

Glazener, C.M.A. and Evans, J.H.C. (2002) 'Desmopressin for nocturnal enuresis in children.' *Cochrane Database of Systematic Reviews 3*: CD002112, doi: 10.1002/14651858.CD002112.

Glazener, C.M.A. and Evans, J.H.C. (2004) 'Simple behavioural and physical interventions for nocturnal enuresis in children.' *Cochrane Database of Systematic Reviews 2*: CD003637, doi: 10.1002/14651858. CD003637.pub2.

Glazener, C.M.A., Evans, J.H.C. and Cheuk, D.K.L. (2005) 'Complementary and miscellaneous interventions for nocturnal enuresis in children.' *Cochrane Database of Systematic Reviews 2*: CD005230, doi: 10.1002/14651858.CD005230.

Glazener, C.M.A., Evans, J.H.C. and Peto, R.E. (2003a) 'Tricyclic and related drugs for nocturnal enuresis in children.' *Cochrane Database of Systematic Reviews 3*: CD002117, doi: 10.1002/14651858.CD002117.

Glazener, C.M.A., Evans, J.H.C. and Peto, R.E. (2003b) 'Drugs for nocturnal enuresis in children (other than desmopressin and tricyclics).' *Cochrane Database of Systematic Reviews 4*: CD002238, doi: 10.1002/14651858.CD002238.

Glazener, C.M.A., Evans, J.H.C. and Peto, R.E. (2004) 'Complex behavioural and educational interventions for nocturnal enuresis in children.' *Cochrane Database of Systematic Reviews 1*: CD004668, doi: 10.1002/14651858.CD004668.

Glazener, C.M.A., Evans, J.H.C. and Peto, R.E. (2005) 'Alarm interventions for nocturnal enuresis in children.' *Cochrane Database of Systematic Reviews 1*: CD002911. doi: 10.1002/14651858.CD002911.

Glickman, G. (2010) 'Circadian rhythms and sleep in children with autism.' *Neuroscience and Biobehavioral Reviews 34*: 755–768.

Glotzbach, S.F., Edgar, D.M. and Ariagno, R.L. (1995) 'Biological rhythmicity in preterm infants prior to discharge from neonatal intensive care.' *Pediatrics 95*(2): 231–237.

Goin-Kochel, R.P., Myers, B.J. and Mackintosh, V.H. (2007) 'Parental reports on the use of treatments and therapies for children with autism spectrum disorders.' *Research in Autism Spectrum Disorders 11*(1): 195–209.

Gold, J.I., Nicolaou, C.D., Belmont, K.A., Katz, A.R. *et al.* (2009) 'Pediatric acupuncture: A review of clinical research.' *Evidence Based Complementary and Alternative Medicine 6*(4): 429–439.

Goldman, S.E., McGrew, S., Johnson, K.P., Richdale, A.L., Clemons, T. and Malow, B.A. (2011) 'Sleep is associated with problem behaviors in children and adolescents with autism spectrum disorders.' *Research in Autism Spectrum Disorders 5*: 1223–1229.

Goldman, S.E., Surdyka, K., Cuevas, R. and Adkins, K. (2009) 'Defining the sleep phenotype in children with autism.' *Developmental Neuropsychology 34*(5): 560–573.

Goldstone, A.P. and Beales, P.L. (2008) 'Genetic obesity syndromes.' *Frontiers in Hormone Research 36*: 37–60.

Gomez-Abellan, P., Hernandez-Morante, J.J., Lujan, J.A., Madrid, J.A. and Garaulet, M. (2008) 'Clock genes are implicated in the human metabolic syndrome.' *International Journal of Obesity 32*: 121–128.

Goodlin-Jones, B.L., Burnham, M.M., Gaylor, E.E. and Anders, T.F. (2001) 'Night waking, sleep-wake organization, and self-soothing in the first year of life.' *Journal of Developmental and Behavioral Pediatrics 22*(4): 226–233.

Goodlin-Jones, B.L., Sitnick, S.L., Tang, K., Liu, J. and Anders, T.F. (2008) 'The children's sleep habits questionnaire in toddlers and preschool children.' *Journal of Developmental and Behavioral Pediatrics 9*(2): 82–88.

Gordon, D.W., Rosenthal, G., Hart, J., Sirota, R. and Baker A.L. (1995) 'Chaparral ingestion: The broadening spectrum of liver injury caused by herbal medications.' *Journal of the American Medical Association 273*: 489–490.

Gordon, J., King, N.J., Gullone, E., Muris, P. and Ollendick, T.H. (2007) 'Treatment of children's nighttime fears: The need for a modern randomised controlled trial.' *Clinical Psychology Review 27*(1): 98–113.

Gottesmann, C. (2001) 'The golden age of rapid eye movement sleep discoveries. 1. Lucretius–1964.' *Progress in Neurobiology 65*: 211–287.

Gozal, D. (2008) 'Obstructive sleep apnea in children: Implications for the developing central nervous system.' *Seminars in Pediatric Neurology 15*(2): 100–106.

Gozal, D., Kheirandish-Gozal, L., Capdevila, O.S., Dayyat, E. and Kheirandish, E. (2008) 'Prevalence of recurrent otitis media in habitually snoring school-aged children.' *Sleep Medicine* 9(5): 549–554.

Gradisar, M., Lack, L., Richards, H., Harris, J. *et al.* (2007) 'The Flinders Fatigue Scale: Preliminary psychometric properties and clinical sensitivity of a new scale for measuring daytime fatigue associated with insomnia.' *Journal of Clinical Sleep Medicine* 3(7): 722–728.

Grave, J. and Blissett, J. (2004) 'Is cognitive behavior therapy developmentally appropriate for young children? A critical review of the evidence.' *Clinical Psychology Review* 24: 399–420.

Graven, S.N. and Browne, J.V. (2008) 'Sleep and brain development: The critical role of sleep in fetal and early neonatal brain development.' *Newborn and Infant Nursing Reviews* 8(4): 173–179.

Graw-Panzer, K.D., Muzumdar, H., Jambhekar, S., Goldstein, N.A. and Rao, M. (2010) 'Effect of increasing body mass index on obstructive sleep apnea in children.' *Open Sleep Journal* 3: 19–23.

Gray, C.A. and Garand, J.D. (1993) 'Teaching Children with Autism to "Read" Social Situations.' In K. Quill (ed.) *Teaching Children with Autism: Strategies to Enhance Communication and Socialization.* New York, NY: Delmar.

Graziano, A.M. and Mooney, K.C. (1982) 'Behavioral treatment of "nightfears" in children: Maintenance of improvement at 2½- to 3-year follow-up.' *Journal of Consulting and Clinical Psychology* 50(4): 598–599.

Greaves, M.W. (1969) 'Scarring due to enuresis blankets.' *British Journal of Dermatology* 81(6): 440–442.

Greenaway, M. and Elbe, D. (2009) 'Focus on aripiprazole: A review of its use in child and adolescent psychiatry.' *Journal of the Canadian Academy of Child and Adolescent Psychiatry* 18(3): 250–260.

Gregory, A.M., Rijsdijk, F.V., Lau, J.Y.F., Dahl, R.E. and Eley, T.C. (2009) 'The direction of longitudinal associations between sleep problems and depression symptoms: A study of twins aged 8 and 10 years.' *Sleep* 32(2): 189–199.

Grigg-Damberger, M., Gozal, D., Marcus, C.L., Quan, S.F. *et al.* (2007) 'The visual scoring of sleep and arousal in infants and children.' *Journal of Clinical Sleep Medicine* 3(2): 201–240.

Groer, M.W. and Morgan, K. (2007) 'Immune, health and endocrine characteristics of depressed postpartum mothers.' *Psychoneuroendocrinology* 32: 133–139.

Gruber, R. and Sadeh, A. (2004) 'Sleep and neurobehavioral functioning in boys with attention-deficit/ hyperactivity disorder and no reported breathing problems.' *Sleep* 27: 267–273.

Gruber, R., Sadeh, A. and Raviv, A. (2000) 'Instability of sleep patterns in children with attention-deficit/ hyperactivity disorder.' *Journal of the American Academy of Child and Adolescent Psychiatry* 39: 495–501.

Gruber, R., Xi, T., Frenette, S., Robert, M., Vannasinh, P. and Carrier, J. (2009) 'Sleep disturbances in prepubertal children with attention deficit hyperactivity disorder: A home polysomnography study.' *Sleep* 32(3): 343–350.

Gruenwald, J. and Skrabal, J. (2003) 'Kava ban highly questionable: A brief summary of the main scientific findings presented in the "In-depth investigation on EU member states market restrictions on kava products".' *Seminars in Integrative Medicine* 1(4): 199–210.

Grundy, S.M., Brewer, H.B., Jr, Cleeman, J.I., Smith, S.C. Jr *et al.* (2004) 'Definition of metabolic syndrome: Report of the National Heart, Lung, and Blood Institute/American Heart Association Conference on scientific issues related to definition.' *Circulation* 109: 433–438.

Grunstein, R., Wilcox, I., Yang, T.S., Gould, Y. and Hedner, J. (1993) 'Snoring and sleep apnea in men: Association with central obesity and hypertension.' *International Journal of Obesity Related Metabolic Disorders* 17(9): 533–540.

Guenole, F. and Baleyte, J.M. (2010) 'Effectiveness of melatonin for sleep problems in autism spectrum disorders: Evidence grows but research is still needed.' *Journal of Autism and Developmental Disorders* 41(7): 974–975.

Guest, A.H. (2005) *Labanotation: or, Kinetography Laban: The System of Analyzing and Recording Movement,* 4th edn. New York, NY: Routledge.

Guilleminault, C., Cathala, J.P. and Castaigne, P. (1973) 'Effects of 5-Hydroxytryptophan on sleep of a patient with brain-stem lesion.' *Electroencephalography and Clinical Neurophysiology* 34: 177–184.

Guilleminault, C., Stoohs, R., Kim, Y.D., Chervin, R., Black, J. and Clerk, A. (1995) 'Upper airway sleep-disordered breathing in women.' *Annals of Internal Medicine* 122(7): 493–501.

Gunlicks, M.L. and Weissman, M.M. (2008) 'Change in child psychopathology with improvement in parental depression: A systematic review.' *Journal of the American Academy of Child and Adolescent Psychiatry 47*(4): 379–389.

Gutkowska, J., Jankowski, M., Mukaddam-Daher, S. and McCann, S.M. (2000) 'Oxytocin is a cardiovascular hormone.' *Brazilian Journal of Medical and Biological Research 33*: 625–633.

Guyda, H.J. (2005) 'Use of dietary supplements and hormones in adolescents: A cautionary tale.' *Paediatrics and Child Health 10*(10): 587–590.

Gyllenhaal, C., Merritt, S.L., Peterson, S.D., Block, K.I. and Gochenour, T. (2000) 'Efficacy and safety of herbal stimulants and sedatives in sleep disorders.' *Sleep Medicine Reviews 4*(3): 229–251.

Haack, M., Sanchez, E. and Mullington, J.M. (2007) 'Elevated inflammatory markers in response to prolonged sleep restriction are associated with increased pain experience in healthy volunteers.' *Sleep 30*(9): 1145–1152.

Halberg, F., Cornelissen, G., Matalova, G., Siegelova, J. *et al.* (2009) 'C. Mendel's legacy: Omnis cyclus e cosmo: Mendel's chronoastrobiological legacy for transdisciplinary science in personalized health care.' Symposium on non-invasive methods in cardiology, Masaryk University, Faculty of Medicine, Brno, Czech Republic: 77–111. Available at http://static.msi.umn.edu/rreports/2009/304.pdf, accessed 13 September 2011.

Halbower, A.C., McGinley, B.M. and Smith P.L. (2008) 'Treatment alternatives for sleep-disordered breathing in the pediatric population.' *Current Opinion in Pulmonary Medicine 14*(6): 551–558.

Hallböök, T., Lundgren, J. and Rosén, I. (2007) 'Ketogenic diet improves sleep quality in children with therapy-resistant epilepsy.' *Epilepsia 48*(1): 59–65.

Haller, C.A. and Benowitz, N.L. (2000) 'Adverse cardiovascular and central nervous system events associated with dietary supplements containing ephedra alkaloids.' *New England Journal of Medicine 343*: 833–838.

Haller, C.A., Meier, K.H. and Olson, K.R. (2005) 'Seizures reported in association with use of dietary supplements.' *Clinical Toxicology 43*(1): 23–30.

Halpern, A., Mancini, M.C., Magalhães, M.E.C., Fisberg, M. *et al.* (2010) 'Metabolic syndrome, dyslipidemia, hypertension and type 2 diabetes in youth: From diagnosis to treatment.' *Diabetology & Metabolic Syndrome 2*: 55. Available at www.dmsjournal.com/content/2/1/55, accessed 13 September 2011.

Hanzel, D.A., Proia, N.G. and Hudgel, D.W. (1991) 'Response of obstructive sleep apnea to fluoxetine and protryptiline.' *Chest 100*: 416–421.

Hao, H. and Rivkees, S.A. (1999) 'The biological clock of very premature primate infants is responsive to light.' *Proceedings of the National Academy of Science 96*: 2426–2429.

Harada, T., Hitotani, M., Maeda, M., Nomura, H. and Takeuchi, H. (2007) 'Correlation between breakfast tryptophan content and morningness-eveningness in Japanese infants and students aged 0–15 yrs.' *Journal of Physiological Anthropology 26*(2): 201–207.

Hardeland, R. (2009) 'New approaches in the management of insomnia: Weighing the advantages of prolonged-release melatonin and synthetic melatoninergic agonists.' *Neuropsychiatric Disease and Treatment 5*: 341–354.

Hare, D.J., Jones, S. and Evershed, K. (2006) 'Objective investigation of the sleep-wake cycle in adults with intellectual disabilities and autistic spectrum disorders.' *Journal of Intellectual Disability Research 50*(10): 701–710.

Harinath, K., Malhotra, A.S., Pal, K., Prasad, R. *et al.* (2004) 'Effects of Hatha yoga and Omkar meditation on cardio-respiratory performance, psychologic profile, and melatonin secretion.' *Journal of Alternative and Complementary Medicine 10*: 261–268.

Harnack, L. and Stang, J. (1999) 'Story M. Soft drink consumption among US children and adolescents: Nutritional consequences.' *Journal of the American Dietetic Association 99*: 436–441.

Harrell, D.B., Schreck, K.A. and Richdale, A.L. (2008) 'Sleep in the world of autism.' *Sleep Review: The Journal of Sleep Specialists* (online). Available at www.sleepreviewmag.com/issues/articles/2008-03_01. asp, accessed 13 September 2011.

Harrington, J.W., Rosen, L., Garnecho, A. and Patrick, P.A. (2006) 'Parental perceptions and use of complementary and alternative medicine practices for children with autistic spectrum disorders in private practice.' *Journal of Developmental and Behavioral Pediatrics 27*: S156–S161.

Harrington, M. (2010) 'Location, location, location: Important for jet-lagged circadian loops.' *Journal of Clinical Investigation 120*(7): 2265–2267.

Harris, J.C. and Allen, R.P. (1996) 'Is excessive daytime sleepiness characteristic of Prader-Willi syndrome: The effects of weight change.' *Archives of Pediatrics and Adolescent Medicine 150*: 120–128.

Harris, L.S. and Purohit, A.P. (1977) 'Bladder training and eneuresis: A controlled trial.' *Behaviour Research and Therapy 15*: 485–490.

Harsh, J.R., Easley, A. and LeBourgeois, M.K. (2002) 'A measure of sleep hygiene.' *Sleep 25*: A316.

Harvey, A.G. (2009) 'A transdiagnostic approach to treating sleep disturbance in psychiatric disorders.' *Cognitive Behaviour Therapy 38*(suppl.1): 35–42.

Harvey, A.G., Murray, G., Chandler, R.A. and Soehner, A. (2010) 'Sleep disturbance as transdiagnostic: Consideration of neurobiological mechanisms.' *Clinical Psychology Review 31*(2): 225–235.

Hasegawa, Y., Morishita, M. and Suzumura, A. (1998) 'Novel chromosomal aberration in a patient with a unique sleep disorder.' *Journal of Neurology, Neurosurgery and Psychiatry 64*: 113–116.

Haslam, D. (1992) *Sleepless Children: A Handbook for Parents.* London: Piatkus Books.

Hasler, B. and Germain, A. (2009) 'Correlates and treatments of nightmares in adults.' *Sleep Medicine Clinics 4*(4): 507–517.

Hauri, P.J., Silber, M.H. and Boeve, B.F. (2007) 'The treatment of parasomnias with hypnosis: A 5-year follow-up study.' *Journal of Clinical Sleep Medicine 3*(4): 369–373.

Haus, E. (2007) 'Chronobiology in the endocrine system.' *Advanced Drug Delivery Reviews 59*: 985–1014.

Hayashi, E. (2001) 'Seasonal changes in sleep and behavioral problems in a pubescent case with autism.' *Psychiatry and Clinical Neurosciences 55*(3), 223–224.

He, Y., Jones, C.R., Fujiki, N., Xu, Y. *et al.* (2009) 'The transcriptional repressor DEC2 regulates sleep length in mammals.' *Science 325*(5942): 866–870.

Heath, A.C., Kendler, K.S., Eaves, L.J. and Martin, N.G. (1990) 'Evidence for genetic influences on sleep disturbance and sleep pattern in twins.' *Sleep 13*(4): 318–335.

Heckman, M.A., Weil, J. and de Mejia, G. (2010) 'Caffeine (1, 3, 7-trimethylxanthine) in foods: A comprehensive review of consumption, functionality, safety and regulatory matters.' *Journal of Food Science 75*(3): R77–87.

Hedges, D.W., Woon, F.L. and Hoopes, S.P. (2009) 'Caffeine-induced psychosis.' *CNS Spectrums 14*(3): 127–129.

Helmer, R. (2007) 'Treating paediatric bed-wetting with Chinese medicine.' *Journal of Chinese Medicine 83*: 25–28.

Henderson, J. and Jordan, S.S. (2010) 'Development and preliminary evaluation of the Bedtime Routines Questionnaire.' *Journal of Psychopathology and Behavioral Assessment 32*: 271–280.

Henderson, J.A., Barry, T.D., Bader, S.H. and Jordan, S.S. (2011) 'The relation among sleep, routines, and externalizing behavior in children with an autism spectrum disorder.' *Research in Autism Spectrum Disorders 5*: 758–767.

Hendricks, J.C., Sehgal, A. and Pack, A.I. (2000) 'The need for a simple animal model to understand sleep.' *Progress in Neurobiology 61*: 339–351.

Herbert, M. (1987) *Behavioural Treatment of Children with Problems: A Practice Manual.* Maryland Heights, MO: Academic Press.

Hering, E., Epstein, R., Elroy, S., Iancu, D.R. and Zelnik, N. (1999) 'Sleep patterns in autistic children.' *Journal of Autism and Developmental Disorders 29*: 143–147.

Herr, J.R. (2003) Letter to the Editor: 'Re: autism—ear infections—glue ear—sleep disorders.' *Journal of Autism and Developmental Disorders 33*(5): 557.

Hertz-Picciotto, I., Croen, L.A., Hansen, R., Jones, C.R. *et al.* (2006) 'The CHARGE Study: An epidemiologic investigation of genetic and environmental factors contributing to autism.' *Environmental Health Perspectives 114*: 1119–1125.

Heussler, H., Harris, D., Cooper, C., Dakin, S., Suresh, S. and Williams, G. (2008) 'Hypersomnolence in Prader Willi syndrome.' *Journal of Intellectual Disability Research 52*(10): 814.

Hill, C.M., Hogan, A.M. and Karmiloff-Smith, A. (2007) 'To sleep, perchance to enrich learning?' *Archives of Disease in Childhood 92*: 637–643.

Hill, G.B. and Powell, L.F. (1934) *Boswell's Life of Johnson*, volume ii. Oxford: Clarendon Press.

Hill, P. and Taylor, E. (2001) 'An auditable protocol for treating attention deficit hyperactivity disorder.' *Archives of Disease in Childhood 84*(5): 404–409.

Hindmarch, I., Dawson, J. and Stanley, N. (2005) 'A double-blind study in healthy volunteers to assess the effects on sleep of pregabalin compared with alprazolam and placebo.' *Sleep 28*(2): 187–193.

Hirota, T., Lee, J.W., Lewis, W.G., Zhang, E.E. *et al.* (2010) 'High-throughput chemical screen identifies a novel potent modulator of cellular circadian rhythms and reveals CKIa as a clock regulatory kinase.' *PLoS Biology 8*(12): e1000559 doi:10.1371/journal.pbio.1000559.

Hiscock, H. and Wake, M. (2002) 'Randomised controlled trial of behavioural infant sleep intervention to improve infant sleep and maternal mood.' *British Medical Journal 324*: 1062–1068.

Hoban, T. (2003) 'Rhythmic movement disorder in children.' *CNS Spectrums 8*(2): 135–138.

Hobson, J.A. (1990) 'Sleep and dreaming.' *Journal of Neuroscience 10*(2): 371–382.

Hobson, J.A. (2005) 'Sleep is of the brain, by the brain and for the brain.' *Nature 437*: 1254–1256.

Hobson, J.A. (2009) 'REM sleep and dreaming: Towards a theory of protoconsciousness.' *Nature Reviews: Neuroscience 10*: 803–813.

Hobson, J.A. and McCarley, R. (1977) 'The brain as a dream state generator: An activation-synthesis hypothesis of the dream process.' *American Journal of Psychiatry 134*: 1335–1348.

Hobson, J.A. and Pace-Schott, E.F. (2002) 'The cognitive neuroscience of sleep: Neuronal systems, consciousness and learning.' *Nature Reviews: Neuroscience 3*: 679–693.

Hobson, R.P. and Bishop, M. (2003) 'The pathogenesis of autism: Insights from congenital blindness.' *Philosophical Transactions of the Royal Society of London, Series B 358*: 335–344.

Hoffman, C.D., Sweeney, D.P., Gilliam, J.E. and Lopez-Wagner, M.C. (2006) 'Sleep problems in children with autism and in typically developing children.' *Focus on Autism and Other Developmental Disabilities 21*(3): 146–152.

Hoffman, C.D., Sweeney, D.P., Lopez-Wagner, M.C., Hodge, D. *et al.* (2008) 'Children with autism: Sleep problems and mothers' stress.' *Focus on Autism and Other Developmental Disabilities 23*(3), 155–165.

Hofstra, W.A. and de Weerd, A.W. (2008) 'How to assess circadian rhythm in humans: A review of literature.' *Epilepsy & Behavior 13*: 438–444.

Hofstra, W.A. and de Weerd, A.W. (2009) 'The circadian rhythm and its interaction with human epilepsy: A review of literature.' *Sleep Medicine Reviews 13*: 413–420.

Högl, B., Oertel, W.H., Stiasny-Kolster, K., Geisler, P. *et al.* (2010) 'Treatment of moderate to severe restless legs syndrome: 2-year safety and efficacy of rotigotine transdermal patch.' *BMC Neurology 10*: 86, doi:10.1186/1471-2377-10-86.

Holland, P.W.H., Booth, H.A.F. and Bruford, E.A. (2007) 'Classification and nomenclature of all human homeobox genes.' *BMC Biology 5*: 47, doi:10.1186/1741-7007-5-47.

Holliday, J., Sibbald, B. and Tooley, M. (1987) 'Sleep problems in two year olds.' *Family Practice 4*: 32–35.

Hollinger, P., Khatami, R., Gugger, M., Hess, C.W. and Bassetti, C.L. (2006) 'Epilepsy and obstructive sleep apnea.' *European Neurology 55*(2): 74–79.

Holmgren, B., Urba-Holmgren, R., Trucios, N., Zermeno, M. and Eguibar, J.R. (1985) 'Association of spontaneous and dopaminergic induced yawning and penile erections in the rat.' *Pharmacology, Biochemistry and Behavior 22*(1): 31–35.

Holzberg, D. and Albrecht, U. (2003) 'The circadian clock: A manager of biochemical processes within the organism.' *Journal of Neuroendocrinology 15*: 339–343.

Honda, Y. (1988) 'Clinical Features of Narcolepsy: Japanese Experiences.' In Y. Honda and T. Juji (eds) *HLA in Narcolepsy*. Berlin: Springer-Verlag.

Honomichl, R.D., Goodlin-Jones, B.L., Burnham, M., Gaylor, E. and Anders, T.F. (2002a) 'Sleep patterns of children with pervasive developmental disorders.' *Journal of Autism and Developmental Disorders 32*: 553–561.

Honomichl, R.D., Goodlin-Jones, B.L., Burnham, M.M., Hansen, R.L. and Anders, T.F. (2002b) 'Secretin and sleep in children with autism.' *Child Psychiatry and Human Development 33*(2): 107–123.

Hoque, R. and Chesson, A.L., Jr (2010) 'Pharmacologically induced/exacerbated restless legs syndrome, periodic limb movements of sleep, and REM behavior disorder/REM sleep without atonia: Literature review, qualitative scoring, and comparative analysis.' *Journal of Clinical Sleep Medicine 6*(1): 79–83.

Horner, R.H., Carr, E.G., Halle, J., McGee, G. *et al.* (2005) 'The use of single-subject research to identify evidence-based practice in special education.' *Exceptional Children 71*(2): 165–179.

Horvath, K., Papadimitriou, J.C., Rabsztyn, A., Drachenberg, C. and Tildon, J.T. (1999) 'Gastrointestinal abnormalities in children with autistic disorder.' *Journal of Pediatrics 135*(5): 598–563.

Hoshino, Y., Watanabe, H., Yashima, Y., Kaneko, M. and Kumashiro, H. (1984) 'An investigation on sleep disturbance of autistic children.' *Folia Psychiatrica et Neurologica Japonica 38*: 45–52.

Houghton, P.J. (1988) 'The biological activity of valerian and related plants.' *Journal of Ethnopharmacology 22*: 121–142.

Howell, M.J., Schenck, C.H. and Crow, S.J. (2009) 'A review of nighttime eating disorders.' *Sleep Medicine Reviews 13*(1): 23–34.

Hsu, L.-M., Huang, Y.-S., Tsay, S.-H., Chang, F.-Y. and Shou-Dong Lee, S.-D. (2006) 'Acute hepatitis induced by Chinese hepatoprotective herb, Xiao-Chai-Hu-Tang.' *Journal of the Chinese Medical Association 69*(2): 86–88.

Hu, V.W., Sarachana, T., Kim, K.S., Nguyen, A.-T. *et al.* (2009) 'Gene expression profiling differentiates autism case–controls and phenotypic variants of autism spectrum disorders: Evidence for circadian rhythm dysfunction in severe autism.' *Autism Research 2*(2): 78–97.

Huang, C.-F., Liu, S.-H. and Lin-Shiau, S.-Y. (2007) 'Neurotoxicological effects of cinnabar (a Chinese mineral medicine, HgS) in mice.' *Toxicology and Applied Pharmacology 224*: 192–201.

Hublin, C., Kaprio, J., Partinen, M. and Koskenvuo, M. (1998) 'Sleep bruxism based on self-report in a nationwide twin cohort.' *Journal of Sleep Research 7*(1): 61–67.

Hubner, W.-D. and Kirste, T. (2001) 'Experience with St John's Wort *(Hypericum perforatum)* in children under 12 years with symptoms of depression and psychovegetative disturbances.' *Phytotherapy Research 15*: 367–370.

Hudson, J.L., Gradisar, M., Gamble, A., Schniering, C.A. and Rebelo, I. (2009) 'The sleep patterns and problems of clinically anxious children.' *Behaviour Research and Therapy 47*(4): 339–344.

Hui, D.S. (2009) 'Craniofacial profile assessment in patients with obstructive sleep apnea.' *Sleep 32*(1): 11–12. (A commentary on Lee, Chan *et al.* (2009) 'Craniofacial phenotyping in obstructive sleep apnea – a novel quantitative photographic approach.' *Sleep 31*(1): 37–45, and Lee, Petocz *et al.* (2009) 'Prediction of obstructive sleep apnea with craniofacial photographic analysis.' *Sleep 32*: 46–52).

Hursthouse, M.W. (1973) 'Burns from enuresis alarm apparatus: case report.' *New Zealand Medical Journal 79*(499): 258–259.

Huynh, N., Manzini, C., Rompré, P.H. and J. Lavigne, G.J. (2007) 'Weighing the potential effectiveness of various treatments for sleep bruxism.' *Journal of the Canadian Dental Association 73*(8): 727–730.

Huynh, N.T., Rompré, P.H., Montplaisir, J.Y., Manzini, C. *et al.* (2006) 'Comparison of various treatments for sleep bruxism using determinants of number needed to treat and effect size.' *International Journal of Prosthodontics 19*(5): 435–441.

Iber, C., Ancoll-Israel, S., Chesson, A. and Quan, S.F. (2007) *The American Academy of Sleep Medicine Manual for the Scoring of Sleep and Associated Events: Rules, Terminology and Technical Specifications.* Westchester, NY: American Academy of Sleep Medicine.

Iglowstein, I., Jenni, O.G., Molinari, L. and Largo, R.H. (2003) 'Sleep duration from infancy to adolescence: Reference values and generational trends.' *Pediatrics 111*(2):302–307.

Illnerova, H., Buresova, M. and Presl, J. (1993) 'Melatonin rhythm in human milk.' *Clinical Endocrinology and Metabolism 77*: 838–841.

Imeri, L. and Opp, M.R. (2009) 'How (and why) the immune system makes us sleep.' *Nature Reviews: Neuroscience 10*(3): 199–210.

Insel, T.R., Gingrich, B.S. and Young, L.J. (2001) 'Oxytocin: Who needs it?' *Progress in Brain Research 133*: 59–66.

Ip, M.S., Lam, K.S., Ho, C., Tsang, K.W. and Lam, W. (2000) 'Serum leptin and vascular risk factors in obstructive sleep apnea.' *Chest 118*(3): 580–586.

Iranzo, A. and Aparicio, J. (2009) 'A lesson from anatomy: Focal brain lesions causing REM sleep behavior disorder.' Editorial, *Sleep Medicine 10*(1): 9–12.

Itaka, C., Muyazaki, K., Akaike, T. and Ishida, N. (2005) 'A role for glycogen synthase kinase-3ß in the mammalian circadian clock.' *Journal of Biological Chemistry 280*(33): 29397–29420.

Itoh, S., Marutani, K., Nishijima, T., Matsuo, S. and Itabashi, M. (1995) 'Liver injuries induced by herbal medicine, syo-saiko-to (xiao-chaihu-tang).' *Digestive Diseases and Sciences 40*: 1845–1848.

Ivanenko, A. and Patwari, P.P. (2009) 'Recognition and management of pediatric sleep disorders.' *Primary Psychiatry 16*(2): 42–50.

Ivanenko, A., Tauman, R. and Gozal, D. (2003) 'Modafinil in the treatment of excessive daytime sleepiness in children.' *Sleep Medicine 4*: 579–582.

Jacobs, G.D., Pace-Schott, E.F., Stickgold, R. and Otto, M.W. (2004) 'Cognitive behavior therapy and pharmacotherapy for insomnia: A randomized controlled trial and direct comparison.' *Archives of Internal Medicine 164*: 1888–1896.

Jafferany, M. (2007) 'Psychodermatology: A guide to understanding common psychocutaneous disorders.' *Journal of Clinical Psychiatry 9*: 203–213.

James, D.K., Spencer, C.J. and Stepsis, B.W. (2002) 'Fetal learning: A prospective randomized controlled study.' *Ultrasound Obstetrics and Gynecology 20*: 431–438.

Jan, J.E. and Freeman, R.D. (2004) 'Melatonin therapy for circadian rhythm sleep disorders in children with multiple disabilities: What have we learned in the last decade?' *Developmental Medicine and Child Neurology 46*(11): 776–782.

Jan, J.E., Freeman, R.D., Wasdell, M.B. and Bomben, M.M. (2004) 'A child with severe night terrors and sleep-walking responds to melatonin therapy.' *Developmental Medicine and Child Neurology 46*(11): 789.

Jan, J.E., Reiter, R.J., Bax, M.C., Ribary, U., Freeman, R.D. and Wasdell, M.B. (2010) 'Long-term sleep disturbances in children: A cause of neuronal loss.' *European Journal of Paediatric Neurology 14*(5): 380–390.

Jang, J.H., Jung, W.H., Kang, D-H., Byun, M.S. *et al.* (2011) 'Increased default mode network connectivity associated with meditation.' *Neuroscience Letters 487*(3): 358–362.

Janosky, J.E., Leininger, S.L., Hoerger, M.P. and Libkuman, T.M. (2009) *Single Subject Designs in Biomedicine.* Springer: Dordrecht.

Javaheri, S., Storfer-Isser, A., Rosen, C.L. and Redline, S. (2008) 'Sleep quality and elevated blood pressure in adolescents.' *Circulation 118*(10): 1034–1040.

Javo, C., Ronning, J.A. and Heyerdahl, S. (2004) 'Child-rearing in an indigenous Sami population in Norway: A cross-cultural comparison of parental attitudes and expectations.' *Scandinavian Journal of Psychology 45*(1): 67–78.

Jenni, O.G., Fuhrer, H.Z., Iglowstein, I., Molinari, L. and Largo, R.H. (2005) 'A longitudinal study of bed sharing and sleep problems among Swiss children in the first 10 years of life.' *Pediatrics 115*(suppl.1): 233–240.

Jenni, O.G., Molinari, L., Caflisch, J.A. and Largo, R.H. (2007) 'Sleep duration from ages 1 to 10 years: Variability and stability in comparison with growth.' *Pediatrics 120*(4): e769–776.

Jenni, O.G. and O'Connor, B.B. (2005) 'Children's sleep: An interplay between culture and biology.' *Pediatrics 115*(1): 204–216.

Jevning, R., Wallace, R.K. and Beidebach, M. (1992) 'The physiology of meditation: A review. A wakeful hypometabolic integrated response.' *Neuroscience and Biobehavioral Reviews 16*: 415–424.

Jiménez-Genchi, A., Díaz-Galviz, J.L., García-Reyna, J.C. and Ávila-Ordoñez, M.U. (2007) 'Coexistence of epileptic nocturnal wanderings and an arachnoid cyst.' *Journal of Clincal Sleep Medicine 3*(4): 399–401.

Johns, M.W. (1991) 'A new method for measuring daytime sleepiness: The Epworth Sleepiness Scale.' *Sleep 14*(6): 540–545.

Johns, M.W. (1992) 'Reliability and factor analysis of the Epworth Sleepiness Scale.' *Sleep 15*(4): 376–381.

Johns, M.W. (1993) 'Daytime sleepiness, snoring, and obstructive sleep apnea. The Epworth Sleepiness Scale.' *Chest 103*(1): 30–36.

Johns, M.W. (2000) 'Sensitivity and specificity of the multiple sleep latency test (MSLT), the maintenance of wakefulness test and the Epworth Sleepiness Scale: Failure of the MSLT as a gold standard.' *Journal of Sleep Research* 9(1): 5–11.

Johnson, E.O., Roth, T., Schultz, L. and Breslau, N. (2006) 'Epidemiology of DSM-IV insomnia in adolescence: Lifetime prevalence, chronicity, and an emergent gender difference.' *Pediatrics 117*: e247–256.

Johnson, K. and Malow, B.A. (2008a) 'Sleep in children with autism spectrum disorders.' *Current Neurology and Neuroscience Reports 8*(2), 155–161.

Johnson, K. and Malow, B.A. (2008b) 'Sleep in children with autism spectrum disorders.' *Current Treatment Options in Neurology 10*(5), 350–359.

Johnson, K.P. and Malow, B.A. (2008c) 'Assessment and pharmacologic treatment of sleep disturbance in autism.' *Child and Adolescent Psychiatric Clinics of North America 17*(4): 773–785.

Johnson, K.P., Giannotti, F. and Cortesi, F. (2009) 'Sleep patterns in autism spectrum disorders.' *Child and Adolescent Psychiatric Clinics of North America 18*(4): 917–928.

Johnston, L.D., O'Malley, P.M., Bachman, J.G. and Schulenberg, J.E. (2006) 'Monitoring the future national results on adolescent drug use: Overview of key findings, 2006.' Bethesda, MD: National Institute on Drug Abuse. Available at http://eric.ed.gov/ERICWebPortal/search/detailmini.jsp?_nfpb=true&_&ERICExtSearch_SearchValue_0=ED497304&ERICExtSearch_SearchType_0=no&accno=ED497304, accessed 13 September 2011.

Jolma, I.W., Laerum, O.D., Lillo, C. and Ruoff, P. (2010) 'Circadian oscillators in eukaryotes.' *Systems Biology and Medicine 2*(5): 533–549.

Joly-Mascheroni, R.M., Senju, A. and Shepherd, A.J. (2008) 'Dogs catch human yawns.' *Biology Letters 4*: 446–448.

Jones, D.P.H. and Verduyn, C.M. (1983) 'Behavioural management of sleep problems.' *Archives of Disease in Childhood 58*: 442–444.

Jones, H.S. and Oswald, I. (1968) 'Two cases of healthy insomnia.' *Electroencephalography and Clinical Neurophysiology 24*: 378–380.

Jonsson, L., Ljunggren, E., Bremer, A., Pedersen, C. *et al.* (2010) 'Mutation screening of melatonin-related genes in patients with autism spectrum disorders.' *BMC Medical Genomics 3*: 10, doi:10.1186/1755-9794-3-10.

Joshi, K.G. and Faubion, M.D. (2005) 'Mania and psychosis associated with St. John's Wort and ginseng.' *Psychiatry (Edgmont) 2*(9): 56–61.

Jouvet, M. and Delorme, F. (1965) 'Locus coeruleus et sommeil parodoxal.' *Comptes rendus des seances et memoires de la Societe de Biologie 159*: 1786–1789.

Jung, H.-K., Choung, R.S. and Talley, N.J. (2010) 'Gastroesophageal reflux disease and sleep disorders: Evidence for a causal link and therapeutic implications.' *Journal of Neurogastroenterology and Motility 16*: 22–29.

Junien, C. (2006) 'Impact of diets and nutrients/drugs on early epigenetic programming.' *Journal of Inherited Metabolic Disease 29*: 359–365.

Kahbazi, M., Ghoreishi, A., Rahiminejad, F., Mohammadi, M.R. *et al.* (2009) 'A randomized, double-blind and placebo-controlled trial of modafinil in children and adolescents with attention deficit and hyperactivity disorder.' *Psychiatry Research 168*(3): 234–237.

Kaiser, P.R., Valko, P.O., Werth, E., Thomann, J. *et al.* (2010) 'Modafinil ameliorates excessive daytime sleepiness after traumatic brain injury.' *Neurology 75*(20): 1780–1785.

Kaleyias, J., Cruz, M., Goraya, J.S., Valencia, I. *et al.* (2008) 'Spectrum of polysomnographic abnormalities in children with epilepsy.' *Pediatric Neurology 39*(3):170–176.

Kamiyama, T., Nouchi, T., Kojima, S., Murata, N. *et al.* (1997) 'Autoimmune hepatitis triggered by administration of an herbal medicine.' *American Journal of Gastroenterology 92*: 703–704.

Kandt, R.S., Emerson, R.G., Singer, H.S., Valle, D.L. and Moser, H.W. (1982) 'Cataplexy in variant forms of Niemann-Pick disease.' *Annals of Neurology 12*: 284–288.

Kaplan, B., Karabay, G., Zagyapan, R.D., Ozer, C. *et al.* (2004) 'Effects of taurine in glucose and taurine administration.' *Amino Acids 27*: 327–333.

Kataria, S., Swanson, M.S. and Trevathan, G.E. (1987) 'Persistence of sleep disturbances in preschool children.' *Journal of Pediatrics 110*(4): 642–646.

Kato, K., Hirai, K., Nishiyama, K., Uchikawa, O. *et al.* (2005) 'Neurochemical properties of ramelteon (TAK-375), a selective MT1/MT2 receptor agonist.' *Neuropharmacology 48*: 301–310.

Kato, T., Dal-Fabbro, C. and Lavigne, G.J. (2003) 'Current knowledge on awake and sleep bruxism: Overview.' *The Alpha Omegan 96: 24*

Kato, T. and Lavigne, G.J. (2010) 'Sleep bruxism: A sleep-related movement disorder.' *Sleep Medicine Clinics 5*: 9–35.

Katz, E.S. and D'Ambrosio, C.M. (2010) 'Pediatric obstructive sleep apnea syndrome.' *Clinics in Chest Medicine 31*(2): 221–234.

Kavanau, J.L. (1997) 'Origin and evolution of sleep: Roles of vision and endothermy.' *Brain Research Bulletin 42*(4): 245–264.

Kayley-Isley, L.C., Peterson, J., Fischer, C. and Peterson, E. (2010) 'Yoga as a complementary therapy for children and adolescents: A guide for clinicians.' *Psychiatry (Edgemont) 7*(8): 20–32.

Keenan, M. and Dillenburger, K. (2011) 'When all you have is a hammer: RCTs and hegemony in science.' *Research in Autism Spectrum Disorders 5*: 1–13.

Kellner, R., Neidhardt, J., Krakow, B. and Pathak, D. (1991) 'Changes in chronic nightmares after one session of desensitization or rehearsal instructions.' *American Journal of Psychiatry 149*: 659–663.

Kennaway, D.J. (2002) 'Programming of the fetal suprachiasmatic nucleus and subsequent adult rhythmicity.' *Trends in Endocrinology and Metabolism 13*(9): 398–402.

Kennaway, D.J., Flanagan, D.E., Moore, M.V., Cockington, R.A. *et al.* (2001) 'The impact of fetal size and length of gestation on 6-sulphatoxymelatonin excretion in adult life.' *Journal of Pineal Research 30*: 188–192.

Kennedy, D.O., Little, W. and Scholey, A.B. (2004) 'Attenuation of laboratory-induced stress in humans after acute administration of Melissa officinalis (lemon balm).' *Psychosomatic Medicine 66*(4): 607–613.

Kern, W., Offenheuser, S., Born, J. and Fehm, H.L. (1996) 'Entrainment of ultradian oscillations in the secretion of insulin and glucagon to the nonrapid eye movement/rapid eye movement sleep rhythm in humans.' *Journal of Clinical Endocrinology and Metabolism 81*(4): 1541–1547.

Kerr, S. and Jowett, S. (1994) 'Sleep problems in pre-school children: A review of the literature.' *Child Care Health and Development 20*(6): 379–391.

Kerr, S.M., Jowett, S.A. and Smith, L.N. (1996) 'Preventing sleep problems in infants: A randomized controlled trial.' *Journal of Advanced Nursing 24*: 938–942.

Khalsa. S.B.S. (2004) 'Treatment of chronic insomnia with yoga: A preliminary study with sleep–wake diaries.' *Applied Psychophysiology and Biofeedback 29*(4): 269–278.

Kiddoo, D. (2007) 'Nocturnal enuresis.' *Clinical Evidence (Online), pii:0305*: 1–15. (An open-access *British Medical Journal* online resource.)

Kiesel, K.B., Lutzker, J.R. and Campbell, R.V. (1989) 'Behavioral relaxation training to reduce hyperventilation and seizures in a profoundly retarded epileptic child.' *Journal of the Multihandicapped Person 2*: 179–190.

Kimata, H. (2001) 'Effect of humor on allergen-induced wheal responses.' *Journal of the American Medical Association 285*: 738.

Kimata, H. (2004) 'Laughter counteracts enhancement of plasma neurotrophin levels and allergic skin wheal responses by mobile phone-mediated stress.' *Behavioral Medicine 29*: 149–152.

Kimata, H. (2007) 'Laughter elevates the levels of breast-milk melatonin.' *Journal of Psychosomatic Research 62*(6): 699–702.

King, N., Cranstoun, F. and Josephs, A. (1989) 'Emotive imagery and children's night-time fears: A multiple baseline design evaluation.' *Journal of Behavior Therapy and Experimental Psychiatry 20*(2): 125–135.

Kingston, J., Raggio, C., Spencer, K. Stalaker, K. and Tuchin, P.J. (2010) 'A review of the literature on chiropractic and insomnia.' *Journal of Chiropractic Medicine 9*: 121–126.

Kinney, D.K., Miller, A.M., Crowley, D.J., Huang, E. and Gerber, E. (2008) 'Autism prevalence following prenatal exposure to hurricanes and tropical storms in Louisiana.' *Journal of Autism and Developmental Disorders 38*: 481–488.

Kinney, D.K., Munir, K.M., Crowley, D.J. and Miller, A.M. (2008) 'Prenatal stress and risk for autism.' *Neuroscience and Biobehavioral Reviews 32*: 1519–1532.

Kinnier Wilson, J.V. (1996) 'Diseases of Babylon: an examination of selected texts.' *Journal of the Royal Society of Medicine 89*: 135–140.

Kirsch, I., Montgomery, G. and Sapirstein, G. (1995) 'Hypnosis as an adjunct to cognitive-behavioural psychotherapy: A meta-analysis.' *Journal of Consulting and Clinical Psychology 63*(2): 214–220.

Kiyohara, H., Matsumoto, T. and Yamada, H. (2004) 'Combination effects of herbs in a multi-herbal formula: Expression of Juzen-taiho-to's immuno-modulatory activity on the intestinal immune system.' *Electronic Journal of Complementary and Alternative Medicine (eCAM) 1*(1): 83–91.

Klerman, E.B., Rimmer, D.W., Dijk, D.-J., Kronauer, R.E. *et al.* (1998) 'Nonphotic entrainment of the human circadian pacemaker.' *American Journal of Physiology 274* (*Regulatory Integrative and Comparative Physiology 43*): R991–R996.

Knutsson, U., Dahlgren, J., Marcus, C., Rosberg, S. *et al.* (1997) 'Circadian cortisol rhythms in healthy boys and girls: Relationship with age, growth, body composition, and pubertal development.' *Journal of Clinical Endocrinology and Metabolism 82*: 536–540.

Ko, R. (1999) 'Adverse reactions to watch for in patients using herbal remedies.' *Western Journal of Medicine 171*: 181–186.

Ko, R.J. (2004) 'A U.S. perspective on the adverse reactions from Traditional Chinese Medicines.' *Journal of the Chinese Medical Association 67*: 109–116.

Kobayashi, H., Ishii, M., Takeuchi, S., Tanaka, Y. et al. (2010) 'Efficacy and safety of a traditional herbal medicine, Hochu-ekki-to in the long-term management of Kikyo (delicate constitution) patients with atopic dermatitis: A 6-month, multicenter, double-blind, randomized, placebo-controlled study.' *Evidence Based Complementary and Alternative Medicine 7*(3): 367–373.

Kodak, T. and Piazza, C.C. (2008) 'Assessment and behavioral treatment of feeding and sleeping disorders in children with autism spectrum disorders.' *Child and Adolescent Psychiatric Clinics of North America 17*(4): 887–905.

Koetter, U., Schrader, E., Käufeler, R. and Brattström, A. (2007) 'A randomized, double blind, placebo-controlled, prospective clinical study to demonstrate clinical efficacy of a fixed valerian hops extract combination (Ze 91019) in patients suffering from non-organic sleep disorder.' *Phytotherapy Research 21*(9): 847–851.

Kohler, W.C., Coddington, R.D. and Agnew, H.W. (1968) 'Sleep patterns in 2-year-old children.' *Journal of Pediatrics 72*: 228–233.

Kok, S.W., Meinders, A.E., Overeem, S., Lammers, G.J. *et al.* (2002) 'Reduction of plasma leptin levels and loss of its circadian rhythmicity in hypocretin (orexin)-deficient narcoleptic humans.' *Journal of Clinical Endocrinology and Metabolism 87*: 805–809.

Kong, J., Shepel, P.N., Holden, C.P., Mackiewicz, M., Pack, A.I. and Geiger, J.D. (2002) 'Brain glycogen decreases with increased periods of wakefulness: Implications for homeostatic drive to sleep.' *Journal of Neuroscience 22*(13): 5581–5587.

Konopka, R.J. and Benzer, S. (1971) 'Clock mutants of drosophila melanogaster.' *Proceedings of the National Academy of Science, USA 68*(9): 2112–2116.

Kordas, K., Siegel, E.H., Olney, D.K., Katz, J. *et al.* (2009) 'The effects of iron and/or zinc supplementation on maternal reports of sleep in infants from Nepal and Zanzibar.' *Journal of Developmental and Behavioral Pediatrics 30*(2): 131–139.

Kotagal, P. (2001) 'The relationship between sleep and epilepsy.' *Seminars in Pediatric Neurology 8*(4): 241–250.

Kotagal, S. (2009) 'Hypersomnia in children: Interface with psychiatric disorders.' *Child and Adolescent Psychiatry Clinics of North America 18*(4): 967–977.

Kotagal, S. and Pianosi, P. (2006) 'Sleep disorders in children and adolescents.' *British Medical Journal 332*: 828–832.

Kothare, S.V. and Kaleyias, J. (2008a) 'Narcolepsy and other hypersomnias in children.' *Current Opinion in Pediatrics 20*(6): 666–675.

Kothare, S.V. and Kaleyias, J. (2008b) 'The clinical and laboratory assessment of the sleepy child.' *Seminars in Pediatric Neurology 15*: 61–69.

Krakow, B., Hollifield, M., Johnston, L., Koss, M. *et al.* (2001a) 'Imagery rehearsal therapy for chronic nightmares in sexual assault survivors with posttraumatic stress disorder: A randomized controlled trial.' *Journal of the American Medical Association 286*(5):537–545.

Krakow, B., Kellner, R., Pathak, D. and Lambert, L. (1995) 'Imagery rehearsal treatment for chronic nightmares.' *Behaviour Research and Therapy 33*(7): 837–843.

Krakow, B., Lowry, C., Germain, A., Gaddy, L. *et al.* (2000) 'A retrospective study on improvements in nightmares and post-traumatic stress disorder following treatment for co-morbid sleep-disordered breathing.' *Journal of Psychosomatic Research 49*: 291–298.

Krakow, B., Sandoval, D., Schrader, R., Keuhne, B. *et al.* (2001b) 'Treatment of chronic nightmares in adjudicated adolescent girls in a residential facility.' *Journal of Adolescent Health 29*: 94–100.

Krakowiak, P., Goodlin-Jones, B., Hertz-Picciotto, I., Croen, L.A. and Hansen, R.L. (2008) 'Sleep problems in children with autism spectrum disorders, developmental delays, and typical development: A population-based study.' *Journal of Sleep Research 17*(2): 197–206.

Krenn, L. (2002) 'Die Passionsblume (Passiflora incarnata L.) – ein bewährtes pflanzliches Sedativum.' [Passion Flower (Passiflora incarnata L.) – a reliable herbal sedative] *Wiener Medizinischer Wochenschrift 152*(15–16): 404–406.

Kromhout, H.E., Landstra, A.M., van Luin, M. and van Setten, P.A. (2008) 'Acute coffeïne-intoxicatie na het innemen van "herbal energy"-capsules.' [Acute caffeine intoxication after intake of 'herbal energy' capsules] *Nederlands Tijdschrift voor Geneeskunde 152*(28): 1583–1586.

Krueger, J.M. (2008) 'The role of cytokines in sleep regulation.' *Current Pharmaceutical Design 14*(32): 3408–3416.

Krueger, J.M., Obal, F., Jr and Fang, J. (1999) 'Why we sleep: A theoretical view of sleep function.' *Sleep Medicine Reviews 3*(2): 119–129.

Kruskal, B. (2009) '"It couldn't hurt... Could it?" Safety of complementary and alternative medicine practices.' *Acta Paediatrica 98*: 628–630.

Kryger, M.H., Walld, R. and Manfreda, J. (2002) 'Diagnoses received by narcolepsy patients in the year prior to diagnosis by a sleep specialist.' *Sleep 25*(1): 36–41.

Krystal, A.D. and Davidson, J.R.T. (2007) 'The use of prazosin for the treatment of trauma nightmares and sleep disturbance in combat veterans with post-traumatic stress disorder.' *Biological Psychiatry 61*: 925–927.

Krystal, A.D., Edinger, J.D., Wohlgemuth, W.K. and Marsh, G.R. (2002) 'NREM sleep EEG frequency spectral correlates of sleep complaints in primary insomnia subtypes.' *Sleep 25*: 630–634.

Kuhn, B.R. and Elliott, A.J. (2003) 'Treatment efficacy in behavioral pediatric sleep medicine.' *Journal of Psychosomatic Research 54*: 587–597.

Kulman, G., Lissoni, P., Rovelli, F., Roselli, M.G. *et al.* (2000) 'Evidence of pineal endocrine hypofunction in autistic children.' *Neuro Endocrinology Letters 21*(1): 31–34.

Kumar, R. (2008) 'Approved and investigational uses of modafinil: An evidence-based review.' *Drugs 68*(13): 1803–1839.

Kupfersztain, C., Rotem, C., Fagot, R. and Kaplan, B. (2003) 'The immediate effect of natural plant extract, Angelica sinensis and Matricaria chamomilla (Climex) for the treatment of hot flushes during menopause. A preliminary report.' *Clinical and Experimental Obstetrics and Gynecology 30*: 203–206.

Kurth, S., Ringli, M., Geiger, A., LeBourgeois, M. *et al.* (2010) 'Mapping of cortical activity in the first two decades of life: A high-density sleep electroencephalogram study.' *Journal of Neuroscience 30*(40): 13211–13219.

Kyriacou, C.P. and Hastings, M.H. (2010) 'Circadian clocks: Genes, sleep, and cognition.' *Trends in Cognitive Sciences 14*(6): 259–267.

Laakso, M.L., Lindblom, N., Leinonen, L. and Kaski, M. (2007) 'Endogenous melatonin predicts efficacy of exogenous melatonin in consolidation of fragmented wrist-activity rhythm of adult patients with developmental brain disorders: A double-blind, placebo-controlled, crossover study.' *Sleep Medicine 8*(3): 222–239.

Laberge, L., Petit, D., Simard, C., Vitaro, F., Tremblay, R.E. and Montplaisir, J. (2001) 'Development of sleep patterns in early adolescence.' *Journal of Sleep Research 10*: 59–67.

Laffan, A.M. and Punjabi, N.M. (2008) 'Sleep: A nourisher in life's feast?' *Sleep Medicine Reviews 12*(4): 253–255.

Lakhan, S.E. and Vieira, K.F. (2010) 'Nutritional and herbal supplements for anxiety and anxiety-related disorders: Systematic review.' *Nutrition Journal 9*:42. Available at www.nutritionj.com/content/9/1/42, accessed 14 September 2011.

Lamerz, A., Kuepper-Nybelen, J., Bruning, N., Wehle, C. *et al.* (2005) 'Prevalence of obesity, binge eating, and night eating in a cross-sectional field survey of 6-year-old children and their parents in a German urban population.' *Journal of Child Psychology and Psychiatry 46*: 385–393.

Lamont, E.W., James, F.O., Boivin, D.B. and Cermakian, N. (2007) 'From circadian clock gene expression to pathologies.' *Sleep Medicine 8*: 547–556.

Lancee, J., Spoormaker, V.I., Krakow, B. and van den Bout, J. (2008a) 'A systematic review of cognitive-behavioral treatment for nightmares: Toward a well-established treatment.' *Journal of Clinical Sleep Medicine 4*(5): 475–480.

Lancee, J., Spoormaker, V.I., Peterse, G. and van den Bout, J. (2008b) 'Measuring nightmare frequency: Retrospective questionnaires versus prospective logs.' *Open Sleep Journal 1*: 26–28.

Lancel, M., Kromer, S. and Neumann, I.D. (2003) 'Intracerebral oxytocin modulates sleep–wake behaviour in male rats.' *Regulatory Peptides 114*: 145–152.

Lanfranchi, P.A., Pennestri, M.-H., Fradette, L., Dumont, M. *et al.* (2009) 'Nighttime blood pressure in normotensive subjects with chronic insomnia: Implications for cardiovascular risk.' *Sleep 32*(6): 760–766.

Lang, R., White, P.J., Machalicek, W., Rispoli, M. *et al.* (2009) 'Treatment of bruxism in individuals with developmental disabilities: A systematic review.' *Research in Developmental Disabilities 30*(5): 809–818.

Langdon, N., Shindler, J., Parkes, J.D. and Bandak, S. (1986) 'Fluoxetine in the treatment of cataplexy.' *Sleep 9*(2): 371–373.

La Pine, M.P., Malcomson, F.N., Torrance, J.M. and Marsh, N.V. (2006) 'Night shift: Can a homeopathic remedy alleviate shift lag?' *Dimensions in Critical Care Nursing 25*(3): 130–136.

Largo, R.H. and Hunziker, U.A. (1984) 'A developmental approach to the management of children with sleep disturbances in the first three years of life.' *European Journal of Pediatrics 142*(3): 170–173.

Larson-Prior, L.J., Zempel, J.M., Nolan, T.S., Prior, F.W. *et al.* (2009) 'Cortical network functional connectivity in the descent to sleep.' *Proceedings of the National Academy of Science 106*(11): 4489–4494.

Lask, B. (1988) 'Novel and non-toxic treatment for night terrors.' *British Medical Journal 297*: 592.

Latif, A., Heinz, P. and Cook, R. (2002) 'Iron deficiency in autism and Asperger syndrome.' *Autism 6*: 103–114.

Lavie, P. and Peled, R. (1987) 'Narcolepsy is a rare disease in Israel.' *Sleep 10*: 608–609.

Lavigne, G.J. and Manzine, C. (2000) 'Bruxism.' In M.H. Kryger, T. Roth and W.C. Dement (eds) *Principles and Practice of Sleep Medicine*, 3rd edn. Philadelphia, PA: WB Saunders.

Lavigne, G.J. and Montplaisir, J.Y. (1994) 'Restless legs syndrome and sleep bruxism: Prevalence and association among Canadians.' *Sleep 17*: 739–743.

Leboeuf, C., Brown, P., Herman, A., Leembruggen, K. *et al.* (1991) 'Chiropractic care of children with nocturnal enuresis: A prospective outcome study.' *Journal of Manipulative & Physiological Therapeutics 14*(2): 110–115.

LeBourgeois, M.K. and Harsh, J.R. (2001) 'A new research measure for children's sleep.' *Sleep 24*: A360.

LeBourgeois, M.K., Giannotti, F., Cortesi, F., Wolfson, A. and Harsh, J. (2004) 'Sleep hygiene and sleep quality in Italian and American adolescents.' *Annals of the New York Academy of Science 1021*: 352–354.

LeBourgeois, M.K., Giannotti, F., Cortesi, F., Wolfson, A.R. and Harsh, J. (2005) 'The relationship between reported sleep quality and sleep hygiene in Italian and American adolescents.' *Pediatrics 115*: 257–265.

Lecanuet, J.-P. and Schaal, B. (2002/1) 'Sensory performances in the human foetus: A brief summary of research.' *Intellectica 34*: 29–56.

Lee, C.-M., Wong, H.N.C., Chui, K.-Y., Choang, T.F. *et al.* (1991) 'Miltirone, a central benzodiazepine receptor partial agonist from a Chinese medicinal herb *Salvia Miltiorrhiza.*' *Neuroscience Letters 127*: 237–241.

Lee, H.-J., Macbeth, A.H., Pagani, J. and Young, W.S. (2009) 'Oxytocin: The great facilitator of life.' *Progress in Neurobiology 88*(2): 127–151.

Lee, R.W.W., Chan, A.S.L., Grunstein, R.R. and Cistulli, P.A. (2009) 'Craniofacial phenotyping in obstructive sleep apnea – a novel quantitative photographic approach.' *Sleep 32*(1): 37–45.

Lee, R.W.W., Petocz, P., Prvan, T., Chan, A.S.L. *et al.* (2009) 'Prediction of obstructive sleep apnea with craniofacial photographic analysis.' *Sleep 32*(1): 46–52.

Lei, H., Wang, Y., Liang, F., Su, W. *et al.* (2010) 'Composition and variability of essential oils of *Platycladus orientalis* growing in China.' *Biochemical Systematics and Ecology 30*: 1–7, doi:10.1016/j.bse.2010.09.018.

Lemmon, M.E., Gregas, M. and Jeste, S.S. (2010) 'Risperidone use in autism spectrum disorders: A retrospective review of a clinic-referred patient population.' *Journal of Child Neurology 26*(4): 428–432.

Lenjavi, M.R., Ahuja, M.A., Touchette, P.E. and Sandman, C.A. (2010) 'Maladaptive behaviors are linked with inefficient sleep in individuals with developmental disabilities.' *Journal of Neurodevelopmental Disorders 2*: 174–180.

Lesku, J.A., Roth, T.C., Amlaner, C.J. and Lima, S.L. (2006) 'A phylogenetic analysis of sleep architecture in mammals: the integration of anatomy, physiology, and ecology.' *American Naturalist 168*: 441–453.

Leu, R.M., Beyderman, L., Botzolakis, E.J., Surdyka, K. *et al.* (2010) 'Relation of melatonin to sleep architecture in children with autism.' *Journal of Autism and Developmental Disorders 41*(4): 427–433.

Levitt, P., Eagleson, K.L. and Powell, E.M. (2004) 'Regulation of neocortical interneuron development and the implications for neurodevelopmental disorders.' *TINS* (Trends in Neurosciences) *27*: 400–406.

Levy, S.E., Mandell, D.S., Merhar, S., Ittenbach, R.F. and Pinto-Martin, J.A. (2003) 'Use of complementary and alternative medicine among children recently diagnosed with autistic spectrum disorder.' *Journal of Developmental and Behavioural Pediatrics 24*(6): 418–423.

Lewandowski, A.S., Toliver-Sokol, M. and Palermo, T.M. (2011) 'Evidence-based review of subjective pediatric sleep measures.' *Journal of Pediatric Psychology 58*(3): 699–713.

Lewy, A.J. (2007) 'Melatonin and human chronobiology.' *Cold Spring Harbour Symposia in Quantitative Biology 72*: 623–636.

Li, K.K., Powell, N.B., Riley, R.W., Troell, R.J. and Guilleminault, C. (2000) 'Long-term results of maxillomandibular advancement surgery.' *Sleep and Breathing 4*(3): 137–139.

Li, Y.S. (2000) 'The comparison of the treatment of insomnia in different Chinese Traditional Medicine formula' [in Chinese]. *Zhejiang Journal of Integrated Traditional Chinese and Western Medicine 10*: 169.

Lichstein, K.L., Payne, K.L., Soeffing, J.P., Durrence, H.H. *et al.* (2008) 'Vitamins and sleep: An exploratory study.' *Sleep Medicine 9*(1): 27–32.

Lichstein, K.L., Peterson, B.A., Riedel, B.N., Means, M.K. *et al.* (1999) 'Relaxation to assist sleep medication withdrawal.' *Behavior Modification 23*: 379–402.

Lichstein, K.L., Riedel, B.W., Wilson, N.M., Lester, K.W. and Aguillard, R.N. (2001) 'Relaxation and sleep compression for late-life insomnia: A placebo controlled trial.' *Journal of Consulting and Clinical Psychology 69*: 227–239.

Licinio, J., Mantzoros, C., Negrão, A.B., Cizza, G. *et al.* (1997) 'Human leptin levels are pulsatile and inversely related to pituitary-adrenal function.' *Nature Medicine 3*(5): 575–579.

Licinio, J., Negrao, A.B., Mantzoros, C., Kaklamani, V. *et al.* (1998) 'Sex differences in circulating human leptin pulse amplitude: Clinical implications.' *Journal of Clinical Endocrinology and Metabolism 83*: 4140–4147.

Lieberman, H., Coffey, B. and Kobrick, J. (1998) 'A vigilance task sensitive to the effects of stimulants, hypnotics, and environmental stress: The Scanning Visual Vigilance Test.' *Behavioral Research Methods Instruments and Computation 30*(3): 416–422.

Liebreich, O. (1869) *Das Chloralhydrat: ein neues Hypnoticum und Anaestheticum und dessen Anwendung in der Medicin; eine Arzneimittel-Untersuchung.* Berlin: Müller.

Liederman, P.C., Wasserman, D.H. and Liederman, V.R. (1969) 'Desipramine in the treatment of enuresis.' *Journal of Urology 101*(3): 314–316.

Lim, A., Cranswick, N. and South, M. (2010) 'Adverse events associated with the use of complementary and alternative medicine in children.' *Archives of Disease in Childhood 96*(3): 297–300.

Lima, S.L. and Rattenborg, N.C. (2007) 'A behavioural shutdown can make sleeping safer: A strategic perspective on the function of sleep.' *Animal Behaviour 74*: 189–197.

Limoges, E., Mottron, L., Bolduc, C., Berthiaume, C. and Godbout, R. (2005) 'Atypical sleep architecture and the autism phenotype.' *Brain 128*: 1049–1061.

Limperopoulos, C., Bassan, H., Sullivan, N.R., Soul, J.S. *et al.* (2008) 'Positive screening for autism in ex-preterm infants: Prevalence and risk factors.' *Pediatrics 121*: 758–765.

Lindahl, O. and Lindwall, L. (1989) 'Double blind study of a valerian preparation.' *Pharmacology Biochemistry & Behavior 32*: 1065–1066.

Lindberg, N., Tani, P., Putkonen, H., Sailas, E. *et al.* (2009) 'Female impulsive aggression: A sleep research perspective.' *International Journal of Law and Psychiatry 32*: 39–42.

Linde, K., Berner, M.M. and Kriston, L. (2008) 'St John's wort for major depression.' *Cochrane Database Systematic Reviews 8*(4): CD000448, doi:10.1002/14651858.CD000448.pub3.

Lindsay, W.R., Fee, M., Michie, A. and Heap, I. (1994) 'The effects of cue control relaxation on adults with severe mental retardation.' *Research in Developmental Disabilities 15*: 425–437.

Lipton, A.J. and Gozal, D. (2003) 'Treatment of obstructive sleep apnea in children: Do we really know how?' *Sleep Medicine Reviews 7*: 61–80.

Littner, M., Johnson, S.F., McCall, W.V., Anderson, W.M. *et al.* (2001) 'Practice parameters for the treatment of narcolepsy: An update for 2000.' *Sleep 24*: 451–466.

Liu, J., Shi, J.-Z., Yu, L.-M., Goyer, R.A. and Waalkes, M.P. (2008) 'Mercury in traditional medicines: Is cinnabar toxicologically similar to common mercurials?' *Experimental Biology and Medicine (Maywood) 233*(7): 810–817.

Liu, X., Hubbard, J.A., Fabes, R.A. and Adam, J.B. (2006) 'Sleep disturbances and correlates of children with autism spectrum disorders.' *Child Psychiatry & Human Development 37*(2): 179–191.

Liu, X., Liu, L., Owens, J.A. and Kaplan, D.L. (2005) 'Sleep patterns and sleep problems among schoolchildren in the United States and China.' *Pediatrics 155*: 241–249.

Liu, X., Uchiyama, M., Okawa, M. and Kurita, H. (2000) 'Prevalence and correlates of self-reported sleep problems among Chinese adolescents.' *Sleep 23*(1): 27–34.

Liu, X.C. and Yang, J. (2000) 'The external use of Cinnabaris in children in the treatment of night terror and sleeping difficulties' [in Chinese]. *China's Naturopathy 8*: 21.

Liukkonen, K., Virkkula, P., Aronen, E.T., Kirjavainen, T. and Pitkaranta, A. (2008) 'All snoring is not adenoids in young children.' *International Journal of Pediatric Otorhinolaryngology 72*: 879–884.

Lombroso, C.T. (2000) 'Pavor nocturnus of proven epileptic origin.' *Epilepsia 41*(9): 1221–1226.

Loomis, A.L., Harvey, E.N. and Hobart, G.A. (1937) 'Cerebral states during sleep as studied by human brain potentials.' *Journal of Experimental Psychology 21*(2): 127–144.

Lopez-Wagner, M.C., Hoffman, C.D., Sweeney, D.P., Hodge, D. and Gilliam, J.E. (2008) 'Sleep problems of parents of typically developing children and parents of children with autism.' *Journal of Genetic Psychology 169*(3): 245–259.

Lord, C., Wagner, A., Rogers, S., Szatmari, P. *et al.* (2005) 'Challenges in evaluating psychosocial interventions for autistic spectrum disorders.' *Journal of Autism and Developmental Disorders 35*(6): 695–708.

Lorimer, P.A., Simpson, R.L., Myles, B.S. and Ganz, J.B. (2002) 'The use of social stories as a preventative behavioral intervention in a home setting with a child with autism.' *Journal of Positive Behavioral Intervention 4*(1): 53–60.

Lozoff, B. and Georgieff, M.K. (2006) 'Iron deficiency and brain development.' *Seminars in Pediatric Neurology 13*: 158–165.

Lozoff, B., Wolf, A.W. and Davis, N.S. (1984) 'Cosleeping in urban families with young children in the United States.' *Pediatrics 74*(2): 171–182.

Lozoff, B., Wolf, A.W. and Davis, N.S. (1985) 'Sleep problems seen in pediatric practice.' *Pediatrics 75*(3): 477–483.

Luboshitsky, R., Aviv, A., Hefetz, A., Herer, P. *et al.* (2002) 'Decreased pituitary-gonadal secretion in men with obstructive sleep apnea.' *Journal of Clinical Endocrinology and Metabolism 87*(7): 3394–3398.

Luboshitsky, R., Zabari, Z., Shen-Orr, Z., Herer, P. and Lavie, P. (2001) 'Disruption of the nocturnal testosterone rhythm by sleep fragmentation in normal men.' *Journal of Clinical Endocrinology and Metabolism 86*(3): 1134–1139.

Lucas, A. and St James-Roberts, I. (1998) 'Crying, fussing and colic behaviour in breast and bottle-fed infants.' *Early Human Development 53*(1): 9–18.

Lumeng, J.C. and Chervin, R.D. (2008) 'Epidemiology of pediatric obstructive sleep apnea.' *Proceedings of the American Thoracic Society 5*: 242–252.

Lundgren, J., Allison, K. and Stunkard, A. (2006) 'Familial aggregation in the night eating syndrome.' *International Journal of Eating Disorders 39*(6): 516–518.

Lyman, D. (Trans.) (1856) *The MoralSayings of Publius Syrus A Roman Slave, from the latin*. Cincinnati, OH: L.E.Barnard & Co.

Lyon, C. and Schnall, J. (2010) 'What is the best treatment for nocturnal enuresis in children?' *Journal of Family Practice 54*(10): 905–909.

Ma, C.-L., Arnsten, A.F.T. and Li, B.-M. (2005) 'Locomotor hyperactivity induced by blockade of prefrontal cortical_2-adrenoceptors in monkeys.' *Biological Psychiatry 57*: 192–195.

McArthur, A.J. and Budden, S.S. (1998) 'Sleep dysfunction in Rett syndrome: A trial of exogenous melatonin treatment.' *Developmental Medicine and Child Neurology 40*(3): 186–192.

McCarley, R.W. (2007) 'Neurobiology of REM and NREM sleep.' *Sleep Medicine 8*(4): 302–330.

McClung, C.A. (2007) 'Circadian genes, rhythms and the biology of mood disorders.' *Pharmacological Therapy 114*(2): 222–232.

McDermott, S., Zhou, L. and Mann, J. (2008) 'Injury treatment among children with autism or pervasive developmental disorder.' *Journal of Autism and Developmental Disorders 38*(4): 626–633.

McGowan, P.O., Meaney, M.J. and Szyf, M. (2008) 'Diet and the epigenetic (re)programming of phenotypic differences in behavior.' *Brain Research 1237*: 12–24.

McGrew, S., Malow, B.A., Henderson, L., Wang, L., Song, Y. and Stone, W.L. (2007) 'Developmental and behavioral questionnaire for autism spectrum disorders.' *Pediatric Neurology 37*(2), 108–116.

McIntyre, L.L., Gresham, F.M., Digennaro, F.D. and Reed, D.D. (2007) 'Treatment integrity of school-based interventions with children in the *Journal of Applied Behavior Analysis* 1991–2005.' *Journal of Applied Behavior Analysis 40*(4): 659–672.

McKenna, J.J., Thoman, E., Anders T.E., Sadeh, A. *et al.* (1993) 'Infant–parent co-sleeping in evolutionary perspective: Implications for understanding infant sleep development and the Sudden Infant Death Syndrome (SIDS).' *Sleep 16*: 263–282.

McKenna, J.J., Ball, H.L. and Gettler, L.T. (2007) 'Mother–infant cosleeping, breastfeeding and Sudden Infant Death Syndrome: What biological anthropology has discovered about normal infant sleep and pediatric sleep medicine.' *Yearbook of Physical Anthropology 50*: 133–161.

McKenna, J.J. and McDade, T. (2005) 'Why babies should never sleep alone: A review of the co-sleeping controversy in relation to SIDS, bedsharing and breast feeding.' *Paediatric Respiratory Reviews 6*: 134–152.

McKenna, J.J. and Mosko, S.S. (1994) 'Sleep and arousal, synchrony and independence, among mothers and infants sleeping apart and together (same bed): An experiment in evolutionary medicine.' *Acta Paediatrica 83*: 94–102.

McKenna, J.J., Mosko, S., Dungy, C. and McAninch, J. (1990) 'Sleep and arousal patterns of co-sleeping human mother/infant pairs: A preliminary physiological study with implications for the study of sudden infant death syndrome (SIDS).' *American Journal of Physical Anthropology 83*(3): 331–347.

Macedo, C.R., Silva, A.B., Machado, M.A.C., Saconato, H. and Prado, G.F. (2007) 'Occlusal splints for treating sleep bruxism (tooth grinding).' *Cochrane Database of Systematic Reviews 4*: CD005514, doi: 10.1002/14651858.CD005514.pub2.

Machado-Vieira, R., Viale, C.I. and Kapczinski, F. (2001) 'Mania associated with an energy drink: The possible role of caffeine, taurine, and inositol.' *Canadian Journal of Psychiatry 46*(5): 454–455.

Mackiewicz, M., Shockley, K.R., Romer, M.A., Galante, R.J. *et al.* (2007) 'Macromolecule biosynthesis: A key function of sleep.' *Physiological Genomics 31*: 441–457.

Makley, M.J., English, J.B., Drubach, D.A., Kreuz, A.J. *et al.* (2008) 'Prevalence of sleep disturbance in closed head injury patients in a rehabilitation unit.' *Neurorehabilitation and Neural Repair 22*(4): 341–347.

Malow, B.A. (2004) 'Sleep disorders, epilepsy, and autism.' *Mental Retardation and Developmental Disabilities Research Reviews 10*(2): 122–125.

Malow, B.A. and McGrew, S.G. (2008) 'Sleep disturbances and autism.' *Sleep Medicine Clinics 3*(3): 479–488.

Malow, B.A., McGrew, S.G., Harvey, M., Henderson, L.M. and Stone, W.L. (2006) 'Impact of treating sleep apnea in a child with autism spectrum disorder.' *Pediatric Neurology 34*: 325–328.

Malow, B.A., Marzec, M.L., McGrew, S.G., Wang, L. *et al.* (2006) 'Characterizing sleep in children with autism spectrum disorders: A multidimensional approach.' *Sleep 29*(12): 1559–1567.

Malsch, U. and Kieser, M. (2001) 'Efficacy of kava-kava in the treatment of non-psychotic anxiety, following pretreatment with benzodiazepines.' *Psychopharmacology 157*: 277–283.

Mamelak, M., Black, J., Montplaisir, J. and Ristanovic, R. (2004) 'A pilot study on the effects of sodium oxybate on sleep architecture and daytime alertness in narcolepsy.' *Sleep 27*(7): 1327–1334.

Mammen, A.A. and Ferrer, F.A. (2004) 'Nocturnal enuresis: Medical management.' *Urologic Clinics of North America 31*: 491–498.

Manber, R. and Harvey, A. (2005) 'Historical perspective and future directions in Cognitive Behavioral Therapy for insomnia and behavioral sleep medicine.' *Clinical Psychology Review 25*: 535–538.

Manfredini, D. and Lobbenzoo, F. (2009) 'Role of psychosocial factors in the etiology of bruxism.' *Journal of Orofacial Pain 23*(2): 153–166.

Manheimer, E., Wieland, S., Kimbrough, E., Cheng, K. and Berman, B.M. (2009) 'Evidence from the Cochrane Collaboration for Traditional Chinese Medicine therapies.' *Journal of Alternative and Complementary Medicine 15*(9): 1001–1014.

Manni, R. and Tartara, A. (1997) 'Clonazepam treatment of rhythmic movement disorders.' *Sleep 20*: 812.

Manni, R. and Terzaghi, M. (2010) 'Comorbidity between epilepsy and sleep disorders.' *Epilepsy Research 90*: 171–177.

Mao, A., Burnham, M.M., Goodlin-Jones, B.L., Gaylor, E.E. and Anders, T.F. (2004) 'A comparison of the sleep–wake patterns of cosleeping and solitary-sleeping infants.' *Child Psychiatry and Human Development 35*(2): 95–105.

Maquet, P. (2000) 'Functional neuroimaging of normal human sleep by positron emission tomography.' *Journal of Sleep Research 9*: 207–231.

Maquet, P. (2001) 'The role of sleep in learning and memory.' *Science 294*(5544): 1048–1052.

Maquet, P., Peters, J.-M., Aerts, J., Delfiore, G. *et al.* (1996) 'Functional neuroanatomy of human rapid-eye-movement sleep and dreaming.' *Nature 383*: 163–166.

Maquet, P., Ruby, P., Maudoux, A., Albouy, G. *et al.* (2005) 'Human cognition during REM sleep and the activity profile within frontal and parietal cortices: A reappraisal of functional neuroimaging data.' *Progress in Brain Research 150*: 219–226.

Marcus, R.N., Owen, R., Kamen, L., Manos, G. *et al.* (2009) 'A placebo-controlled, fixed-dose study of aripiprazole in children and adolescents with irritability associated with autistic disorder.' *Journal of the American Academy of Child Adolescent Psychiatry 48*(11): 1110–1119.

Marks, G.A., Shaffery, J.P., Oksenberg, A., Speciale, S.G. and Roffwarg, H.P. (1995) 'A functional role for REM sleep in brain maturation.' *Behavioral Brain Research 69*(1): 1–11.

Marks, I.M. (1978) 'Rehearsal relief of a nightmare.' *British Journal of Psychiatry 135*: 461–465.

Marshall, J. and Meltzoff, A.N. (2011) 'Neural mirroring systems: Exploring the EEG mu rhythm in human infancy.' *Developmental Cognitive Neuroscience 1*(2): 110–123.

Martínez-Rodríguez, J.E., Lin, L., Iranzo, A., Genis, D. *et al.* (2003) 'Decreased hypocretin-1 (Orexin-A) levels in the cerebrospinal fluid of patients with myotonic dystrophy and excessive daytime sleepiness.' *Sleep 26*(3): 287–290.

Martynska, L., Wolinska-Witort, E., Chmielowska, M., Bik, W. and Baranowska, B. (2005) 'The physiological role of orexins.' *Neuroendocrinology Letters 2*(4): 289–292.

Massa, F., Gonsalez, S., Laverty, A., Wallis, C. and Lane, R. (2002) 'The use of nasal continuous positive airway pressure to treat obstructive sleep apnoea.' *Archives of Disease in Childhood 87*: 438–443.

Matos, G., Andersen, M.L., do Valle, A.C. and Tufik, S. (2010) 'The relationship between sleep and epilepsy: Evidence from clinical trials and animal models.' *Journal of the Neurological Sciences 295*(1): 1–7.

Matteson-Rusby, S.E., Pigeon, W.R., Gehrman, P. and Perlis, M.L. (2010) 'Why treat insomnia?' *Primary Care Companion: Journal of Clinical Psychiatry 12*(1): PCC.08r00743, doi: 10.4088/PCC.08r00743bro. (An online resource of the *Journal of Clinical Psychiatry*.)

Mattewal, A., Casturi, L. and Subramanian, S. (2010) 'A child with REM sleep disturbance.' *Journal of Clinical Sleep Medicine 6*(1): 97–100.

Mayer, G., Wilde-Frenz, J. and Kurella, B. (2007) 'Sleep related rhythmic movement disorder revisited.' *Journal of Sleep Research 16*: 110–116.

Mayers, S.D. and Calhoun, S.L. (2009) 'Variables related to sleep problems in children with autism.' *Research in Autism Spectrum Disorders, 3*(4): 931–941.

Mayes, S.D., Calhoun, S.L., Bixler, E.O., Vgontzas, A.N. *et al.* (2009) 'ADHD subtypes and comorbid anxiety, depression, and oppositional-defiant disorder: Differences in sleep problems.' *Journal of Pediatric Psychology 34*(3): 328–337.

Mazzoccoli, G., Giuliani, A., Carughi, S., De Cata, A. *et al.* (2004) 'The hypothalamic-pituitary-thyroid axis and melatonin in humans: Possible interactions in the control of body temperature.' *Neuroendocrinology Letters 25*(5): 368–372.

Means, M.K., Lichstein, K.L., Epperson, M.T. and Johnson, C.T. (2000) 'Relaxation therapy for insomnia: Nighttime and day time effects.' *Behaviour Research and Therapy 38*: 665–678.

Mednick, S., Nakayama, K. and Stickgold, R. (2003) 'Sleep-dependent learning: A nap is as good as a night.' *Nature Neuroscience 6*(7): 697–698.

Meerlo, P., Mistlberger, R.E., Jacobs, B.L., Heller, H.C. and McGinty, D. (2009) 'New neurons in the adult brain: The role of sleep and consequences of sleep loss.' *Sleep Medicine Reviews 13*(3): 187–194.

Mehra, R. and Redline, S. (2008) 'Sleep apnea: A proinflammatory disorder that coaggregates with obesity.' *Journal of Allergy and Clinical Immunology 121*(5): 1096–1102.

Mehta, A. and Hindmarsh, P. (2002) 'The use of somatropin (recombinant growth hormone) in children of short stature. *Pediatric Drugs 4*: 37–47.

Meier-Ewert, H.K., Ridker, P.M., Rifai, N., Regan, M.M. *et al.* (2004) 'Effect of sleep loss on C-reactive protein, an inflammatory marker of cardiovascular risk.' *Journal of the American College of Cardiology 43*: 678–683.

Melendres, M.C., Lutz, J.M., Rubin, E.D. and Marcus, C.L. (2004) 'Daytime sleepiness and hyperactivity in children with suspected sleep disordered breathing.', *Pediatrics, 114*(3): 768–775.

Melke, J., Goubran-Botros, H., Chaste, P., Betancur, C. *et al.* (2008) 'Abnormal melatonin synthesis in autism spectrum disorders.' *Molecular Psychiatry 13*(1): 90–98.

Meltzer, L.J., Johnson, C., Crosette, J., Ramos, M. and Mindell, J.A. (2010) 'Prevalence of diagnosed sleep disorders in pediatric primary care practices.' *Pediatrics 125*: e1410–e1418.

Mennella, J.A. and Garcia-Gomez, P.L. (2001) 'Sleep disturbances after acute exposure to alcohol in mothers' milk.' *Alcohol 25*(3): 153–158.

Merica, H., Blois, R. and Gaillard, J.M. (1998) 'Spectral characteristics of sleep 9. EEG in chronic insomnia.' *European Journal of Neuroscience 10*: 1826–1834.

Merlino, G., Serafini, A., Robiony, F., Valente, M. and Gigli, G.L. (2009) 'Restless legs syndrome: Differential diagnosis and management with rotigotine.' *Neuropsychiatric Disease and Treatment 5*: 67–80.

Miano, S., Bruni, O., Elia, M., Trovato, A. *et al.* (2007) 'Sleep in children with autistic spectrum disorder: A questionnaire and polysomnographic study.' *Sleep Medicine 9*(1): 64–70.

Miano, S., Donfrancesco, R., Bruni, O., Ferri, R. *et al.* (2006) 'REM sleep instability is reduced in children with attention-deficit/hyperactivity disorder.' *Sleep 29*: 797–803.

Miano, S. and Ferri, R. (2010) 'Epidemiology and management of insomnia in children with autistic spectrum disorders.' *Paediatric Drugs 12*(2): 75–84.

Miano, S., Paolino, M.C., Peraita-Adrados, R., Montesano, M. *et al.* (2009) 'Prevalence of EEG paroxysmal activity in a population of children with obstructive sleep apnea syndrome.' *Sleep 32*(4): 522–529.

Mick, E., Biederman, J., Jetton, J. and Faraone, S.V. (2000) 'Sleep disturbances associated with attention deficit hyperactivity disorder: The impact of psychiatric comorbidity and pharmacotherapy.' *Journal of Child and Adolescent Psychopharmacology 10*(3): 223–231.

Middela, S., Polizois, K., Bradley, A.J. and Rao, P.N. (2009) 'Bardet-Biedl syndrome, renal transplant and percutaneous nephrolithotomy: A case report and review of the literature.' *Cases Journal 2*: 6771, doi: 10.4076/1757–1626-2-6771.

Mignot, E. (1998) 'Genetic and familial aspects of narcolepsy.' *Neurology 50*(suppl.1): S16–S22.

Mignot, E. (2008a) 'Excessive daytime sleepiness: Population and etiology versus nosology.' *Sleep Medicine Reviews 12*: 87–94.

Mignot, E. (2008b) 'Why we sleep: The temporal organization of recovery.' *PloS Biology 6*(4): e106, 0661–0669.

Mignot, E., Taheri, S. and Nishino, S. (2002) 'Sleeping with the hypothalamus: Emerging therapeutic targets for sleep disorders.' *Nature Neurosciemce Supplement 5*: 1071–1075.

Mignot, E., van Lammers, G., Ripley, B., Okun, M. *et al.* (2002) 'The role of cerebrospinal fluid hypocretin measurement in the diagnosis of narcolepsy and other hypersomnias.' *Archives of Neurology 59*: 1553–1562.

Millan, M.J., Gobert, A., Lejeune, F., Dekeyne, A. *et al.* (2003) 'The novel melatonin agonist agomelatine (S20098) is an antagonist at 5-hydroxytryptamine2C receptors, blockade of which enhances the activity of frontocortical dopaminergic and adrenergic pathways.' *Journal of Pharmacology and Experimental Therapeutics 306*: 954–964.

Miller, J. (2007) 'Cry babies: A framework for chiropractic care.' *Clinical Chiropractic 10*: 139–146.

Miller, J. and Klemsdal, M. (2008) 'Can chiropractic care improve infants' sleep?' *Journal of Clinical Chiropractic Pediatrics 9*(1): 543–546.

Miller, J.L., Shuster, J., Theriaque, D., Driscoll, D.J. and Wagner, M. (2009) 'Sleep disordered breathing in infants with Prader-Willi syndrome during the first 6 weeks of growth hormone therapy: A pilot study.' *Journal of Clinical Sleep Medicine 5*(5): 448–453.

Miller, K.E. (2008) 'Energy drinks, race, and problem behaviors among college students.' *Journal of Adolescent Health 43*(5): 490–497.

Miller, W.R. and DiPilato, M. (1983) 'Treatment of nightmares via relaxation and desentisation: A controlled evaluation.' *Journal of Consulting Clinical Psychology 51*: 870–877.

Mindell, J.A. (1993) 'Sleep disorders in children.' *Health Psychology 12*(2): 151–162.

Mindell, J.A. (1999) 'Empirically supported treatments in pediatric psychology: Bedtime refusal and night wakings in young children.' *Journal of Pediatric Psychology 24*(6): 465–481.

Mindell, J.A., Emslie, G., Blumer, J., Genel, M. *et al.* (2006) 'Pharmacologic management of insomnia in children and adolescents: Consensus statement.' *Pediatrics 117*: e1223–e1232.

Mindell, J.A., Meltzer, L.J., Carskadon, M.A. and Chervin, R.D. (2009) 'Developmental aspects of sleep hygiene: Findings from the 2004 National Sleep Foundation Sleep in America Poll.' *Sleep Medicine 10*: 771–779.

Mindell, J.A., Telofski, L.S., Wiegand, B. and Kurtz, E.S. (2009) 'A nightly bedtime routine: Impact on sleep in young children and maternal mood.' *Sleep 32*(5): 599–606.

Ming, X., Brimacombe, M., Chaaban, J., Zimmerman-Bier, B. and Wagner, G.C. (2008) 'Autism spectrum disorders: Concurrent clinical disorders.' *Journal of Child Neurology 23*(1): 6–13.

Ming, X., Gordon, E., Kang, N. and Wagner, G.C. (2008) 'Use of clonidine in children with autism spectrum disorders.' *Brain & Development 30*: 454–460.

Ming, X. and Walters, A.S. (2009) 'Autism spectrum disorders, attention deficit/hyperactivity disorder, and sleep disorders.' *Current Opinion in Pulmonary Medicine 15*(6): 578–584.

Mirmiran, M. and Kok, J.H. (1991) 'Circadian rhythms in early human development.' *Early Human Development 26*: 121–128.

Mirmiran, M., Kok, J.H., Boer, K. and Wolf, H. (1992) 'Human circadian rhythms: Role of the foetal biological clock.' *Neuroscience and Biobehavioral Reviews 16*: 371–378.

Mirmiran, M., Maas, Y.G.H. and Ariagno, R.L. (2003) 'Development of fetal and neonatal sleep and circadian rhythms.' *Sleep Medicine Reviews 7*(4): 321–334.

Mitamura, R., Yano, K., Suzuki, N., Ito, Y. *et al.* (1999) 'Diurnal rhythms of luteinizing hormone, follicle-stimulating hormone, and testosterone secretion before the onset of male puberty.' *Journal of Clinical Endocrinology and Metabolism 84*(1): 29–37.

Miyamoto, H. and Hensch, T.K. (2003) 'Reciprocal interaction of sleep and synaptic plasticity.' *Molecular Interventions 3*(7): 404–417.

Moldofsky, H., Broughton, R.J. and Hill, J.D. (2000) 'A randomized trial of the long-term, continued efficacy and safety of modafinil in narcolepsy.' *Sleep Medicine 1*: 109–116.

Moldofsky, H., Lue, F.A., Davidson, J.R. and Gorczynski, R. (1989) 'Effects of sleep deprivation on human immune functions.' *FASEB Journal 3*: 1972–1977.

Montgomery, P. and Dunne, D. (2007) 'Sleep disorders in children.' *Clinical Evidence (Online) 09*: 2304.

Monteleone, P. and Maj, M. (2008) 'The circadian basis of mood disorders: Recent developments and treatment implications.' *European Neuropsychopharmacology 18*: 701–711.

Moon, E.C., Corkum, P. and Smith, I.M. (2011) 'Case study: A case-series evaluation of a behavioral sleep intervention for three children with autism and primary insomnia.' *Journal of Pediatric Psychology 36*(1): 47–54.

Moolla, A. and Viljoen, A.M. (2008) 'Buchu – Agathosma betulina and Agathosma crenulata (Rutaceae): a review.' *Journal of Ethnopharmacology 119*(3): 413–419.

Moore, M., Kirchner, H.L., Drotar, D., Johnson, N. *et al.* (2009) 'Relationships among sleepiness, sleep time, and psychological functioning in adolescents.', *Journal of Pediatric Psychology, 34*(10): 1175–1183.

Moore, M., Meltzer, L.J. and Mindell, J.A. (2008) 'Bedtime problems and night wakings in children.' *Primary Care 35*(3): 569–581.

Moore, P.S. (2004) 'The use of social stories in a psychology service for children with learning disabilities: A case study of a sleep problem.' *British Journal of Learning Disabilities 32*(3): 133–138.

Moore, T. and Ucko, L.E. (1957) 'Night waking in early infancy. Part I.' *Archives of Diseases in Childhood 32*: 333–342.

Morelli, G.A., Rogoff, B., Oppenheim, D. and Goldsmith, D. (1992) 'Cultural variation in infants' sleeping arrangements: Questions of independence.' *Developmental Psychology 28*(4): 604–613.

Morgenthaler, T.I., Kapur, V.K., Brown, T., Swick, T.J. *et al.* (2007) 'Standards of Practice Committee of the American Academy of Sleep Medicine. Practice parameters for the treatment of narcolepsy and other hypersomnias of central origin.' *Sleep 30*(12): 1705–1711.

Morgenthaler, T.I. and Silber, M.H. (2002) 'Amnestic sleep-related eating disorder associated with zolpidem.' *Sleep Medicine 3*(4): 323–327.

Morin, C.M. (1993) *Insomnia – Psychological Assessment and Management.* New York, NY: Guilford Press.

Morin, C.M. (2006) 'Cognitive-behavioral therapy of insomnia.' *Sleep Medicine Clinics 1*: 375–386.

Morin, C.M., Belanger, L., LeBlanc, M. and Ivers, H. (2009) 'The natural history of insomnia: A population-based 3-year longitudinal study.' *Archives of Internal Medicine 169*(5): 447–453.

Morin, C.M., Bootzin, R.R., Buysse, D.J., Edinger, J.D. *et al.* (2006) 'Psychological and behavioral treatment of insomnia: Update of the recent evidence (1998–2004).' *Sleep 29*(11): 1398–1414.

Moroni, F., Nobili, L., Curcio, G., De Carli, F. *et al.* (2007) 'Sleep in the human hippocampus: A stereo-EEG study.' *PLoS ONE 2*(9): e867, doi:10.1371/journal.pone.0000867.

Morton, J. (2004) *Understanding Developmental Disorders: A Causal Modelling Approach.* Oxford: Blackwell.

Moscovitch, A., Partinen, M. and Guilleminault, C. (1993) 'The positive diagnosis of narcolepsy and narcolepsy's borderland.' *Neurology 43*: 55–60.

Motavalli, N., Tuzun, U., Tuna, S., Yargic, I. and Aydogmus, K. (1994) 'Comparison of the effectiveness of three different treatment modalities in enuresis nocturna.' *Noropsikiyatri Arsivi 31*(3): 146–150.

Moturi, S. and Avis, K. (2010) 'Assessment and treatment of common pediatric sleep disorders.' *Psychiatry (Edgemont) 7*(6): 24–37.

Mowrer, O.H. and Mowrer, W.M. (1938) 'Enuresis – a method for its study and treatment.' *American Journal of Orthopsychiatry 8*: 436–459.

Mukaddes, N.M., Kilincaslan, A., Kucukyazici, G., Sevketoglu, T. and Tuncer, S. (2007) 'Autism in visually impaired individuals.' *Psychiatry and Clinical Neurosciences 61*(1): 39–44.

Müller, D., Roehr, C.C. and Eggert, P. (2004) 'Comparative tolerability of drug treatment for nocturnal enuresis in children.' *Drug Safety 27*(10): 717–727.

Muller, S.F. and Klement, S. (2006) 'A combination of valerian and lemon balm is effective in the treatment of restlessness and dyssomnia in children.' *Phytomedicine 13*(6): 383–387.

Muller, U., Steffenhagen, N., Regenthal, R. and Bublak, P. (2004) 'Effects of modafinil on working memory processes in humans.' *Psychopharmacology 177*(1–2): 161–169.

Mulvaney, S.A., Kaemingk, K.L., Goodwin, J.L. and Quan, S.F. (2006) 'Parent-rated behavior problems associated with overweight before and after controlling for sleep disordered breathing.' *BMC Pediatrics 6*: 34, doi:10.1186/1471-2431-6-34.

Murali, H. and Kotagal, S. (2006) 'Off-label treatment of severe childhood narcolepsy-cataplexy with sodium oxybate.' *Sleep 29*(8): 1025–1029.

Muris, P., Merckelbach, H., Gadet, B. and Moulaert, V. (2000) 'Fears, worries, and scary dreams in 4- to 12-year-old children: their content, developmental pattern, and origins.' *Journal of Clinical Child Psychology 29*: 43–52.

Murray, L. and Cooper, P. (eds) (1997) *Postpartum Depression and Child Development.* New York, NY: Guilford Press.

Muthu, M.S. and Prathibha, K.M. (2008) 'Management of a child with autism and severe bruxism: A case report.' *Journal of the Indian Society of Pedodontics and Preventive Dentistry 26*(2): 82–84.

Myers, S.P. and Cheras, P.A. (2004) 'The other side of the coin: Safety of complementary and alternative medicine.' *Medical Journal of Australia 181*(4): 222–225.

Nader, N., Chrousos, G.P. and Kino, T. (2010) 'Interactions of the circadian CLOCK system and the HPA axis.' *Trends in Endocrinology and Metabolism 21*(5): 277–286.

Nappi, C.M., Drummond, S.P.A., Thorp, S.R. and McQuaid, J.R. (2010) 'Effectiveness of imagery rehearsal therapy for the treatment of combat-related nightmares in veterans.' *Behavior Therapy 41*: 237–244.

Nappo, S., Del Gado, R., Chiozza, M.L., Biraghi, M., Ferrara, P. and Caione, P. (2002) 'Nocturnal enuresis in the adolescent: A neglected problem.' *BJU International 90*: 912–917.

Naruse, H., Yhayashi, T., Takesada, M., Nakane, A. and Yamazaki, K. (1989) 'Metabolic changes in aromatic amino acids and monoamines in infantile autism and development of new treatment related to the finding' [in Japanese]. *No To Hattatsu 21*(2): 181–189.

Naudé, D.F., Couchman, I.M.S. and Maharaj, A. (2010) 'Chronic primary insomnia: Efficacy of homeopathic simillimum.' *Homeopathy 99*: 63–68.

Nedeltcheva, A.V., Kilkus, J.M., Imperial, J., Kasza, K. *et al.* (2009) 'Sleep curtailment is accompanied by increased intake of calories from snacks.' *American Journal of Clinical Nutrition 89*: 126–133.

Newell, K.M., Incledon, T., Bodfish, J.W. and Sprague, R.L. (1999) 'Variability of stereotypic body-rocking in adults with mental retardation.' *American Journal of Mental Retardation 104*: 279–288.

Ng, B.-Y. and Lee, T.-S. (2008) 'Hypnotherapy for sleep disorders.' *Annals of the Academy of Medicine of Singapore 37*: 683–688.

Ng, D.K., Chow, P.-Y., Chan, C.-H., Kwok, K.-L., Cheung, J.M. and Kong, F.Y. (2006) 'An update on childhood snoring.' *Acta Pædiatrica 95*: 1029–1035.

Nguyen, A.-T., Rauch, T.A., Pfeifer, G.P. and Hu, V.W. (2010) 'Global methylation profiling of lymphoblastoid cell lines reveals epigenetic contributions to autism spectrum disorders and a novel autism candidate gene, *RORA*, whose protein product is reduced in autistic brain.' *FASEB Journal 24*(8): 3036–3051.

Nguyen, B.H., Pérusse, D., Paquet, J., Petit, D. *et al.* (2008) 'Sleep terrors in children: A prospective study of twins.' *Pediatrics 122*(6): e1164–1167.

Nicholas, B., Rudrasingham, V., Nash, S., Kirov, G., Owen, M.J. and Wimpory, D.C. (2007) 'Association of Per1 and Npas2 with autistic disorder: Support for the clock genes/social timing hypothesis.' *Molecular Psychiatry 12*: 581–592.

Nickels, K.C., Katusic, S.K., Colligan, R.C., Weaver, A.L. *et al.* (2008) 'Stimulant medication treatment of target behaviors in children with autism: A population-based study.' *Journal of Developmental and Behavioural Pediatrics 29*(2): 75–81.

Nickelsen, T., Samel, A., Vejvoda, M., Wenzel, J., Smith, B. and Gerzer, R. (2002) 'Chronobiotic effects of the melatonin agonist LY 156735 following a simulated 9h time shift: Results of a placebo-controlled trial.' *Chronobiology International 19*: 915–936.

Nicolau, G.Y. and Haus, E. (1994) 'Chronobiology of the Hypothalamic-pituitary-thyroid Axis.' In Y. Touitou and E. Haus (eds) *Biologic Rhythms in Clinical and Laboratory Medicine*, 2nd edn. New York, NY: Springer-Verlag.

Nielsen, T. and Levin, R. (2007) 'Nightmares: A new neurocognitive model.' *Sleep Medicine Reviews 11*: 295–310.

Nielsen, T.A., Stenstrom, P. and Levin, R. (2006) 'Nightmare frequency as a function of age, gender, and September 11, 2001: Findings from an internet questionnaire.' *Dreaming 16*(3): 145–158.

Nieto, F.J., Peppard, P.E. and Young, T.B. (2009) 'Sleep disordered breathing and metabolic syndrome.' *Western Medical Journal 108*(5): 263–265.

Nir, I. (1995) 'Biorhythms and the biological clock involvement of melatonin and the pineal gland in life and disease.' *Biomedical and Environmental Sciences 8*(2): 90–105.

Nir, I., Meir, D., Zilber, N., Knobler, H. *et al.* (1995) 'Brief report: Circadian melatonin, thyroid-stimulating hormone, prolactin, and cortisol levels in serum of young adults with autism.' *Journal of Autism and Developmental Disorders 25*: 641–654.

Nishida, M., Pearsall, J., Buckner, R.L. and Walker, M.P. (2009) 'REM sleep, prefrontal theta, and the consolisation of human emotional memory.' *Cerebral Cortex 19*: 1158–1166.

Nixon, G.M. and Brouillette, R.T. (2002) 'Sleep and breathing in Prader-Willi syndrome.' *Pediatric Pulmonology 34*(3): 209–217.

Nobili, L., Francione, S., Mai, R., Cardinale, F. *et al.* (2007) 'Surgical treatment of drug-resistant nocturnalfrontal lobe epilepsy.' *Brain 130*(2): 561–573.

Nofzinger, E.A., Mintun, M.A., Wiseman, M.-B., Kupfer, D.J. and Moore, R.Y. (1997) 'Forebrain activation in REM sleep: An FDG PET study.' *Brain Research 770*: 192–201.

Nolan, C. (2010) *Inception.* Legendary Pictures, Syncopy Films; Distributor: Warner Bros.

Nonogaki, K., Ohashi-Nozue, K. and Oka, Y. (2006) 'A negative feedback system between brain serotonin systems and plasma active ghrelin levels in mice.' *Biochemical and Biophysical Research Communications 341*: 703–707.

Obál, F. Jr, Garcia-Garcia, F., Kacsóh, B., Taishi, P. *et al.* (2005) 'Rapid eye movement sleep is reduced in prolactin-deficient mice.' *Journal of Neuroscience 25*(44): 10282–10289.

Obermann, M., Schorn, C.F., Mummel, P., Kastrup, O. and Maschke, M. (2006) 'Taurine induced toxic encephalopathy?' *Clinical Neurology and Neurosurgery 108*: 812–813.

O'Brien, F. (1937) *At Swim-Two-Birds.* London: Longman's Green & Co.

O'Brien, L.M., Holbrook, C.R., Mervis, C.B., Klaus, C.J. *et al.* (2003) 'Sleep and neurobehavioral characteristics of 5- to 7-year-old children with parentally reported symptoms of attention-deficit/hyperactivity disorder.' *Pediatrics 111*(3): 554–563.

O'Brien, L.M., Ivanenko, A., Crabtree, V.M., Holbrook, C.R. *et al.* (2003) 'The effect of stimulants on sleep characteristics in children with attention deficit/hyperactivity disorder.' *Sleep Medicine 4*(4): 309–316.

O'Callaghan, F.J., Clarke, A.A., Hancock, E., Hunt, A. and Osborne, J.P. (1999) 'Use of melatonin to treat sleep disorders in tuberous sclerosis.' *Developmental Medicine and Child Neurology 41*: 123–126.

O'Connor, M.-F., Bower, J.E., Cho, H.J., Creswell, J.D. *et al.* (2009) 'To assess, to control, to exclude: Effects of biobehavioral factors on circulating inflammatory markers.' *Brain, Behavior, and Immunity 23*: 887–897.

O'Connor, T.G., Caprariello, P., Blackmore, E.R., Gregory, A.M. *et al.* (2007) 'Prenatal mood disturbance predicts sleep problems in infancy and toddlerhood.' *Early Human Development 83*(7): 451–458.

OECD (2009) *Society at a Glance 2009 – OECD Social Indicators.* Available at www.oecd.org/els/social/indicators/SAG, accessed 14 September 2011.

Oguni, H. (2011) 'Treatment of benign focal epilepsies in children: When and how should be treated?' *Brain and Development 33*(3): 207–212.

Ohayon, M.M. (2008a) 'Excessive daytime sleepiness: Population and etiology versus nosology.' *Sleep Medicine Reviews 12*: 87–94.

Ohayon, M.M. (2008b) 'From wakefulness to excessive sleepiness: What we know and still need to know.' *Sleep Medicine Reviews 12*: 129–141.

Ohayon, M.M., Guilleminault, C. and Priest R.G. (1999) 'Night terrors, sleepwalking, and confusional arousals in the general population: Their frequency and relationship to other sleep and mental disorders.' *Journal of Clinical Psychiatry 60*(4): 268–276.

Ohayon, M.M. and Roth, T. (2002) 'Prevalence of restless legs syndrome and periodic limb movement disorder in the general population.' *Journal of Psychosomatic Research 53*: 547–554.

Ohta, T., Ando, K., Iwata, T., Ozaki, N. *et al.* (1991) 'Treatment of persistent sleep-wake schedule disorders in adolescents with methylcobalamin (vitamin B12).' *Sleep 14*: 414–418.

Okawa, M., Mishima, K., Nanami, T., Shimizu, T. *et al.* (1990) 'Vitamin B-12 treatment for sleep-wake disorders.' *Sleep 13*: 15–23.

Oken, B.S. (ed.) (2004) *Complementary Therapies in Neurology: An Evidence-Based Approach.* Boca Raton, FL: Parthenon Publishing, CRC Press.

Olivier, J.D., Blom, T., Arentsen, T. and Homberg, J.R. (2010) 'The age-dependent effects of selective serotonin reuptake inhibitors in humans and rodents: A review.' *Progress in Neuropsychopharmacology and Biological Psychiatry 35*(6): 1400–1408.

Olson, E.J., Boeve, B.F. and Silber, M.H. (2000) 'Rapid eye movement sleep behaviour disorder: Demographic, clinical and laboratory findings in 93 cases.' *Brain 123*: 331–339.

Ommerborn, M.A., Schneider, C., Giraki, M., Schafer, R. *et al.* (2007) 'Effects of an occlusal splint compared with cognitive-behavioral treatment on sleep bruxism activity.' *European Journal of Oral Science 115*(1): 7–14.

O'Neill, J.S. and Reddy, A.B. (2011) 'Circadian clocks in human red blood cells.' *Nature 469*: 498–504.

Orav, A., Raal, A. and Arak, E. (2010) 'Content and composition of the essential oil of Chamomilla recutita (L.) Rauschert from some European countries.' *Natural Product Research 24*(1): 48–55.

Orbach, D., Ritaccio, A. and Devinsky, O. (2003) 'Psychogenic, nonepileptic seizures associated with Video-EEG-Verified sleep.' *Epilepsia 44*(1): 64–68.

O'Reardon, J.P., Stunkard, A.J. and Allison, K.C. (2004) 'Clinical trial of sertraline in the treatment of night eating syndrome.' *International Journal of Eating Disorders 35*(1): 16–26.

O'Reilly, M.F. (1995) 'Functional analysis and treatment of escape-maintained aggression correlated with sleep deprivation.' *Journal of Applied Behaviour Analysis 28*: 225–226.

Orr, W.C., Robert, J.J.T., Houck, J.R., Giddens, C.L. and Tawk, M.M. (2009) 'The effect of acid suppression on upper airway anatomy and obstruction in patients with sleep apnea and gastroesophageal reflux disease.' *Journal of Clinical Sleep Medicine 5*(4): 330–334.

Ortega-Albás, J.J., López-Bernabé, R., García, A.L. and Gómez, J.R. (2010) 'Suicidal ideation secondary to sodium oxybate.' *Journal of Neuropsychiatry and Clinical Neuroscience 22*(3): e26.

Oshikoya, K.A., Senbanjo, I.O., Njokanma, O.F. and Soipe, A. (2008) 'Use of complementary and alternative medicines for children with chronic health conditions in Lagos, Nigeria.' *BMC Complementary and Alternative Medicine 8*: 66, doi:10.1186/1472-6882-8-66.

Osorio, I. and Daroff, R.B. (1980) 'Absence of REM and altered NREM sleep in patients with spinocerebellar degeneration and slow saccades.' *Annals of Neurology 7*(3): 277–280.

Ospina, M.B., Seida, J.K., Clark, B., Karkhaneh, M. *et al.* (2008) 'Behavioural and developmental interventions for autism spectrum disorder: A clinical systematic review.' *PLoS ONE 3*(11): e3755, doi:10.1371/journal.pone.0003755.

Owen, R., Sikich, L., Marcus, R.N., Corey-Lisle, P. *et al.* (2009) 'Aripiprazole in the treatment of irritability in children and adolescents with autistic disorder.' *Pediatrics 124*(6): 1533–1540.

Owens, J.A. (2005) 'The ADHD and sleep conundrum: A review.' *Developmental and Behavioral Pediatrics 26*(4): 312–322.

Owens, J.A. (2009) 'A clinical overview of sleep and attention-deficit/hyperactivity disorder in children and adolescents.' *Journal of the Canadian Academy of Child and Adolescent Psychiatry 18*(2): 92–102.

Owens, J.A. and Dalzell, V. (2005) 'Use of the 'BEARS' sleep screening tool in a pediatric residents' continuity clinic: A pilot study.' *Sleep Medicine 6*: 63–69.

Owens, J., France, K.G. and Wiggs, L. (1999) 'Behavioural and cognitive-behavioural interventions for sleep disorders in infants and children: A review.' *Sleep Medicine Reviews 3*(4): 281–302.

Owens, J.A., Opipari, L., Nobile, C. and Spirito, A. (1998) 'Sleep and daytime behavior in children with obstructive sleep apnea and behavioral sleep disorders.' *Pediatrics 102*(5): 1178–1184.

Owens, J.A., Palermo, T.M. and Rosen, C.L. (2002) 'Overview of current management of sleep disturbances in children: II–Behavioural interventions.' *Current Therapeutic Research 63*(suppl.B): B38–B52.

Owens, J.A., Rosen, C.L., Mindell, J.A. and Kircher, H.L. (2010) 'Use of pharmacotherapy for insomnia in child psychiatry practice: A national survey.' *Sleep Medicine 11*(7): 692–700.

Owens, J.A., Spirito, A. and McGuinn, M. (2000) 'The Children's Sleep Habits Questionnaire (CSHQ): Psychometric properties of a survey instrument for school-aged children.' *Sleep 23*: 1043–1051.

Owens, J.A., Spirito, A., McGuinn, M. and Nobile, C. (2000) 'Sleep habits and sleep disturbance in elementary school-aged children.' *Journal of Developmental and Behavioral Pediatrics 21*: 27–36.

Oxman, A.D., Flottorp, S., Havelsrud, K., Atle Fretheim, A. *et al.* (2007) 'A televised, web-based randomised trial of an herbal remedy (valerian) for insomnia.' *PLoS ONE 2*(10): e1040, doi:10.1371/journal.pone.0001040.

Oyama, K., Takahashi, T., Shoji, Y., Oyamada, M. *et al.* (2006) 'Niemann-Pick disease type C: Cataplexy and hypocretin in cerebrospinal fluid.' *Tohoku Journal of Experimental Medicine 209*: 263–267.

Øyane, N.M.F. and Bjorvatn, B. (2005) 'Sleep disturbances in adolescents and young adults with autism and Asperger syndrome.' *Autism 9*(1): 83–94.

Paavonen, E.J., Vehkalahti, K., Vanhala, R., von Wendt, L. *et al.* (2008) 'Sleep in children with Asperger syndrome.' *Journal of Autism and Developmental Disorders 38*: 41–51.

Paavonen, E.J., Nieminen-von.Wendt, T., Vanhala, N.R., Aronen. E.T. and von Wendt, L. (2003) 'Effectiveness of melatonin in the treatment of sleep disturbances in children with Asperger disorder.' *Journal of Child and Adolescent Psychopharmacology 13*: 83–95.

Pace-Schott, E.F., Solms, M., Blagrove, M. and Harnad, S. (2003) *Sleep and Dreaming: Scientific Advances and Reconsiderations.* Cambridge and New York, NY: Cambridge University Press.

Pack, A., Black, J.E., Schwartz, J.R. and Matheson, J.K. (2001) 'Modafinil as adjunct therapy for daytime sleepiness in obstructive sleep apnea.' *American Journal of Respiratory and Critical Care Medicine 164*: 1675–1681.

Pagel, J.F. and Parnes, B.L. (2001) 'Medications for the treatment of sleep disorders: A review.' *Journal of Clinical Psychiatry 3*: 118–125.

Palace, E.M. and Johnston, C. (1989) 'Treatment of recurrent nightmares by the dream reorganization approach.' *Journal of Behavior Therapy and Experimental Psychiatry 20*(3): 219–226.

Palagini, L. and Rosenlicht, N. (2010) 'Sleep, dreaming, and mental health: A review of historical and neurobiological perspectives.' *Sleep Medicine Reviews 15*(3): 179–186.

Pallesen, S., Nordhus, I.H., Nielsen, G.H., Havik, O.E. *et al.* (2001) 'Prevalence of insomnia in the adult Norwegian population.' *Sleep 24*(7): 771–779.

Palombini, L., Pelayo, R. and Guilleminault, C. (2004) 'Efficacy of automated continuous positive airway pressure in children with sleep-related breathing disorders in an attended setting.' *Pediatrics 113*: e412–e417.

Panayiotopoulos, C.P., Michael, M., Sanders, S., Valeta, T. and Koutroumanidis, M. (2008) 'Benign childhood focal epilepsies: Assessment of established and newly recognized syndromes.' *Brain 131*: 2264–2286.

Papageorgiou, P., Katsambas, A. and Chu, A. (2000) 'Phototherapy with blue (415 nm) and red (660 nm) light in the treatment of acne vulgaris.' *British Journal of Dermatology 142*(5): 973–978.

Paparrigopoulos, T.J. (2005) 'REM sleep behaviour disorder: Clinical profiles and pathophysiology.' *International Review of Psychiatry 17*(4): 293–300.

Park, S.A., Lee, B.I., Park, S.C., Lee, S.J. *et al.* (1998) 'Clinical courses of pure sleep epilepsies.' *Seizure 7*(5): 369–377.

Parkin, T.M. and Fraser, M.S. (1972) 'Poisoning as a complication of enuresis.' *Developmental Medicine and Child Neurology 14*(6): 727–730.

Patel, S.R., Malhotra, A., White, D.P., Gottlieb, D.J. and Hu, F.B. (2006) 'Association between reduced sleep and weight gain in women.' *American Journal of Epidemiology 164*: 947–954.

Patel, S.R., Zhu, X., Storfer-Isser, A., Mehra, R. *et al.* (2009) 'Sleep duration and biomarkers of inflammation.' *Sleep 32*(2): 200–204.

Paterson, C., Unwin, J. and Joire, D. (2010) 'Outcomes of traditional Chinese medicine (traditional acupuncture) treatment for people with long-term conditions.' *Complementary Therapies in Clinical Practice 16*(1): 3–9.

Paterson, L.M., Knutt, D.J., Ivarsson, M., Hutson, P.H. and Wilson, S.J. (2009) 'Effects on sleep stages and microarchitecture of caffeine and its combination with zolpidem or tradozone in healthy volunteers.' *Journal of Psychopharmacology 23*(5): 487–494.

Patterson, G.R. (1982) *A Social Learning Approach 3: Coercive Family Process.* Eugene, OR: Castalia Press.

Patwardhan, B., Warude, D., Pushpangadan, P. and Bhatt, N. (2005) 'Ayurveda and Traditional Chinese Medicine: A comparative overview.' *eCAM 2*(4): 465–473, doi:10.1093/ecam/neh140.

Patzold, L.M., Richdale, A.L. and Tonge, B.J. (1998) 'An investigation into sleep characteristics of children with autism and Asperger's Disorder.' *Journal of Paediatrics and Child Health 34*: 528–533.

Pedersen, C.A. and Prange, A.J., Jr (1979) 'Induction of maternal behavior in virgin rats after intracerebroventricular administration of oxytocin.' *Proceedings of the National Academy of Science 76*(12): 6661–6665.

Peirano, P.D., Algarín, C.R., Chamorro, R., Reyes, S. *et al.* (2009) 'Sleep and neurofunctions throughout child development: Lasting effects of early iron deficiency.' *Journal of Pediatric Gastroenterology and Nutrition 48*(suppl. 1): S8–15.

Peirano, P.D., Algarín, C.R., Chamorro, R.A., Reyes, S.C. *et al.* (2010) 'Sleep alterations and iron deficiency anemia in infancy.' *Sleep Medicine 11*(7): 637–642.

Peirano, P., Algarín, C., Garrido, M., Algarín, D. and Lozoff, B. (2007) 'Iron-deficiency anemia is associated with altered characteristics of sleep spindles in NREM sleep in infancy.' *Neurochemical Research 32*(10): 1665–1672.

Peirano, P.D, Algarín, C.R., Garrido, M.I. and Lozoff, B. (2007) 'Iron deficiency anemia in infancy is associated with altered temporal organization of sleep states in childhood.' *Pediatric Research 62*(6): 715–719.

Pelayo, R. and Dubik, M. (2008) 'Pediatric sleep pharmacology.' *Seminars in Pediatric Neurology 15*: 79–90.

Pelc, K., Cheron, G., Boyd, S.G. and Dan, B. (2008) 'Are there distinctive sleep problems in Angelman syndrome?' *Sleep Medicine 9*(4): 434–441.

Pelsser, L.M., Frankena, K., Buitelaar, J.K. and Rommelse, N.N. (2010) 'Effects of food on physical and sleep complaints in children with ADHD: A randomized controlled pilot study.' *European Journal of Pediatrics 169*(9): 1129–1138.

Peppard, P.E., Young, T., Palta, M. and Skatrud, J. (2000) 'Prospective study of the association between sleep disordered breathing and hypertension.' *New England Journal of Medicine 342*(19): 1378–1384.

Peracchi, M., Bardella, M.T., Caprioli, F., Massironi, S. *et al.* (2006) 'Circulating ghrelin levels in patients with inflammatory bowel disease.' *Gut 55*: 432–433.

Perfect, M.M. and Elkins, G.R. (2010) 'Cognitive-behavioral therapy and hypnotic relaxation to treat sleep problems in an adolescent with diabetes.' *Journal of Clinical Psychology 66*(11): 1205–1215.

Perlis, M.L., Smith, M.T., Andrews, P.J., Orff, H. and Giles, D.E. (2001) 'Beta/gamma EEG activity in patients with primary and secondary insomnia and good sleeper controls.' *Sleep 24*: 110–117.

Perreau-Lenz, S., Zghoul, T. and Spanagel, R. (2007) 'Clock genes running amok: Clock genes and their role in drug addiction and depression.' *EMBO Reports 8*(Special Issue): S20–S23.

Perry, A., Bentin, S., Shalev, I., Israel, S. *et al.* (2010) 'Intranasal oxytocin modulates EEG mu/alpha and beta rhythms during perception of biological motion.' *Psychoneuroendocrinology 35*(10): 1446–1453, doi:10.1016/j.psyneuen.2010.04.011.

Peters, J.M., Camfield, C.S. and Camfield, P.R. (2001) 'Population study of benign rolandic epilepsy: Is treatment needed?' *Neurology 57*(3): 537–539.

Peterson, J.L. and Peterson, M. (2003) *The Sleep Fairy.* Omaha, NE: Behave'n Kids Press.

Petroczi, A., Taylor, G. and Naughton, D.P. (2010) 'Mission impossible? Regulatory and enforcement issues to ensure safety of dietary supplements.' *Food and Chemical Toxicology 49*(2): 393–402.

Peyron, C., Faraco, J., Rogers, W., Ripley, B. *et al.* (2000) 'A mutation in a case of early onset narcolepsy and a generalized absence of hypocretin peptides in human narcoleptic brains.' *Nature Medicine 6*(9): 991–997.

Piazza, C.C. and Fisher, W. (1991) 'A faded bedtime with response cost protocol for treatment of multiple sleep problems in children.' *Journal of Applied Behaviour Analysis 24*: 129–140.

Picchietti, D., Allen, R.P., Walters, A.S., Davidson, J.E. *et al.* (2007) 'Restless legs syndrome: Prevalence and impact in children and adolescents – The Peds REST study.' *Pediatrics 120*: 253–266.

Picchietti, D.L., England, S.J., Walters, A.S., Willis, K. and Verrico, T. (1998) 'Periodic limb movement disorder and restless leg syndrome in children with attention deficit hyperactivity disorder.' *Journal of Child Neurology 13*: 588–594.

Picchietti, D.L., Rajendran, R.R., Wilson, M.P. and Picchietti, M.A. (2009) 'Pediatric restless legs syndrome and periodic limb movement disorder: Parent–child pairs.' *Sleep Medicine 10*: 925–931.

Picchietti, D.L. and Stevens, H.E. (2008) 'Early manifestations of restless legs syndrome in childhood and adolescence.' *Sleep Medicine 9*: 770–781.

Picchietti, D.L., Underwood, D.J. and Farris, W.A. (1999) 'Further studies on periodic limb movement disorder and restless legs syndrome in children with Attention-Deficit Hyperactivity Disorder.' *Movement Disorders 14*: 1000–1007.

Picchietti, M.A. and Picchietti, D.L. (2008) 'Restless legs syndrome and periodic limb movement disorder in children and adolescents.' *Seminars in Pediatric Neurology 15*: 91–99.

Pierce, C.J. and Gale, E.N. (1988) 'A comparison of different treatments for nocturnal bruxism.' *Journal of Dental Research 67*(3): 597–601.

Pierce, K. (2011) 'Early functional brain development in autism and the promise of sleep fMRI.' *Brain Research 1380*: 162–174.

Pierce, K., Conant, D., Hazin, R., Stoner, R. and Desmond, J. (2010) 'Preference for geometric patterns early in life as a risk factor for autism.' *Archives of General Psychiatry*, September, doi:10.1001/archgenpsychiatry.2010.11.

Pigeon, W.R. and Yurcheshen, M. (2009) 'Behavioral sleep medicine interventions for restless legs syndrome and periodic limb movement disorder.' *Sleep Medicine Clinics 4*: 487–494.

Piggins, H.D. (2002) 'Human clock genes.' *Annals of Medicine 34*(5): 394–400.

Pillai, M. and James, D. (1990) 'Are the behavioural states of the newborn comparable to those of the fetus?' *Early Human Development 22*: 39–49.

Piravej, K., Tangtrongchitr, P., Chandarasiri, P., Paothong, L. and Sukprasong, S. (2009) 'Effects of Thai traditional massage on autistic children's behavior.' *Journal of Alternative and Complementary Medicine 15*(12): 1355–1361.

Platek, S.M., Critton, S.R., Myers, T.E, and Gallup, G.G., Jr (2003) 'Contagious yawning: The role of self-awareness and mental state attribution.' *Cognitive Brain Research 17*: 223–227.

Plymate, S.R., Tenover, J.S. and Bremner, W.J. (1989) 'Circadian variation in testosterone, sex hormone-binding globulin and calculated non-sex hormone-bonding globulin bound testosterone in healthy young and elderly men.' *Journal of Andrology 10*: 366–372.

Pohlandt, F. (1974) 'Cystine: A semi essential amino acid in the newborn infant.' *Acta Paediatrica Scandinavica 63*: 801–804.

Polimeni, M.A., Richdale, A.L. and Francis, A.J. (2005) 'A survey of sleep problems in autism, Asperger's disorder and typically developing children.' *Journal of Intellectual Disability Research 49*(4): 260–268.

Polimeni, M., Richdale, A.L. and Francis, A.J. (2007) 'The impact of children's sleep problems on the family and behavioural processes related to their development and maintenance.' *E-Journal of Applied Psychology 3*(1): 76–85.

Ponde, M.P., Novaes, C.N. and Losapio, M.F. (2010) 'Frequency of symptoms of attention deficit and hyperactivity disorder in autistic children.' *Arquivos de Neuro-psychiatria 68*(1): 103–106.

Popoviciu, L. and Corfariu, O. (1983) 'Efficacy and safety of midazolam in the treatment of night terrors in children.' *British Journal of Clinical Pharmacology 16*: 97S–102S.

Porkka-Heiskanen, T. (2003) 'Gene expression during sleep, wakefulness and sleep deprivation.' *Frontiers in Bioscience 8*: s421–437.

Powell, E.M., Campbell, D.B., Stanwood, G.D., Davis, C. *et al.* (2003) 'Genetic disruption of cortical interneuron development causes region- and GABA cell type-specific deficits, epilepsy, and behavioral dysfunction.' *Journal of Neuroscience 23*(2): 622–631.

Powers, M.E. (2001) 'Ephedra and its application to sport performance: Another concern for the athletic trainer?' *Journal of Athletic Training 36*(4): 420–424.

Prats Vinas, J.M., Madoz, P. and Martin, R. (1976) 'Trigliceridos de cadena media en la epilepsia infantile terapeuticamente rebelde.' *Revue Espanole Pediatria 187*: 111–122.

Prinz, P. (2004) 'Sleep, appetite, and obesity – what is the link?' *PLoS Medicine 1*(3): e61.

Prokopenko, I., Langenberg, C., Florez, J.C., Saxena, R. *et al.* (2008) 'Variants in MTNR1B influence fasting glucose levels.' *Nature Genetics 41*: 77–81.

Provine, R.R. (1989) 'Faces as releasers of contagious yawning: An approach to face detection using normal human subjects.' *Bulletin of the Psychonomic Society 27*: 211–214.

Puigjaner, J., Fabrega, J., de Diego, I., Subirada, F., Durany, O. and Rivero-Urgell, M. (2007) 'Two circadian infant formulas produce differential cerebellum gene expression in lactating rat neonates.' *Genes and Nutrition 2*: 129–131.

Punjabi, N.M., Shahar, E., Redline, S., Gottlieb, D.J. *et al.* (2004) 'Sleep-disordered breathing, glucose intolerance, and insulin resistance: The Sleep Heart Health Study.' *American Journal of Epidemiology 160*(6): 521–530.

Quillin, S.I. (1997) 'Infant and mother sleep patterns during 4th postpartum week.' *Issues in Comprehensive Pediatric Nursing 20*(2): 115–123.

Quillin, S.I. and Glenn, L.L. (2004) 'Interaction between feeding method and co-sleeping on maternal-newborn sleep.' *Journal of Obstetric Gynecologic and Neonatal Nursing 33*: 580–588.

Rajaratnam, S.M.W., Polymeropoulos, M.H., Fisher, M., Roth, T. *et al.* (2009) 'Melatonin agonist tasimelteon (VEC-162) for transient insomnia after sleep-time shift: Two randomised controlled multicentre trials.' *Lancet 373*(9662): 482–491.

Ralph, M.R. and Menaker, M. (1988) 'A mutation of the circadian system in golden hamsters.' *Science 241*, 1225–1227.

Ramchandani, P., Wiggs, L., Webb, V., Hospice, W. and Stores, G. (2000) 'A systematic review of treatment of settling problems and night waking in young children.' *British Medical Journal 320*: 209–213.

Ramoz, N., Cai, G., Reichert, J.G., Corwin, T.E. *et al.* (2006) 'Family-based association study of TPH1 and TPH2 polymorphisms in autism.' *American Journal of Medical Genetics B: Neuropsychiatric Genetics 141B*(8): 861–867.

Rana, S.K. and Sanders, T.A.B. (1986) 'Taurine concentrations in the diet, plasma, urine and breast milk of vegans compared with omnivores.' *British Journal of Nutrition 56*: 17–27.

Rand, C.S., Macgregor, A.M. and Stunkard, A.J. (1997) 'The night eating syndrome in the general population and among post operative obesity surgery patients.' *International Journal of Eating Disorders 22*: 65–69.

Randazzo, A.C., Muehlbach, M.J., Schweitzer, P.K. and Walsh, J.K. (1988) 'Cognitive function following acute sleep restriction in children ages 10–14.' *Sleep 21*(8): 861–868.

Randler, C. (2008) 'Morningness-eveningness comparison in adolescents from different countries around the world.' *Chronobiology International 25*(6): 1017–1028.

Rantala, H. and Putkonen, T. (1999) 'Occurrence, outcome and prognostic factors of infantile spasms and Lennox-Gastaut syndrome.' *Epilepsia 40*: 286–289.

Rao, V., Spiro, J., Vaishnavi, S., Rastogi, P. *et al.* (2008) 'Prevalence and types of sleep disturbances after traumatic brain injury.' *Brain Injury 22*(5): 381–386.

Raskind, M.A., Peskind, E.R., Hoff, D.J., Hart, K.L. *et al.* (2007) 'A parallel group placebo controlled study of prazosin for trauma nightmares and sleep disturbance in combat veterans with post-traumatic stress disorder.' *Biological Psychiatry 61*: 928–934.

Raskind, M., Peskind, E., Kanter, E., Petrie, E.C. *et al.* (2003) 'Reduction of nightmares and other PTSD symptoms in combat veterans by prazosin: A placebo-controlled study.' *American Journal of Psychiatry 160*: 371–373.

Rattenborg, N.C., Lesku, J.A., Martinez-Gonzalez, D. and Lima, S.L. (2007) 'The non-trivial functions of sleep.' *Sleep Medicine Reviews 11*: 405–409.

Rechtschaffen, A. and Kales, A. (eds) (1968) *A Manual of Standardized Terminology, Techniques and Scoring System for Sleep Stages of Human Subjects.* Washington, DC: Public Health Service.

Rector, D.M., Schei, J.L., Van Dongen, H.P.A., Belenky, G. and Krueger, J.M. (2009) 'Physiological markers of local sleep.' *European Journal of Neuroscience 29*(9): 1771–1778.

Redcay, E. and Courchesne, E. (2008) 'Deviant functional magnetic resonance imaging patterns of brain activity to speech in 2–3-year-old children with autism spectrum disorder.' *Biological Psychiatry 64:* 589–598.

Redline, S., Storfer-Isser, A., Rosen, C.L., Johnson, N.L. *et al.* (2007) 'Association between metabolic syndrome and sleep-disordered breathing in adolescents.' *American Journal of Respiratory and Critical Care Medicine 176*: 401–408.

Reed, M.D. and Findling, R.L. (2002) 'Overview of current management of sleep disturbances in children: I-pharmacotherapy.' *Current Therapeutic Research 63*(suppl.B): B18–B37.

Reed, W.R., Beavers, S., Reddy, S.K. and Kern, G. (1994) 'Chiropractic management of primary nocturnal enuresis.' *Journal of Manipulative & Physiological Therapeutics* 17(9): 596–600.

Reghunandanan, V. and Reghunandanan, R. (2006) 'Neurotransmitters of the suprachiasmatic nuclei.' *Journal of Circadian Rhythms* 4: 2, doi:10.1186/1740-3391-4-2.

Reid, K.J., Baron, K.G., Lu, B., Naylor, E. *et al.* (2010) 'Aerobic exercise improves self-reported sleep and quality of life in older adults with insomnia.' *Sleep Medicine* 11(9): 934–940.

Reid, M.J., Walter, A.L. and O'Leary, S.G. (1999) 'Treatment of young children's bedtime refusal and nighttime wakings: A comparison of "standard" and graduated ignoring procedures.' *Journal of Abnormal Child Psychology* 27(1): 5–16.

Reilly, J.J., Armstrong, J., Dorosty, A.R., Emmett, P.M. *et al.* (2005) 'Early life risk factors for obesity in childhood: Cohort study.' *British Medical Journal* 330: 1357.

Reiser, M.F. (2001) 'The dream in contemporary psychiatry.' *American Journal of Psychiatry* 158: 351–359.

Reissig, C.J., Strain, E.C. and Griffiths, R.R. (2009) 'Caffeinated energy drinks – a growing problem.' *Drug and Alcohol Dependency* 99(1–3): 1–10.

Remington, G., Sloman, L., Konstantareas, M., Parker, K. and Gow, R. (2001) 'Clomipramine versus haloperidol in the treatment of autistic disorder: A double-blind, placebo-controlled, crossover study.' *Journal of Clinical Psychopharmacology* 21(4): 440–444.

Repp, A.C. (1983) *Teaching the Mentally Retarded.* New York, NY: Prentice-Hall.

Revonsuo, A. (2000) 'The reinterpretation of dreams: An evolutionary hypothesis of the function of dreaming.' *Behavioral and Brain Sciences* 23: 877–901.

Revonsuo, A. and Valli, K. (2008) 'How to test the threat simulation theory.' *Consciousness and Cognition* 17: 1292–1296.

Reynolds, A. (2004) 'Sleep disorders in Fragile X syndrome.' *The National Fragile X Foundation Quarterly* (Summer/Fall): 16–19.

Reynolds, A.M. and Malow, B.A. (2011) 'Sleep and autism spectrum disorders.' *Pediatric Clinics of North America* 58: 685–698.

Rial, R.V., Nicolau, M.C., Gamundi, A., Akaarir, M. *et al.* (2007) 'The trivial function of sleep.' *Sleep Medicine Reviews* 11: 311–325.

Ribeiero, J.A. and Sebastiao, A.M. (2010) 'Caffeine and adenosine.' *Journal of Alzheimer's Disease* 20(suppl.1): 3–15.

Richardson, H.L., Walker, A.M. and Horne, R.S.C. (2009) 'Maternal smoking impairs arousal patterns in sleeping infants.' *Sleep* 32(4): 515–521.

Richdale, A.L. (1999) 'Sleep problems in autism: Prevalence, cause, and intervention.' *Developmental Medicine and Child Neurology* 41: 60–66.

Richdale, A.L. and Prior, M.R. (1992) 'Urinary cortisol circadian rhythm in a group of high-functioning autistic children.' *Journal of Autism and Developmental Disorders* 22(3): 443–447.

Richdale, A.L. and Prior. M.R. (1995) 'The sleep/wake rhythm in children with autism.' *European Journal of Child and Adolescent Psychiatry* 4: 175–186.

Richdale, A.L. and Schreck, K.A. (2009) 'Sleep problems in autism spectrum disorders: Prevalence, nature, & possible biopsychosocial aetiologies.' *Sleep Medicine Reviews* 13: 403–411.

Richdale, A.L. and Wiggs, L. (2005) 'Behavioral approaches to the treatment of sleep problems in children with developmental disorders. What is the state of the art?' *International Journal of Behavioral and Consultation Therapy* 1(3): 165–189.

Richman, N. (1981a) 'A community survey of characteristics of 1–2 year olds with sleep disruptions.' *Journal of the American Academy of Child Psychiatry* 20: 281–91.

Richman, N. (1981b) 'Sleep problems in young children.' *Archives of Disease in Childhood* 56: 491–493.

Richman, N., Stevenson, J.E. and Graham, P.J. (1975) 'Prevalence of behaviour problems in 3-year-old children: An epidemiological study in a London borough.' *Journal of Child Psychology and Psychiatry* 16(4): 277–287.

Rickert, V.I. and Johnson, C.M. (1988) 'Reducing nocturnal awakening and crying episodes in infants and young children: A comparison between scheduled awakenings and systematic ignoring.' *Pediatrics* 81(2): 203–212.

Riemann, D. and Perlis, M.L. (2009) 'The treatments of chronic insomnia: A review of benzodiazepine receptor agonists and psychological and behavioral therapies.' *Sleep Medicine Reviews 13*(3): 205–214.

Ritvo, E., Ritvo, R., Yuwiler, A. and Brother, A. (1993) 'Elevated daytime melatonin concentrations in autism: A pilot study.' *European Child and Adolescent Psychiatry 2*: 75–78.

Rivkees, S.A. (2003) 'Developing circadian rhythmicity in infants.' *Pediatrics 112*: 373–381.

Rivkees, S.A., Mayes, L., Jacobs, J. and Gross, S.J. (2004) 'Rest-activity patterns of premature infants are regulated by cycled lighting.' *Pediatrics 113*: 833–839.

Robert, W. (1886) *Der Traum als Naturnothwendigkeit erklärt.* Hamburg: Seippel.

Rodriguez-Fragoso, L., Reyes-Esparza, J., Burchiel, S., Herrera-Ruiz, D. and Torres, E. (2008) 'Risks and benefits of commonly used herbal medicines in México.' *Toxicology and Applied Pharmacology 227*(1): 125–135.

Roenneberg, T., Kuehnle, T., Juda, M., Kantermann, T. *et al.* (2010) 'Epidemiology of the human circadian clock.' *Sleep Medicine Reviews 11*: 429–438.

Roenneberg, T., Kuehnle, T., Pramstaller, P.P., Ricken, J. *et al.* (2004) 'A marker for the end of adolescence.' *Current Biology 14*(24): R1038–R1039.

Roffwarg, H.P., Muzio, J.N. and Dement, W.C. (1966) 'Ontogenetic development of the human sleep-dream cycle.' *Science 152*: 604–619.

Rohdin, M., Fernell, E., Eriksson, M., Albåge, M., Lagercrantz, H. and Katz-Salamon, M. (2007) 'Disturbances in cardiorespiratory function during day and night in Rett syndrome.' *Pediatric Neurology 37*(5): 338–344.

Roky, R., Obál, F., Jr, Valatx, J.L., Bredow, S. *et al.* (1995) 'Prolactin and rapid eye movement sleep regulation.' *Sleep 18*(7): 536–542.

Rolland, A., Fleurentin, J., Lanhers, M.C., Younos, C. *et al.* (1991) 'Behavioural effects of the American traditional plant Eschscholzia californica: Sedative and anxiolytic properties.' *Planta Medica 57*(3): 212–216.

Rolland, A., Fleurentin, J., Lanhers, M.C., Misslin, R. *et al.* (2001) 'Neurophysiological effects of an extract of *Eschscholzia californica* Cham (Papaveraceae).' *Phytotherapy Research 15*: 377–381.

Romcy-Pereira, R.N., Leite, J.P. and Garcia-Cairasco, N. (2009) 'Synaptic plasticity along the sleep–wake cycle: Implications for epilepsy.' *Epilepsy & Behavior 14*: 47–53.

Rose, S.R. and Nisula, B.C. (1989) 'Circadian variation of thyrotropin in childhood.' *Journal of Clinical Endocrinology and Metabolism 68*: 1086–1090.

Rosenwasser, A.M. (2009) 'Functional neuroanatomy of sleep and circadian rhythms.' *Brain Research Reviews 61*: 281–306.

Roth, T. (2007) 'Insomnia: definition, prevalence, etiology, and consequences.' *Journal of Clinical Sleep Medicine 3*(suppl.5): S7–S10.

Roth II, T.C., Lesku, J.A., Amlaner, C.J. and Lima, S.L. (2006) 'A phylogenetic analysis of the correlates of sleep in birds.' *Journal of Sleep Research 15*: 395–402.

Roth II, T.C., Rattenborg, N.C. and Pravosudov, V.V. (2010) 'The ecological relevance of sleep: The trade-off between sleep, memory and energy conservation.' *Philosophical Transactions of the Royal Society B 365*: 945–959.

Rowe, P.H., Racey, P.A., Lincoln, G.A., Ellwood, M. *et al.* (1975) 'The temporal relationship between the secretion of luteinizing hormone and testosterone in man.' *Journal of Endocrinology 64*: 17–26.

Russell, W., Harrison, R.F., Smith, N., Darzy, K. *et al.* (2008) 'Free triiodothyronine has a distinct circadian rhythm that is delayed but parallels thyrotropin levels.' *Journal of Clinical Endocrinology and Metabolism 93*(6): 2300–2306.

Rutter, J., Reick, M. and McKnight, S.L. (2002) 'Metabolism and the control of circadian rhythms.' *Annual Review of Biochemistry 71*: 307–331.

Rybarczyk, B., Lopez, M., Benson, R., Alsten, C. and Stepanski, E. (2002) 'Efficacy of two behavioral treatment programs for comorbid geriatric insomnia.' *Psychology of Aging 17*: 288–298.

Sack, U., Burkhardt, U., Borte, M., Schadlich, H. *et al.* (1998) 'Age-dependent levels of select immunological mediators in sera of healthy children.' *Clinical and Diagnostic Laboratory Immunology 5*(1): 28–32.

Sadeghi, M., Daniel, V., Naujokat, C., Weimer, R. and Opelz, G. (2005) 'Strikingly higher interleukin (IL)1a, IL-1b and soluble interleukin-1 receptor antagonist (sIL-1RA) but similar IL-2, sIL-2R, IL-3, IL-4, IL-6, sIL-6R, IL-10, tumour necrosis factor (TNF)-a, transforming growth factor (TGF)-b 2 and interferon IFN-g urine levels in healthy females compared to healthy males: Protection against urinary tract injury.' *Clinical and Experimental Immunology 142*(2): 312–317.

Sadeh, A. (1994) 'Assessment of intervention for infant night waking: Parental reports and activity-based home monitoring.' *Journal of Consulting and Clinical Psychology 62*: 63–68.

Sadeh, A. (2004) 'A brief screening questionnaire for infant sleep problems: Validation and findings for an internet sample.' *Pediatrics 113*(6): 570–577.

Sadeh, A. (2005) 'Cognitive–behavioral treatment for childhood sleep disorders.' *Clinical Psychology Review 25*: 612–628.

Sadeh, A., Raviv, A. and Gruber, R. (2000) 'Sleep patterns and sleep disruptions in school-age children.' *Developmental Psychology 36*: 291–301.

Sadeh, A. and Sivan, Y. (2009) 'Clinical practice: Sleep problems during infancy.' *European Journal of Pediatrics 168*(10): 1159–1164.

Sajith, S.G. and Clarke, D. (2007) 'Melatonin and sleep disorders associated with intellectual disability: A clinical review.' *Journal of Intellectual Disability Research 51*(1): 2–13.

Sakurai, S., Nishijima, T., Takahashi, S., Yamauchi, K., Arihara, Z. and Takahashi, K. (2004) 'Clinical significance of daytime plasma orexin-A-like immunoreactivity concentrations in patients with obstructive sleep apnea hypopnea syndrome.' *Respiration 71*: 380–384.

Salzarulo, P. and Chevalier, A. (1983) 'Sleep problems in children and their relationship with early disturbances of the waking-sleeping rhythms.' *Sleep 6*: 47–51.

Sánchez-Ortuño, M.M., Bélanger, L., Ivers, H., LeBlanc, M. and Morin, C.M. (2009) 'The use of natural products for sleep: A common practice?' *Sleep Medicine 10*: 982–987.

Sangal, B., Owens, J., Allen, A., Sutton, V. *et al.* (2006) 'Effects of atomoxetine and methylphenidate on children with attention deficit hyperactivity disorder.' *Sleep 29*(12): 1573–1585.

Sanodiya, B.S., Thakur, G.S., Baghel, R.K., Prasad, G.B. and Bisen, P.S. (2009) 'Ganoderma lucidum: A potent pharmaceutical macrofungus.' *Current Pharmaceutical Biotechnology 10*(8): 717–742.

Saper, C.B., Chou, T. and Scammell, T.E. (2001) 'The sleep switch: Hypothalamic control of sleep and wakefulness.' *Trends in Neuroscience 24*: 726–731.

SARC (2001) *Within Our Reach: 2000 Annual Report,* Southwestern Autism Research Center (SARC), 1002 E. McDowell Rd., Suite A, Phoenix, AZ, 85006, USA.

Sarris, J. and Byrne, G.J. (2010) 'A systematic review of insomnia and complementary medicine.' *Sleep Medicine Reviews 15*(2): 99–106.

Scharf, M.T., Naidoo, N., Zimmerman, J.E. and Pack, A.I. (2008) 'The energy hypothesis of sleep revisited.' *Progress in Neurobiology 86*: 264–280.

Schenck, C.H., Hurwitz, T.D., O'Connor, K.A. and Mahowald, M.W. (1993) 'Additional categories of sleep-related eating disorders and the current status of treatment.' *Sleep 16*(5): 457–466.

Schenck, C.H., Hurwitz, T.D., Bundlie, S.R. and Mahowald, M.W. (1991) 'Sleep related eating disorders: Polysomnographic correlates of a heterogeneous syndrome distinct from daytime eating disorders.' *Sleep 14*: 419–431.

Schenck, C. and Mahowald, M. (1990) 'A polysomnographic, neurologic, psychiatric and clinical outcome report on 70 consecutive cases with REM sleep behavior disorder (RBD): Sustained clonazepam efficacy in 89.5% of 57 treated patients.' *Cleveland Clinic Journal of Medicine 57*(suppl.): 9–23.

Schenck, C.H. and Mahowald, M.W. (2002) 'REM sleep behavior disorder: Clinical, developmental and neuroscience perspectives 16 years after its formal identification in SLEEP.' *Sleep 25*(2): 120–138.

Schenck, C.H. and Mahowald, M.W. (2006) 'Topiramate therapy of sleep related eating disorder (SRED).' *Sleep 29*: A268.

Schenck, C.H., Connoy, D.A., Castellanos, M., Johnson, B. *et al.* (2005) 'Zolpidem-induced sleep-related eating disorder (SRED) in 19 patients.' *Sleep 28*: A259.

Schiller, H., Forster, A., Vonhoff, C., Hegger, M. *et al.* (2006) 'Sedating effects of *Humulus lupulus L.* extracts.' *Phytomedicine 13*(8): 535–541.

Schmoll, C., Lascaratos, G., Dhillon, B., Skene, D. *et al.* (2010) 'The role of retinal regulation of sleep in health and disease.' *Sleep Medicine Reviews 15*(2): 107–113.

Schnetz-Boutaud, N.C., Anderson, B.M., Brown, K.D., Wright, H.H. *et al.* (2009) 'Examination of tetrahydrobiopterin pathway genes in autism.' *Genes Brain and Behavior 8*(8): 753–757.

Schreck, K.A. (1997/1998) 'Preliminary analysis of sleep disorders in children with developmental disorders.' (Doctoral dissertation, Ohio State University, 1997. *Dissertation Abstracts International 58,* 3934.

Schreck, K.A. (2001) 'Behavioral treatments for sleep problems in autism: Empirically supported or just universally accepted?' *Behavioral Assessments 16*(4): 265–278.

Schreck, K.A. (2010) 'Sleep disorders the forgotten variable in behavior assessment: A guide for practitioners.' *Journal of Behavioral Health and Medicine 1*(1): 65–78.

Schreck, K.A.and Mulick, J.A. (2000) 'Parental report of sleep problems in children with autism.' *Journal of Autism and Developmental Disorders 30*(2): 127–135.

Schreck, K.A., Mulick, J.A. and Rojahn, J.A. (2003) 'Development of the behavioral evaluation of disorders of sleep scale.' *Journal of Child and Family Studies 12*(3): 349–360.

Schreck, K.A., Mulick, J.A. and Smith, A.F. (2004) 'Sleep problems as possible predictors of intensified symptoms of autism.' *Research in Developmental Disabilities 25*: 57–66.

Schuessler, P., Uhr, M., Ising, M., Schmid, D. *et al.* (2005) 'Nocturnal ghrelin levels-relationship to sleep EEG, the levels of growth hormone, ACTH and cortisol-and gender differences.' *Journal of Sleep Research 14*: 329–336.

Schulman, S. (2003) 'Addressing the potential risks associated with ephedra use: A review of recent efforts.' *Public Health Reports 118*: 487–492.

Schultz, S.T., Klonoff-Cohen, H.S., Wingard, D.L., Akshoomoff, N.A. *et al.* (2006) 'Breastfeeding, infant formula supplementation, and autistic disorder: The results of a parent survey.' *International Breastfeeding Journal 1*: 16, doi:10.1186/1746-4358-1-16.

Schwartz, J.R.L. (2008) 'Modafinil in the treatment of excessive sleepiness.' *Drug Design, Development and Therapy 2*: 71–85.

Schwartz, J., Hirshkowitz, M., Erman, M.K. and Schmidt-Nowara, W. (2003) 'Modafinil as adjunct therapy for daytime sleepiness in obstructive sleep apnea: A 12-week, open-label study.' *Chest 124*: 2192–2199.

Seicean, A., Redline, S., Seicean, S., Kirchner, H.L. *et al.* (2007) 'Association between short sleeping hours and overweight in adolescents: Results from a US Suburban High School survey.' *Sleep and Breathing 11*: 285–293.

Sejnowski, T.J. and Destexhe, A. (2000) 'Why do we sleep?' *Brain Research 886*: 208–223.

Seligman, M.E. and Yellen, A. (1987) 'What is a dream?' *Behaviour Research and Therapy 25*(1): 1–24.

Senju, A., Maeda, M., Kikuchi, Y., Hasegawa, T. *et al.* (2007) 'Absence of contagious yawning in children with autism spectrum disorder.' *Biology Letters 3*: 706–708.

Shakelle, P.G., Hardy, M.L., Morton, S.C., Maglione, M. *et al.* (2003) 'Efficacy and safety of ephedra and ephedrine for weight loss and athletic performance: a meta-analysis.' *Journal of the American Medical Association 289*: 1537–1545.

Shearer, W.T., Reuben, J.M., Mullington, J.M., Price, N.J. *et al.* (2001) 'Soluble TNF-alpha receptor 1 and IL-6 plasma levels in humans subjected to the sleep deprivation model of spaceflight.' *Journal of Allergy and Clinical Immunology 107*: 165–170.

Shibley, H.L., Malcolm, R.J. and Veatch, L.M. (2008) 'Adolescents with insomnia and substance abuse: Consequences and comorbidities.' *Journal of Psychiatric Practice 14*: 146–153.

Shimizu, I. (2000) 'Sho-saiko-to: Japanese herbal medicine for protection against hepatic fibrosis and carcinoma.' *Journal of Gastroenterology and Hepatology 15*(suppl.): 84–90.

Shinno, H., Kamei, M., Nakamura, Y., Inami, Y. and Horiguchi, J. (2008) 'Successful treatment with Yi-Gan San for rapid eye movement sleep behavior disorder.' *Progress in Neuropsychopharmacology and Biological Psychiatry 32*: 1749–1751.

Shirani, A. and St Louis, E.K. (2009) 'Illuminating rationale and uses for light therapy.' *Journal of Clinical Sleep Medicine 5*(2): 155–163.

Siegel, J.M. (2005a) 'Clues to the functions of mammalian sleep.' *Nature 437*: 1264–1271.

Siegel, J.M. (2005b) 'Functional implications of sleep development.' *PLoS Biology* 3(5): e178. doi: 10.1371/journal.pbio.0030178

Siegel, J.M. (2008) 'Do all animals sleep?' *Trends in Neurosciences* 31(4): 208–213.

Siegel, J.M. (2009a) 'The neurobiology of sleep.' *Seminars in Neurology* 29(4): 277–296.

Siegel, J.M. (2009b) 'Sleep viewed as a state of adaptive inactivity.' *Nature Neuroscience* 10: 747–753.

Silber, M.H., Ehrenberg, B.L., Allen, R.P., Buchfuhrer, R.A. *et al.* (2004) 'An algorithm for the management of restless legs syndrome.' *Mayo Clinic Proceedings* 79: 916–922.

Silvia, M. and Raffaele, F. (2010) 'Epidemiology and management of insomnia in children with autistic spectrum disorders.' *Pediatric Drugs* 12(2): 75–84.

Simakajornboon, N., Gozal, D., Vlasic, V., Mack, C. *et al.* (2003) 'Periodic limb movements in sleep and iron status in children.' *Sleep* 26: 735–738.

Simakajornboon, N., Kheirandish-Gozal, L., Gozal, D., Sharon, D. *et al.* (2006) 'A long term follow-up study of periodic limb movement disorders in children after iron therapy.' *Sleep* 29(suppl.): A76.

Simard, V., Nielsen, T.A., Tremblay, R.E., Boivin, M. and Montplaisir, J.Y. (2008) 'Longitudinal study of bad dreams in preschool-aged children: Prevalence, demographic correlates, risk and protective factors.' *Sleep* 31(1): 62–70.

Simon, C. and Brandenberger, G. (2002) 'Ultradian oscillations of insulin secretion in humans.' *Diabetes* 51(suppl.1): S258–S261.

Simonds, J.F. and Parraga, H. (1982) 'Prevalence of sleep disorders and sleep behaviors in children and adolescents.' *Journal of the American Academy of Child Psychiatry* 21: 383–388.

Simone, K.E. (2004) 'Abuse of dietary supplements is common and dangerous.' *Clinical and Forensic Toxicology News* September, 2–6.

Simonoff, E.A. and Stores, G. (1987) 'Controlled trial of trimeprazine tartrate for night waking.' *Archives of Disease in Childhood* 62: 253–257.

Simpson, D. (1998) 'Buchu – South Africa's amazing herbal remedy.' *Scottish Medical Journal* 43(6): 189–191.

Sinha, M.K., Ohannesian, J.P., Heiman, M.L., Kriauciunas, A. *et al.* (1996) 'Nocturnal rise of leptin in lean, obese, and non-insulin-dependent diabetes mellitus subjects.' *Journal of Clinical Investigation* 97: 1344–1347.

Siriwardena, A.N., Qureshi, M.Z., Dyas, J.V., Middleton, H. and Orner, R. (2008) 'Magic bullets for insomnia? Patients' use and experiences of newer (Z drugs) versus older (benzodiazepine) hypnotics for sleep problems in primary care.' *British Journal of General Practice* 58: 417–422.

Sitnick, S.L., Goodlin-Jones, B.L. and Anders, T.F. (2008) 'The use of actigraphy to study sleep disorders in preschoolers: Some concerns about detection of nighttime awakenings.' *Sleep* 31(3): 395–401.

Skinner, M.K. and Guerrero-Bosagna, C. (2009) 'Environmental signals and transgenerational epigenetics.' *Epigenomics* 1(1): 111–117.

Slifer, K.J., Avis, K.T. and Frutchey, R.A. (2008) 'Behavioral intervention to increase compliance with electroencephalographic procedures in children with developmental disabilities.' *Epilepsy and Behavior* 13(1): 189–195.

Smellie, J.M., McGrigor, V.S., Meadow, S.R., Rose, S.J. and Douglas, M.F. (1996) 'Nocturnal enuresis: A placebo controlled trial of two antidepressant drugs.' *Archives of Disease in Childhood* 75: 62–66.

Smith, A., Sturgess, W. and Gallagher, J. (1999) 'Effects of a low dose of caffeine given in different drinks on mood and performance.' *Human Psychopharmacology: Clinical and Experimental* 14(7): 473–482.

Smith, G.C.S. and Pell, J.P. (2003) 'Parachute use to prevent death and major trauma related to gravitational challenge: Systematic review of randomised controlled trials.' *British Medical Journal* 327: 1459–1461.

Smith, R., Ronald, J., Delaive, K., Walld, R. *et al.* (2002) 'What are obstructive sleep apnea patients being treated for prior to this diagnosis?' *Chest* 121: 164–172.

Smith, T., Scahill, L., Dawson, G., Guthrie, D. *et al.* (2007) 'Designing research studies on psychosocial interventions in autism.' *Journal of Autism and Developmental Disorders* 37(2): 354–366.

Snodgrass, W.R. (2001) 'Herbal products: Risks and benefits of use in children.' *Current Therapeutic Research* 62(10): 724–737.

Solberg, E.E., Holen, A., Ekeberg, O., Osterud, B. *et al.* (2004) 'The effects of long meditation on plasma melatonin and blood serotonin.' *Medical Science Monitor* 10: CR96–101.

Solms, M. (2000) 'Freudian dream theory today.' *The Psychologist 13*(12): 618–619.

Solms, M. (2004) 'Freud returns.' *Scientific American*, May, 81–88.

Souders, M.C., Mason, T.B.A., Valladares, O., Bucan, M. *et al.* (2009) 'Sleep behaviors and sleep quality in children with autism spectrum disorders.' *Sleep 32*(12): 1566–1578.

Spanagel, R., Pendyala, G., Abarca, C., Zghoul, T. *et al.* (2005) 'The clock gene *Per2* influences the glutamatergic system and modulates alcohol consumption.' *Nature Medicine 11*: 35–42.

Spiegel, K., Follenius, M., Simon, C., Saini, J. *et al.* (1994) 'Prolactin secretion and sleep.' *Sleep 17*: 20–27.

Spiegel, K., Tasali, E., Penev, P. and Van, C.E. (2004) 'Brief communication: Sleep curtailment in healthy young men is associated with decreased leptin levels, elevated ghrelin levels, and increased hunger and appetite.' *Annals of Internal Medicine 141*(11): 846–850.

Spock, B. (1946) *The Commonsense Book of Baby and Child Care*. New York, NY: Duell, Sloane & Pearce.

Spock, B. rev. and updated by Needleman, R. (2004) *The Commonsense Book of Baby and Child Care*, 8th edn. New York, NY: Pocket Books.

Spoormaker, V.I. (2008) 'A cognitive model of recurrent nightmares.' *International Journal of Dream Research 1*(1): 15–22.

Spoormaker, V.I. and Montgomery, P. (2008) 'Disturbed sleep in post-traumatic stress disorder: Secondary symptom or core feature.' *Sleep Medicine Reviews 12*: 169–184.

Spruyt, K. and Gozal, D. (2008) 'Mr. Pickwick and his child went on a field trip and returned almost empty handed… What we do not know and imperatively need to learn about obesity and breathing during sleep in children!' *Sleep Medicine Reviews 12*(5): 335–338.

Staunton, H. (2005) 'Mammalian sleep.' *Naturwissenschaften 92*: 203–220.

Stein, M.A. (1999) 'Unravelling sleep problems in treated and untreated children with ADHD.' *Journal of Child and Adolescent Psychopharmacology 9*(3): 157–168.

Stepanova, I., Nevsimalova, S. and Hanusova, J. (2005) 'Rhythmic movement disorder in sleep persisting into childhood and adulthood.' *Sleep 28*: 851–857.

Stepanski, E.J. and Wyatt, J.K. (2003) 'Use of sleep hygiene in the treatment of insomnia.' *Sleep Medicine Reviews 7*(3): 215–225.

Stephenson, J.B.P. (1990) *Fits and Faints. Clinics in Developmental Medicine, 109*. London: Mackeith Press.

Steptoe, A., Peacey, V. and Wardle, J. (2006) 'Sleep duration and health in young adults.' *Archives of Internal Medicine 166*: 1689–1692.

Stickgold, R. (2005) 'Sleep-dependent memory consolidation.' *Nature 437*: 1272–1278.

Stickgold, R.J., Malia, A., Maguire, D., Roddenberry, D. and O'Connor, M. (2000) 'Replaying the game: Hypnagogic images in normals and amnesics.' *Science 290*: 350–353.

Stigler, K.A., Posey, D.J. and McDougle. C.J. (2006) 'Ramelteon for insomnia in two youths with autistic disorder.' *Journal of Child and Adolescent Psychopharmacology 16*(5): 631–636.

Stojanovski, S.D., Rasu, R.S., Balkrishnan, R. and Nahata, M.C. (2007) 'Trends in medication prescribing for pediatric sleep difficulties in US outpatient settings.' *Sleep 30*(8): 1013–1017.

Stolz, S. and Aldrich, M. (1991) 'REM sleep behavior disorder associated with caffeine abuse.' *Sleep Research 20*: 341.

Stores, G. (1999) 'Recognition and management of narcolepsy.' *Archives of Disease in Childhood 81*: 519–524. (This appears in PubMed incorrectly as 1998.)

Stores, G. (2001) 'Dramatic parasomnias.' *Journal of the Royal Society of Medicine*, *94*(4):173–176.

Stores, G. and Wiggs, L. (1998) 'Abnormal sleep patterns associated with autism: A brief review of research findings, assessment methods and treatment strategies.' *Autism 2*: 157–169.

Stores, G., Zaiwalla, Z. and Bergel, N. (1991) 'Frontal lobe complex partial seizures in children: a form of epilepsy at particular risk of misdiagnosis.' *Developmental Medicine and Child Neurology 3*: 998–1009.

Strausz, T., Ahlberg, J., Lobbezoo, F., Restrepo, C.C. *et al.* (2010) 'Awareness of tooth grinding and clenching from adolescence to young adulthood: A nine-year follow-up.' *Journal of Oral Rehabilitation 37*(7): 497–500.

Strean, W.B. (2009) 'Laughter prescription.' *Canadian Family Physician 55*: 965–967.

Striegel-Moore, R.H., Dohm, F.A., Hook, J.M., Schreiber, G.B. *et al.* (2005) 'Night eating syndrome in young adult women: Prevalence and correlates.' *International Journal of Eating Disorders 37*: 200–206.

Stroe, A.F., Roth, T., Jefferson, C., Hudgel, D.W. *et al.* (2010) 'Comparative levels of excessive daytime sleepiness in common medical disorders.' *Sleep Medicine 11*(9): 890–896.

Stunkard, A.J., Allison, K.C., Lundgren, J.D., Martino, N.S. *et al.* (2006) 'A paradigm for facilitating pharmacotherapy at a distance: Sertraline treatment of the night eating syndrome.' *Journal of Clinical Psychiatry 67*(10): 1568–1572.

Su, C., Miao, J., Liu, Y., Liu, R. *et al.* (2009) 'Multiple forms of rhythmic movements in an adolescent boy with rhythmic movement disorder.' *Clinical Neurology and Neurosurgery 111*: 896–899.

Tabandeh, H., Lockley, S.W., Buttery, R., Skene, D.J. *et al.* (1998) 'Disturbance of sleep in blindness.' *American Journal of Ophthalmology 126*: 707–712.

Tachibana, N., Shinde, A., Ikeda, A., Akiguchi, I., Kimura, J. and Shibasaki, H. (1996) 'Supplementary motor area seizure resembling sleep disorder.' *Sleep 19*: 811–816.

Tager-Flusberg, H. (1999) 'A psychological approach to understanding the social and language impairments in autism.' *International Review of Psychiatry 11*(4): 325–334.

Taheri, S., Lin, L., Austin, D., Young, T. and Mignot, E. (2004) 'Short sleep duration is associated with reduced leptin, elevated ghrelin, and increased body mass index.' *PLoS Medicine 1*: e62.

Tahmaz, L., Kibar, Y., Yildirim, I., Ceylan, S. and Dayanc, M. (2000) 'Combination therapy of imipramine with oxybutynin in children with enuresis nocturna.' *Urologia Internationalis 65*(3): 135–139.

Taibi, D.M., Landis, C.A., Petry, H. and Vitiello, M.V. (2007) 'A systematic review of valerian as a sleep aid: Safe but not effective.' *Sleep Medicine Reviews 11*: 209–230.

Taira, M., Takase, M. and Sasaki, H. (1998) 'Sleep disorder in children with autism.' *Psychiatry and Clinical Neurosciences 52*(2): 182–183.

Takahashi, Y., Kipnis, D. and Daughaday, W. (1968) 'Growth hormone secretion during sleep.' *Journal of Clinical Investigation 47*(9): 2079–2090.

Takase, M., Taira, M. and Sasaki, H. (1998) 'Sleep-wake rhythm of autistic children.' *Psychiatry and Clinical Neurosciences 52*(2): 181–182.

Taneja, P., Ogier, M., Brooks-Harris, G., Schmid, D.A. *et al.* (2009) 'Pathophysiology of locus ceruleus neurons in a mouse model of Rett syndrome.' *Journal of Neuroscience 29*(39): 12187–12195.

Tanguay, P.E. *et al.* (1976) 'Rapid eye movement (REM) activity in normal and autistic children during REM sleep.' *Journal of Autism and Child Schizophrenia 6*(3): 275–288.

Tani, P., Lindberg, N., Nieminen-von Wendt, T., von Wendt, L. *et al.* (2003) 'Insomnia is a frequent finding in adults with Asperger syndrome.' *BMC Psychiatry: 3.* Available at www.biomedcentral.com/1471-244X/3/12, accessed 14 September 2011.

Tani, P., Lindberg, N., Joukamaa, M., Nieminen-von Wendt, T. *et al.* (2004) 'Sleep in young adults with Asperger syndrome.' *Neuropsychobiology 50*: 147–152.

Taveras, E.M., Rifas-Shiman, S.L. Oken, E. Gunderson, E.P. and Gillman, M.W. (2008) 'Short sleep duration in infancy and risk of childhood overweight.' *Archives of Pediatric and Adolescent Medicine 162*(4): 305–311.

Taylor, D.J., Mallory, L.J., Lichstein, K.L., Durrence, H.H. *et al.* (2007) 'Comorbidity of chronic insomnia with medical problems.' *Sleep 30*: 213–218.

Taylor, F.B., Martin, P., Thompson, C., Williams, J. *et al.* (2008) 'Prazosin effects on objective sleep measures and clinical symptoms in civilian trauma posttraumatic stress disorder: A placebo-controlled study.' *Biological Psychiatry 63*: 629–632.

Taylor, J., Holmes, G. and Walshe, F. (eds) (1958) *Selected writings of John Hughlings Jackson: Evolution and Dissolution of the Nervous System.* London: Staples.

Temple, J.L. (2009) 'Caffeine use in children: What we know, what we have left to learn, and why we should worry.' *Neuroscience and Biobehavioral Reviews 33*(6): 793–806.

Terman, M. (2007) 'Evolving applications of light therapy.' *Sleep Medicine Reviews 11*(6): 497–507.

Thannickal, T.C., Nienhuis, R. and Siegel, J.M. (2009) 'Localized loss of hypocretin (orexin) cells in narcolepsy without cataplexy.' *Sleep 32*(8): 993–998.

Thapan, K., Arendt, J. and Skene, D.J. (2001) 'An action spectrum for melatonin suppression: Evidence for a novel non-rod, non-cone photoreceptor system in humans.' *Journal of Physiology 535*(1): 261–267.

Thelander, G., Johnsson, A.K., Personne, M., Forsberg, G.S. *et al.* (2010) 'Caffeine fatalities – do sales restrictions prevent intentional intoxications?' *Clinical Toxicology 48*(4): 354–358.

Thien, F.C. (2001) 'Chamomile tea enema anaphylaxis.' *Medical Journal of Australia 175*(1): 54.

Thirumalai, S., Shubin, R. and Robinson, R. (2002) 'Rapid eye movement sleep behavior disorder in children with autism.' *Journal of Child Neurology 17*(3): 173–178.

Thomas, A., Nallur, D.G., Jones, N. and Deslandes, P.N. (2009) 'Diphenhydramine abuse and detoxification: A brief review and case report.' *Journal of Psychopharmacology 23*(1): 101–105.

Thompson, B.L. and Levitt, P. (2010) 'The clinical-basic interface in defining pathogenesis in disorders of neurodevelopmental origin.' *Neuron 67*: 702–712.

Thompson, M.D., Comings, D.E., Abu-Ghazalah, R., Jereseh, Y. *et al.* (2004) 'Variants of the orexin2/hcrt2 receptor gene identified in patients with excessive daytime sleepiness and patients with Tourette's syndrome comorbidity.' *American Journal of Medical Genetics B: Neuropsychiatric Genetics 129B*(1): 69–75.

Thompson, S.B.N. (2010) 'The dawn of the yawn: Is yawning a warning? Linking neurological disorders.' *Medical Hypotheses 75*: 630–633.

Thorburn, P.T. and Riha, R.L. (2010) 'Skin disorders and sleep in adults: Where is the evidence?' *Sleep Medicine Reviews 14*: 351–358.

Tikotzky, L. and Sadeh, A. (2010) 'The role of cognitive–behavioral therapy in behavioral childhood insomnia.' *Sleep Medicine 11*: 686–691.

Tinuper, P., Provini, F., Bisulli, F., Vignatelli, L. *et al.* (2007) 'Movement disorders in sleep: Guidelines for differentiating epileptic from non-epileptic motorphenomena arising from sleep.' *Sleep Medicine Reviews 11*: 255–267.

Toma, C., Rossi, M., Sousa, I., Blasi, F. *et al.* (2007) 'Is ASMT a susceptibility gene for autism spectrum disorders? A replication study in European populations.' *Molecular Psychiatry 12*: 977–979.

Tononi, G. and Cirelli, C. (2006) 'Sleep function and synaptic homeostasis.' *Sleep Medicine Reviews 10*: 49–62.

Tooley, G.A., Armstrong, S.M., Norman, T.R. and Sali, A. (2000) 'Acute increases in night-time plasma melatonin levels following a period of meditation.' *Biological Psychology 53*: 69–78.

Tordjman, S., Anderson, G.M., Pichard, N., Charbuy, H. and Touitou, Y. (2005) 'Nocturnal excretion of 6-sulphatoxymelatonin in children and adolescents with autistic disorder.' *Biological Psychiatry 57*(2): 134–138.

Toro, R., Konyukh, M., Delorme, R., Leblond, C. *et al.* (2010) 'Key role for gene dosage and synaptic homeostasis in autism spectrum disorders.' *Trends in Genetics 20*: 1–10, doi:10.1016/j.tig.2010.05.007.

Touchon, J., Baldy-Moulinier, M., Billiard, M., Besset, A. *et al.* (1987) 'Organisation du sommeil dans l'epilepsie recente du lobe temporal avant et apres traitment par carbamazepine.' [Sleep organisation in recent-onset temporal lobe epilepsy before and after treatment with carbamazepine]. *Revue Neurologique 143*: 462–467.

Tovar, R.T. and Petzel, R.M. (2009) 'Herbal Toxicity.' *Disease-a-Month 55*(10): 592–641.

Tractenberg, R.E. and Singer, C.M. (2007) 'Sleep and sleep disturbance: From genes to dreams.' *Cellular and Molecular Life Sciences 64*: 1171–1173.

Trachtman, J.N. (2010) 'Vision and the hypothalamus.' *Optometry 81*: 100–115.

Trenell, M.I., Marshall, N.S. and Rogers, N.L. (2007) 'Sleep and metabolic control: Waking to a problem?' *Clinical and Experimental Pharmacology and Physiology 34*(1): 1–9.

Trenkwalder, C., Hening, W.A., Montagna, P., Oertel, W.H. *et al.* (2008) 'Treatment of restless legs syndrome: An evidence-based review and implications for clinical practice.' *Movement Disorders 23*: 2267–2302.

Troxel, W.M. (2010) 'It's more than sex: Exploring the dyadic nature of sleep and implications for health.' *Psychosomatic Medicine 72*(6): 578–586.

Tung, A., Takase, L., Fornal, C. and Jacobs, B. (2005) 'Effects of sleep deprivation and recovery sleep upon cell proliferation in adult rat dentate gyrus.' *Neuroscience 134*: 721–723.

Turek, F.W. and Gillette, M.U. (2004) 'Melatonin, sleep, and circadian rhythms: Rationale for development of specific melatonin agonists.' *Sleep Medicine 5*: 523–532.

Turk, J. (2003) 'Melatonin supplementation for severe and intractable sleep disturbance in young people with genetically determined developmental disabilities: Short review and commentary.' *Journal of Medical Genetics 40*(11): 793–796.

Turker, A.U. and Camper, N.D. (2002) 'Biological activity of common mullein, a medicinal plant.' *Journal of Ethnopharmacology 82*: 117–125.

Ueno, L.M., Drager, L.F., Rodrigues, A.C.T., Rondon, M.U.P.B. *et al.* (2009) 'Effects of exercise training in patients with chronic heart failure and sleep apnea.' *Sleep 32*(5): 637–647.

Valenti, G., Laera, A., Gouraud, S., Pace, G. *et al.* (2002) 'Low-calcium diet in hypercalciuric enuretic children restores AQP2 excretion and improves clinical symptoms.' *American Journal of Physiology – Renal Fluid & Electrolyte Physiology 283*(5): F895–F903.

Valenstein, E.S. (2005) *The War of the Soup and the Sparks – the Discovery of Neurotransmitters and the Dispute over How Nerves Communicate.* New York, NY: Columbia University Press.

Valicenti-McDermott, M.R. and Demb, H. (2006) 'Clinical effects and adverse reactions of off-label use of aripiprazole in children and adolescents with developmental disabilities.' *Journal of Child and Adolescent Psychopharmacology 16*(5): 549–560.

Valldeoriola, F., Santamaria, J., Graus, F. and Tolosa, E. (1993) 'Absence of REM sleep, altered NREM sleep and supranuclear horizontal gaze palsy caused by a lesion of the pontine tegmentum.' *Sleep 16*(2): 184–188.

Valli, K., Revonsuo, A., Palkas, O., Ismail, K.H. *et al.* (2005) 'The threat simulation theory of the evolutionary function of dreaming: Evidence from dreams of traumatized children.' *Consciousness and Cognition 14*: 188–218.

Vallieres, A., Morin, C.M. and Guay, B. (2005) 'Sequential combinations of drug and cognitive behavioural therapy for chronic insomnia: An exploratory study.' *Behaviour Research and Therapy 43*: 1611–1630.

Van Cauter, E. and Knutson, K.L. (2008) 'Sleep and the epidemic of obesity in children and adults.' *European Journal of Endocrinology 159*: S59–S66.

Van Cauter, E., Leproult, R. and Plat, L. (2000) Age-related changes in slow-wave sleep and REM sleep in relationship with growth hormone and cortisol levels in healthy men.' *Journal of the American Medical Association 284*: 961–868.

van der Heijden, K.B., Smits, M.G. and Gunning, W.B. (2006) 'Sleep hygiene and actigraphically evaluated sleep characteristics in children with ADHD and chronic sleep onset insomnia.' *Journal of Sleep Research 15*: 55–62.

Van de Walle, J., Stockner, M., Raes, A. and Nørgaard, J.P. (2007) 'Desmopressin 30 years in clinical use: A safety review.' *Current Drug Safety 2*(3): 232–238.

Van de Walle, J., Van Herzeele, C. and Raes, A. (2010) 'Is there still a role for desmopressin in children with primary monosymptomatic nocturnal enuresis?: A focus on safety issues.' *Drug Safety 33*(4): 261–271.

Van IJzendoorn, M.H., Goossens, F.A., Tavecchio, L.W.C., Vergeer, M.M. and Hubbard, F.O.A. (1983) 'Attachment to soft objects: Its relationship with attachment to the mother and with thumbsucking.' *Child Psychiatry and Human Development 14*(2): 97–105.

van Leeuwen, W.M.A., Lehto, M., Karisola, P., Lindholm, H. *et al.* (2009) 'Sleep restriction increases the risk of developing cardiovascular diseases by augmenting proinflammatory responses through IL-17 and CRP.' *PLoS ONE 4*(2): e4589, doi:10.1371/journal.pone.0004589.

van Liempt, S., Vermetten, E., Geuze, E. and Westenberg, H. (2006) 'Pharmacotherapeutic treatment of nightmares and insomnia in posttraumatic stress disorder: An overview of the literature.' *Annals of the New York Academy of Science 1071*: 502–507.

van Litsenburg, R.R., Waumans, R.C., van den Berg, G. and Gemke, R.J. (2010) 'Sleep habits and sleep disturbances in Dutch children: A population-based study.' *European Journal of Pediatrics 169*(8): 1009–1015.

Vandekerckhove, M. and Cluydts, R. (2010) 'The emotional brain and sleep: An intimate relationship.' *Sleep Medicine Reviews 14*: 219–226.

van Poecke, A.J. and Cunliffe, C. (2009) 'Chiropractic treatment for primary nocturnal enuresis: A case series of 33 consecutive patients.' *Journal of Manipulative and Physiological Therapy 32*: 675–681.

Varan, B., Saatci, U., Ozen, S., Bakkaloglu, A. and Besbas, N. (1996) 'Efficacy of oxybutynin, pseudoephedrine and indomethacin in the treatment of primary nocturnal enuresis.' *Turkish Journal of Pediatrics 38*(2): 155–159.

Varmus, H. (2010) *The Art and Politics of Science*. New York, NY: Norton.

Veerman, S.R., Dijkstra, H.N. and Liefting-Kluft, I. (2010) 'Levensbedreigende onthoudingsverschijnselen door gammahydroxyboterzuur.' [Life threatening symptoms of withdrawal of gamma-hydroxybutyrate] *Tijdschrift voor Psychiatrie 52*(6): 411–416.

Vendrame, M., Havaligi, N., Matadeen-Ali, C., Adams, R. and Kothare, S.V. (2008) 'Narcolepsy in children: A single-center clinical experience.' *Pediatric Neurology 38*(5): 314–320.

Vera, F.M., Manzaneque, J.M., Maldonado, E.F., Carranque, G.A. *et al.* (2009) 'Subjective sleep quality and hormonal modulation in long-term yoga practitioners.' *Biological Psychology 81*: 164–168.

Verkasalo, P.K., Lillberb, K., Stevens, R.G., Hublin, C. *et al.* (2005) 'Sleep duration and breast cancer: A prospective cohort study.' *Cancer Research 65*(20): 9595–9600.

Vernet, C. and Arnulf, I. (2009) 'Idiopathic hypersomnia with and without long sleep time: A controlled series of 75 patients.' *Sleep 32*(6): 753–759.

Vetrugno, R., Manconi, M., Ferini-Strambi, L., Provini, F. *et al.* (2006) 'Nocturnal eating: Sleep-related eating disorder or night eating syndrome? A videopolysomnographic study.' *Sleep 29*: 949–954.

Vickers, A., Zollman, C. and Lee, R. (1999) 'Herbal medicine.' *British Medical Journal 319*: 1050–1053.

Viola, H., Wasowski, C. and Levi de Stein, M. (1995) 'Apigenin, a component of *Matricaria recutita* flowers, is a central benzodiazepine receptors-ligand with anxiolytic effects.' *Planta Medica 61*: 213–216.

Visser, G.H.A., Poelmann-Weesjes, G., Cohen, T.M.N. and Bekedam, D.J. (1987) 'Fetal behavior at 30 to 32 weeks of gestation.' *Pediatric Research 22*: 655–658.

Vgontzas, A.N., Zoumakis, E., Bixler, E.O., Lin, H.-M. *et al.* (2004) 'Adverse effects of modest sleep restriction on sleepiness, performance, and inflammatory cytokines.' *Journal of Clinical Endocrinology & Metabolism 89*(5): 2119–2126.

Vogt, M., Lehnert, T., Till, H. and Rolle, U. (2010) 'Evaluation of different modes of combined therapy in children with monosymptomatic nocturnal enuresis.' *British Journal of Urology International 105*(10): 1456–1459.

von Schantz, M. (2008) 'Phenotypic effects of genetic variability in human clock genes on circadian and sleep parameters.' *Journal of Genetics 87*: 513–519.

von Schantz, M. and Archer, S.N. (2003) 'Clocks, genes and sleep.' *Journal of the Royal Society of Medicine 96*: 486–489.

Vorona, R.D. (2008) 'Sleep, Sleep Disorders, and the Endocrine System.' In C.W. Attwood, Jr (ed.) *ACCP Sleep Medicine Board Review Syllabus Book*. Northwood, IL: American College of Chest Physicians (available from www.chestnet.org).

Vorona, R.D. and Ware, J.C. (2002) 'Exacerbation of REM sleep behavior disorder by chocolate ingestion: A case report.' *Sleep Medicine 3*: 365–367.

Wachowski, A. and Wachowski, L. (1999) *The Matrix*. Village Roadshow Pictures, Silver Pictures; Distributor: Warner Bros.

Wafford, K.A. and Ebert, B. (2006) 'Gaboxadol – a new awakening in sleep.' *Current Opinion in Pharmacology 6*(1): 30–36.

Wagner, M.H. and Berry, R.B. (2007) 'An obese female with Prader-Willi syndrome and daytime sleepiness.' *Journal of Clinical Sleep Medicine 3*(6): 645–647.

Waldschutz, R. and Klein, P. (2008) 'The homeopathic preparation Neurexan® vs. valerian for the treatment of insomnia: An observational study.' *The Scientific World Journal 8*: 411–420.

Walker, M.P. (2009) 'The role of sleep in cognition and emotion.' The Year in Cognitive Neuroscience 2009: *Annals of the New York Academy of Science 1156*: 168–197.

Walker, M.P., Brakefield, T., Hobson, J.A. and Stickgold, R. (2003) 'Dissociable stages of human memory consolidation and reconsolidation.' *Nature 425*: 616–620.

Walker, M.P., Brakefield, T., Seidman, J., Morgan, A. *et al.* (2003) 'Sleep and the time course of motor skill learning.' *Learning and Memory 10*: 275–284.

Walker, M.P. and Harvey, A.G. (2010) 'Obligate symbiosis: Sleep and affect.' *Sleep Medicine Reviews 14*: 215–217.

Walters, A.S., Mandelbaum, D.E., Lewin, D.S., Kugler, S. *et al.* (2000) 'Dopaminergic therapy in children with restless legs/periodic limb movements in sleep and ADHD, Dopaminergic Therapy Study Group.' *Pediatric Neurology 22*: 182–186.

Walters, A.S., Silvestri, R., Zucconi, M., Chandrashekariah, R. and Konofal, E. (2008) 'Review of the possible relationship and hypothetical links between attention deficit hyperactivity disorder (ADHD) and the simple sleep related movement disorders, parasomnias, hypersomnias, and circadian rhythm disorders.' *Journal of Clinical Sleep Medicine 4*(6): 591–600.

Wang, Q., Yang, X., Zhang, B., Yang, X. and Wang, K. (2007) 'The anxiolytic effect of cinnabar involves changes of serotonin levels.' *European Journal of Pharmacology 565*: 132–137.

Wanmuang, H., Leopairut, J., Kositchaiwat, C., Wananukul, W. and Bunyaratvej, S. (2007) 'Fatal fulminant hepatitis associated with Ganoderma lucidum (Lingzhi) mushroom powder.' *Journal of the Medical Association of Thailand 90*(1): 179–181.

Watanabe, K., Matsuura, K., Gao, P., Hottenbacher, L. *et al.* (2010) 'Traditional Japanese Kampo Medicine: Clinical research between modernity and traditional medicine – the state of research and methodological suggestions for the future.' *CAM. Evidence-Based Complementary and Alternative Medicine*, 513842, doi:10.1093/ecam/neq067

Waters, W.F., Hurry, M.J., Binks, P.G., Carney, C.E. *et al.* (2003) 'Behavioral and hypnotic treatments for insomnia subtypes.' *Behavioral Sleep Medicine 1*(2): 81–101.

Weaver, T.E. (2001) 'Outcome measurement in sleep medicine practice and research. Part 1: assessment of symptoms, subjective and objective daytime sleepiness, health-related quality of life and functional status.' *Sleep Medicine Reviews 5*(2): 103–128.

Wehrle, R., Kaufmann, C., Wetter, T.C., Holsboer, F. *et al.* (2007) 'Functional microstates within human REM sleep: First evidence from fMRI of a thalamocortical network specific for phasic REM periods.' *European Journal of Neuroscience 25*: 863–871.

Weidong, W., Fang, W., Yang, Z., Menghan, L. and Xueyu, L. (2009) 'Two patients with narcolepsy treated by hypnotic psychotherapy.' *Sleep Medicine 10*: 1167–1169.

Weikel. J.C., Wichniak, A., Ising, M., Brunner, H. *et al.* (2003) 'Ghrelin promotes slow-wave sleep in humans.' *American Journal of Physiology, Endocrinology and Metabolism 284*(2): E407–415.

Weiskop, S., Richdale, A. and Matthews, J. (2005) 'Behavioural treatment to reduce sleep problems in children with autism or Fragile X syndrome.' *Developmental Medicine and Child Neurology 47*: 94–104.

Weiss, L.A., Kosova, G., Delahanty, R.J., Jiang, L. *et al.* (2006) 'Variation in ITGB3 is associated with whole-blood serotonin level and autism susceptibility.' *European Journal of Human Genetics 76*: 1050–1056.

Werneke, U., Turner, T. and Priebe, S. (2006) 'Complementary medicines in psychiatry: Review of effectiveness and safety.' *British Journal of Psychiatry 188*: 109–121.

Werner, H., LeBourgeois, M.K., Geiger, A. and Jenni, O.G. (2009) 'Assessment of chronotype in four- to eleven-year-old children: Reliability and validity of the Children's Chronotype Questionnaire.' *Chronobiology International 26*(5): 992–1014.

Whelan-Goodinson, R., Ponsford, J., Johnston, L. and Grant, F. (2009) 'Psychiatric disorders following traumatic brain injury: Their nature and frequency.' *Journal of Head Trauma Rehabilitation 24*(5): 324–332.

Widmalm, S.E., Christiansen, R.L. and Gunn, S.M. (1995) 'Oral parafunctions as temporomandibular disorder risk factors in children.' *Cranio: the Journal of Craniomandibular Practice 13*(4): 242–246.

Wietske, R., Kox, D., den Herder, C., van Tintern, H. and de Vries, N. (2007) 'One stage multilevel surgery (uvulopalatopharyngoplasty, hyoid suspension, radiofrequent ablation of the tongue base with/ without genioglossus advancement), in obstructive sleep apnea syndrome.' *European Archives of Oto-Rhino-Laryngology 264*(4): 439–444.

Wiggs, L. and Stores, G. (1996) 'Severe sleep disturbance and daytime challenging behaviour in children with severe learning disabilities.' *Journal of Intellectual Disability Research 40*(6): 518–528.

Wiggs, L. and Stores, G. (2004) 'Sleep patterns and sleep disorders in children with autistic spectrum disorders: Insights using parent report and actigraphy.' *Developmental Medicine and Child Neurology 46*: 372–380.

Williams, K., Wheeler, D.M., Silove, N. and Hazell, P. (2010) 'Selective serotonin reuptake inhibitors (SSRIs) for autism spectrum disorders (ASD).' *Cochrane Database Systematic Reviews* Aug 4(8): CD004677.

Williams, P.G., Sears, L.L. and Allard, A. (2004) 'Sleep problems in children with autism.' *Journal of Sleep Research 13*: 265–268.

Williams, T.I. (2006) 'Evaluating effects of aromatherapy massage on sleep in children with autism: A pilot study.' *eCAM 3*(3): 373–377.

Williams, K., Scheimann, A., Sutton, V., Hayslett, E. and Glaze, D.G. (2008) 'Sleepiness and sleep disordered breathing in Prader-Willi syndrome: Relationship to genotype, growth hormone therapy, and body composition.' *Journal of Clinical Sleep Medicine, 4*(2): 111–118.

Willis, J. (2009) 'How students' sleepy brains fail them.' *Kappa Delta Pi Record*, Summer: 158–162.

Wilson, M.A. and McNaughton, B.L. (1994) 'Reactivation of hippocampal ensemble memories during sleep.' *Science 265*: 676–679.

Wilson, S.J., Nutt, D.J., Alford, C., Argyropoulos, S.V. *et al.* (2010) 'British Association for Psychopharmacology consensus statement on evidence-based treatment of insomnia, parasomnias and circadian rhythm disorders.' *Journal of Psychopharmacology 24*(11): 1577–1601.

Wimpory, D., Nicholas, B. and Nash, S. (2002) 'Social timing, clock genes and autism: A new hypothesis.' *Journal of Intellectual Disability Research 46*(4): 352–358.

Wing, Y.K. (2001) 'Herbal treatment of insomnia.' *Hong Kong Medical Journal 7*(4): 392–402.

Winkelman, J.W. and James, L. (2004) 'Serotonergic antidepressants are associated with REM sleep without atonia.' *Sleep 27*: 317–321.

Winrow, C.J., Williams, D.L., Kasarskis, A., Millstein, J. *et al.* (2009) 'Uncovering the genetic landscape for multiple sleep-wake traits.' *PLoS ONE 4*(4): e5161, doi:10.1371/journal.pone.0005161.

Wirojanan, J., Jacquemont, S., Diaz, R., Bacalman, S. *et al.* (2009) 'The efficacy of melatonin for sleep problems in children with autism, fragile X syndrome, or autism and fragile X syndrome.' *Journal of Clinical Sleep Medicine 5*: 145–150.

Wise, M.S., Arand, D.L., Auger, R.R., Stephen N. *et al.* (2007) 'Treatment of narcolepsy and other hypersomnias of central origin: An American Academy of Sleep Medicine review.' *Sleep 30*(12): 1712–1727.

Wise, M.S. and Lynch, J. (2001) 'Narcolepsy in children.' *Seminars in Pediatric Neurology 8*: 198–206.

Wojtowicz, J.M., Yarema, M.C. and Wax, P.M. (2008) 'Withdrawal from gamma-hydroxybutyrate, 1, 4-butanediol and gamma-butyrolactone: A case report and systematic review.' *Canadian Journal of Emergency Medicine 10*(1): 69–74.

Wolfson, A., Futterman, A. and Lacks, P. (1992) 'Effects of parent training on infant sleeping patterns, parents' stress, and perceived parental competence.' *Journal of Consulting and Clinical Psychology 60*: 41–48.

Wolfson, A.R. and Carskadon, M.A. (1998) 'Sleep schedules and daytime functioning in adolescents.' *Child Development 69*(4): 875–887.

Wolfson, A.R. and Carskadon, M.A. (2003) 'Understanding adolescents' sleep patterns and school performance: A critical appraisal.' *Sleep Medicine Reviews 7*(6): 491–506.

Wolfson, P. and Hoffmann, D.L. (2003) 'An investigation into the efficacy of scutellaria lateriflora in healthy volunteers.' *Alternative Therapies in Health and Medicine 9*: 74–78.

Wong, M.M., Brower, K.H. and Zucker, R.A. (2009) 'Childhood sleep problems, early onset of substance use and behavioral problems in adolescence.' *Sleep Medicine 10*(7): 787–796.

Wood, J.J., Piacentini, J.C., Southam-Gerow, M. and Sigman, M. (2006) 'Family cognitive behavioral therapy for child anxiety disorders.' *Journal of the American Academy of Child and Adolescent Psychiatry 45*(3): 314–321.

Wrangham, R. (2009) *Catching Fire: How Cooking Made Us Human.* London: Profile Books.

Wright, A. (2008) 'Evidence-based assessment and management of childhood enuresis.' *Paediatrics and Child Health 18*(12): 561–567.

Wright, B., Sims, D., Smart, S., Alwazeer, A. *et al.* (2010) 'Melatonin versus placebo in children with autism spectrum conditions and severe sleep problems not amenable to behaviour management strategies: A randomized controlled crossover trial.' *Journal of Autism and Developmental Disorders 41*(2): 175–184.

Wright, C.E., Valdimarsdottir, H.B., Erblich, J., and Bovbjerg, D.H. (2007) 'Poor sleep the night before an experimental stress task is associated with reduced cortisol reactivity in healthy women.' *Biological Psychology 74*: 319–327.

Wu, H.Q. and Han, X.W. (1999) 'The treatment of insomnia with a combination of Radix salviae miltiorrhizae and Fructus schisandrae in 48 patients' [in Chinese]. *China's Naturopathy 7*: 38.

Wulff, K., Porcheret, K., Cussans, E. and Foster, R.G. (2009) 'Sleep and circadian rhythm disturbances: Multiple genes and multiple phenotypes.'*Current Opinion in Genetics and Development 19*: 237–246.

Wyatt, R.J., Engelman, K., Kupfer, D.J., Fram, D.H. *et al.* (1970) 'Effects of l-tryptophan (a natural sedative) on human sleep.' *The Lancet 2*(7678): 842–846.

Wyder-Westh, C., Lienert, C., Pihan, H. and Steinlin, M. (2005) 'An unusual cause of stridor in childhood due to focal epileptic seizures.' *European Journal of Pediatrics 164*: 648–649.

Yamabe, N. and Yokozawa, T. (2006) 'Activity of the Chinese prescription Hachimi-jio-gan against renal damage in the Otsuka Long-Evans Tokushima fatty rat: A model of human type 2 diabetes mellitus.' *Journal of Pharmacy and Pharmacology 58*(4): 535–545.

Yang, A., Palmer, A.A. and de Wit, H. (2010) 'Genetics of caffeine consumption and responses to caffeine.' *Psychopharmacology 211*(3): 245–257.

Yang, S., Liu, A., Weidenhammer, A., Cooksey, R.C. *et al.* (2009) 'The role of *mPer2* clock gene in glucocorticoid and feeding rhythms.' *Endocrinology 150*: 2153–2160.

Yanik, G., Glaum, S. and Radulovacki, M. (1987) 'The dose-response effects of caffeine on sleep in rats.' *Brain Research 403*: 177–180.

Yeung, C.K., Sreedhar, B., Sihoe, J.D., Sit, F.K. and Lau, J. (2006) 'Differences in characteristics of nocturnal enuresis between children and adolescents: A critical appraisal from a large epidemiological study.' *British Journal of Urology International 97*: 1069–1073.

Yi, P.-L., Lin, C.-P., Tsai, C.-H., Lin, J.-G. and Chang, F.-C. (2007) 'The involvement of serotonin receptors in suanzaorentang-induced sleep alteration.' *Journal of Biomedical Science 14*: 829–840.

Young, D., Nagarajan, L., de Klerk, N., Jacoby, P. *et al.* (2007) 'Sleep problems in Rett syndrome.' *Brain and Development 29*(10): 609–616.

Yu-lian, X., Xiao-yun, L. and Chun-hua, D. (2002) 'Treatment observations & results of 50 cases of pediatric enuresis with Yi Niao Ling Fang' [in Chinese]. *Xin Zhong Yi* [New Chinese Medicine] *12*: 27–28. Translation by R. Helmer available at www.goldenneedleonline.com/blog/2009/08/09/treatment-observations-results-of-50-cases-of-pediatric-enuresis-with-yi-niao-ling-fang-effective, accessed 15 September 2011.

Yurdakok, M., Kinik, E., Guvenc, H. and Beduk, Y. (1987) 'Viloxazine versus imipramine in the treatment of enuresis.' *Turkish Journal of Pediatrics 29*(4): 227–230.

Zadeh, M.A., Moslemi, M.K. and Zadeh, G.K. (2010) 'Comparison between imipramine and imipramine combined with pseudoephedrine in 5–12-year-old children with uncomplicated enuresis: A double-blind clinical trial.' *Journal of Pediatric Urology 7*(1): 30–33.

Zanquetta, M.M., Corrêa-Giannella, M.L., Monteiro, M.B. and Villares, S.M.F. (2010) 'Body weight, metabolism and clock genes.' *Diabetology & Metabolic Syndrome 2*: 53. Available at www.dmsjournal.com/content/2/1/53, accessed 15 September 2011.

Zee, P.C. and Manthena, P. (2007) 'The brain's master circadian clock: Implications and opportunities for therapy of sleep disorders.' *Sleep Medicine Reviews 11*: 59–70.

Zeitzer, J.M., Dijk, D.J., Kronauer, R.E., Brown, E.N. and Czeisler, C.A. (2000) 'Sensitivity of the human circadian pacemaker to nocturnal light: Melatonin phase resetting and suppression.' *Journal of Physiology 526*(3): 695–702.

Zeitzer, J.M., Nishino, S. and Mignot, E. (2006) 'The neurobiology of hypocretins (orexins), narcolepsy and related therapeutic interventions.' *Trends in Pharmacological Sciences 27*(7): 368–374.

Zhao, Q., Sherrill, D.L., Goodwin, J.L. and Quan, S.F. (2008) 'Association between sleep disordered breathing and behavior in school-aged children: The Tucson Children's Assessment of Sleep Apnea Study.' *Open Epidemiology Journal 1,* 1–9.

Zhdanova, I.V., Wurtman, R.J. and Wagstaff, J. (1999) 'Effects of a low dose of melatonin on sleep in children with Angelman syndrome.' *Journal of Pediatric Endocrinology and Metabolism 12*(1): 57–67.

Zhong, Y.-Q., Fu, J.-J., Liu, X.-M., Diao, X. *et al.* (2010) 'The reporting quality, scientific rigor, and ethics of randomized placebo-controlled trials of Traditional Chinese Medicine compound formulations and the differences between Chinese and non-Chinese trials.' *Current Therapeutic Research 71*(1): 30–49.

Zingone, F., Siniscalchi, M., Capone, P., Tortora, R. *et al.* (2010) 'The quality of sleep in patients with coeliac disease.' *Alimentary Pharmacology and Therapeutics 32*(8): 1031–1036.

Zucconi, M., Ferini-Strambi, L., Erminio, C., Pestalozza, G. and Smime, S. (1993) 'Obstructive sleep apnea in the Rubinstein-Taybi syndrome.' *Respiration 60*(2): 127–132.

Zuckerman, B., Stevenson, J. and Bailey, V. (1987) 'Sleep problems in early childhood: Continuities, predictive factors, and behavioral correlates.' *Paediatrics 80*: 664–671.

INDEX